Sustainable Innovation
The Organisational, Human and Knowledge Dimension

Sustainable Innovation

THE ORGANISATIONAL, HUMAN AND KNOWLEDGE DIMENSION

CONTRIBUTING EDITOR
RENÉ JORNA

Greenleaf
PUBLISHING

2006

To
ISABEL IRENE JORNA
(one of the future generation)

© 2006 Greenleaf Publishing Ltd

Published by Greenleaf Publishing Limited
Aizlewood's Mill
Nursery Street
Sheffield S3 8GG
UK
www.greenleaf-publishing.com

Printed in Great Britain on acid-free paper by Antony Rowe Ltd, Chippenham, Wiltshire.
Cover by LaliAbril.com.

All rights reserved. No part of this publication may be reproduced, stored in a retrieval system, or transmitted, in any form or by any means, electronic, mechanical, photocopying, recording or otherwise, without the prior permission in writing of the publishers.

British Library Cataloguing in Publication Data:

ISBN-10: 1-874719-99-3
ISBN-13: 978-1-874719-99-1

Contents

Foreword viii
    John Elkington

Preface x

Part A: Sustainable innovation: the organisational, human and knowledge dimension 1

  1 Knowledge creation for sustainable innovation: the KCSI programme 2
    René J. Jorna

  2 Innovation: many-headed and certainly important 15
    René J. Jorna and Jan Waalkens

  3 Sustainability: from environment and technology to people and organisations ... 28
    René J. Jorna and Niels R. Faber

  4 Levels of description, kinds of entities and systems 42
    René Jorna and Henk Hadders

  5 Organisation: artefact and principle 57
    René J. Jorna and Laura Maruster

  6 Knowledge as a basis for innovation: management and creation 74
    René J. Jorna

Part B: Instruments and models 97

7 A method for the identification of stakeholders............98
  Janita F.J. Vos and Marjolein C. Achterkamp

8 A cognitive map of sustainability: a method for assessing mental images.........111
  Derk Jan Kiewiet

9 Knowledge systems and reasoning with cases (and rules).............123
  Henk Hadders and René J. Jorna

Part C: The organisational (business) projects 135

10 Biosoil: sustainable remediation............136
  Else J.M. Boutkan and René J. Jorna

11 KunstStoffenHuis and synthetics innovation within the small business sector 148
  Cees van Dijk, Koos Zagema and Han van Kasteren

12 Know what you're blending! A tool for a sustainable paper industry 165
  Niels Faber and Kristian Peters

13 Philips and the long road towards social sustainability 187
  Floortje Smit and Niels R. Faber

14 Knowledge systems for sustainable innovation of starch potato production: achieving more with less............204
  Niels R. Faber and Rob van Haren

15 Sustainability of knowledge within mental healthcare: knowledge infrastructure, knowledge management and learning............227
  Henk Hadders and Derk Jan Kiewiet

16 The University Medical Centre Groningen. Sustainable innovation in postgraduate medical education: a knowledge and learning approach.........247
  Marjolein C. Achterkamp and Jan Pols

17 Grontmij: co-operation in the light of sustainability 259
  Janita F.J. Vos and Nico J. Rommes

18 Sociocracy and the sustainability of knowledge: Reekx, ATOL and Endenburg Elektrotechnics............275
  René J. Jorna and Nico Rommes

Part D: Theory and practice: results from the organisational projects 287

19 The focus of innovation: what have we established? 288
René J. Jorna

20 Business (organisational) practices: recurring themes of sustainability 298
René J. Jorna

21 Business practice: recurring themes in and around knowledge 303
René J. Jorna and Henk Hadders

22 Further steps towards a systematic perspective on sustainability 311
Niels R. Faber, René J. Jorna and Jo van Engelen

23 Assessing and determining social sustainability: an onset and an attempt 321
Niels R. Faber, Laura Maruster and René J. Jorna

Abbreviations 346
References 348
About the contributors 359
Index of subjects 363
Index of names 370

Foreword

As challenges such as demographic pressures, ethnic tensions, terrorism, global poverty, pandemics and abrupt climate change force their way into mainstream politics and business, so we see growing interest in innovation, entrepreneurial solutions and, critically, issues such as how to ensure successful solutions replicate and scale. The book—*Sustainable Innovation*—you hold in your hands is part of that shift. Instead of simply focusing on environmental and technological matters, it adopts a wider-angle perspective based on the 3P approach my colleagues and I pioneered over a decade ago, focusing on 'People,' 'Planet' and 'Prosperity'.

The subtitle—*The Organisational, Human and Knowledge Dimension*—underscores the authors' determination to view and evaluate innovation-for-sustainability in terms of the human, social and management challenges and responses. They argue that a just, efficient and sustainable balancing of the 3Ps is best achieved by the development of new knowledge, and by the evolution of better means both of embedding that emerging knowledge in organisations and institutions, and of managing the relevant flows of information, knowledge and (crucially, I believe) wisdom.

The authors stress that claims that a particular product, production process or service are sustainable usually assume—and certainly imply—that an appropriate balance has been achieved between the 3Ps. The problem here, they note, is that calculating the sustainability of such things, let alone of complex systems such as enterprises or economies, can be hugely complex. Instead of 'sustainability', they favour the use of terms such as 'making sustainable', emphasising that in dynamic operating environments organisational processes are changing constantly, whether or not they are under effective strategic control by management.

Innovation, too, is dynamic by definition. But the argument developed in the following pages is that there must be a constant focus on the triple bottom line of economic, social and environmental value creation during the innovation process. Hence the authors' observation that sustainability is formulated as follows: *'a matter, object or construct is sustainable if its internal structure is in a dynamic balance with its social and natural environment'* (p. 10). At times it's easier to understand what all this implies when observing the work of a leading social entrepreneur, for example; but if theory—

at its best—is our attempt to capture emerging collective wisdom, then the authors have done us a service.

Sustainable Innovation helped expand my own thinking on the first 'P', People. And with the looming 20th anniversary of the 1987 publication of the Brundtland Commission's report *Our Common Future*, which ushered the notion of sustainable development into the political mainstream, it is increasingly important that we honestly assess our progress to date and that we build our ability to handle the human, social, economic and—crucially—political dimensions of the profound transformation we must now make in the ways in which we manage the resources of our Planet to achieve lasting Prosperity for all.

John Elkington, Founder and Chief Entrepreneur, SustainAbility (www.sustainability.com); originator of the 'triple bottom line' and '3P' concepts

Preface

In contrast to what some sceptics may think, sustainability issues are here to stay. Resources are diminishing, the overall climate is changing more rapidly than we could ever have imagined and we, the industrial worlds, believe that we are entitled to conquer and absorb all earthly assets as quickly as possible. On a timescale of many thousands of years this can be considered as the ups and downs of a natural dynamic system. Why bother? In the end, the present-day exhaustions and sufferings will be merely wrinkles in the ocean of time. For some this may be a comforting idea, especially when sustainability issues are positioned against economic growth. 'Economic growth must go on, even if it is restricted by natural, human and organisational constraints.' Some clever jokers have even coined the term 'sustainable growth'. In our view this is a perverse line of thought, frustrating the essence of sustainability, which is always about the dynamic interaction between system and the natural and social environment. Whether we like it or not, at this moment this interaction or balance is disturbed as far as our future position is concerned.

When discussing sustainability issues in this book, we try to combine three things: innovation, knowledge and organisational structures. First, we tackle innovation from what may be an unexpected point of view. In our view innovation does not primarily deal with technology or new gadgets in audio or video equipment. Innovation is about undertaking new or renewed activities with humans in organisational structures and co-ordination mechanisms. Innovation, therefore, is not the ultimate medicine to achieve economic growth; it is a continuous process of human actions with the aim of better adjusting a system or adapting it to the natural or social environment. Second, knowledge is the motor, the fuel and the realisation of human existence. The fact that we, humans, can reason, remember and use symbols makes us a unique species on earth. In all these cognitive activities the basic element is knowledge. Organisational structures, or, better, conscious organisational structures and co-ordination mechanisms, are the tools that human beings use to deal with complexity, insufficiency, their own limitations and those of their multi-aspect environment. And, returning to our opening sentence about exhausting resources, climate change and asset exploitation, these are not natural processes only. No, these processes are taking place because innovation, knowledge, knowledge creation and organisational structuring make them happen. The human, organisational and knowledge dimensions are just as crucial for the decline of our habitat as for a possible improvement of our natural and social *Umwelt*. Sustainable innovation as a continuous process of natural, social and human adaptation is the main topic of this book. If we, humans, do not adapt ourselves, we will be adapted, either for better or for worse.

This book is an indirect result of a programme (2001–2004) of the National Institute for Sustainable Development (NIDO) in the Netherlands. In 2004 NIDO was terminated by the (conservative) Dutch government. In their infinite wisdom this government declared sustainability to be of minor importance. We still do not believe they were right. On the other hand, sustainability issues are like the Hydra, a multi-headed monster. If you cut off one head, at least two heads appear anew. We look upon this book as the Hydra's 'offspring'. NIDO is now history, the business projects described lie both partly in the past and in the present, while future ideas concerning sustainability have yet to be developed. With regards to the latter we are thinking about second-generation knowledge management and the development and use of McElroy's (2005) social footprint metrics.

Several organisations and people have made this book possible. First of all, NIDO itself. I would like to thank Colette Alma and Theo van Bruggen for their continuous stimulation and criticism of our programme of Sustainable Innovation. Further, without the extra (financial) support from the Faculty of Management and Organisation (University of Groningen), the work of Jessica Bakker on the translations and corrections, and Sonja Abels for taking on all kinds of secretarial activities, this book would not have been possible. Finally, I would like to thank NIAS (an institute of the Royal Dutch Academy of Science [KNAW]) for inviting me to stay there from September 2004 until July 2005. During my stay I was able to enlarge my knowledge of sustainability and reflect on the chapters of this book. I hope that those interested will find this book as stimulating to read as I found it a challenge to write and compile it.

René Jorna
Groningen, 4 July 2006

Part A
Sustainable innovation: the organisational, human and knowledge dimension

1
Knowledge creation for sustainable innovation
THE KCSI PROGRAMME

René J. Jorna

There is something peculiar about innovation in the Netherlands, and probably in other countries too. On the one hand, various independent sources both internal and external (Weggeman 2003; van Ees and Postma 2002; European Commission 2004) indicate that innovation is in bad shape. The growing tendency is to import technologically educated people from outside rather than produce them 'in-house'. Budgets for innovation and research at university level are decreasing. In addition, Dutch multinationals, comprising companies such as Shell, Philips, AKZO-Nobel and Unilever, are reducing their participation in innovation.

On the other hand, according to the Dutch Central Bureau for Statistics (CBS 2004), sufficient new products are nevertheless being developed. However, these products do not find their way commercially into society as one would hope. Furthermore, and this is not insignificant, in the Netherlands there is a rich tradition—in universities, in R&D units of companies, and in government agencies—which ensures a solid foundation in overcoming deficiencies.

This combination of positive and negative features is typical for the theme of innovation, not only in the Netherlands but also in many other European countries. Simply, innovation means either realising something new out of nothing or realising something new based on what already exists (Schumpeter 1934). There are some important differences between these two approaches. With the former there is no need to be competitive or to change the existing cognitive and social landscape. But it is a different case with the latter. Then, it is a matter of what Schumpeter describes as 'creative destruction'. It is worth noting, however, that Schumpeter is mainly referring to economics and sociology: that is, to a high aggregation level for innovation. He does not discuss the effects of innovation on people's thinking, knowledge and behaviour. We return to this in Chapter 6.

With regard to the processes and aims of innovation, we have several observations to make. First, many innovations are long-term activities. For example, the development of haemodialysis equipment took more than 100 years (Cijsouw *et al.* 2004). This is an extreme example, although periods of 10–15 years are common in *radical* innovations regardless of the domain or product. A great deal of time, effort and money needs to be invested.

Second, innovations are not guaranteed to succeed. Many innovations fail, but it is very difficult to determine precisely the reasons for failure—lack of financial and/or human resources, incomplete knowledge, poor co-operation, absence of materials, etc. Failure is likely to be due to a matrix of factors, with knowledge a key one; but how a potentially successful innovation turns into a failure, and at what phase in the innovation process, is often impossible to determine.

Third, traditional discussions about innovation are often one-dimensional, tending to refer only to material aspects. Moreover, this view is shared by a large number of rating systems within, for example, the Dutch Ministry of Economic Affairs and the EU. In this way innovatory approaches tend to be restricted to product or production process innovations. This is inadequate. Innovations can also relate to new services, organisational forms and ways of working. In this book we will make a case for a much broader vision than the traditional one.

Fourth, we believe that the importance of technology in innovation is strongly overestimated. This is, we should stress, not the current consensus in the Netherlands where universities bemoan the lack of resources available for technological innovation and the lack of interest in, and value placed upon, the exact sciences. This is true in the sense that over the past few years there has been little growth in the number of students signing up for the exact sciences. However, it is not true if one considers the large number of (natural) scientists who no longer work in their own disciplines but are occupied in management, consultancy and business policy matters.

Fifth, innovation is tied to knowledge. Innovation starts with knowledge, it elaborates that knowledge or generates new knowledge, and produces knowledge as the final outcome. Thus, knowledge is the engine of innovation (see Chapter 6). Furthermore, innovation is directly linked to people who realise new knowledge or extend existing knowledge. Without such people there would be no innovation. People are the carriers of knowledge. Their culture and society is largely immaterial, although the importance of background is less strong for technological innovation than for non-technological innovation. If the influx of people from other cultures is too large, the role of people as carriers of knowledge is affected. Foreign researchers who develop knowledge will return to their home countries after some time. This means that knowledge will flow away, which creates problems regarding the continuation of education in the education-giving countries. As we will discuss, knowledge is not a free-floating commodity, as economists believe. Knowledge, without human beings, socially and culturally embedded, is not possible. Innovation is also a process. Besides creating and producing knowledge, it also requires that knowledge is transferred, available, accessible and usable.

Sixth, nowadays individuals rarely realise innovations. Even the most brilliant inventor needs other people to work out details and to conduct tests and case studies, as well as to convince others that the innovation is as brilliant as the inventor thinks it is. Innovation means working together to exchange knowledge and information. In the modern climate of innovation the individual inventor or innovator has become an exception—the current state of affairs requires teamwork. And, in order to be useful, innovations need to be introduced, accepted and adopted.

In summary, we conclude that innovations take time, there is no guarantee of success and there is currently too little focus on services and organisational forms. Furthermore, it can be stated that innovation is not just a scientific exercise, but that in principle it is about knowledge, with people as the carriers of this knowledge. Thus, innovation will succeed only if people co-operate. This book deals with these subjects in a theoretical sense as well as from the practical perspective of a number of organisations.

Regarding the aforementioned issues we take the following positions:

- Innovation is about products, services and organisational forms
- Innovation is about knowledge carried in the minds of people
- Innovation requires co-operation
- Innovation should be seen as an ongoing and enduring process

We think the phrase **sustainable innovation** effectively describes these four positions. We will explain this in greater detail in the next section. This will be followed by an overview of the Netherlands Initiative for Sustainable Development (NIDO[1]). Then, we go on to discuss the conceptual core of NIDO—the Knowledge Creation for Sustainable Innovation (KCSI) programme. This book is an extended description of, and reflection on, the KCSI programme. Finally, we explain the structure of this book.

Sustainable innovation

In the previous section we noted that the innovation theme evokes a large amount of debate. Indeed, it appears that we have complicated the situation by postulating the idea of sustainable innovation. At first sight sustainable innovation seems to deal with two things—sustainability and innovation. However, we do not go along with the obvious interpretation that sustainability is related only to ecology and the green environment, and that innovation mainly refers to technological matters. This would imply that sustainable innovation is about technological modernisation in the field of the environment and ecology. Instead, we are eager to define our own interpretation of sustainable innovation. We believe that sustainability in the environmental sense is always directly or indirectly connected to the way in which people possess and organise knowledge. In general, managing and making this knowledge operational takes place in

---

1   The Nationaal Initiatief Duurzame Ontwikkeling foundation was established by the government of Prime Minister Wim Kok between 1999 and 2004 as a means of investing in the knowledge infrastructure.

organisations, firms, enterprises and institutes. In Chapter 3 we return to various definitions of sustainability.

As mentioned previously, innovation can mean that something already in existence is renounced or abandoned and something new replaces it. As well as products, services and organisations themselves can be innovated; a good innovation always means that, within a certain context, knowledge has been created. In this book we want to focus on sustainable innovation in the human and organisational sense.

Sustainable innovation is accomplished by **knowledge creation**, and the ways and structures that embed this knowledge in organisations need to be analysed and stimulated. A proper innovation process results in making knowledge sustainable. The essence of sustainable innovation is shaped by a process perspective on sustainability. Whenever we say that a particular product, production process or service is sustainable, we mean that a balance has been achieved between the three pillars of sustainable development—'planet', 'profit' and 'people', where 'planet' is often the key pillar. A car can be sustainable because it runs on hydrogen, or electricity can be sustainable because it is generated by biomass. In the same way we say that innovation can be sustainable. For example, a new material has been discovered that is less environmentally damaging or a particular production process has been developed that produces less harmful emissions. These are obvious examples of sustainable innovation.

However, there is more to it than this. It is very hard for complex systems, such as firms, enterprises and organisations, or for complex transactions, such as innovations, to determine a state of sustainability. One cannot simply measure the degree of sustainability of an enterprise or an innovation as this changes over time. We therefore suggest transforming the term 'sustainability' to 'making sustainable'. By 'making sustainable' we want to raise the issue that the organisational processes in the organisation are constantly changing. The same goes for innovation. An innovation is not there for a limited period of time, after which it is finished. Innovations endure as processes rather than projects. However, in the innovation process there has to be a constant focus on sustainability. Consequently, from the perspective of the human and organisational sciences, design rules have to be formulated and implemented such that the innovation process is able to sustain itself.

In the KCSI programme sustainability and knowledge are combined in two ways. First, it is important to know whether sustainability concerns planet, people or profit. This holds for the usual processes in organisations as well as for innovation processes. We call this **knowledge of sustainability** (KoS). Second, it is also important to know whether this knowledge is used efficiently, whether it is shared, whether the conditions for innovation creation are sufficient and whether it has a human dimension. We term this **sustainability of knowledge** (SoK). We will explain KoS and SoK later in this chapter and in more detail in Chapter 3.

NIDO: the organisational context

This book is one of the achievements to arise from the NIDO foundation's KCSI programme. NIDO brings together enterprises, governments, social organisations and scientific institutions in programmes aimed at putting sustainability into practice. Such co-operation leads to solutions which receive concrete support within organisations or enterprises. In this way a solid basis is formed for the further spread of sustainable development within society. The aim of NIDO is to link prosperity to well-being by ensuring that economic growth and environmental improvements go hand in hand. An important second objective of NIDO is to strengthen the knowledge infrastructure in the Netherlands. NIDO sees its task as building bridges between various knowledge disciplines and social sections. In its programmes NIDO stimulates public–private co-operation.

NIDO translates society's demands for sustainable economic development into practical reality. This requires a joint effort in order to combine the experience and insights of people from the corporate world, social organisations, knowledge institutions and the government. To achieve this, NIDO is engaged in drawing up programmes around key themes. Themes in previous years were:

- From financial to sustainable efficiency—about financial auditing
- Sustainable outsourcing—about relations between different enterprises
- Values of water—about the behaviour of governments regarding the management and usage of water
- Market opportunities for sustainable products—about the role of marketing within the frame of sustainable products and services

The KCSI programme takes a central place in this book with its main theme of innovation and its subtheme of how sustainability in innovation and innovation processes can be determined and stimulated.

In particular, NIDO tries to show what a sustainable approach achieves. This will emerge in Part C of this book which deals with projects in organisations and firms. NIDO works together with current initiatives and continues these so that faster and bigger leaps can be made in sustainable development. In the next section, we will discuss the contents of the KCSI programme, how it is structured, what its objectives are and what results are intended.

Knowledge creation for sustainable innovation

Orientation

The KCSI programme aims at the sustainability of innovation processes. The process of innovation and the role of knowledge and of the people who possess that knowledge form its basis. In this context, sustainable innovation can have two meanings (see also McElroy 2003).

In the first place within an organisation the innovation itself can be aimed at sustainable services, products or production processes. Take, for example, the hydrogen technology that is increasingly considered as a key technology for the near future, provided hydrogen is not produced by burning natural gas, oil or coal. Hydrogen as an energy source is efficient, it can also be used at a small-scale level, and has a high output. It neither has the ecological disadvantages that are attached to the use of biomass and fossil fuels nor the cost problem of the solar energy collectors or the low efficiency of the harnessing of wind energy. Take an enterprise that by means of innovation develops an efficient method to change from gas and oil as energy carriers to hydrogen technology as an energy provider. This enterprise is practising sustainable innovation.

In the second place sustainable innovation may refer to structuring an innovation in such a way that it becomes sustainable. This means that the organisation of innovation as a *process* is structured in such a way that it is a component of the value chain of an organisation. Consequently, in this (second) sense, sustainable innovation touches the core of an enterprise or organisation: namely, the knowledge processes. The aim here is to influence the way in which (the people in) the organisation deal(s) with knowledge: that is, the way in which knowledge is created and produced, the way it is made accessible and is shared, and the way (people make sure) it is used.

In essence, sustainable innovation is about knowledge processes that form the core of an organisation. It influences the ways in which the organisation deals with knowledge. The innovation process is inextricably connected with all kinds of knowledge creation and management. It is very difficult for organisations as complex systems or innovations and transitions as complex situations to determine a condition of sustainability. An enterprise or innovation cannot be measured by a certain degree of sustainability since sustainability is a dynamic process and innovations and enterprises are constantly changing.

Sustainable innovation is realised by knowledge creation. The aim is to stimulate and facilitate this knowledge creation which is linked to the ways and structures to embed knowledge in organisations. According to Argyris and Schön (1978), knowledge creation is **second-order learning**, which means **learning to learn**. By contrast, **first-order learning** is increasing or accelerating existing knowledge. This first-order learning is important, though Argyris and Schön also make it clear that in order to achieve actual renewal 'learning to learn' must be included. Only then is knowledge created. A sound **process of innovation** ensures preserving the SoK.

The essence of the KCSI programme entails this process perspective with respect to sustainability. Whenever we say that a product, product process or service is sustainable, we want to indicate that a balance in the three pillars of planet, profit and people is achieved. In the same way one can say that an innovation is sustainable. For the sake of convenience we call this the **static interpretation** of sustainable development. Sustainability is a condition by which—according to certain criteria—it can be determined, whether or not it has been achieved. We return to various interpretations of sustainability in Chapter 3.

The aforementioned formulation of sustainable innovation also applies to conducting business in a sustainable way. This means that the business processes are structured and embedded in such a way that the organisation or firm does not exploit the environment or the society in which it operates, but rather interacts with it on a mutually beneficial and ongoing basis. Preserving sustainability in both innovations and organisations leads to a continuous stacking, restructuring and adjusting of the process itself. This stacking means that existing knowledge is being adjusted and complemented. In addition, new knowledge is created and existing knowledge is elaborated. Our **process perspective** is inextricably connected with all aspects of knowledge creation and management. Empathy with, and awareness of, sustainability can take innovation to a higher level and, in this way a continuous impetus can be given to preserve sustainability.

An organisation consists of layers

Organisations can be classified in a number of ways: for example, by primary and secondary processes or by functional areas such as marketing, logistics and finance. In Chapters 4 and 5 we will come back to these classifications.

If we consider sustainable innovation as an ongoing and enduring process we can also consider organisations in the same dynamic way, especially in relation to the intervention levels. These levels are combined with an ontological classification of organisations. Going from top to bottom, we then say that an organisation has the following levels:

- Organisational objectives
- Organisational processes
- Behaviour and knowledge of the employees
- Learning abilities of the employees

All four are important for effective innovation, but the last two particularly so. How can the creation of a **learning organisation** be stimulated in such a way as to generate awareness of the fact that one is dealing with SoK?

Making change happen is likely to be very different at each of these intervention levels (van Raaij 2001). Changing the objectives of an organisation is quite easy, as is bringing in KoS at this level. With a little imagination an objective can be reformulated in an instant. It only consists of words. It is harder to change processes where an organisation's structure may be at risk, and even harder to change people's behaviour. Hardest of all is changing learning ability (see Table 1.1). In summary, deep changes are more difficult but also more effective. In our terms, they are more sustainable. While at an abstract level within the organisation one can simply speak of SoK, its implementation at the operational level may cause enormous problems. After all, SoK requires an organisation to consist of **learning people** (who make up the so-called learning organisation). This means that a sufficient number of stakeholders must be involved.

	Increase in KoS	Increase in SoK
Organisational objectives	Easy	Easy
Organisational processes	Easy	Difficult
Behaviour/knowledge	Difficult	Extremely difficult
Learning/self-evaluation	Difficult	Extremely difficult

TABLE 1.1 Changing sustainability in relation to preserving sustainability, according to levels of intervention

It may be clear that this new way of business development cannot be carried out without a fundamental approach to the knowledge infrastructure and the help of knowledge management (see Chapters 6–8). In the remainder of this section, we will elaborate on the different factors dealing with knowledge. Business and knowledge processes are aimed at knowledge creation and knowledge production, knowledge use and knowledge management (McElroy 2003).

A conceptual framework for sustainable innovation

In previous sections we dealt with the main terms **innovation** and **sustainability**. We have also presented the concepts of **knowledge** and **organisation**. How, then, are these concepts connected or, to put it another way, how do they form a framework? To provide a renewing perspective on innovation and sustainability we will start from the central terms 'organisation' and 'knowledge'.

There are two ways—internal and external—of looking at an organisation's right to exist. An organisation's internal reason to exist lies in the fact that there are many things that individuals cannot achieve alone. Providing insurance services, manufacturing a car or publishing a book require collaborative effort. This leads to a division of labour, functions or tasks that need to be co-ordinated (see Chapters 5 and 6).

Organisations' external reason to exist is to supply a product or service for which there is a market demand. Business development is the result of a successful match between supply and demand, and business processes are organised in such a way as to attune these two elements. These processes are basically transformation processes converting a particular input (such as raw materials) to a particular output (a product or service) by the addition of knowledge. Since a large number of parties are either directly or indirectly involved in the organisation (stakeholders, employees, governments and customers), structuring an organisation is a complex matter and requires a system-oriented approach.

Whether the reason for existence is internal or external, it is the employees who take centre stage as they are the ones who possess, share, develop, use and distribute knowledge. So, an organisation consists of people, artefacts (such as buildings and computers) and social constructs (such as opening hours and hierarchies) (see Chapter 6).

Three principles of classification

The theme of people and organisation brings us to the first classification principle in this book. We can make a classification of people through groups and teams, according to departments, enterprises and also according to society and culture as a whole. This can be described in terms of levels of aggregation: for example, from low to high or from micro through meso to macro levels. This will be discussed more thoroughly in Chapter 4.

In carrying out tasks people create, share and use knowledge. This knowledge dimension is the key to our second classification principle for two reasons. In the first place it characterises us as humans. Without knowledge we would simply rely on instinctive reflexes, standard responses and behaviour patterns. Second, knowledge is the raw material, the engine and the final outcome of innovation. Whether it concerns knowledge about materials, technical knowledge, organisational knowledge, creativity or design knowledge, innovation cannot do without it. A distinction can be made between **knowledge content** and **knowledge type**. Knowledge content is what is known, for example, with regard to disease (see Chapter 16), water management or synthetics manufacture (see Chapter 11). Knowledge type refers to the way in which knowledge is presented and shown. For example, knowledge can be expressed by behaviour, speech, in writing or through visual imagery. A further distinction is between knowledge in the **primary process** of an organisation and knowledge in the **secondary process**. The primary process refers to the main objective of an enterprise or organisation while the secondary process relates to management, finances, planning and administration. The distinction between knowledge content and knowledge type applies to both types of process. The classification shows in which process and for which task knowledge is used and also the nature of the division of knowledge types. This is discussed further in Chapter 6.

Innovation and knowledge are closely linked. Since innovation is such a vast concept and takes a central place in the KCSI programme it is dealt with in detail in Chapter 2.

Next to the classification dimensions of **aggregation level** and **knowledge distinction**, there is a third classification principle. This principle is related to the sustainability concept itself—a term frequently used and interpreted in many different ways (Faber, Jorna and van Engelen 2005). The most influential definition of sustainability was the one made by the Brundtland Commission in 1987. It defined sustainable development as (WCED 1987, as reported in Garcia and Calantone 2002: 112):

> a process of change in which the use of resources, the direction of investments, the orientation of the technological development and institutional change are all in harmony and do not compromise both current and future possibilities to meet human needs and wishes.

In its definition the Brundtland Commission gave a central place to development—a process that makes use of various resources. This use of resources has to be such that not only current generations but also future ones will be able to utilise them. Another definition of sustainability was articulated by John Elkington (1997). He refers to sustainability as finding a balance between the 'triple P-areas' of planet, people and profit.

In this book we will try to follow and further apply the Brundtland Commission's and Elkington's definitions by considering sustainability as the balance between the matter, object or construct and its social and natural environment. Therefore, a matter, object or construct is sustainable if its internal structure is in a dynamic balance with its social and natural environment. A dynamic balance means that the environment can be used, but also that the environment itself 'uses' the matter, object or construct. This formulation is derived from a remark made by Herman Wijffels, chair of the Dutch Social Economic Council, at a NIDO meeting in April 2002 where he said: 'Sustainability is realising a reduction in offload(ing) or in devolvement.' **Offloading** means burdening, destroying or exploiting the environment. Reducing the degree of offloading reduces environmental damage both in the short and long term, thus conforming to the Brundtland Commission's position that sustainability must take account of future generations. The idea of sustainability as a reduction in the degree of offloading enables us to deal with sustainability in a more operational way. Thus, discussions can focus on how to reduce offloading, who is responsible, how long it is likely to take and whether there are any disadvantages. Such an analysis helps to formulate effective measures to reduce offloading. This approach to sustainability results in the third classification principle and is discussed in detail in Chapter 3.

The organisation of the programme

The focus on both sustainability and the preservation of sustainability is expressed in two so-called **leap projects**. These are projects that are apt to realise leaps forward resulting in discontinuous positive changes. The aim of leap project 1 is to deal in a better, more transparent and more effective way with KoS in its broadest sense, especially in innovations. The KoS leap project consists of a number of business projects in which each organisation works on a product, service or market innovation in order to embed the concomitant KoS more thoroughly. Participating organisations are: Biosoil (Chapter 10); Synthetics House (Chapter 11); Optichem (Chapter 12); Philips (Chapter 13); and AVEBE (Chapter 14). The various business projects within KoS are parallel projects, but also interactive ones. Leap project 1 focuses on the people and planet pillars of sustainability.

Leap project 2 aims to sustain knowledge in business processes, tasks and other types of organisational activities in order to realise SoK. This leap project puts more emphasis on the process approach than does the KoS project. SoK is directed at using knowledge without wasting it, preserving knowledge and structuring business processes in such a way that innovation as a process of knowledge creation continues to take place. The aim of SoK is to give concrete form to the people perspective of sustainability in particular. The participants in leap project 2 are: the Dutch mental healthcare sector (Chapter 15); Academisch Ziekenhuis Groningen[2] (AZG) (Chapter 16); Grontmij (Chapter 17); and Sociocracy in Reekx, ATOL and Endenburg (Chapter 18).

Objectives of the programme

For the research programme as a whole, as well as the individual business projects, objectives have been formulated at various levels. At the level of the separate organisation it is important to give an impetus to the innovation in question. In addition, within each organisational project an objective is formulated in the field of KoS or SoK: for example, the re-use of knowledge concerning a particular content area of sustainability or increasing the co-operation with external parties with respect to soil remediation (see Chapter 10). One level higher combines organisational projects within a leap project in order to provide an insight into the preconditions for realising either KoS or SoK. These are objectives at the level of the leap projects. The highest level of the whole research KCSI programme deals with two kinds of objectives—designing instruments and methodologies on the one hand, and exploring and testing empirically a conceptual framework in the field of sustainable innovation on the other. In the overall programme, methodologies and structures are developed by means of instrumental objectives enabling organisations to preserve the sustainability of their innovations. Further, software has been developed to support and implement the aforementioned methods

---

2 Academic Hospital Groningen. Changed to the University Medical Centre Groningen in 2005.

and structures in organisations (see Part B and various business projects in Part C). With regard to the conceptual framework, sustainability in relation to innovation will be further defined and stipulated in terms of knowledge and (second-generation) knowledge management. This implies that insights and methods will be developed that enable organisations to recognise existing knowledge and to deploy this knowledge for the benefit of sustainable innovation. Through this range of objectives the sustainability of innovations can be embedded in a methodological and scientific way into knowledge management in and around the innovation process.

Methodology applied in the programme

The programme outlined in this book has both a conceptual and an empirical component or, in other words, theoretical and practical components. The conceptual framework is laid down according to three lines of classification, namely:

- Various aggregation levels
- Knowledge content and knowledge type in primary and secondary processes
- Applying sustainability as a reduction in offload (or devolvement)

In the organisational projects, the empirical component is realised. These projects have not been selected as representative random examples out of a large collection of possible projects; they have been selected from the perspectives of innovation, the discussion about sustainability and the theme of knowledge creation and knowledge management. Caution should be used in generalising the experiences reported here to all types of innovations and discussions concerning sustainability. This is certainly not our presumption. Methodologically speaking we are dealing here with explorative research rather than research based on testing hypotheses. In this context, we find ourselves in the pre-stage of the empirical cycle (de Groot 1961). At the same time this programme includes design research carried out according to a step-by-step plan going from analysis and diagnosis via design towards change. In each of the organisational projects, analysis, diagnosis and design are dealt with, one way or another.

The structure of the book

The book consists of four main parts. Part A presents the conceptual framework. Part B contains a number of instruments, questionnaires and methodologies. Part C, the largest, deals with the organisational projects that are subdivided into the KoS and SoK leap projects. Part D contains conclusions and a checklist. The various parts and chapters are structured as follows.

Part A describes the conceptual framework in six chapters. Chapters 2 and 3 deal with the basic terms of innovation and sustainability. In Chapter 2 we discuss different kinds of innovation, phases in innovation and the difference in radical and imitative innovations while in Chapter 3 we discuss sustainability. Chapter 4 deals with levels of aggregation, from individual to organisational. These are elaborated in Chapters 5 and

6, with Chapter 5 taking an integrated stance concerning organisational forms and co-ordination mechanisms, business development, business models and management. In Chapter 6 the theme of knowledge, knowledge management and knowledge creation is discussed.

In Part B, instruments and methods of analysis are described based on the work of others or developed by ourselves. We discuss these instruments and methods separately because they go beyond the individual organisational projects or domains. In Chapter 7 a **stakeholders' analysis instrument** is discussed while Chapter 8 presents a method to **map domain images**: for example. of sustainability. Chapter 9 deals with a different way of classifying knowledge than with the classical production rules by using **case-based reasoning**. Many issues in sustainability are difficult to categorise and cannot be easily dealt with by simple causal chains. In these situations case-based thinking may offer an alternative.

In Part C the KoS and SoK business projects are discussed separately. In each business project the related research is described, but attention is also paid to the three themes of innovation, sustainability and knowledge type.

- The KoS leap projects are:
    - **Chapter 10:** Biosoil—designing a stakeholder instrument to support decision-making for soil remediation
    - **Chapter 11:** SyntheticsHouse—the development of a chain of innovation in small and medium-sized businesses (SMEs) in order to lift synthetics innovation to a higher plane
    - **Chapter 12:** Optichem—the development of software in the form of a **decision-support system** (DSS) to improve the use of chemical substances in the paper and cardboard industry
    - **Chapter 13:** Philips—the formulation of social focus areas in product development
    - **Chapter 14:** AVEBE (a global agro-starch company)—the development of an improved DSS for various groups of potato growers
- The SoK leap projects are:
    - **Chapter 15:** Sustainability within the Dutch mental healthcare system—knowledge infrastructure, knowledge management and learning
    - **Chapter 16:** AZG—improving the deployment of knowledge and skills in the curriculum innovations of medical specialists
    - **Chapter 17:** Grontmij—analysing inter-firm alliances to improve the integration of knowledge of sustainability
    - **Chapter 18:** Sociocracy and the sustainability of knowledge—Reekx, ATOL and Endenburg

Finally, in Part D we deal more thoroughly with the final outcomes of all the projects, incorporating the themes of sustainability, knowledge creation, knowledge type, organisational forms and innovation. As already mentioned, the overall research programme does not test hypotheses. Therefore, the projects should not be regarded as representative case studies. Our aim is to study actual practice in a systematic way. At the outset of the KCSI research programme, we found ourselves short of a coherent conceptual frame in the field of innovation and sustainability. We consider Part D to be a representation of the final outcomes of our research, both in a theoretical and in a practical sense. In Chapters 19, 20 and 21 we provide some conclusions regarding, respectively, innovation, sustainability and knowledge. In Chapter 22 we further operationalise the concept of sustainability as a reduction in offload or devolvement and, in Chapter 23, we provide a short checklist for organisations involved with, or interested in becoming involved with, sustainable innovation.

2
Innovation
MANY-HEADED AND CERTAINLY IMPORTANT

René J. Jorna and Jan Waalkens*

At present, innovation is seen as a panacea for modern society's social, technical and economic ills. Criticisms such as: 'Conservatism is the general mentality'; 'Our economic climate is too weak'; 'The entrepreneurial spirit has to be stimulated'; and 'Our youth shows too little interest in technology' are always answered with: 'We have to put more effort into innovation'. But are we really dealing here with a cure-all or should our approach be more differentiated?

Our answer is, in most cases, that the challenges are much more complicated and, therefore, a single remedy will not work. This is because innovation is a concept that lends itself to a multitude of meanings. What is striking, though, is that innovation is closely linked to economic growth. This can be explained quite simply by the argument that, when there is innovation, the rate of economic growth will increase. Innovation leads to the development and production of new products and services thus creating demand. In this way, as economic activity increases so does growth. This line of reasoning starts from the perception that everyone knows what innovation is and that it simply has to be realised. In our opinion this perception is incomplete and, to a significant extent, incorrect.

In this chapter we deal with the different aspects of innovation in detail in order to set straight this one-sided view of the concept. We define innovation and explain why it is important, and not just economically. We discuss the subdivision of innovation in its different phases and show that innovation is more than simply product innovation or technical innovation, as is often claimed. The different types of innovation are dis-

---

* With thanks to Henk Hadders and Jo van Engelen for their comments on earlier versions of this chapter.

cussed and we put forward some suggestions on how innovation can be measured. In conclusion, the chapter looks at the role of knowledge in innovation.

The importance of innovation and a choice of definition

From an organisational process perspective innovation can be approached in three different ways. First, large companies and organisations may have an R&D department which has innovation as its core activity. The oldest example in the Netherlands is the physics laboratory of Philips. However, smaller companies often cannot afford to have a separate R&D department so a second approach may be to focus on innovation throughout the whole organisation. Although there is no separate R&D department, the organisation as a whole is nevertheless engaged in innovation. A well-known example is the Dutch company Nedap which provides innovative and sustainable solutions in the fields of security and electronic control units as well as automation, management and information for organisations. Third, there is the individual. Whether separate departments are concerned or whether innovation is practised throughout the entire organisation, in each case individuals are involved. Innovations have to be conceived, worked out and realised. On all kinds of levels this requires knowledge, and knowledge is something that only people can develop, use and maintain.

Ideally, these three approaches take place simultaneously within the same organisation. A separate R&D department can coincide with an innovative attitude throughout the whole organisation. But, because separate R&D departments are more common in large multinationals which due to their size are forced to have more formal procedures and bureaucracy in place, this combined approach is rare. In any case, one essential condition is the presence of individuals who are willing to try things, who possess knowledge and skills and, crucially, who are not afraid to fail as the failure rate of innovations greatly exceeds the success rate.

Innovations are important for both external and internal reasons. By external reasons we mean that within an organisation's environment (which can include other companies in the form of purchasers or suppliers and also consumers and customers) there exists an urgency for renewal. Common motives for responding to these external reasons are competitive advantage and profit maximisation.

There may also be internal reasons for organisations to engage in innovation: for example, as a way of improving existing products and services or unlocking employees' creativity. The internal reasons basically come down to interacting and dealing adequately with the intrinsic motivation of employees.

It is often the case that internal and external stimuli occur simultaneously. However, it is wise to keep these stimuli apart because they both have different advantages and disadvantages. For example, an advantage of an internal stimulus is that it is initiated by the organisation itself which means that employees are more likely to identify with it. A disadvantage can be that internally something promising is achieved without knowing whether it will work externally. An advantage of an external stimulus is that one continuously has to adjust to changing external circumstances and this is exactly what an adaptive system, such as an organisation, should do. A disadvantage of external stimuli is that they have no 'individual quality' (von Hippel 1988).

Innovations are often defined as entirely novel and successful entities. We do not agree with this view, as will be shown later by our choice of definition.

There are many definitions of innovation. In general these consist of three elements. The first is **change** or doing things in a different way (Schumpeter 1934) and thus undertaking something new. **Newness** is the second element and this is often interpreted in an absolute way. This element is dominated by the technical approach. This is because once a device, a machine or design has been invented it is easy to repeat the process. The disadvantage of a merely technical viewpoint is that it fails to take account of the human dimension which requires that people actually have to understand and accept the innovation. We argue for a combined perspective comprising both technical and organisational aspects. An example of a non-technical innovation clarifies this. If a company appoints new personnel to deal with extra workload this is not considered to be an innovation. This is because the additional employees will continue to perform the same kind of work. However, appointing staff with new skills in response to customer demands for a new service or product can be seen as an innovation. Innovation may also be realised by new ways of working: for example, self-steering teams. No-one could say that either of these approaches is novel, but they are nevertheless innovative for the organisations concerned. We call this **organisation innovation**.

The third element in almost all definitions of innovation is that of **performance improvement**. Schumpeter links performance to economic achievement. According to this one-sided economic view, innovation creates value in terms of rewards for entrepreneurs. However, this view has not remained unchallenged. For example, it could be both innovative and economically highly profitable to make new products with the aid of highly polluting production processes. Such an approach to value adding could not, however, be described as sustainable.

In the course of time and under the influence of psychological and sociological research, the one-sided economic view of value adding has become more differentiated. The focus now is increasingly on overall improvement in the performance of companies and organisations, both with respect to task execution and organisational structures and systems. So, an organisational improvement within a hospital that leads to shorter waiting lists and less work pressure can be called an innovation. We come back to this aspect of innovation later in this chapter.

There are many definitions of innovation. We identify the following as among the most important. Paraphrasing Schumpeter (1934), innovation is doing things differently in the realm of economic life. In this respect he also refers to the 'realisation of new combinations, by which he means that existing things and products are further developed. What is implicit in his description, though, is that when making or designing something new, some existing things have to be broken down or abandoned. The OECD (1996: 9) gives the following description of innovation:

> [it is the] implementation/commercialisation of a product with improved performance characteristics such as to deliver objectively new or improved services to a customer. A technological process innovation is the implementation/adaptation of new or significantly improved production or delivery methods. It may involve changes in equipment, human resources, working methods or a combination of these.

What is striking in this description is its focus on technology, market and commercial success. Such a definition suggests that a non-commercial institution, such as a hospital or university, would be unable to realise innovations.

Another interesting description is that of Nonaka (1994: 14):

> Innovation can be better understood as a process in which the organisation creates and defines problems and then actively develops new knowledge to solve them.

Nonaka's description very much resembles the perspective of Newell and Simon (1972) on human reasoning and behaviour. They consider all human activities as some form of problem-solving. We will return to this later.

Nonaka's description emphasises what happens at the process side of an innovation. It does not define what innovation is. Since we choose a relative approach to innovations, we follow the description as formulated by West and Farr (1990: 9):

> An innovation is the intended or premeditated introduction or application — within a particular role, group or organisation—of ideas, processes, products or procedures which are new to the relevant adoption-unity, with the aim of being clearly beneficial to the individual, the group, the organisation or society as a whole.

In this description, an innovation is context-bound. In addition, it is not merely limited to commercial environments. Moreover, an innovation does not necessarily have to be complete, radical and new in the sense that it has never been realised before. A particular renewal may already have been invented elsewhere, but not yet in this particular company or organisation. Furthermore, the description allows the possibility of including individuals, teams and organisations. It also enables one to consider the things that happen when an innovation takes place as a form of problem-solving. The term **relevant adoption-unity** also makes clear that an innovation has to develop as well as to be understood.

Phases within the innovation

From the perspectives of both the individual (psychology) and the organisation (management, economy or sociology) an innovation has two phases—invention or creation and implementation (Nonaka and Takeuchi 1995). During the phase of invention or creation an individual—or in most cases a group of individuals—conceives something new. The actual process of creation is often considered as taking place at the individual level, but defining creation is difficult. For example, Boden (1994) uses the dictionary definition of creativity as 'bringing something into existence' or 'making something out of nothing'. Csikszentmihalyi (1996) states that creativity is a process whereby a symbolic domain within a culture is being changed.

Howard Gardner (1984) defines the creative person as someone who regularly solves problems, gives new products shape or thinks of new questions in fields and in ways that are perceived as new and which are ultimately accepted in a specific cultural environment. Once a person has invented particular ideas or when inventions or new developments start playing a role in an organisation, a highly complicated process starts to emerge. The inventor(s) needs to convey the innovation to others in the organisation so they can turn it into a new product, service or way of working. During this process various forms of knowledge take alternate turns. The implementation phase of the innovation is not the end-point. The innovation must also be accepted by those that need to engage with it, whether within the organisation itself, in other organisations or in the wider community or society. In order for an innovation to be realised, there will always need to be interaction with other individuals.

Within the innovation literature (see, for example, Dosi 1988; Senker 1995) a categorisation into processes is also applied, for example:

- Initiation or starting phase
- Development phase
- Implementation and completion phase

In some cases a maintenance and control phase is added (Cooper and Kleinschmidt 1990). The first phase is focused more on the individual, the other phases more on the team or on the group. Both phase categorisations have their value, however, from different perspectives.

In summary, we conclude that an innovation differs from an invention. An invention deals with the creative process of thinking of, designing and realising new things or constructs. An innovation means that, apart from its design, it has to be realised or implemented. It may be obvious that the creative or inventive part mainly takes place because individuals invent or combine things. This does not mean that they do not talk about or discuss it with others, but the starting point lies with the single individual. The spark originates from the individual, but it must be fanned by other individuals if the innovation is to catch fire.

In the implementation phase other people need to be convinced, swept along and become intimately involved in the project. Here, sociological aspects will dominate over psychological ones. But, even if an internal group agrees on the value of a particular innovation, this does not mean that others will be persuaded. Further adjustment, elaboration and argument may still be needed.

Innovation of products, product processes, services and organisations

In general, it seems that innovations tend to be defined as new products and processes, such as hydrogen fuel cells. This approach is too narrow. First, many renewals in the form of services, social artefacts and constructs can also be depicted as innovations. For example, the complete renewal of one of the medical specialist training courses in the Academic Hospital Groningen (Chapter 16) is clearly an innovation since a better balance between study and working hours results in a better service to the patients and so can be described as a service innovation. Also, the development of new organisational forms, such as **sociocracy**, possibly by means of or with the aid of new information and communication technology, are innovations. This is because, when compared against the three criteria of innovation—change, newness and performance—the new curriculum and the organisational form are clearly innovations.

The chapters dealing with the organisational projects in Part C are about different kinds of innovations in the field of products, services, production processes and organisations. We illustrate our point with an anonymous example from an actual business. In the lease contracts of a large manufacturer of copying machines it was arranged that the machines could be returned after the contract period. This arrangement was so successful that at some point the manufacturer's warehouse was completely filled with returned copying machines which were full of chemical pollutants. The situation in the warehouses became so problematic that the manufacturer asked the entire organisation to come up with an innovative solution. The marketing department came up with the idea of 'repiping' the bearings in the machines and selling at a lower price the reconditioned machines to companies and organisations that could not afford new copiers. The partly renewed machines were, for example, sent to Egypt as excellent reconditioned products. As a result of this re-use initiative, the manufacturer gained new technical knowledge that was also applicable to new copying machines. Although it may not have been the primary motivation, the initiative was highly beneficial to both the planet and people pillars of sustainability, helping organisations that may otherwise not have been able to afford good-quality equipment.

The example shows that innovations do not necessarily start with products. Often existing products can be given a new direction with the aid of marketing innovations. However, it also appears that marketing initiatives can have consequences for products, product parts or production processes. The example demonstrates an implicit advantage with respect to environmental sustainability. The occurrence of harmful substances in the returned machines was not the reason for initiating the innovation, and neither was sustainability the primary objective of the process. The outcome of the innovation was nevertheless a more sustainable use of resources and an increase in technical know-how on the part of the manufacturer. In addition, the manufacturer obtained the insight that an adequate management of knowledge and the sharing and combining of this knowledge are essential for the success of an innovation. As a result, knowledge itself becomes sustainable as the re-use of knowledge contributes to the KoS (knowledge of sustainability).

In the past few years there has been a steadily growing interest in the importance of non-technical innovations, although this interest has not yet spread to institutions such as the Dutch Central Bureau for Statistics or the EU. Damanpour (1987) made the distinction between technical and administrative innovations. He defines technical innovations as those (Damanpour 1987: 677):

> that occur in the technical systems of an organisation and are directly related to the primary work activity of the organisation. A technical innovation can be the implementation of an idea for a new product or a new service, or the introduction of new elements in an organisation's production or service operations.

Administrative innovations, on the other hand, are defined as (Damanpour 1987: 677):

those that occur in the social system of an organisation . . . the implementation of a new way to recruit personnel, allocate resources and structure tasks, authority and rewards. It comprises innovations in organisational structure and in the management of people.

In this respect it should be noted that administrative innovations are related to both material and immaterial matters (constructs and artefacts) (see Chapters 3 and 5).

An example of an administrative innovation is a transaction innovation. Take, for example, the way in which we withdraw money from the bank. In the early days we had to go to the desk in a bank office. We often had to wait in a queue. Nowadays money is withdrawn from an ATM and waiting times have been dramatically reduced. This transaction innovation has had two organisational consequences. Parts of the banking tasks have been made into standard activities which are dealt with by computers. Second, this rationalisation of the service process has resulted in a reduction in staff. Another example is the emergence of supermarkets. In traditional grocery shops the customer stood still while the shopkeeper walked around, whereas in the supermarket the customer walks around and the checkout operator sits behind the till. This entirely new way of working has had a radical impact on the structure and organisation of the retail trade.

Important aspects in the classification of innovations are those of **newness, change** and **improvements in performance** or realisation. These aspects have to be determined for products, services, production processes and organisations. Below, we will first go into a further differentiation of the term 'newness', and after that we will come back to the other aspects of change and performance improvement.

Innovations can be categorised in terms of newness based on a dimension that runs from radical via incremental to imitation. Radical innovations are based on fundamental inventions that are 'new to the world'. When we think of the **relevant adoption-unity** (West and Farr 1990) we do not speak of 'the' world, but 'a' world. The effects of **radical innovations** are very far-reaching, for they change the rules of the game. To put it briefly, when something is completely new it will lead to a completely new (market) infrastructure (O'Connor 1998; Song and Montoya-Weiss 1998). Radical and fundamental innovations are commonly followed by a large number of innovations connected with them. For example, think of the first integrated circuits and the consequences for electronics technology.

Somewhat less far-reaching is the **really new innovation**. A completely new product or service is being developed which leads to a discontinuity in the market or in the technology itself. A good example of this is the cell phone. As opposed to the computer this product and its use are not radical innovations because telephones already existed, so at the macro level the break from the existing technology is not complete. Cell phones have, however, led to a discontinuity in the market and the product. The production process of the mobile telephone has in fact been designed from scratch, so only in this sense can one speak of a radical innovation.

Somewhat less renewing are **discontinuous innovations**, the so-called **game changers**. These innovations offer the possibility of realising an improvement in performance of 5–10 times, to reduce costs by 30–50%, or to introduce an existing item with completely new characteristics (Rice, O'Connor and Peters 1998). An example is the introduction of broadscreen televisions in the late 1990s.

Next, we have **incremental innovations**. These are strongly focused on renewal and improvement. Here, rules are not changed, but the game is played better. These innovations lead to products and services that provide existing technology in an existing market with new qualities, revenues or improvements (Garcia and Calantone 2002). The ongoing development of Microsoft operating systems is an example.

Finally, at the opposite pole of the newness dimension are **imitative innovations**— innovations that are new for a particular company or organisation. However, they are not new in terms of product, service or process, nor do they offer any kind of renewal in terms of the market (Garcia and Calantone 2002). The most obvious example of imitative innovations is the copying of Western designer brands and goods by Chinese manufacturers, offered at much cheaper prices due to extremely low labour costs. About 30 years ago Japan followed a similar path but, in later years, it turned to other types of innovations.

The dimension of newness demonstrates that innovations involve the following aspects (Garcia and Catalone 2002):

- Science as well as the state of the knowledge in physics and the behavioural sciences
- The product, the service or the process and the structure itself
- The market, other companies, consumers and customers
- The company or the organisation itself

An innovation is radical if there is discontinuity in all four aspects; an innovation is merely an imitation if there is only a new company or organisation involved (see Table 2.1).

	Radical	Really new	Discontinuous	Incremental	Imitative
Science/technology	✓				
Production/service	✓	✓	✓		
Environment of organisation	✓	✓		✓	
Organisation/firm	✓	✓	✓	✓	✓

TABLE 2.1 Types of innovation and aspects on which innovation is based

The dimension of newness also shows that the more radical an innovation, the more uncertainty and risk is involved. In the case of radical innovations the chances of failure are therefore much more severe than for incremental innovations. Another factor concerns complexity. This factor can be measured by the number of components involved in an innovation which is, in turn, related to the number of disciplines (Kleinknecht, Reijnen and Smits 1992). The more disciplines involved, the more complex and, as a result, the more risky the innovation.

Measuring innovations: but on which level of aggregation?

In addition to the dimension of newness there are also aspects of change and improvement in performance. How can we deal with these aspects and how should they be classified? If one speaks of an improvement in performance it is implicitly assumed that a measurement or a comparison has occurred between a new innovation and an older one. We can accept that there is renewal, so for now we will leave that out of consideration. On the basis of which measurements are innovations compared? Let us say straight away that there is no answer to this question. Too many factors are involved. What is helpful to begin with, though, is to make a distinction in terms of aggregation levels: namely, that of the individual, the team, the department, the network and society. With respect to each of these levels a limited number of factors can be considered.

The discussion about assessing the value of innovations has been initiated by, among others, Porter (1985) who asks why some stimulation measures work for innovations where others do not. Porter illustrates this by pointing at clusters of particular organisations on the regional level which are very successful in certain combinations. Using Silicon Valley as an example, the combination of good universities, a tradition of entrepreneurship in which failure is no deadly sin, the availability of particular flows and forms of capital and the mutual network approach of companies have resulted in many successful innovations. A large number of countries have tried to realise their own Silicon Valleys, but unambiguous success has not been achieved. As aggregation levels Porter has in particular chosen the region as well as value adding which, under certain preconditions, can develop into a cluster of organisations.

When starting at the lowest level of aggregation, namely that of the individual, we see that research into innovations is especially concentrated on working methods, individual skills and work goals. Without unambiguous results a great deal of research has been conducted on the personality characteristics of innovators or inventors (see Rogers 1962). In this kind of research, however, the social aspect is often ignored. Early on, Burns and Stalker (1961) claimed that the fixed notion of the brilliant individual is a myth. More recently, however, too much emphasis has been put on the social character of innovations (Nonaka and Takeuchi 1995), and this leads to the impression that innovations are not based on a particular individual's creation.

A more moderate position can be taken by stating that organisations and innovations are **multi-actor systems**. The multi-actor perspective sees people as combinations of functions, roles and expertise who, in combination with communication patterns and organisational forms, have to achieve implementation after invention (Kratzer 2001). In this respect, factors that can be measured include multidisciplinarity, knowledge dispersal, research climate, safety and trust as well as experience and expertise.

Since individuals are not capable of realising innovations on their own, it is wise to look at teams as well. This is because creativity can only be given form by interaction, and a team is an effective and efficient instrument for this purpose. It is important that the various team members have a proper balance between diversity and depth, but also that there is a sufficient degree of coherence to ensure both individual self-determination and the integration of functions. To achieve this, communication and knowledge sharing are very important (Kratzer 2001). Factors that play a role here are staff member satisfaction, the participation of individuals in several innovation projects and the possibility of knowledge accumulation.

When looking at a higher aggregation level we end up with the organisation. What is of importance to the organisation here is its size, organisational structure (Kanter 1983) and its **absorptive capacity** (Cohen and Levinthal 1990). The latter refers to the extent to which an organisation is capable of taking up new ideas coming from the outside. This is mostly organised in R&D units. Research has shown that an innovation requires a small-sized (internal) organisation in which the interaction among people is informal and which is led by a decisive figure who can make decisions supported by management (van de Ven et al. 1999). As regards organisation size, it should be noted that only (very) large companies can actually afford an R&D department.

On the level of the company or organisation within its network or in the market, a great deal of research has been conducted in the value chain (see von Hippel 1988) and in strategy and network management (Miles and Snow 1978). The productivity of innovations has been studied by comparing R&D expenses and patents obtained. All these measures have an economic basis in the sense that innovations are being compared in terms of money spent and acquired. In this respect, Porter has pointed at the acquisition of patents. Without criticising the necessity of measurement, the disadvantage of a calculation in terms of finances or number of patents is that only the outcome counts—measured, moreover, in a very specific way—rather than the process that led to it. Besides, with regard to measurement in terms of patents, the emphasis is on who comes first. From a social perspective in which competition is the basis for a good performance, for example in the US, this may work. The view here is that the gains—investments and revenues—of the innovations are to be attributed to the private organisation. However, in a social structure in which public and private are much more interwoven, as in Europe, this is almost impossible.

On the level of countries, the debate on the measurement of innovations is conducted almost entirely in macroeconomic terms. This has led to discussions about quantifications in which decisions are hard to make, such as the number of graduates of technical universities within a country (input indicator) or the number of innovation projects (output indicator). Some people speak of system innovation in terms of changes at the national or international level. The latter are dramatic social changes on a very high aggregation level with a running time of 30–50 years (Rotmans 2003). No measurements can in fact be given on this level of aggregation.

From the aforementioned, it is obvious that there are no uniform, generally accepted measures for innovation. With each aggregation level there are controversial measures. What is important, however, is the interplay of individuals, teams, organisations, an adequate educational infrastructure and organisational forms that are more informal. Combining these issues into one measure is a task for the future.

Conclusions: problem-solving, innovation and knowledge

Our first point of departure has been that of the individual. It is always individuals who, in one way or another, carry out activities. And this also applies to innovations. The individuals are, however, not economic subjects but human information processors with all kinds of cognitive possibilities and limitations (Newell and Simon 1972). This is reflected by their ways of problem-solving, co-operation and the exchange of knowledge. People are rational to a limited degree, they cannot know everything and, even if this were the case, they would not be able to process all this information cognitively (Simon 1960). This means that often people settle for solutions that are 'satisfying' rather than for those that are 'optimal'.

The perspective we have on innovations as such is, following Simon, that of problem-solving. Whenever a problem has to be solved, it must first be observed. We could give a complex description of what a problem is, but what it basically comes down to is the observation of a difference between a present situation and a desired situation. The observation of a discrepancy is the motivator for seeking new possibilities (March and Simon 1958). An innovation will not be initiated if the current situation is experienced as sufficient. People are, in this respect, 'satisfiers' (they settle for what is sufficient) rather than 'optimisers' (they only settle for the best). This is in line with people's limited cognitive processing capabilities and the principle of 'the least amount of effort' (March and Simon 1958).

So, considering innovation as solving a problem enables us to look at the (cognitive and behavioural) qualities of the problem-solver, but also at the problem-solving process itself. According to Newell and Simon (1972) problem-solving consists of two main steps. First, a **problem space** has to be defined and, second, within a particular problem space the **best solution** (in practice, often the most sufficient) has to be found. Given a problem space that is relatively well known, most human activities entail the second step—finding solutions. This is no easy task, however. It can involve a great deal of thinking and investigation.

Innovations are different in this respect as the problem space is often removed, restricted or expanded. Once a problem space is removed, a new one has to be found or defined. This costs time, often requires new terminology and is, to a large degree, uncertain and therefore difficult to predict.

In the innovation literature, the two steps in problem-solving processes are also called the phases of **exploitation** and of **exploration** (March 1991). Exploitation is then the search for new solutions in an already existing or slightly adjusted problem space, whereas exploration comes down to creating new problem spaces. A contradiction strongly arises here. March himself indicates that exploration and exploitation have to be placed on a continuum as two poles of extremity. This makes it possible to consider or rephrase a radical innovation as exploration and an incremental innovation as exploitation.

The different phases in innovation, the kinds of innovation and the psychological and sociological perspectives on innovation do not change the fact that innovation is actually knowledge creation. This means that in any discussion on innovation, knowledge is central. To put it simply, knowledge is both the primary source and the outcome of an innovation. We will come back to this in Chapter 6. Here, it suffices to limit ourselves to the discussion of the various phases in innovation when dealing with knowledge. While doing this we make no choice between individuals and teams. In each of the phases both of them occur with a different emphasis. Apart from creating knowledge, the key activity in innovation is sharing knowledge. No matter how brilliant a new invention or service may be, if it is not transferred, shared or used, the innovation will not be successful.

26 SUSTAINABLE INNOVATION

From a knowledge management perspective the following phases can be distinguished: knowledge creation; knowledge encoding; knowledge storage and maintenance; knowledge access and availability; and knowledge use. Elaborating on our objective to stimulate the SoK (sustainability of knowledge), it should be obvious that sustainability will increase as the phases are better connected with each other, are more transparent and have the proper organisational forms.

Knowledge creation → Knowledge encoding → Knowledge acquisition and storage → Knowledge dispersal/ sharing → Knowledge management/ maintenance → Knowledge use (have knowledge used)

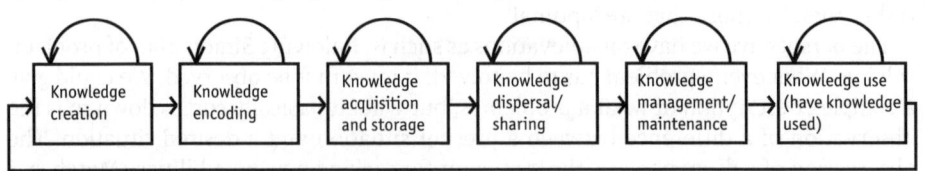

FIGURE 2.1 The consecutive knowledge phases of innovations

Although in Figure 2.1 the consecutive phases have been depicted linearly they in fact occur iteratively. This means that there are a large number of feedback loops. Also, knowledge creation itself starts with something. An actual *creatio ex nihilo* (creation from nothing) does not occur in innovations. Within this sequence, the content of knowledge can be looked at phase by phase, with regard to the people involved, the form in which the knowledge is presented and the importance of the individual and the team.

With this brief explanation of the essential importance of knowledge in innovations (see also Chapter 6) we end this chapter. Based on the foregoing we can draw the following conclusions:

- Innovation is a form of problem-solving whereby a distinction is made between expanding a problem space (exploration) and searching within the problem space (exploitation)

- Regardless of what technicians and economists might say about the subject, an innovation is and remains the work of people. This means that attention should explicitly be paid to the way in which people think and reason, the way in which they are organised and the way in which their co-operation is structured

- An innovation is knowledge creation in which knowledge is the primary source, is involved in the process and constitutes the final outcome

- Innovations cannot be measured objectively. The measurement depends on the aggregation level of people, team, department, organisation, network and country. On each of these levels different variables to be measured can be indicated

- Making innovations sustainable implies that within the different phases knowledge is dealt with in an adequate manner. 'Adequate' means, in this context, transparent, with a clearer focus on re-use and more adequate knowledge sharing and dispersal. The organisational forms and co-ordination mechanisms must be attuned to these goals

- Innovation also means learning in its various aspects—learning by undertaking action, learning by understanding, learning by sharing and learning by being more aware of the facts. All these types of learning have a bearing on the knowledge and skills of individual people, on their mutual understanding of complex problems and, therefore, also on their co-operation

3
Sustainability
FROM ENVIRONMENT AND TECHNOLOGY TO PEOPLE AND ORGANISATIONS

René J. Jorna and Niels R. Faber

In discussions about possible solutions to problems of sustainability there exists a clear focus on the environment and technology. Although there is nothing wrong with this, this focus may paint an incomplete and inadequate picture. In spite of the logical association of ecology and environment with sustainability, various interpretations of this concept have been conceived over time. In this respect we refer to the economic and social perspectives, the so-called 'profit' and 'people' pillars of sustainability.

In the economic perspective, growth received a great deal of attention as a source of sustainable development. Growth is often connected with profitability and is one of the motives for the activities of a commercial organisation. A company can fund its renovations by the profits resulting from its entrepreneurial activities. It is this renovation that can be a source of sustainability. Unfortunately, in countries where the economic system has banished this stimulus completely, often an enormous backlog appears with respect to the sustainability.

Another theme is social structuring as a fundamental aspect of sustainable development. However, until now, it has not been actively used as a concept. Efforts within the framework of this component are mostly made within a certain social ideology based on solidarity and eradication of poverty. Concrete initiatives in this respect are, for example, developmental co-operation or remittance of the debts of developing countries. Here, the focus is especially on reducing the gap between the poor and the rich. **Social capital**, the business-oriented translation of this social component, introduced in the concept of the **triple bottom line**, has received a considerable amount of attention (Sauvante 2001). Social capital is subdivided into human capital and capital in the form of social systems. Healy and Côté (2001) refer to social capital as the norms and networks enabling co-operation among and within groups. We will return to this subject in Chapters 5 and 6.

This introductory discussion about the ecological, economic and social components of sustainability makes clear that this concept is anything but unambiguous and, especially with respect to the social component, has not yet been operationalised properly. Since sustainability is one of the core concepts in this book we will discuss it thoroughly. We will do this by first addressing related issues, such as **socially accountable entrepreneurship** (SAE), **corporate social responsibility** (CSR) and **corporate governance** (CG). Then we will discuss a number of definitions of sustainability and categorise them with respect to three dimensions: type of artefact, absolute–relative and static–dynamic. We then explain our description of sustainability as a **reduction in offload** and, finally, we indicate how this can be operationalised.

Social-organisational developments in the framework of sustainability

What makes sustainability different from concepts such as SAE, CSR and CG? In fact, they are highly similar and are often put on the same footing. SAE and CSR involve interpretations of sustainability while CG deals with adequate company management. SAE means that a company is aware that it is part of a greater whole, both in an environmental and a social sense. Entrepreneurship is not a goal in itself but is placed in a broader social context. This could involve external social organisational policies, such as adopting a school or a hospital, or making company facilities available for neighbourhood events. Or it could mean adopting policies such as choosing not to sack employees immediately when the economic climate deteriorates.

CSR means that an organisation has responsibilities that go beyond the optimisation of profits. This could imply taking account of the views of stakeholders (see Chapter 7) within and around the organisation rather than considering only the shareholders. Often, these activities are not directly related to the management of the organisation but they are connected with its corporate image. Because of its responsibility component, CSR is more oriented towards ethic-normative issues than is SAE. Nevertheless, CSR and SAE have a lot in common. In the discussion about sustainability they both emphasise the people pillar of sustainability, placing the organisation in its wider social context, and are both focused on the short as well as the long term. The key difference between them is that SAE puts more emphasis on the business economic aspects and CSR more on the ethical aspects.

In the past few years the discussion about CG has changed. Through its CG an organisation tries to show that managing a business is more than simply pursuing short-term profits. Until some five years ago sustainability was not an issue. In the Netherlands, under the influence of the Tabaksblat Committee (2004),[1] aspects of the incorruptible and socially responsible organisation have received a great deal of attention in the dis-

---

1 The Tabaksblat Committee issued a proposal in 2001 in favour of responsible behaviour by boards of directors, executives and commissioners.

cussion about CG. Although the term 'sustainability' is not explicitly mentioned in this discussion, risk control and transparency in communication with stakeholders are key issues. As a result, in the light of adequate CG, sustainability is an element that has increased in importance. However, in SAE and CSR the sustainability concept is a core theme which we will now discuss more thoroughly.

Sustainability is a complex concept with a contradictory quality. It seems to imply that our resources should be inexhaustible or that they should replenish themselves. Moreover, we as people want to have them at our disposal for our entire lives. Indeed, we want to live even longer than nature allows. We want to be sustainable ourselves. In this way, sustainability touches both us and our surroundings. Before elaborating on the sustainability concept in a more structured way, we would first like to illustrate the sustainability theme with one example. We will do this by primarily starting from the planet perspective—resource consumption.

The history of sustainability in the ecological sense shows that in the past various resources were addressed and left to dry up again. Van Zon and Kuipers (2002) describe the development of the timber industry, the mining industry and population growth. With regard to the timber industry, all the wood currently in existence could never be sufficient for all our needs. The mining sector also has serious limitations. Therefore, in Europe coal mining has, for the greater part, been abandoned. Nevertheless, new materials have been developed to compensate for the shortages and to complement them. A similar story can be told about population growth. In the 1800s, Malthus (1798) predicted a world in the year 2000 that would collapse under its human burden. This did not happen. It seems that, in one way or another, we realise and maintain sustainability. It seems that where equilibrium is lost it can be retrieved. The question is whether this is a technological success, a human success or an organisational success. Or perhaps we are fooling ourselves and equilibrium cannot, once lost, be retrieved. One planet is all we have at the moment. In order to answer these questions we should approach the sustainability concept more thoroughly. Where does it come from, how is it defined and where will it lead us?

Some definitions of sustainability

Anyone who is confronted with sustainability for the first time will soon realise that, although the concept has been discussed by many and used by even more, a sharp unambiguous definition is lacking. To place sustainability in a usable framework, it has to be made clear what it is that distinguishes sustainability as a concept from other similar concepts, such as continuity, durability or permanency. For that matter, there is a problem with the Dutch term for sustainability, *duurzaamheid*, as it is a more general term related to the English concepts of sustainability, durability and renewability. Therefore, this chapter will not provide a precise definition of sustainability either. The best we can do is to map out, in a descriptive way, the context within which the concept has meaning.

Let us begin by establishing that sustainability is not a concept that stands on its own. It is a quality ascribed to certain issues. We ascribe this quality to things, matters and constructs, both tangible and intangible. For example, we speak of 'sustainable coffee', a 'sustainable society' and 'sustainable development'. By ascribing sustainability to a particular matter, both the sustainable nature and the degree of sustainability are indicated. However, ascribing sustainability to a particular matter remains meaningless if it is not clear what it entails.

Several meanings have been assigned to the sustainability concept. The Dutch classical dictionary Van Dale describes it as follows (1996: 737):

> Sustainable: suited to exist for a long time, durable, consistent; long lasting, continuous; a lasting memory; to be permanently divorced; to persist durably.

From this description it can be concluded that ascribing sustainability to a particular matter or thing refers to the degree to which the matter or thing is suitable to exist over a long period of time. However, the term 'sustainable coffee' does not, of course, refer to coffee that cannot be used. So the definition offered here does not clarify what is meant by a long existence or which factors determine that a particular matter can exist for a long period of time. After some more reflection we will come to the conclusion that the term 'sustainable coffee' refers to the *process* of producing coffee.

The way in which sustainability is used at the present moment is based on the English term 'sustainability' which is an expression of the possibility of a certain matter to be supported. Apart from the term 'sustainability', the English language also knows the closely related terms of 'durability' and 'endurability'. Freely translated, these terms mean, respectively, wear-resistant or lasting and bearable (easy to bear). This range of terms does not make the discussion about sustainability any easier. However, there are similarities in these terms. According to the given description, ascribing sustainability to a particular matter expresses the possibility that this matter can exist for a long(er) period of time. In line with the term 'sustainability', the matter can exist longer because it can be supported. Therefore, as a result, sustainability is not just a characteristic of a particular issue, it connects the issue to its environment. Thus, the term 'sustainability' reflects the possibility that a particular matter can be supported by its environment for a longer period of time. In this way it can be directly distinguished from the related concepts of durability and endurability. These terms respectively express the built-in capacity of a particular matter to fend off or bear external influences. Rather than connecting the matter to its environment, they merely express its inherent quality.

The word 'sustainable' is often especially used in the area of energy where it is referred to as 'renewable'. This means that the use of this type of energy, such as wind, wave and solar, has no limitations because it can be regained. In particular, hydrogen fuel-cell technology, which is rapidly gaining momentum, claims to be completely sustainable. By means of sun, wind, tidal or water energy, water can be split into hydrogen and oxygen. The hydrogen stored in a hydrogen cell provides energy and results in water. In turn, energy can be retrieved from the sun, wind or water (white current). As already observed, sustainability is considered as an obvious framework for dealing wisely with energy and resources.

More than 50 official definitions of sustainability can be found. The number of indicator lists based on these definitions, which are intended to make sustainability operational, is a multiple of this (Faber, Jorna and van Engelen 2005). To give an impression of the large number of descriptions of sustainability we will offer a few:

> Meeting the needs of the present without compromising the ability of the future generations to meet their own needs. (WCED 1987: 43)
>
> Sustainable development is a process of change in which the use of resources, the direction of the investments, the orientation of technological development and institutional change are all in harmony, and (all) increase both the current and the future possibilities to meet the human needs and wishes. (WCED 1987; as reported in Garcia and Calantone 2002: 112)
>
> It [sustainability] not only applies to not harming the possibilities for future generations, but also the actual creation of more and better opportunities for future generations. (Kaptein and Wempe 1999: 93)
>
> I defined the business end of sustainable development in terms of value creation across the 'triple bottom line' of economic, social and environmental added—or destroyed. To make the concept more appetising for ordinary people I also introduced the 3P formula 'People, Planet and Profit', or as some preferred 'Prosperity'. (Elkington 1997: 67-96)
>
> A sustainable development of the world economy can only then be achieved if acceptable relations are established in the relationship between South and North, between poor and rich. We cannot force our trading partners in the South to meet our demands to approach the environment respectfully if we ourselves are not even capable to respect them by means of rewarding them adequately for their efforts in producing their goods. (Stephan Peijnenburg, managing director Max Havelaar Foundation [personal communication])
>
> I associate sustainability with concepts such as 'being in balance with one's surroundings', 'robust' and 'long-lasting". In my view a sustainable system is a system which functions, whenever possible, on the basis of natural resources and processes. (Den Blanken, NV PWN Water Board North Netherlands [personal communication]).

What is striking in the descriptions above is that, apart from that of WCED, no definition is actually given of sustainability. WCED connects sustainability with the notion that not only the 'here and now' need to be considered, but also the 'elsewhere and later'.

In fact, 'sustainability' and 'sustainable' again function as bulk terms. In these examples we can recognise two categories. The first is especially aimed at society and the second is more focused on the organisation. The above quotations show that one is concerned about the future of the earth, about human society and a balanced division of goods, resources and means in the world. Clashing interests are recognised, both with respect to society and organisation. In many of the quotations there is an underlying ethical discussion about which goals humanity should pursue. Most quotations implicitly refer to a kind of ideal typical final state. This final state seems to be directional to the situation of today. In the next section we will return to this observation of a directional end state.

What arouses our attention in the quotation from Den Blanken is the notion of a balance. We will investigate this idea later. The issues called 'sustainable' in the quotations mostly refer to abstract matters—the planet, human life, the living environment, society and the basis of existence. Sustainable products, sustainable services or sustainable production processes are not mentioned.

To go back into history, sustainability was first given worldwide attention by the Brundtland Report (WCED 1987: 43). Here, sustainability means 'providing for the needs of the current generations, without putting at risk the possibility for future generations to fulfil their needs'. The Brundtland Report distinguishes three fundamental components of sustainable development. The first is environmental protection and resource conservation. This is achieved by a gradual adjustment to the way in which technology is developed and used. The second involves economic growth. Brundtland argued that economic growth should be stimulated, with developing countries given the opportunity to experience a growth similar to that of the developed countries. The third component of sustainable development is social (re)structuring. The Brundtland Report warns that a worldwide gap between rich and poor will result in environmental decline in developing countries. So one important aspect of sustainable development is to tackle inequalities between the haves and the have-nots.

Another approach is that of the triple bottom line or the triple P of people, planet and profit. The triple P offers a more general approach to sustainability. Although it includes the three elements of sustainable development, it does not view these solely from the perspective of environmental protection. All three aspects contribute to achieving sustainability. In this respect the planet component is mostly considered in terms of biological and physical terminology and variables, the profit component in terms of financial terminology and variables, and the people component in terms of social structuring, social capital or social justice. The problem with the last component is that it is hardly operational. Since social capital in the sense of human and organisational possibilities is considered as the core of sustainable innovation, we will come back to it later.

When we look at the essence of the aforementioned descriptions of sustainability, we see that sustainability is linked to a number of issues. However, an example such as sustainable coffee involves other factors than do either sustainable development or sustainable energy. So, sustainability is always interpreted in a specific way, depending on the issue itself and the context. Sustainability is an issue, service, product or construct if it is considered within the context in which it has been established and exists.

Our general point of view is that a particular matter (thing, service or construct) that is referred to as sustainable has, with respect to its existence and functioning, a certain interaction with its supporting environment. And, depending on the nature of the matter (thing, construct, etc.), certain parts of that environment are addressed—people, planet and profit or the social, ecological and economic components. Some also refer to 'man', 'environment' and 'surplus value'. In this respect it is not the absolute value of the individual components that is relevant, but the combination of the total range of components.

Within the triple-bottom-line concept we can go to an even deeper level. The cause and effect relations of the three Ps can differ a great deal. A lack of ecological sustainability is often considered a reason to interfere (technically). Here, the relation of cause and effect is that of planet (technical intervention) with planet. However, often a lack of sustainability is the consequence of a particular design of a company, organisation or society. In the work of Carson (1972), Naess (1973) and Sessions (1995) the environmental issue is considered as resulting from a certain design or configuration of organisations, from knowledge use and from fundamental starting points on which our way of working is based. The Norwegian philosopher and argumentation theorist Arne Naess made the first steps towards this view. In a speech at the Third World Future Congress in 1972 Naess made a significant distinction between **shallow ecology** and **deep ecology**. Shallow ecology is not primarily eco-oriented; it is people-oriented and, in many cases, especially aimed at people in the West. More complex environmental solutions are often found in the export or purchasing of pollution. One only has to think of the trade in carbon emissions which, despite being strongly criticised, was accepted as the best that could be achieved. Naess puts it as follows (quoted from McElroy 2002: 3):

> The essence of deep ecology is to ask deeper questions. The adjective 'deep' stresses that we ask why and how, where others do not. For instance, ecology as a science does not ask what kind of society would be the best for maintaining a particular ecosystem; that is considered a question for value theory, for politics, for ethics. As long as ecologists keep narrowly to their science, they do not ask such questions. What we need today is a tremendous expansion of ecological thinking in what I call ecosophy. Sophy comes from the Greek term sophia, 'wisdom', which relates to ethics, norms, rules and practice. Ecosophy, or deep ecology, then, involves a shift from science to wisdom. For example, we need to ask questions like: why do we think that economic growth and high levels of consumption are so important? The conventional answer would be to point to the economic consequences of not having economic growth. But in deep ecology, we ask whether the present society fulfils basic human needs like love and security and access to nature, and, in so doing, we question our society's underlying assumptions. We ask which society, which education, which form of religion is beneficial for all life on the planet as a whole, and then we ask further what we need to do in order to make the necessary changes. We are not limited to a scientific approach; we have an obligation to verbalise a total view.

Deep ecology is, in principle, ecocentric rather than anthropocentric. Obviously, it is about the well-being of people, but that is not the only issue. It is aimed at the interaction between humans and their environment, not only the natural and biological environment, but also the social, mental and knowledge environment. Deep ecology sees a biosphere consisting of people rather than one evolving around people. Deep ecology asks questions that touch at the core of our ways of working and organising things. This does not mean that technology and science are *either* the problem *or* the answer. Science and technology are *both* the problem *and* the answer. We will return to this later in this chapter.

The discussion about deep ecology leads to four conclusions regarding sustainable innovation. First, Naess makes clear that sustainability does not refer to people *or* the environment, but to people *and* the environment or, rather, to people *and* organisations *and* the environment. Second, the debate on sustainability should begin by asking the right questions. Asking questions leads to knowledge creation. Not only is existing knowledge used or built upon, it is also produced. By asking the (proper) questions knowledge creation begins which can lead to a leap in thinking (see Chapter 1). Third, Naess's line of thought shows that increasing complexity asks for a system approach since everything is connected. Fourth, it is not true that technology is the cause of all deficiencies and mistakes. On the contrary, technology has played and will continue to play a crucial role in solving these deficiencies and mistakes. This does not alter the fact that aspects relating to social and organisational issues will always play a role, simply because people design, implement and use technology.

The discussion about the meaning of sustainability clarifies a number of issues. It is a general term which has often been interpreted in different ways. Its basic meaning is positive. How could anyone not wish to be sustainable? In addition, with respect to the sustainability concept, several components can be distinguished—ecological, economic and social. Further, anything that is sustainable is part of a context. The key question therefore is: is it still possible to make sense of this maze of meanings? In order to do so, we have to engage in a discussion about the conceptual foundations of sustainability and its definitions.

Classifying the definitions: thing–construct, absolute–relative, static–dynamic

When considering the various descriptions of the sustainability concept, the question 'sustainability of what?' instantly springs to mind. Sustainability is used to describe the quality of a type of thing or construct. In case of sustainable energy or the relation between the global ecology and economic developments (Meadows et al. 1972), it is about constructs. Sustainability reflects a relationship between an artefact and its supporting environment with respect to a specific aspect of this artefact. And, in principle, this relationship is a continuous one. In other words, there is a balance between the artefact and its supporting environment without the occurrence of disadvantageous effects for either party. In this respect, sustainability focuses on equilibrium. Logically speaking, sustainability should not be seen as a one-placed (monadic) operator, but as a two-placed (dyadic) one; thus, X is sustainable in relation to Y. By contrast, the term 'endurable' is a monadic operator. It says something about the inherent potential of a thing or artefact to resist the harmful influences of the external environment. Something continues to exist, but the fact that it does so does not actually say anything about its connection with the environment in which it exists.

On the basis of this first step of categorisation a classification has been made (Faber, Jorna and van Engelen 2005) which, with respect to the sustainability definitions, uses three dimensions to which sustainability is deemed applicable:

- To an entity (thing) or construct (both to be considered as an artefact)
- The point of reference regarding sustainability
- The nature of the relation of the good (asset), thing or construct with the environment

The first aspect concerns 'sustainability of what'. It involves the concreteness of something called sustainable. In a general sense we speak of an artefact. Herbert Simon (1969) was one of the first to deal with this subject in a systematic way. He accordingly implies that artefacts are made by people and can take many forms, from concrete to abstract. We will call concrete artefacts 'things' and abstract artefacts 'constructs'. So we may speak of sustainable cars, sustainable development and also of sustainable innovation. The first artefact is directly visible, the last two merely indirectly. Naturally, a consequence of using artefacts that cannot be seen as wholes is that in determining sustainability there are always different characteristics involved.

The second aspect concerns the point of reference used to determine when an artefact is sustainable and when it is not. In this respect we can distinguish between an absolute and a relative standard. The absolute approach starts from a continuum with two extremes—not sustainable and sustainable. An artefact has a sustainability value if it fits somewhere on this continuum; the value is determined by the distance between the established situation and the most remote extremity. Starting from the most extreme poles this can be called the absolute evaluation. This absolute evaluation of sustainability is in line with Beth's view (1959) on Aristotle's principle of the absolute which he used for a large number of change perspectives in philosophy. By means of this principle Beth wanted to indicate that according to many philosophers there is an **ultimate good** which motivates all human actions. Beth deliberately uses the name of Aristotle instead of Plato because the latter is more clearly associated with the ultimate good. Contrary to what many think, Beth argues that Aristotle does not differ from Plato on this issue.

Beth's reconstructive analysis is as follows. Each activity is carried out to achieve something **good**. This is only possible if there is actually a good at which all things aim. There are three different goals (goods):

- Activities aiming at a direct goal
- Activities serving a goal that is subordinate to a higher goal (of which one may be unaware)
- The possibility that there is a higher goal which is subordinate to an even higher goal (of which one may be unaware)

This last step in Aristotle's principle of the absolute is reflected in the statement that 'the aim of all our activities has to be a good and even a highest good'. By formulating this principle Beth indicates that there is a good and even a **highest good**. If we replace 'good' by 'sustainable' we have a similar line of reasoning. We should realise though, that the 'most sustainable' has in fact become unreachable. It seems to give direction, but it is actually an empty concept likely to be counterproductive. Because nobody knows the most sustainable, achieving it implies that one is either free to pursue a (dangerous) illusion or undertake no action whatsoever. Beth saw that many philosophers applied the principle he formulated (**the real truth**, **the good life** or **the classless society**). We can also see this principle being applied by ideologists in our era as **the real market** and by scientists as **the one force**.

In contrast to the absolute approach, a relative approach can be presented. If the notion of an existing ultimate good is put aside, there will, as a consequence, be no ultimate goal left to pursue. Instead, the alternative is a more pragmatic perspective which leads to a valuation of the sustainability concept by taking a relative approach. A relative approach starts from the existing situation and begins by mapping out existing problems that people try subsequently to solve. A relative approach tends to start from the here and now and aims at repairing the existing situation. Some people call this piecemeal engineering since improvements will be incremental. And faults or mistakes can, if necessary, be redressed quickly. In contrast with the absolute approach, the focus of the relative approach is not the ultimate good, but the less bad or the better.

The third aspect concerns the distinction between static and dynamic and deals with the dynamics of the artefact and its environment. The artefact may be subjected to changes resulting from internal components that alter its structure. However, this can also happen as the result of external changes in the environment to which, in turn, the artefact reacts. Labelling an artefact as 'sustainable' can either refer to changes in both or in none. A static view of sustainability is applicable when the artefact is either static or dynamic, while the environment is static and remains so. The relation between the components and the internal structure of the artefact and its environment remains unaltered. In the balance between both, the only important thing is the scale of the interaction. The artefact's sustainability especially depends on its potential to change in connection with the dynamic environment.

From a dynamic perspective both artefact and environment are subject to changes that influence the balance of sustainability. The artefact can anticipate these changes by following those taking place in the environment and by adjusting to them internally. In this way, the sustainability balance remains intact. Take, for example, an organisation. It can be sustainable only if the organisation not only considers itself as a whole in relation to the environment, but is also capable of making internal changes to improve the balance with its environment. Also, the autonomous internal changes within the organisation should be dealt with in such a way that they are attuned to the environment. One can speak of a dynamic perspective on sustainability if both the artefact's internal powers and the environment's external powers continuously lead to adjustments.

Broader definitions of sustainability (Faber, Jorna and van Engelen 2005) from between 1970 and 2002 show that the way in which sustainability has been defined through the years is undergoing a conceptual development. It is becoming more complex because it is more and more often referred to in terms of constructs rather than things. The basic assumption of an artefact and its relation to the environment is gaining momentum. Moreover, a shift can be observed from the absolute approach to sustainability starting from a static environment to the notion that sustainability is relative and, in addition, should be placed within a dynamic environment.

Our definition: a dynamic balance and a reduction in offload

It is the connection between an artefact and its environment that distinguishes our definition from related terminology. By advocating a relative rather than an absolute position of the sustainability concept we formulate it as follows:

> An artefact (thing, construct, issue) is sustainable if its internal structure is in a dynamic balance with its environment. A dynamic balance means that the environment can be used, but that the environment itself also 'uses' the artefact.

In line with this definition and following Wijffels[2] we consider sustainability as the attempt to achieve a reduction in offloading. Offloading involves burdening, harming,

2 See Chapter 1, page 10.

destroying or exploiting the environment. Conduct of this kind is unacceptable and must cease, for in the long term it is harmful both to the environment and to the artefact itself.

There are many examples of **occurrence of offload** and **reduction in offload**. A reduction in offload can be achieved by including removal fees in the purchase of new appliances as well as by applying the Brundtland definition (1987) in which sustainability takes into account the needs of later generations. After all, we often do things and leave it to people elsewhere (or later) to cope with the consequences. In this sense, working and living in a sustainable way also means reducing the burden on our children. On the other hand, leaving behind waste in the natural environment as well as exhausting resources without replacing them are also forms of offload. Another example is a company which, in economically difficult times, dismisses a large number of its employees, who will, as a result, become a public charge. If, in addition, the company has tampered with the payment of premiums, it is clearly offloading onto the socioeconomic environment. A better example would be a company with a good occupational pension scheme.

In Figure 3.1 we depict sustainability according to its relative and dynamic description. Based on the assumption that an artefact is sustainable if it is in a dynamic balance with its environment, we see a reduction in offload as the central issue in making sustainability operational. As regards this reduction in offload, four aspects have to be described as accurately as possible:

- What is subjected to offload?
- Who transfers the what to whom?
- In what time horizon does this offload take place?
- What does a reduction in offload imply (again considered from the points of view of the what, the who and the time span)?

These aspects will be dealt with in each of the business projects described in Part C of this book. Part D elaborates on these issues from a more general perspective.

Figure 3.1 especially depicts the 'who'. The balance is good when there is an equilibrium between the levels of aggregation and bad when there is offload onto other levels. In that case we have a distorted equilibrium; the scales are out of balance. When the offload takes place from individual to organisation or society it is called centrifugal (see Fig. 3.1). A good example is the Dutch Disablement Insurance Act (1966). In the 1980s in the Netherlands, both employers and employees left their employment problems to be dealt with by society. People who were fired were diagnosed as sick and transferred onto benefits under the Act. In this case it was a matter of offload from the organisation to society or, in other words, from the inside to the outside. However, if there is an offload from society to the individual or organisation it is called centripetal. Examples are shifts in public to private matters which have increasingly occurred over the past 20 years. In the Netherlands, the transfer of education from public to private paid schools is an example. We can call this an offload from the outside to the inside.

Another example is the social rearrangement of sustainable energy. If every individual could arrange his/her own energy, local optimisation would be a possible consequence. However, this also means that a global suboptimisation may occur. The adverse

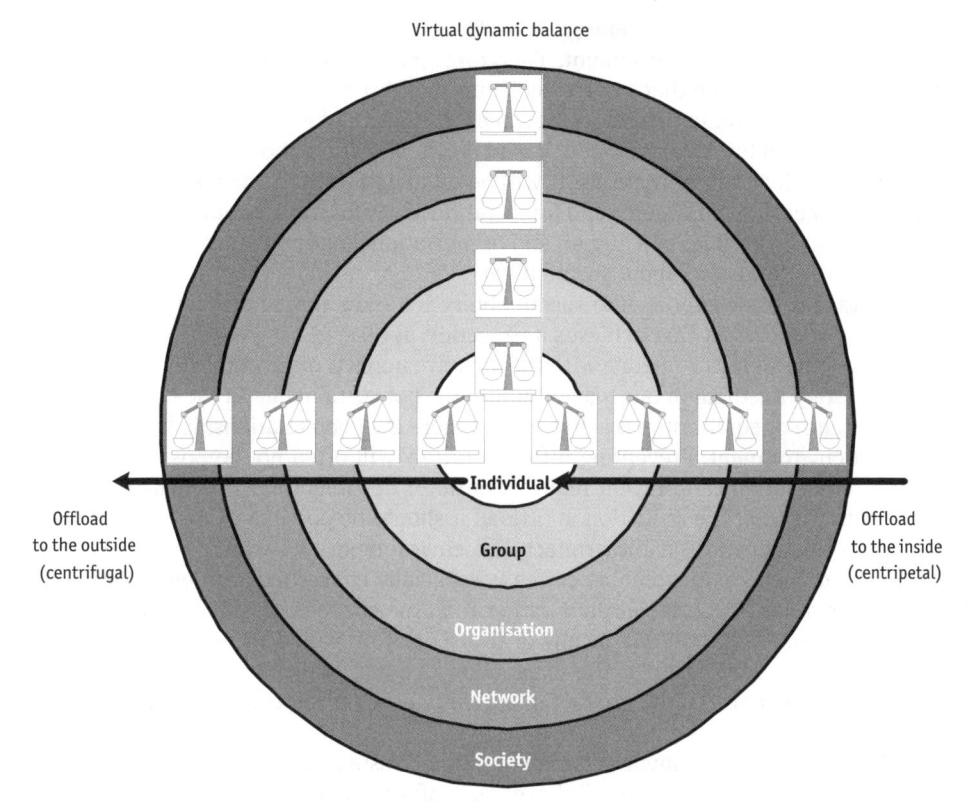

3. FROM ENVIRONMENT AND TECHNOLOGY TO PEOPLE AND ORGANISATIONS *Jorna and Faber*   39

FIGURE 3.1 NIDO Offload Model (NOM)

effects of this situation could entirely counteract the favourable effects of the summation of the individual situations. So, in this example, there is no reduction in offload.

Conclusions and making the reduction in offload operational

The debate on sustainability conducted so far provides the ingredients to structure and make operational the sustainability concept from a social perspective. We will give a summarised overview of this debate by presenting a number of points of interest while making use of examples related to sustainable coffee, sustainable energy and sustainable development.

In the first place a statement about the sustainability of something should always ask what it is that is sustainable. This is important with respect to determining the characteristics of this something: for example, emissions from a so-called sustainable car or the generation of sustainable energy. It is also important because an artefact is always in interaction with its environment. Therefore, this environment must also be classified. After all, we argue that an artefact is sustainable only if it is in a dynamic balance with its environment. In this respect it can be useful to make a distinction according to the triple bottom line of planet, people and profit. It is also important to find quantitative variables for each of these Ps. It will be quite easy to find chemical and physical variables for ecological systems and financial variables for the economy. It will be more difficult to find variables of a human and organisational nature that can be made operational in the discussion about sustainability.

Second, our basic approach to sustainability is a reduction in offload. The activity, act, thing or construct that achieves a reduction in offload can be called sustainable. Saddling something or someone with the negative impacts of current activities without compensating for them in one way or another is not sustainable. In the optimal situation a balance or equilibrium is achieved and there is a good relationship between artefact and environment. Preventing offload entirely will often not be possible, but the notion of reduction can prevent many harmful or detrimental consequences. On the basis of this idea of the reduction in offload it should be possible to apply a standard. Naturally this depends on the artefact, the environment and which characteristic is subjected to offload. Sustainable coffee is especially concerned with ensuring a reasonable price for the coffee farmers rather than the cheapest possible price for Western consumers. A sustainable means of transportation would focus on reducing the emission of harmful gases or the exhaustion of fossil fuels. So, a discussion about offload always concerns the artefact or a quality of the artefact in relation to its environment.

Third, offload always involves a time horizon. Waste products, polluting emissions or unhealthy living conditions will have a harmful effect in the long run. To increase people's awareness of sustainability a short time span between activity and harmful effect would be the most effective. However, there are often decades, sometimes centuries, between an activity and any resultant environmental effects. This leads many to think that things will get better and that in due time (technical) solutions will be found. Where there is a shorter gap between the activity and its environmental effects, there is more likely to be a realisation that certain activities should not take place: for example, global warming or ozone depletion. Artefacts concern matters created by people, either consciously or unconsciously, and this applies just as much to artefacts causing favourable effects as it does to those causing unfavourable effects. Timely prevention or intervention is often preferable than trying to repair total derailments.

Fourth, we state that when considering the aggregation levels of individuals, groups, organisations and society, offload can go in two directions (see Fig. 3.1). An individual could subject the group to offload which in turn could subject the company to it and then society. The reverse situation also occurs with offload by society onto organisations and organisations onto the individual.

Our debate on sustainability leads us to conclude that sustainability applies to artefacts, both in the form of things and constructs. These should be regarded as:

- Relative rather than absolute
- Context-bound and determined on the basis of their situation

- Changing in response to dynamic interaction with the environment
- Enormously complex

Returning to sustainable innovation, this type of innovation is a process that has no ending. As an artefact and a process, innovation must exist in connection with its 'supporting' environment: that is to say, the organisation. Innovation itself stands or falls with knowledge and is in fact the creation of knowledge. Innovations will work and continue only if the supporting environment is equipped for them. Here, the reduction in offload pays itself back instantly—innovations are successful if they are designed to be ongoing and if they fit into adequate organisational forms. Simply, people's knowledge should not be wasted and a co-ordination mechanism should not function inefficiently with respect to innovation in the value chain. This is the key to creating sustainable innovation in a sustainable society.

4
Levels of description, kinds of entities and systems

René Jorna and Henk Hadders

The basic perspective in our approach to sustainability is that of the human dimension. In our view of innovations, humans possess, create and share knowledge of various domains, with the emphasis on the domain of sustainability. Humans also make decisions, solve problems, create organisations and use them to make things happen. Especially in organisations, humans work, by definition, with other humans. An organisation is a mixture of the division and co-ordination of labour, actions and, of course, knowledge. Although inherently cohesive entities, organisations, mostly because of their financial and legal structures, do not operate in a void; they are interconnected with other organisations, which we may call **networks**. Networks can, like organisations, be informal or formal. Organisations and networks operate within larger structures, such as cultures and societies.

Humans, organisations, networks and societies are entities operating at different levels of **aggregation**. The latter are always included by the former or, to phrase it differently, the latter always consists of the former. Organisations consist of humans and 'things', such as buildings and other artefacts, just as a society consists of organisations of various kinds—firms, institutions and companies. Thus, we are dealing here with multi-layered systems.

In Chapter 2 we introduced the terms **system** and **actor**, in the sense that a system is a coherent whole consisting of its constituent parts whereas an actor is a coherent (intelligent) entity suitable for performing actions. Chapter 2 described an organisation as a **multi-actor system**. In Chapter 5 we will further discuss the various perspectives on and divisions in organisations. In this chapter we will concentrate on the multi-layering of the various entities. The overall perspective that we have on all these entities is that they are systems (Simon 1969; Lit 1992; von Bertalanffy 1968; Ashby

1956). Humans, organisations, networks and societies are systems, with different kinds of control, and made up of parts, feedback loops, boundaries and physical carriers.

If sustainability is viewed as a **reduction in offload**, further expressed in terms of X (entity) offloads W (something, what) to Y (entity) within t (time horizon) (see Chapter 3), it is important to know, besides W, who or what X and Y are as entities. This identification has consequences for the opportunities and possibilities in the process of reducing offload. Therefore, entities, systems and/or actors, either multi-layered or operating at different levels of aggregation, have to be discussed in greater detail. There are, however, two problems related to the discussion of different levels of aggregation and the various types of entities. First, it is difficult to strictly distinguish the levels from one another and, second, it is difficult to strictly determine the precise nature of the entities at the various levels of aggregation. The determination of a human (entity) is quite easy, but the determination of an organisation is more difficult and that of networks and societies is extremely hard. As a consequence, it is very difficult to find an easy way to approach or measure the higher-level entities in quantitative terms.

In this chapter we will try to give a description of kinds of layers and types of entities and their properties. Layers and entities have been discussed in other areas, especially in the philosophy of science and in epistemology (Bunge 1998). Recently, an extended discussion took place about levels of description in the domain of cognition (Newell 1990; Pylyshyn 1984). We will use this discussion as an exemplar. We will therefore begin by addressing the analogue situation in the study of cognitive systems to illustrate the reasons and the implications of the division into various levels of description. We will then describe the various entities, such as the individual, group, organisation or network, in greater detail. Then we will deal with two particular aspects of the various entities—the system's perspective as such and the complexity and adaptation of entities. Finally, we will present the first steps towards a systematic approach to sustainability.

Levels of description and the issue of reductionism

The way in which scientists study and describe phenomena depends on the perspective they use. Tangible phenomena require different perspectives compared to intangible. Within biology one can study separate microorganisms but also complete ecosystems. Examining the intriguing intangible phenomenon of the human mind also requires simultaneous perspectives. These perspectives depend on certain levels of aggregation, also called **levels of description**. According to Newell (1990: 118):

> Levels are clearly abstractions, being alternative ways of describing the same system, each level ignoring some of what is specified at the level beneath it.

To make clear what the issue of the levels of description means, we will first look explicitly at a detailed example from the domain of cognitive science. Next, we will extend this discussion to the main topic of this book—sustainability. We will first discuss cognition—that what enables a human to think, reason, remember, talk and understand—in short, our mental processes.

The idea of levels of description or explanation for a cognitive system has been worked out most elegantly by Dennett (1978, 1987, 1991). He distinguishes three independent levels or stances:

- Physical
- Design (or functional)
- Intentional

Other authors (Newell 1982, 1990; Pylyshyn 1984) have given similar accounts albeit with different numbers of levels. Newell says (1990: 46):

> Often we describe the same system in multiple ways . . . The choice of what description to use is a pragmatic one, depending on our purpose and our own knowledge of the system and its character.

In the following paragraphs we use Dennett's explanation of levels (1978, 1987). The physical stance explains behaviour in terms of physical properties of the states and behaviour of the system under concern. For its proper functioning the human organism requires a complex interaction with its parts as well as with the external world. The central nervous and the endocrine system are there to transmit information that reveals the state of one part of the system to other parts. We can also mention the transmission of currents in the synaptic system of neurons. Within cognition, this physical or physiological stance is the end-point of the ontological reduction.

The second level is the functional design of a system. In a functional description it is important to know the components of a cognitive system, how they are defined and how the components and subcomponents of systems are connected with one another. In other words, if the input and output of each component are known, the resulting behaviour can be predicted on the basis of characteristics of the components by using a particular input at the system's beginning. The behaviour of a system is considered as the result of the interaction among a number of functional components or processes. The physical structure of the system is not explicitly taken into account, although it may impose constraints on the behaviour of the system. The capacity limitations of human cognition will, for instance, impose a boundary on the complexity of decision-making.

In the third place Dennett distinguishes the intentional stance. According to some criteria of optimality, complex behaviour that is adapted to the prevailing circumstances is said to be rational or intelligent. A behaving system to which we can successfully attribute rationality or intelligence qualifies as an intentional system. It is not necessary for a behaving system to 'really' possess rationality or intelligence, as long as the assumption allows us to correctly predict the behaviour of the system on the basis of our knowledge of the circumstances in which it is operating.

One may deal with this level's distinction in two essentially different ways. By making this distinction Dennett (1978) has taken a strictly instrumentalist perspective, claiming only a pragmatic validity. Summarising his position 20 years later, he wrote (Dennett 1998: 119):

> As I have put it, physical stance predictions trump design [or functional] stance predictions which trump intentional stance predictions—but one pays for the power with a loss of portability and a (usually unbearable) computational cost.

In contrast to Dennett, authors such as Fodor (1975), Newell (1990) and Pylyshyn (1984) assign an ontological meaning to each level. The higher levels introduce emergent qualities into human behaviour that make no sense if we maintain an instrumentalist point of view.

Dennett's threefold distinction is applicable to cognitive systems in a broader environment. It also fits the multidisciplinary approach taken in cognitive science where neuroscientists emphasise the physical or physiological level of description, cognitive psychologists emphasise the functional or symbolic level and social psychologists and economists emphasise the intentional level of description. The fundamental proposition of cognitive science is to explain phenomena at the intentional level in terms of descriptions at the functional or symbolic level. Other cognitive scientists, such as Smolensky (1988), have studied the inter-level between the physical/physiological and the functional by proposing connectionism with its symbolic and subsymbolic processes.

The discussion about the various levels has, of course, consequences for the relations among the levels. This is a recurring debate (Nagel 1961). Some cognitive scientists (Churchland 1984) argue that the distinction of the levels for cognition will ultimately show that the intentional levels will be reduced to functional levels and, in turn, the functional levels to physical levels. In the philosophy of science this debate is called **reductionism**. Simply said, reductionism claims that higher levels are in one way or another reducible to lower levels. Just as psychology should be reduced to biology, and biology to chemistry and physics, in cognitive science intentional statements should be reducible to physiological or neurological ones. This so-called vertical reductionism presupposes the existence of bridging laws which can entirely explain the concepts of the one level in terms of the other lower level. In contrast to reductionism is **emergentism** which implies that properties studied at a higher level are more than just compositions of properties and concepts at a lower level. Higher levels can never completely be understood in terms of the properties at the lower level.

Despite the classical philosophical flavour of this debate about reductionism, taking a position influences the research agenda for all science not just cognitive psychology. From the 1960s to the 1990s the relevance of the separate levels was accepted within cognitive science with the acknowledgment that neurological structures determine the boundaries of the higher levels. In other words, the lower levels **underdetermine** the higher levels. Newell and Simon's (1976) physical symbol system hypothesis is an example of this position.

Although working in the field of cognitive science, Newell (1990) also used levels of description analysis for research into computer systems. A computer as an empirical phenomenon consisting of hardware and software can be described at different levels—as a composition of electronic devices, as a set of electrical circuits, as a set of logical circuits, as a combination of programmes and, possibly, as a knowledge system. At the same time, it can be described as a hierarchy, where at each level the laws and the medium can be formulated. As for electronic devices, the laws are taken from electron physics and the medium consists of electrons, whereas with respect to the logical circuits the laws are based on Boolean algebra, and the medium consist of bits.

A principal characterisation applying to computer systems as well as to cognition is that they can both be described at different levels. The question is what happens if, rather than computers or cognition, we are referring instead to organisations and, related to that, if we claim that an organisation realises sustainable innovation. Can an organisation also be described as a single phenomenon at different levels? The answer is, conditionally, yes. As we discuss in Chapter 5, organisations can be described in terms of processes, tasks, actors and groups. The condition refers to the reality of the entities involved. In this respect computers and human actors are different from organisations and networks; the former are tangible, whereas the latter are intangible. Organisations are constructs or intangible artefacts which only exist in the eyes of the beholder. A reification of the entity 'organisation' is therefore tempting, but misleading. This misleading aspect shows itself in the applicability of certain properties or features. It seems common usage to speak of organisations' learning capabilities or memory (Nooteboom 2000), but this is a metaphorical way of speaking. Organisations do not literally learn or remember. The reason is a simple one—the physical carriers of these properties are humans. The metaphorical way of speaking has its advantages but also its limitations. The danger of making a category mistake is imminent.

This implies that the question whether the phenomenon of an organisation can be described at different levels is qualified. Yes, organisations can be described as constellations of processes, tasks and groups but, at the same time, organisations are artefacts, constructed by humans. They only exist because humans, as information processing entities, have a representation of these artefacts and behave interactively as social entities. In this sense an organisation is not one phenomenon, but an artefact or a construct that cannot be described at different levels. Within this perspective various kinds of properties can be ascribed to the organisation entity. For example, one may say that an organisation has decided to make an investment, but one has to realise that it is the members of the management team that have made this decision not the 'organisation'. 'The organisation has decided' is shorthand for the actual processes and perhaps also related to the legal and financial structures that institutionalise the organisation. In many cases a reduction in the constituent individuals in the organisation is relevant, in other situations the shorthand description suffices. However, we would like to argue that humans are always involved, and the behaviour of the collective is a weighted summation of individual behaviours and representations shared by means of communication. This also implies that in the discussion about whether an organisation exhibits or performs sustainable innovation, human behaviour has to be involved in (almost) all cases. Not only does KoS require the presence of carriers of that knowledge, SoK requires humans to prevent knowledge wastage and to ensure that knowledge is better used, better shared and better created.

In the next section we will discuss in more detail the various entities that may be involved in the X and Y of a reduction in offload, where X devolves W to Y over time horizon t and where X and Y may be individuals, groups, organisations, networks or societies.

Kinds of entities

Individual

Although as humans we retrieve information from knowledge processing systems we are clearly changing towards new forms of consuming and working. In tomorrow's world a synthesis is required between teamwork and individual capacities, between organisational and personal development. It seems that an individual can only be certain of things by looking at and including himself or herself. Compared with even one generation ago, the individual no longer engages in enduring relations; he or she is likely to be a member of several teams or groups simultaneously. The future is for powerful individuals who connect and disconnect easily and are able continuously to adjust their personal meaning, their personal significance. This seems a positive perspective but, by speaking of 'the corrosion of character', Sennett (1998) has also indicated the negative aspects to this development. Individuals are no longer consistent entities but are moved from project to project, from relation to relation, from friend to friend and from partner to partner. It takes really strong and powerful individuals to remain coherent. It requires **empowerment**. Block (1998) defines empowerment as that which individuals can do to reduce feelings of futility while, at the same time, expressing through work the depth of our own values. Increasing individualisation requires a redefinition of commitment. A new interpretation of commitment is based on the formal organisation that has a mission directed at a new course, in a culture in which there is interaction and interchange between the individual and the organisation as well as between the individual and his or her cognitive and behavioural learning possibilities.

Learning consists of processing concrete experiences, observations and reflections, adjusting mental models or representations and testing adapted models in new situations (Kolb 1984; Bower and Hilgard 1981; see also Chapters 22 and 23). Individuals learn all the time, although they forget most of what they experience and encounter. In the learning processes, sensory, coded and theoretical knowledge (see Chapter 6) is enriched and enlarged (Jentjens 2001). However, we need information to be able to learn. This information is integrated into existing knowledge and applied in relevant situations. In Chapter 6 we go into details of various aspects of knowledge, but we can already state that individuals are increasingly supposed to behave as **knowledge workers** within knowledge intensive organisations. Knowledge is their main contribution. Therefore, organisations have to be fit to make this learning and knowledge creation possible. It is in this context that notions such as **organisational learning** and the **learning organisation** make sense. However, organisations can only learn by virtue of the learning capacities of the individuals within them.

Group and organisation

A group is a collection of more than two individuals. A special kind of group is the community (a **cohesive group**). Many communities can be distinguished, such as communities of interest, communities of religion and communities of practice (Wenger 1998). The interaction processes within communities—communication, co-operation, co-ordination, learning and social interaction—are very different. In addition, the goals and binding effects of communities can be diverse. Communities can be oriented towards problem-solving, product or service development, innovations and individual learning. In the case of simple everyday problem-solving we speak of **single-loop learning** whereas in cases of innovation we refer to **second-loop learning** (see Chapter 23). The boundaries of the community can also differ. Some communities are open whereas others are closed to outsiders.

Communities can be designed and implemented formally from top to bottom and informally from bottom to top. In a top-down structure, management usually selects the members. Communities can differ in size, but cannot be too large; they can also differ in composition. They can consist of experts only or of both experts and novices. Some communities are virtual, which means that no face-to-face meetings take place, others only communicate face to face. Communities also differ in the way ICT is implemented. Within organisations communities of practice increasingly develop as centres where knowledge is created and shared. At each of the various levels important key performance indicators (KPIs) are formulated as realised advantages: individual (knowledge, satisfaction and social relations); group (status, attractiveness and innovations); and organisation (productivity, success of implementation and customer satisfaction).

By combining individual learning processes with interactions among people, learning processes become valuable for the organisation. In this way individual learning is connected to organisational learning. Senge (1990) defines a learning community as 'a group of people continually enhancing their capability to create what they want to create'. Organisational or community learning can be seen as learning by individuals and groups within the organisation whereas a learning organisation can be regarded as learning by the organisation as a system. Storing coded knowledge is one of the most important ways to make individual knowledge available and accessible at a group or organisation level. Nonaka and Takeuchi (1995) make a distinction between four processes to exchange implicit (sensory) and explicit (coded) knowledge. The four knowledge conversion processes are: socialisation; externalisation; combination; and internalisation.

The creation of knowledge can take place only individually and in groups because sensory knowledge can only be shared through intensive co-operation where people are physically close to each another. Effective collective learning can take place only if the members know one another's background theories and mental models and the interpretations that can be given of them. Within organisations, groups and teams are the important link between individual learning and learning by the organisation. The culture and structure of an organisation should enable people to work together in multidisciplinary groups and make knowledge freely accessible.

The development of organisational and business architectures is increasingly influenced by developments in society. One of the trends is that, starting from machine bureaucracies with a vertical command-and-control structure, organisations are first developing into business-unit structures and thereafter into various kinds of horizontal networks. As a result these organisations will change from teaching into learning structures. In a teaching structure, someone tells you what and when to learn whereas in a learning structure you decide yourself what to learn and when. On the road towards these new structures, Nonaka and Takeuchi (1995) describe the **hypertext organisation** consisting of three layers—the knowledge layer, the business system layer and the project team layer. A hypertext organisation consists of a combination of these three and functions as an interactive model representing both hierarchy and non-hierarchy or equality. The knowledge level includes implicit knowledge related to the culture and procedures of the organisation and explicit knowledge in the form of documents, archives, databases, etc. This layer is very important for the learning potential of the organisation and is directed at the development, storage, combination and use of knowledge in the creation of new products, services and processes. We are speaking here of **corporate repository** or **collective memory** in terms of a **corporate university**. Within the present knowledge intensive organisations it is increasingly becoming clear that the business systems layer is neither adequate for the optimal flow of knowledge nor for innovation. According to Nonaka and Takeuchi (1995), the process of organisational knowledge creation is a dynamic cycle of knowledge and information transfer among the three layers.

Besides developments in organisations, something else is going on. Technology and globalisation make the economy unpredictable worldwide. The new organisation or the new entrepreneur has to be adaptive. Organisations are no longer isolated players in a stable economy; they are the centre of their own ecosystems, the centre of a dynamic and unpredictable network of partners, suppliers, buyers, consumers and competitors. An adaptive organisation tries to react to the dynamics in the market. ICT is essential in actually realising this business model in a changing world. Future organisations have to learn to deal with the boundary between order and chaos; they 'live on the edge'.

Organisations are increasingly becoming knowledge-intensive; the demand for new products increases and the 'time-to-market' shortens. The role of knowledge workers becomes more important and they have to strengthen their learning capabilities. We already stated that, if various kinds and types of knowledge are important in the learning processes of the collective, the group has to be limited in size to make these processes effective (Jentjes 2001). Within the organisation, the exchange of coded knowledge is more or less standardised. Learning and critiquing require that the organisation adopts learning strategies, that it has a flexible organisational structure and a culture where making mistakes is accepted but also where lessons are learned from mistakes—trial and error should be combined with trial and success. The core competencies of organisations determine the knowledge that is important for them. With regard to the core competencies four types of learning are relevant and should be balanced: internal learning (knowledge sharing by individuals); learning by feedback (stakeholders, customers, etc.); learning from others (libraries, education, retraining and new personnel); and creative learning (self-development of new knowledge).

Network and society

Within networks of organisations we see on the one hand the autonomy of various partners and on the other the common goals. Or, to put it differently, is it possible to combine multi-formity and the tension between co-operation and competition? Networks develop at the interfaces of organisations and branches, horizontally as well as vertically within the company and firm structures. Network management is primarily a matter of managing interfaces. In network management it is important to give and take, to dominate and to counterbalance and to combine self-interest with mutual dependency. Managing an organisational network means finding a balance between self-creation and mutual solutions (Damhuis *et al* 2002). In some business projects (see Chapters 11, 12 and 16) networks of firms are the essential tools to make the intended innovation successful. In this respect knowledge of sustainability and innovation within networks is important. Requirements should be formulated for goals, tasks, structures, systems and communication in the network. One has to determine what the most important success factors are. How can innovations take place within networks and how can they be managed? Besides demand control, transparency and organisational or governance innovation, this issue requires an adequate infrastructure. In this context knowledge management becomes knowledge network management, involving public and private partners operating in a network in which system innovations are emphasised without the use of a separate co-ordination centre.

Although inter-organisational learning differs from intra-organisational learning, there are also many similarities. Also, here we have individuals and groups that learn. Knowledge is an important asset for an organisation in relation to its competitors. This may raise a dilemma. In the tension between co-operation and competition, collaboration is necessary to learn from each other and to reach a synergy in sharing and developing knowledge in order to enable sensory, coded and theoretical knowledge to grow as a result of the interaction among the partners. A better use of existing knowledge will result in completion and an increase in efficiency. On the other hand, all parties feel the need to exploit others to maximise their own organisational advantages (i.e. to take more than to give). Mistrust develops easily, as a result of which the learning processes and learning potential within the network could rapidly become distorted. Important factors in the learning processes at the level of the organisational networks include trust, the images the parties have of one another, added value and past experiences.

At the societal level, the three main developmental processes are globalisation, increasing use of ICT and individualisation. At present the developments seem to be disjointed rather than smooth. In addition to the main sociological analyses of Marx and Weber in the 19th and 20th century, Castells (1996a) describes the societal changes of the 21st century as follows. Within a network society the most important driver of societal and economic dynamics is ICT. The network and information society is heading towards a global economy with worldwide flows of money, knowledge and information in which individuals, organisations and institutions are mutually connected within networks. This will result in a system without central governance, self-evident rules or control structures. The global networks will mainly strive towards an increase in production and competition. This is a new kind of capitalism without a ruling class.

The open and dynamic character of these future networks will result in an increase in uncertainty and unpredictability. Besides the contrasts already existing in the world (rich and poor, North and South), a new contrast will emerge; one between those who are connected to the network system and those who are not. According to Castells, the relation between public and private will change drastically as will the role of nations on the world stage (the fall and rise of Russia, the emerging economies of China and India and the development of a fourth world consisting of those who are not connected to the global network). New forms of social organisations and social interactions will emerge, and, because individuals will be relatively powerless against these global networks of power, money and information they will look for new cultural connections and relations, new ties and sense-making within small communities ('tribes').

With regard to the above, Dutch and other European societies have many persistent and complex problems. Creating a sustainable society requires not only individual and group learning, but also innovation at the societal level. As Rotmans (2003) suggests with respect to learning processes and transition management, the old societal systems will have to be changed into new ones through transitions. At the Lisbon summit in 2000, the EU agreed that by 2010 the bloc should have established a knowledge economy comparable to that of the US. It seems that this can be realised only by strong economic growth and significant investment in innovation, research and development. There are two problems with realising this utopia. The first is that economic growth is in contradiction with sustainability, regardless of whether it concerns 'people' or 'planet', and, secondly, realising innovation as well as research at a product, service and production process level requires new ways of organising, new governance structures and an increased emphasis on the knowledge creation and learning abilities of people. In their essay *Rethinking the Dutch Innovation Agenda* for the Dutch Ministry of Economic Affairs, Volberda and Van den Bosch (2004) emphasise the necessary improvements in management and organisation. This issue not only holds for the Netherlands, it is important for almost every European country. At the management level a change is required from exploitation towards exploration. The present focus on efficiency and similar matters has to change to absorb new knowledge and engender more experimentation. Another important focal point is self-organisation. The knowledge worker has to combine knowledge domains and, therefore, the organisational structure needs to be flatter and the accessibility of networks has to increase. This implies that there must be a balance between exploration which is directed at innovation, renewal and efficiency.

A systems perspective and adaptation

In this section we will shift from the various kinds of entities at their consecutive levels of description described in the former section towards a system's perspective. Although the different characteristics of the entities are important in relation to their behaviour and interaction in the specific areas and levels, the system's perspective focuses on entities in terms of complexity, adaptation, composition of parts, and boundaries between system and environment. The first extended literature on systems originates from the 1950s (Boulding 1956). Here, a system is a set of subentities that have mutual relations as well as relations with the environment (see also Chapter 22). Strictly speaking, an organisation is not a system, it is a (mental) construct, but it can be considered as a system. It is a system that realises its results by means of activities. This model can be applied to all kinds of entities both concrete and abstract and, as we have earlier indicated, can be formulated at different levels of aggregation. Here, aggregation relates to the amount of detail. The less the detail, the rougher or higher the level of aggregation.

If we consider an organisation as a social system—as a system of humans—we have to take into account the multifacetedness of the human components, the subentities. Humans are not only instruments; they are also stakeholders who act on the basis of self-interest, team interest or sense-making (the **social action model**). From the perspective of sustainable innovation, the dynamics of knowledge creation and knowledge artefacts are essential. With respect to the various levels of cognition described earlier, the same discussion can be applied to humans as cognitive systems which also consist of various subentities, such as memory or perception. Memory can, in turn, also be considered as a system in which recursive analysis proceeds. However, at every level different system characteristics dominate and constrain the activities of the system as a whole.

We continue the system's perspective with an organisation as a system and the society as the environment. With regard to knowledge we see a model of the main functions of the organisation comprising four levels: execution; development; programming; and 'goaling' or policy-making. This model can be applied to processes taking place in any ordered goal-seeking system regardless of whether it concerns individuals, teams, units or organisations, but it can also be applied to robots, animals and even smaller organisms such as cells and bacteria.

When studying problems (in our case sustainability and sustainable innovation), it is very important to determine the system boundaries precisely. The problem determination has to lead to defining the system's boundaries and to filling in the content of the model in terms of concrete processes. Determination of the goal always takes place within the system. The contribution of a system (individual or group) to a larger whole is ultimately determined by this system (individual or group) and by valuing its possible or desirable outcome. This valuation is carried out by the system on the basis of its perception of the possibilities—external and internal desires and constraints. In the end, the autonomous system will always have the liberty to say 'yes' or 'no', although this could result in its complete destruction (Adriaanse and Malotaux 1975).

Within the main function model, and with regard to desires and results, two different process dimensions can be discerned—the **production dimension** and the **policy-making dimension**. The production dimension is a horizontal 'in-through-out' process whereas the policy-making dimension is a vertical process that regulates the in-through-out process. Both dimensions are schematically depicted in a conceptual framework (see Fig. 4.1).

Within the conceptual framework we also discern aspects. In our view these are the various types of knowledge related to goal, process and outcome. Sensory, coded and theoretical knowledge are combined with the production dimension (the knowledge process) and the policy-making process (the knowledge management process). Types of knowledge can be discerned; they cannot be separated (see Chapter 6).

If we assess a system (an organisation) on the basis of the knowledge aspects relevant in 2001 and 2004 it is possible to compare the situations. What we also see is that the process of a system's change is embedded in the development process of the larger whole, the societal culture. It is therefore necessary to add this change process as the third dimension related to the production and policy-making dimension. This again illustrates the essence of our approach to sustainability—it is a relative and dynamic concept with changes taking place both within the system as well as outside it (see Chapter 3). Sustainability is not just relevant within the system; it has become a cultural value which is influenced by the system (the organisation, the individual or the group, whatever entity is chosen), but which also influences the environment of the system. This leads to a dynamic systems theory containing a model in which the societal 'here and now' (which constitutes the organisational 'here and now') moves along a cultural dimension (see Fig. 4.1).

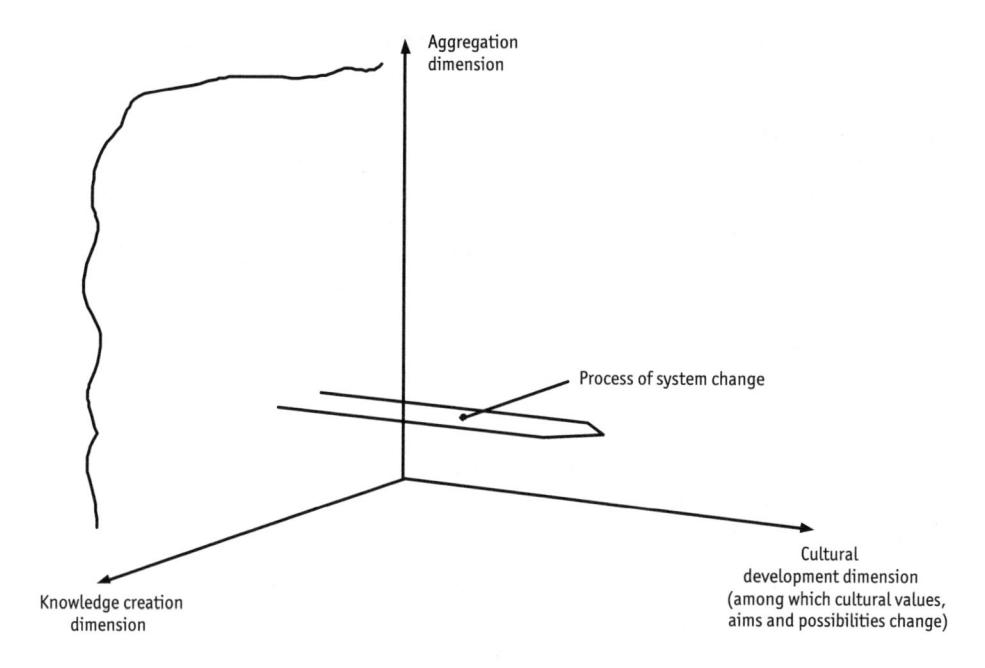

4. LEVELS OF DESCRIPTION, KINDS OF ENTITIES AND SYSTEMS *Jorna and Hadders*

FIGURE 4.1 The three axes of the conceptual framework

Important in our approach to sustainability or sustainable innovation is the dynamic balance between system and environment—the notion of homeostasis (von Bertalanffy 1968). As a biologist, von Bertalanffy described homeostasis as the way living organisms maintain a steady state through feedback mechanisms, but others apply this concept, often as a metaphor, to economic systems and organisations (de Leeuw 1986) and, in cognitive psychology, to human cognition. Phenomena such as growth in living systems as well as in organisations can be understood in terms of a dynamic balance between the system and its environment. For all kind of systems, laws of nature or regularities can be formulated (Lit 1992). Concerning openness, adaptive self-stabilisation, adaptive self-organisation, optimal balance and autonomy, the following laws can be used literally (concrete system) as well as metaphorically (abstract system) (van der Plaats 1994).

Openness means an exchange of energy, matter or information between system and environment. In case of continuous exchange the system's internal situation has to lead to adaptive self-stabilisation. This also implies that the internal situation has to be relatively constant; this forms part of auto-regulation. Feedback and feedforward loops occur within and between processes. Auto-regulation may also partly mean that functions and structures adapt to long-lasting changes. This also implies that there is a partial order which may consist of internal information processing. An open system can export energy (or information) to the environment: that is, to a larger system. In such a system attempts will be made to restore the balance which has positive effects on the lower systems. Open systems strive towards a maximum balance in which the subsystems also function at optimal balance. The higher the level of the subsystem the more

54 SUSTAINABLE INNOVATION

it is capable of and inclined to perform these activities. In this respect autonomy also means that a system is relatively stable with regard to external influences.

Chaos theory and complexity theory have strongly influenced the development of dynamic systems theory. All living systems are complex systems. Complex systems consist of interacting actors. Individuals, groups and organisations are also complex adaptive systems. Compared with complex mechanical systems it is quite difficult to predict the behaviour of complex adaptive systems when responding to stimuli. The parts of a complex adaptive system are semi-independent and are free to react to stimuli because this type of system consists of parts that can change themselves. As the different parts act more or less autonomously, new behaviour easily emerges. This behaviour is also non-linear which means that small changes have large effects.

Complex systems are intrinsically chaotic and are not predictable in detail. In addition, because they are often part of larger systems, the context (i.e. the larger system) is vital (Plesk, Lindenberg and Zimmerman 1997). Another characteristic of complex adaptive systems is the use of simple rules. Changes in these rules may lead to large innovative alterations of the system. The difference between complex mechanical and complex adaptive systems is that different instruments are applicable to direct changes. We illustrate this in Figure 4.2.

In zone 1 ('order') we see activities that have a high degree of certainty. The results are in line with the predicted results of the activities. We are referring here to classical management processes in which suitable instruments are being applied, such as plan-

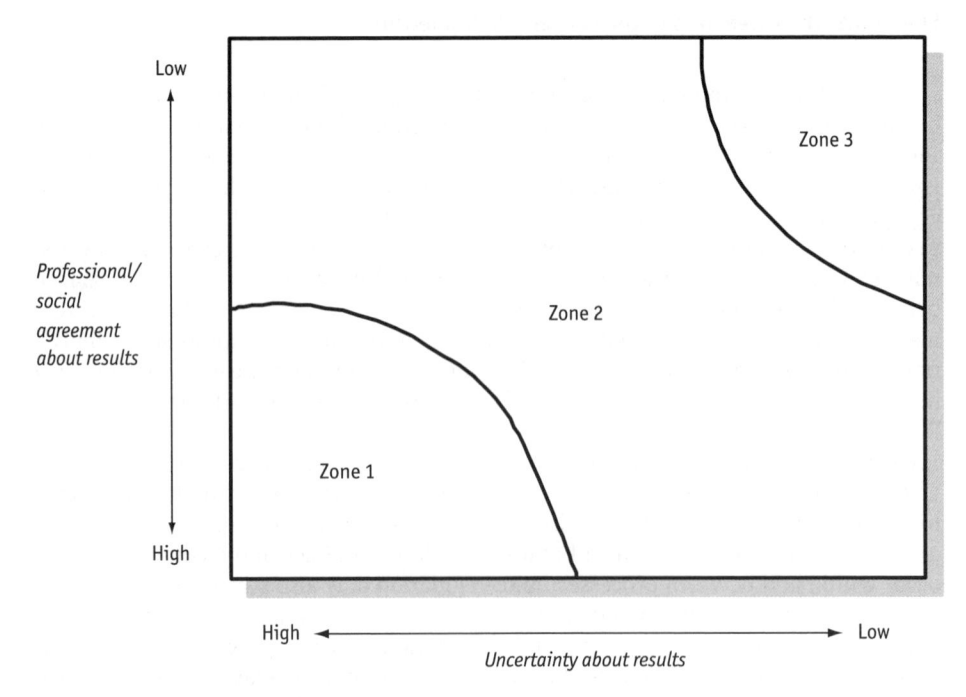

FIGURE 4.2 Certainty-agreement diagram (Stacey's model)

Source: Based on Stacey 1996

ning, rationality, standardisation, measurement and control. In zone 3 ('disorder'), we have activities with a low predictive value and very little agreement between expectations and results. In between we find zone 2, the area of complexity. A complex system is neither orderly nor disorderly; it is a system continuously balancing on the edge of instability. In dynamic situations, such as in governing innovative changes, instruments used in zone 1 (planning and control) and zone 2 (simple rules) are applied (Ravensbergen and Mik 2003).

Dynamic systems theory presupposes that organising takes place within complex dynamic systems in which actors (as information-processing systems) continuously interact and make sense of events. Here, the boundaries between organisations fade away. The system produces and creates, and so does the environment. In relation to these circular patterns of interaction we see negative feedback which leads to restoring stability and positive feedback which enforces renewals resulting in instability. These dynamics are the everlasting source of innovation in which the organisation as a unit of renewal merges into the organisational networks within the environment.

First steps towards a systematic approach to sustainability

In the Netherlands, Lit (1992) has used general system theory to develop a model for multidisciplinary domains in medical practices which we can also apply to sustainable innovation. We use this model to analyse the various aspects of sustainable innovation in terms of kinds of entities and layers of description. It should enable us to describe a 'healthy' stable or dynamic balance among systems and between systems and their environment. In line with the layers of aggregation defined, a system theoretical elaboration is made in which all relevant data and facts are presented in response to things we know about the system we are dealing with and the characteristics of that system. For every system detail, the knowledge results from the assessment of the following aspects:

- The 'normal' structure, development and function
- The research methods applicable to this system
- Symptoms and phenomena indicating problematic functioning or misbehaviour of system characteristics
- The determinants of disorders occurring at one particular level of aggregation
- The influences of disorders at one level of functioning on other levels (offloading)
- The way in which other levels function (including offloading or devolvement)
- Intervention methods applicable at this level of functioning
- The system's factors which have a predictive value in changing the system

The explanations of each of the aspects are relevant to further analysis. They will give a first indication of the entities, the levels of aggregation, the characteristics of the entities at each level and possible directions of change of the reduction in offload. In Part D of this book we will come back to the various issues discussed in this chapter, albeit with a different orientation. Because in Part C we will discuss the various business projects, in Part D we can be clearer about the follow-up steps concerning entity, characteristics, level of aggregation and interaction. The determination of offload from the high to the lower level (i.e. from organisation to individual) and from the low to the higher level (i.e. from organisation to society) may result in clear directions with respect to the reduction in offload.

5
Organisation
ARTEFACT AND PRINCIPLE

René J. Jorna and Laura Maruster

In its essence an organisation is not much more than a complex composition of **division** and **co-ordination**. Division is important because not every individual or business component (operating more or less independently, but forming part of a greater whole) can deal with a task or activity entirely on its own. Therefore, activities have to be divided. Co-ordination is important in the sense that these various individuals or business components have to perform again as a whole. This simple description instantly becomes complex if all types of aspects and details are filled in. Without giving an exhaustive overview, we will first briefly deal with the various aspects and then go into more detail in the different sections.

In the first place, **organisation** can have two meanings. It can be a **principle** or an **object**, an **artefact** or a **construct**. If it concerns a principle, the nature of the principle must be determined. We then enter the field of co-ordination (**tuning**) mechanisms. If co-ordination concerns an object, artefact or construct, it is important to determine what exactly it entails.

A human individual is an object who acts as a whole but consists of many parts, both functional and physical. The individual acts in a co-ordinated way. The same applies to a car. This object also consists of many parts (which in general can be replaced more easily than those of a human) and also functions as a whole. In both cases we are dealing with physical objects that are very different in nature. In contrast, take a company such as Grontmij (see Chapter 17). This is an organisation consisting of many parts (3,000 employees) which also functions as a whole. However, both the whole and the parts are not physical objects as such. As an organisation Grontmij is a construct or artefact. The various Grontmij buildings exist physically and many people consider themselves, as employees, to be part of Grontmij; but the organisation does not exist in the same physical sense as do people or cars. In this second meaning of organisation—as an artefact or construct—the nature of the parts is essential. In actual practice, the first and second meanings of organisation—as a principle or as an object or artefact—are intertwined. We will deal with the nature of one of the parts—the **actors**—in more detail in the next section. We will then go on to elaborate the ways to divide an organisation, company or institution as well as what exactly is divided. This division can be carried out in terms of processes, functions or tasks. Then we will deal further with the organisation as a principle. We will discuss examples of co-ordination mechanisms, organisational forms, governance, dependencies or interdependencies and deal with the subject of management. Finally, we will discuss organisational dynamics and changes as well as business development. Like people, organisations do not stand still. They either change more or less autonomously on the basis of an internal vision or strategy, or because of stimuli and events issuing from the external environment.

The organisation: the nature of humans as parts

An organisation as a company or institution consists of people and other physical entities, such as buildings, furniture, computers and other electronic devices. But these are not the first things that organisation and business experts (as well as sociologists and economists) think of when referring to organisations. The first things that spring to mind with respect to organisations are regulations, structures and processes on the one hand and groups of people or teams and departments on the other.

Herbert Simon (1969) was one of the first scientists explicitly to acknowledge that addressing organisations in this way means that one is referring to an **artificial world**. Simon also called this the world of artefacts made by people. He distinguished two kinds of artefacts—physical and the immaterial. Examples of the first are buildings or cars while examples of the second are meetings, company policies and departments. In addition, there are natural objects, such as trees, stones or water.

The study of natural objects has been classified according to scientific disciplines, such as physics, biology and chemistry. The study of physical artefacts has been categorised in engineering sciences, from architectural design to chemical technology. The study of immaterial artefacts has been classified according to subject areas, such as economics, business studies and sociology. Psychology deals both with natural objects, such as the human brain, but also with non-material artefacts, such as cognition and personality. By looking at the classical sciences in this way, Simon revealed similarities. With respect to the study of non-material artefacts he refers to the artificial and, by doing so, throws a different light on themes such as architecture, complexity, and the possibility of division and dependency. An important aspect of Simon's approach is the development of a conceptual framework in which the various themes and subject areas are adequately represented. For this purpose Simon uses and elaborates on existing **systems theory**.

This book does not deal with natural objects and physical artefacts. Instead, it focuses on **non-material artefacts**—in this case organisations and their components: the individuals and structures that make up the organisation. In general, an organisation without people is inconceivable, and this especially applies in relation to knowledge and innovation.

Following Simon's line of reasoning on cognition, which he developed together with Newell after 1960 (Newell and Simon 1972; Newell 1990), we consider people as knowledge and information-processing systems. People use their intelligence in performing all sorts of tasks. Thus, people are dealing with tasks as problem-solvers. They show intelligence in displaying, explicitly or inexplicitly, purposive behaviour. In contrast with the view, often shared by economists, that people are always and in every respect rational, Simon is of the opinion that people's rationality is limited (**bounded**) in two respects. First, because we cannot have a complete knowledge of reality and, second, because our rationality is bounded as a result of the system limitations in our cognitive apparatus. We have a limited memory and perception, we are not good at estimating probabilities and it is extremely hard for us to unlearn things once we have learned them. The first category of rationality is limited in an epistemological/ontological sense and the second is limited in a cognitive sense.

Based on the cognitive approach that the human brain is an information-processing system, we distinguish three essential elements related to cognition: a cognitive architecture; mental representations; and operations based on these mental representations (Jorna 1990). Because the rules, regulations, appointments and other non-material artefacts in organisations require material carriers (i.e. humans), we will briefly explain the three elements related to cognition.

First, there is the cognitive architecture—the layout or structure of cognitive functions. Among others, this means functional components, such as memory, processing capacity and perception. The structure and the system limitations of these functional components form an aspect of what has been called **bounded rationality**. For example, our short-term memory can process only seven plus or minus two memory chunks, and it takes at least five seconds to retrieve information from long-term to short-term memory.

Second, there are mental representations. These refer, for example, to the stories we have been told, the things we have seen and our relationships with others. All this knowledge exists in our memory in the form of representations or images that can be retrieved. Some of these representations are in the form of images, others in the form of language expressions and others in the form of events.

Third, we use these representations continuously; and we alter them, complement them and combine them. Cognitive science calls this the manipulation or operation on representations.

In this view, which sees people as knowledge and information-processing systems, representations are basically symbolic. Hence, Newell and Simon speak of the human cognitive system as a system that adapts and processes symbols (Newell and Simon 1976; Gazendam, Jorna and Cijsouw 2003).

Thus, if we consider organisations as non-material artefacts, humans are the essential elements in these artefacts. However, because of the fact that they are intelligent human individuals, these elements have a number of characteristics that determine the continuation and coherence of the greater whole. To put it bluntly, without people there would be no organisations. This is true in two respects. First, it is people who make up a group, team or company and, second, people know how to co-operate with others. In other words, apart from the buildings and the other materials, an organisation exists by virtue of the fact that people have mental representations of the organisation. They make up the organisation and give it a reason to exist by thinking about it.

Shared mental representations hold organisations together. These include shared conceptions about who does what in the organisation and the way things are co-ordinated. In principle, these representations differ per individual, but there is also a significant overlap with respect to all kinds of representations shared among individuals, from the way in which events take place within the organisation to the decision-making hierarchies. Later in this chapter we will discuss a hierarchy as a co-ordination mechanism. However, this hierarchy is a construct that has to exist as a mental representation in the minds of at least two people, showing a great deal of overlap as well as many differences. The superior is aware of his/her position and that of the subordinate, just as the subordinate knows that the superior functions in that capacity. Thus, they partly share the representations of the norms and rules belonging to a hierarchy. We call these norms and rules **social constructs** which exist as mental representations in the minds of the different employees within the organisation (Helmhout, Gazendam and Jorna 2004).

The human component is therefore crucial in every organisation and, thus, in every discussion about organisations. In more general terms, we can also see people as actors and thus the organisation as a **multi-actor system**. The term 'actor' refers back to our discussion about humans as cognitive systems while the notion of 'multi' instantly shows that between actors there must be co-ordination.

In brief, we state that an organisation is a multi-actor system in which actors within organisations perform tasks (often) forming part of processes, and that in performing these tasks knowledge is used. The actors, tasks and processes are the backbone of the organisation.

The organisation: ways of division

Introduction

If an organisation is conceptualised in terms of a multi-actor system, the division into actors, processes and tasks has to be organised in a particular way. In management literature this is called **co-ordination** or **structuring**. We will successively discuss processes, tasks, the classification of functions and co-ordination.

Primary and secondary processes

The issue of co-ordination comes after division. There are many forms of division within organisations. On the process level it is common to divide an organisation into **primary** and **secondary processes**. The primary processes refer to what an organisation produces and its activities. Briefly, the primary processes indicate why an organisation exists. For example, a hospital 'produces' health by curing and caring for patients while a baker produces bread. In both examples substantial specialised knowledge of the respective subject areas is required to execute the primary processes—medical knowledge in the case of the hospital and knowledge about baking in the case of the baker. The way in which the primary processes are structured, classified and co-ordinated (in other words **connected**) makes up the secondary processes (Porter 1985). The interplay of primary and secondary processes can be organised in many ways.

In the first place, secondary processes can be interwoven with primary processes. In this case the co-ordination of baking machinery or operating theatres cannot be separated from the primary process. Co-ordination, co-operation and everything that is connected with these issues form the constituent elements of the primary process. We call it the **integrated organisational processes**. Often (but not always) this situation applies to small businesses. Large companies may also have many reasons to interweave the primary and secondary processes. One wants to make a division but is unable to do so or, because of the company's particular size, the tasks are expanded through the secondary process, the execution of which is considered a little time-consuming. Another reason could be that within the organisation a large degree of task complexity exists, making this integration necessary.

Second, the organising processes can be separated from the primary processes. This situation is described by the term **separated organisational processes**. The secondary processes can be regarded as supporting, co-ordinating or service-providing processes. In general, most of these processes are carried out in separate units or departments. They have been especially established for this purpose; examples include a financial department, a planning department or an administrative centre.

Third, organisational processes can be completely separated from the original organisation. They are then placed within a new organisation or in a completely separate organisation responsible for their own results. The primary process of this new organisation constitutes the execution of the organisational processes themselves. We would like to call this situation a **second-order primary process**. From the perspective of an organisation this third situation can be considered as an innovation. It is a new way of organising. An example is a company whose primary process is making timetables and schedules for other organisations. Outsourcing administrative tasks to separate companies is also an example of this complete separation.

From an extended perspective on sustainability it is of less importance whether one speaks of the integrated, separated organisational processes or second-order primary processes. However, within the framework of an organisational innovation this distinction could be important. This is because each of the three possibilities has both advantages and disadvantages. In order not to make matters too complicated, we will henceforth deal only with the separated organisational processes, usually assigned to separate departments belonging to the same company or firm. It is likely that interwoven primary and secondary processes occur only in particular content domains. They demand only a small organisational scope or a high degree of knowledge specialisation. Separated processes often lead to an increase in the development of regulations and a great deal of red tape. Secondary processes as second-order primary processes in a new organisation may lead to a loss of knowledge in the former company.

Secondary processes: tasks

Secondary or organisational processes can be described in terms of the tasks of which they are composed. Examples of these are control, planning, administration, following (monitoring), communication, maintenance (and, to a certain degree, contracting), arranging offers and closing contracts (Daft 2001). 'Control' refers to tasks allowing the capability and power to give commands, to decide and to judge. 'Planning' involves the task of arranging on a tactical and strategic level the current affairs and the proper tuning of personnel, products, machines, transportation means and activities. 'Administration' involves the task of selecting and registering all relevant information about, and for the benefit of, the primary (and organisational) processes. 'Monitoring' (following) deals with mapping out and following the status and progress of products, services and primary processes within the organisation. 'Communication' is the task of keeping contact with others within and outside the organisation, both written and orally. 'Maintenance' and 'contracting' involve the support and proper preservation of providing service and production means. 'Drawing up and closing contracts' entails carrying out in a (legal) manner the management and arrangement of promises and agreements within and outside the organisation.

Over the past few decades, many of the organisational or secondary processes have been computerised to a large degree. This was possible because of the high level of standardisation of a large number of organisational processes. In addition, the knowledge acquired in these processes is fairly easy to define and to model, and the execution of the tasks is strongly repetitive. This repetitive nature lends itself easily to being supported by means of databases, management information systems and systems that support the decision-making process. However, a marginal note should be made. Software support for administration, control, contracting, arranging offers and closing contracts is highly developed, but for planning and communication it is not. This is due to the complexity and the weak structure of the planning and communication processes (Jorna et al. 1996, van Wezel and Jorna 2002; van Wezel, Jorna and Meystel 2006).

Next to the distinction between primary and secondary processes there are two other ways of division. First, a classification into tasks which involves a lower aggregation level and, second, a division into the functional parts of an organisation or firm.

Classification into tasks

From a process perspective an organisation is considered from top to bottom. This organisational point of view is also called a **helicopter** or **bird's-eye view**. We can observe this in the discussion about primary and secondary processes. Although necessary, the bird's-eye view has a number of disadvantages. It suggests that processes form the lowest level of aggregation in an organisation. In addition, a normative orientation is often linked to a process analysis. A model is made which, ideally, depicts how a process should be executed. It is often wrongly suggested that there is only one bird's-eye view of the arrangement of the processes. Finally, the most essential objection to process analysis is that the impression is given that carriers of processes are not required. It seems that the implementation of the processes and mechanisms is a highly abstract matter that barely involves empirical reality. The concrete and factual realisation is often not considered thoroughly enough.

Therefore, apart from the bird's-eye view, we suggest a **mammal's perspective** on organisations in which, next to processes and structures, people and tasks are central. A mammal's perspective considers the organisation from bottom to top. Fundamentally, it is about the people who execute tasks. They carry out these tasks in the framework of the functions they have, and the tasks have their place within the primary and secondary processes of the organisation. Normally, several people carry out comparable tasks. In practice, this means that, although people sometimes execute tasks alone, mostly they are carried out by groups who use their intelligence and knowledge to interpret the tasks. The co-ordination of the tasks is in the hands of the people themselves or forms part of another person's function.

A task orientation has two advantages. It explicitly involves people in analysing the organisation and it makes clear where the knowledge of the task execution can be found (Vicente 1999). For this reason an adequate analysis of tasks starts with a **cognitive task analysis**. In this type of analysis the human actor and the task are joined. With reference to the human actor and the knowledge, it is about mental representations and collections of mental operations in the form of cognitive strategies. As regards the task, it is about an initial situation which is transformed into an end situation by means of a (structured) range of actions (Waern 1989). In a cognitive task analysis the interaction between the task (or subtask) and the cognitive strategy to carry out the task is central. The aspect of the human actor as information processor has already been discussed in the previous section. We will now go into the task issue in more detail.

A task is the execution of a number of actions to achieve a particular goal. No less than a process, a task is a natural unity. Naturally, all kinds of prior conditions play a role (Waern 1989). This means that divisions of tasks can be made along many lines: for example, according to time. A touch (i.e. a task) on the keyboard takes between 20 and 200 milliseconds. However, making a decision that demands more than a day's hard thinking is also a task. Another form of division is on the basis of what people do. In this case, a person's task load is made up of the complete range of activities they performed. The composition of another person's task load would be different.

We can use another method of division, namely one based on the characteristics of the task. In this division a distinction is made in tasks that unravel, combine and alter. One may also speak of **analytic**, **synthetic** and **modifying tasks** (Breuker and Van de Velde 1994). Examples of analytic tasks are classification and prediction. In the most concrete sense this entails making diagnoses and monitoring (following). Examples of synthetic tasks are configuration, making schedules, design, and planning. Examples of modifying tasks are reparation and improvement. In this method of division the general point of departure is that we are dealing with generic tasks each involving different related domains but with which the process in execution is similar. Taking as an example a diagnostic task carried out by a doctor or a car mechanic seeking to 'repair' a human body or a car respectively, the process of reasoning follows similar steps, even though they operate in completely different content domains.

The division in tasks means that, in principle, within each task subtasks can be distinguished. The above-mentioned approach to tasks also means that one starts from a problem-solution method (Schreiber *et al.* 2000). In terms of problem-solving this means that a situation is described as an initial state. After the initialisation, a desired situation (or end state) must be achieved by carrying out a certain range of activities. Once again, the advantage of division in terms of tasks rather than of processes is that the aspects of knowledge and human beings as information processors are explicitly involved in what takes place within an organisation. A disadvantage of an analysis based on tasks is that, in some cases, there may be too much detail on task execution within an organisation.

Classification according to function

Without being exhaustive, there is another way to divide organisations. Termed **functional classification** (Davis and Olson 1985), this takes the perspective of a high level of aggregation and sees an organisation as having an input, a transformation (transfer or throughput) and an output. In terms of departments, purchase, acquisition and, possibly, marketing are involved in input. Production and service provision are examples of departments involved in transfer or throughput while forwarding, shipping, stock control and, again, possibly marketing, are examples of departments involved in output. As well as these there are the logistics and personnel departments, IT, accounts, administration and R&D. Of course not every organisation has all these departments. Furthermore, there is a large difference between companies that are profit-oriented and those operating in the public sector. Many of the latter do not have separate marketing or R&D departments and so have no inherent structures for innovation. It is not our aim to discuss in detail all aspects of this functional classification; we simply wanted to show another justifiable classification than one based on processes or tasks. However, whether one is dealing with company functions, processes or tasks, when it comes to knowledge it is always the human individual who is the knowledge carrier on behalf of the organisation.

The organisation: organisational forms and co-ordination mechanisms

As already explained, processes as well as tasks and actors form the backbone of an organisation. However, the processes should be organised in one way or another. In management literature this is called co-ordination, management or governance. The organisational forms that classify this co-ordination and governance have a variety of terms: for example, bureaucracy, adhocracy, hierarchy or mutual adjustment. Other forms can also be relevant, such as clan, network or co-operation.

Many names and labels for the organisational forms and the co-ordination mechanisms are discussed in the literature (Sorge 2001), but in relation to sustainable innovation we will focus on the forms referred to by Thompson (1967), Mintzberg (1983) and Boisot (1995) (see also Gazendam 1993). In their overviews these authors provide an adequate picture for our purposes. With respect to organisational forms, Thompson (1967) describes co-ordination within an organisation in terms of task or process **interdependencies**. If an organisation has no interdependencies, organisation and individual coincide. An entire organisation then consists of one individual and interdependency is a completely cognitive affair. From the management point of view the more interesting forms are pooled, sequential and reciprocal interdependency.

Common (pooled) interdependency involves independent departments, mostly given shape by means of a division structure. If there are three departments A, B, and C, where A is central and B and C issue from A, the dependencies between B and C only take place via A. Sequential interdependency refers to the situation where the output of A is the input for B. In a reciprocal interdependency the output of A is the input of B and, in turn, the output of B is the input of A.

Mintzberg (1983) gives a description of the development of organisations through five different forms:

- Simple structure
- Machine bureaucracy
- Professional bureaucracy
- Divisional form
- Adhocracy

On the one hand, the different forms indicate a type of evolution of a particular company as an organisation through time. On the other hand, with this typology, an assessment of each organisation's **centre of gravity** can be made in terms of the dominance of the operational core, the strategic top or the techno-structure.

Boisot (1995), who deals in a similar manner with the evolution of organisations, distinguishes according to the classifications of feudal system, clan, market and bureaucracy. Boisot classifies organisations in terms of informational aspects, that is to say their **encoding**, **concreteness** and **diffusion**.

Irrespective of what subdivision is applied, it is striking that knowledge, representations and tasks are not mentioned, let alone used as a relevant dimension to distinguish organisational forms.

The organisational forms discussed by Thompson, Mintzberg and Boisot are based on decomposition structures and co-ordination mechanisms. In this respect we see that, in general, a subdivision is made either according to processes or according to functional lines, such as marketing and production. Irrespective of which organisational form is chosen, what makes an organisation function are the people who form and shape co-ordination within it. They do this in three ways: first, by having representations of the organisational forms; second, by following the design of structures and forms; and, third, by knowing, often implicitly, the reasons why co-ordination mechanisms are used and why they work. With regard to the latter, we mean the mechanisms behind the organisational forms. With respect to co-ordination mechanisms we can distinguish three types:

- Standardisation
- Power and authority based on various backgrounds
- Trust, competition and distrust

Standardisation is impersonal in nature, while power, authority and trust are personal. Standardisation means that a structure has been designed for tasks and processes in combination with co-ordination, which functions, so to speak, all by itself. Here, we come close to **institutional factors**, as Williamson (1975) called it, both within organisations and in their environment. Of course in any organisation, people who act in an intelligent way are required, but tuning and coherence is organised in such a way that the degree of freedom in the execution of the actions is minimal. Standardisation can be designed for tasks: for example, the layout of car factories, in which people and robots perform the work in a fixed order. Standardisation also applies to call centres which stipulate precisely the steps that should be taken in a particular process. In this way co-ordination is interwoven with the tight standard order of tasks and processes. In all situations in which there is no or incomplete standardisation, co-ordination is based on personal relations.

There are many mechanisms of a personal nature that serve as co-ordination mechanisms within organisational forms. First, there is power and authority. In a hierarchy of two one person is the boss and the other is the subordinate. However, this situation requires a representation to be shared by both, as discussed earlier. Being the 'boss' can be based on a formal organisational structure, but may also be based on charisma, expertise regarding content or other forms of power. In this respect, the aspect of 'ruling' should not be underestimated. It makes coercion, imposing sanctions or granting rewards possible, with the boss making the decisions. In this context we can also mention the authority relation. Here, one can think of the subdivisions of monarchy, bureaucracy, aristocracy, meritocracy, democracy and technocracy (see also Sorge and Warner 2001). In their diversity the many forms suggest that the leading principle (the 'archy' or 'cracy') is interpreted as a representation of the leading entity/principle dictating how one behaves.

Second, a large number of psychological notions are important as mechanisms behind the issues of co-ordination and organisation: for example, trust, distrust, competition, competitiveness and reliability in agreements. In this way a clan is based on trust but a market is based on competition and rivalry because every participant can continuously start new relations and end them on the basis of distrust. Bureaucracies are based on the reliability of the rules.

Management (in the sense of the set of activities consisting of managing, controlling, governing, decision-making, influencing and arranging) tries to carry out the co-ordination within the existing organisational forms. In this respect management sometimes aims at processes, sometimes at tasks and, naturally, always at people. A fundamental characteristic of management in this sense seems to be leadership. However, there is no consensus on this because, as some argue, a managed organisation leads itself. In an organisation of this kind, affairs are run in a natural way, requiring no or little attention. We could also describe this as a culture within an organisation in which habits, behaviour, norms, knowledge and manners exist more or less as a matter of fact. It is not our intention to raise the subject of culture here as this cannot be done briefly. It is possible, however, to place the subject of culture into our first explanation of shared representations. In this way a culture is a social construct shared by the members of the organisation as a representation and existing within the organisation as an artefact and a principle.

We will first briefly discuss a number of organisational forms while also dealing with the knowledge aspect. We will then go into the organisational mechanisms that are instrumental in co-ordination and governance. As examples of organisational forms we will consecutively discuss clan, feudal system, divisional form, machine bureaucracy, professional bureaucracy, market and network. In addition to knowledge aspects, we are characterising these organisational forms considering leading principles that are prevailing within one organisation; these are autonomy or dependence, co-operation or competition, rules or own initiative, hierarchy or heterarchy, openness or closeness, centralisation or decentralisation, shared knowledge or private knowledge and specialisation or generalisation (Sorge and Warner 2001). The discussion about knowledge aspects refers to knowledge types and learning.

A clan consists of a limited group of individuals (actors) who co-operate on the basis of trust (the mechanism behind co-ordination). Sometimes this concerns family relations and, sometimes, very close and long-lasting friendships. Boisot (1995: 259) states that 'the term "clan" refers to a non-hierarchical group of limited size transacting on the basis of shared intangible knowledge and values'. The norms and values remain implicit as they are well known to the members of the group, but are very hard to formulate. Clans are often small and local. Trust, loyalty, responsibility and obedience are essential. If a clan is big it is often divided into subclans in order to recreate the required physical proximity, personal familiarity and involvement. The organisational process within a clan, based on loyalty and trust, does not work in impersonal relationships. An explanation of a rule or habit is not explicitly given, but rather in terms of 'it has always been this way' and, usually, that is all that is needed. Dependence tends to prevail in clans rather than autonomy. Clans are characterised by co-operation based on trust. However, obeying rules leaves little space for the development of own initiative. Neither shared knowledge nor private knowledge predominate in a clan. Rather, the authority is heterarchical (i.e. is determined by knowledge and function). Clans are based on closeness and are rather decentralised. Learning is mostly done by doing.

Strong dependence and hierarchy characterise feudal systems. This form of organisation is based on rules rather than own initiative. Like clans, organisations resembling feudal systems are based on closeness. Centralisation prevails. Regarding the dimensions co-operation–competition and specialisation–generalisation, neither is specifically relevant. Knowledge is private, rarely coded, is generally difficult to put into words (sensory) and is available only to a few people. Most members of the organisation do not know precisely what they are doing. Moreover, knowledge is controlled by just a few people. Learning is mostly done by doing.

In the divisional form, middle management (or, in Mintzberg's [1983] terminology, the 'middle line') is responsible for the development of new industrial activities and controlling operations. Often within a large organisation divisions are formed that operate independently but still have to communicate with other divisions. The organisational processes that require co-ordination, co-operation and communication are based on rules and procedures often available in coded form and used accordingly. The divisions belong to a large organisation as a whole. The co-ordination processes take place on the basis of structures and explicit arrangements.

Machine bureaucracies are known (some say notoriously) for their continuous and autonomous quest for procedures, regulations and rules. Everything within an organisation has to be 'arranged', otherwise it is neither useful nor usable. If, by any chance, implicit habit forming takes place (often in the form of an exception or deviation), this is translated into new rules as quickly as possible. Often an explanation of the 'why' is seen as undermining the rules and procedures. In this form of organisation, dependency, rules, hierarchy, closeness and centralisation are very strong and generalisation prevails. This form of organisation is a very good example of the situation where coded knowledge alone is dominant since everything within the organisational process must be coded; otherwise it is neither suitable nor usable. Sensory knowledge (see Chapter 6) is avoided but, if it does turn up, it will be converted into coded knowledge. Theoretical knowledge is also absent because the rules are seen as self-evident. Explanations in terms of theories, models or scientific regularities or laws are not used. Often these theories are considered to undermine the procedures and rules formulated in codes. Learning is done by using documents and other written materials.

In a professional bureaucracy (Mintzberg 1983) the operational core consists of highly educated, very specialised experts, many with an academic background. This means that the organisational processes of co-ordination, control and planning are executed in close connection with substantial tasks and processes: that is, to say the primary processes. Examples of this type of organisation are hospitals, universities and government departments within certain subject domains, such as agriculture, traffic and public works, justice and the economy. In contrast with government departments, local authorities are, in general, machine bureaucracies, precisely because of the absence of certain kinds of knowledge (see Chapter 6). To explain why things are done in a certain way civil servants at a local level apply rules and procedures rather than theories and models. The knowledge professional bureaucracies use is coded in the sense that it is represented and documented in rules, procedures and scripts. The knowledge is also theoretical because in answer to 'questions why' explanations, theories and 'logical necessities' can be formulated. Very little knowledge is sensory, illustrated by the long explicitly structured training period the new recruits in this type of organisation have to undergo. Learning is done mainly by education and training or the self-study of manuals.

A market is characterised by many autonomous organisations, small and large. Co-ordination as an organisational process between organisations is dealt with by a combination of an 'invisible hand' and competition. We look at a market here from a perspective that is external *vis-à-vis* the organisation. The interaction of organisations is based on rivalry and competition. In theory it is argued that within a market perspective all organisations are equal, but in actual practice they are very unequal. Co-ordination within an organisation can never be solely based on a market structure. Competition and rivalry within an organisation are detrimental to that organisation in the long run. Internally, organisations work on the basis of local information while the external comparison and contacts often take place in terms of prices. A market can be characterised by strong autonomy, competition, specialisation and decentralisation. Own initiative prevails. Knowledge is shared, and authority is based on heterarchy.

A market is a special type of network. Because organisations are so diversified in reality, the implication is that an organisation with much sensory knowledge competes with an organisation with much coded and theoretical knowledge and that two organisations with dominant coded knowledge could negotiate with one another. The variety of organisations involved in the market explains the presence of all types of knowledge (see Chapter 6). It also explains the complexity of market situations. One could also reason the other way around and call a market a co-ordination, co-operation and communication structure without the dominance of any kind of knowledge. Principally it does not matter whether none or all knowledge types are dominant but, for reasons of the assumed intelligence of the actors within the organisation, we prefer the overall dominance of knowledge types. Learning is done by doing, but also by studying documents and other materials.

Another example of a network is a web. As a neutral term a network is a coherent connection of actors and relations. Within a web the co-ordination of the actors is based on trust. A web is also based on autonomy, own initiative, shared knowledge, heterarchy, openness and decentralisation. As in the case of markets, all knowledge types are dominant. Learning is done by doing, but also by studying documents and other materials.

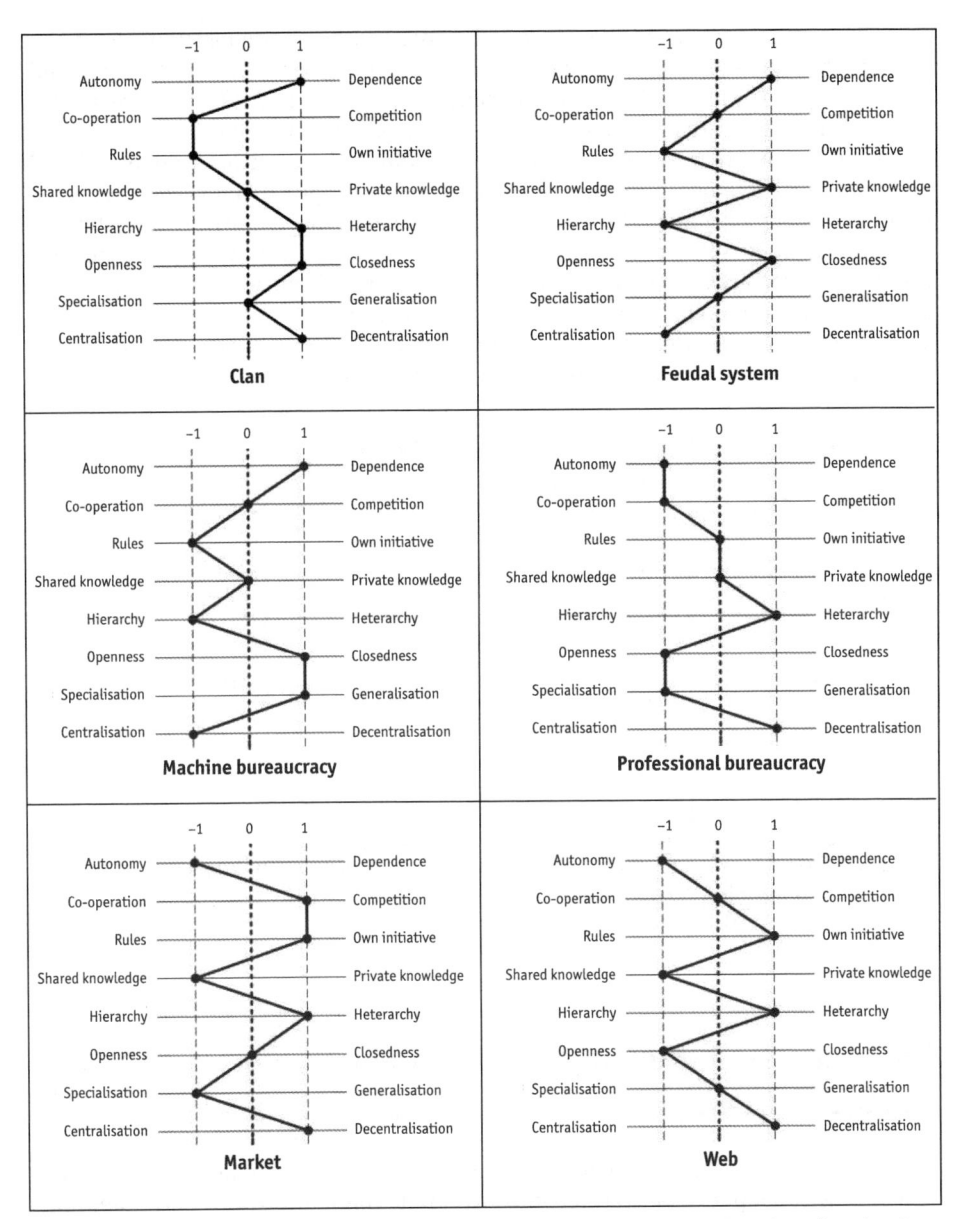

5. ORGANISATION: ARTEFACT AND PRINCIPLE *Jorna and Maruster*

Clan	Feudal system
Autonomy — Dependence	Autonomy — Dependence
Co-operation — Competition	Co-operation — Competition
Rules — Own initiative	Rules — Own initiative
Shared knowledge — Private knowledge	Shared knowledge — Private knowledge
Hierarchy — Heterarchy	Hierarchy — Heterarchy
Openness — Closedness	Openness — Closedness
Specialisation — Generalisation	Specialisation — Generalisation
Centralisation — Decentralisation	Centralisation — Decentralisation

Machine bureaucracy	Professional bureaucracy
Autonomy — Dependence	Autonomy — Dependence
Co-operation — Competition	Co-operation — Competition
Rules — Own initiative	Rules — Own initiative
Shared knowledge — Private knowledge	Shared knowledge — Private knowledge
Hierarchy — Heterarchy	Hierarchy — Heterarchy
Openness — Closedness	Openness — Closedness
Specialisation — Generalisation	Specialisation — Generalisation
Centralisation — Decentralisation	Centralisation — Decentralisation

Market	Web
Autonomy — Dependence	Autonomy — Dependence
Co-operation — Competition	Co-operation — Competition
Rules — Own initiative	Rules — Own initiative
Shared knowledge — Private knowledge	Shared knowledge — Private knowledge
Hierarchy — Heterarchy	Hierarchy — Heterarchy
Openness — Closedness	Openness — Closedness
Specialisation — Generalisation	Specialisation — Generalisation
Centralisation — Decentralisation	Centralisation — Decentralisation

Value −1 corresponds to the predominance of the 'left' concept (for instance, on the autonomy–dependence dimension, the concept of autonomy) while the value 1 corresponds to the predominance of the 'right' concept (for instance, on the autonomy–dependence dimension, the concept of dependence). The value 0 means an indefinite value (i.e. one that reflects no dominance of either concept or the dimension is not relevant).

TABLE 5.1 Charts illustrating the characterisation of six organisational forms with respect to leading principles

70 SUSTAINABLE INNOVATION

To illustrate better what we have said so far about different organisational forms, we provide two characterisations. The first is in Table 5.1 where we profile the six organisational forms—clan; feudal system; machine bureaucracy; professional bureaucracy; market; and web—with respect to the leading principles of autonomy–dependence; co-operation–competition; rules–own initiative; hierarchy–heterarchy; openness–closedness; centralisation–decentralisation; shared knowledge–private knowledge; and specialisation–generalisation. The profiles are not based on empirical data, but are indications based on aforementioned literature (partly empirical) and our own insights. The second characterisation is in Table 5.2. This refers to the characterisation of the six organisational forms with respect to knowledge types and learning modality. The details of the knowledge types are discussed in Chapter 6. These representations also allow for the different organisational forms to be compared.

Organisational form	Knowledge types (see Table 5.3 [page 73] for an explanation)			Learning
	Sensory	*Coded*	*Theoretical*	
Clan	+	–	–	• By doing
Feudal system	+	+/–	–	• By doing
Machine bureaucracy	–	+	–	• Documents, materials
Professional bureaucracy	–	+	+	• Education, training
Market	+	+/–	+	• By doing • Documents, materials
Web	+	+	+	• By doing • Documents, materials

TABLE 5.2 Characterisation of the organisational forms in terms of knowledge types and learning modalities

The organisation: business development, dynamics and change

We have already suggested that an organisation can be considered as a multi-actor system in which an input is transformed into an output. This is an abstract and system-theoretical formulation. What has been left out here is why an organisation exists and how it develops. For whom does it supply products, services or even knowledge?

An organisation's reason to exist concerns the realisation of a match between product or service supply and customer, user or market demand. Business is the result of such a successful match or **tuning**. The primary and secondary processes have to be arranged in such a way that this tuning is stimulated. The processes basically concern transformation processes in which a particular input (e.g. resources, knowledge and other artefacts), complemented by existing or new knowledge, is transformed into a particular output (e.g. product, service or knowledge). Given the large number of parties directly or indirectly involved in the organisation, such as stakeholders, employees, governments and customers, the layout of an organisation is a complex matter. This also explains the usability of a system-oriented approach.

As long as there have been companies and organisations, changes and renewals have occurred. Bolwijn and Kumpe (1990) tried to map out the development of organisations from the 1960s. The related social and market trends are the cause of this development. Bolwijn and Kumpe (1990) looked at organisational developments in a systematic way and formulated for each period so-called **ideal types**. These ideal types are formulated in terms of efficiency, quality, flexibility and innovation (see Fig. 5.1). Besides this, Bolwijn et al. saw an alteration in the dominance of structural and cultural factors in organisations. Structural refers to design and configuration of organisations, cultural to the people orientation.

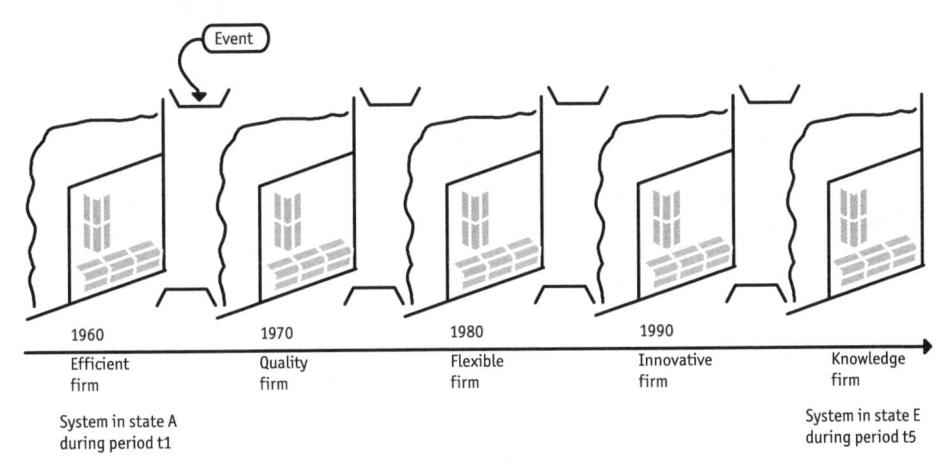

FIGURE 5.1 **Ideal types of organisational developments**

Source: Bolwijn and Kumpe 1990

In the 1960s, efficiency in particular was a central issue. Production costs had to be kept as low as possible and companies were held accountable for this. Within the organisation the focus was therefore mainly on structural aspects, such as hierarchy and specialisation.

In the 1970s, next to efficiency the predominant indicator of an organisation's success was quality. Communication and co-operation were considered important characteristics of a flexible organisation, resulting in a particular focus on cultural rather than structural factors.

In the 1980s, companies were forced to produce as flexibly as possible. They had to offer a vast range of products and services that were modularly structured. Here, again, the focus was on structural aspects of the organisation.

The 1990s was a period of innovative enterprises. Unique, new and innovative products and services were very important to companies. Because innovation has to ensue from the company's people and the organisation itself, cultural aspects were also an issue here. To realise innovation an adequate organisational environment had to be created.

The different phases can be considered as evolutionary developments in which each phase built on an earlier one. Innovation came after flexibility which again was built on quality and efficiency. Instead of ideal typical companies we can speak of role models. When continuing this line of company development we see that after the 1990s the subject of knowledge gained considerable momentum (Grant 1996b). Companies had to concern themselves with knowledge otherwise they could not perform properly. Here, we encounter a cultural aspect. However, if this means that, for the sake of knowledge, companies have to look further than their own organisation then this aspect will mainly consist of structural characteristics. We are now referring to the situation from the late 1990s onwards and this process will certainly continue until the end of 2010. At the moment a clear interest in sustainability is emerging. It has not yet been crystallised sufficiently, but a shift can be observed towards an interest in the three Ps (Faber, Jorna and van Engelen 2005). This shift does not concern only environmental sustainability but also social sustainability.

Bolwijn and Kumpe (1990) highlight a development involving many companies at the sector or branch level. However, individual companies or organisations do not stand still either. An organisation is a non-material artefact which alters itself on the basis of the idea that business development is aimed at renewals as regards combining product/service on the one hand and purchaser/user/market on the other. Simply formulated, one can say that: B(usiness) = P(roduct) + M(arket). If we express a change as Δ, we get different formulae: $\Delta B = P + \Delta M$ or $\Delta B = \Delta P + M$ or $\Delta B = \Delta(P + M)$. A change in one's own business means either a renewal in the products or services or in the groups of purchasers, users or markets (or in both).

By combining KoS, SoK (see Chapter 1) and the various aspects of sustainability within organisations we want to make clear that it is very difficult to change structural and cultural factors. This concerns the level of an organisation's goals, the organisational processes as well as knowledge, learning and the behaviour of people. As already argued, changing an organisation's goals is not that difficult, even if it concerns the provision of knowledge at this level. But it becomes really difficult if we enter the stage of learning or self-evaluation, especially if this is related to the SoK (see also Chapter 1).

In brief, if changes are more intensive they are more difficult, but if they are more intensive they are also more effective. In our terms they are more sustainable. While at an abstract level within an organisation one can simply speak of KoS and SoK, at an operational level the implementation may result in enormous problems. After all, SoK demands a learning organisation on all levels—individuals, groups and departments. Business development is aimed at the proper development of companies and organisations, at making companies and organisations sustainable. It may be obvious that business development cannot do without a thorough approach to the knowledge infrastructure, knowledge creation and knowledge management.

In Figure 5.2 we combine the various axes of our conceptual framework. Two of the axes are already discussed separately in Chapter 3 on sustainability and in Chapter 4 on levels of aggregation. In Chapter 6 we will explicitly deal with the axis of knowledge. In Figure 5.2 the x axis depicts the cultural development dimension in which, for the greater part, the sustainability issue and the debate on the reduction in offload can be placed. The y axis depicts the different levels of aggregation. We call this the aggrega-

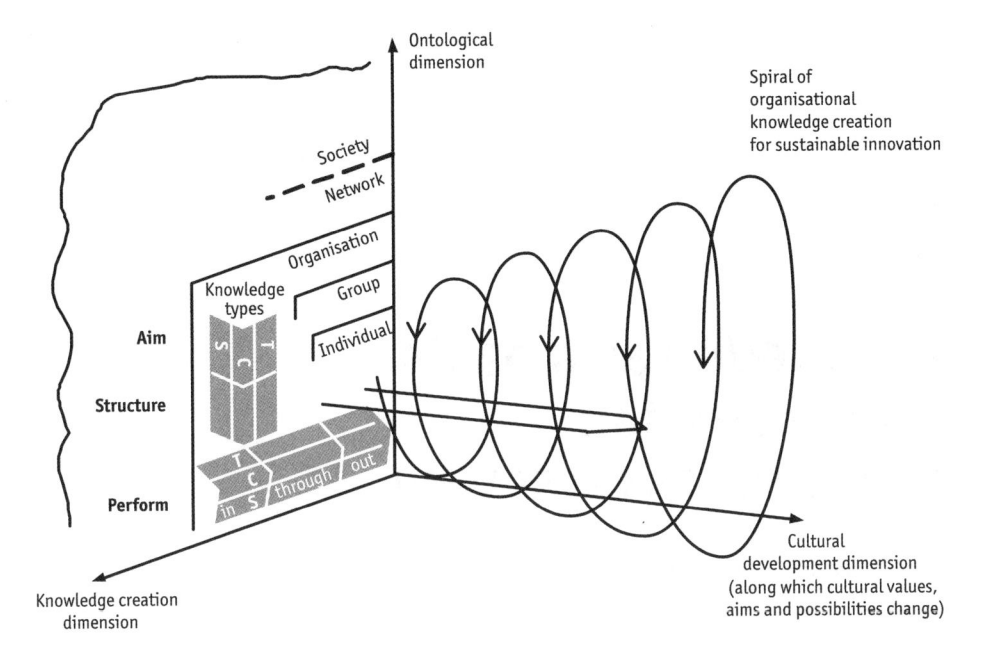

5. ORGANISATION: ARTEFACT AND PRINCIPLE *Jorna and Maruster*

FIGURE 5.2 Three dimensions of sustainability, levels of aggregation and knowledge

tion dimension (or the ontological dimension). The z axis shows the knowledge dimension within the context of primary and secondary processes. We refer here to the knowledge types—sensory, coded and theoretical—and their mutual relation. We go into the details of 'knowledge' in the next chapter.

Sensory knowledge Rough ↔ Detailed	Knowledge that cannot be put into words. It is about concrete experiences, and it can be shared only with those who are co-present. This knowledge can be rough or detailed
Coded knowledge Weak ↔ Strong	Knowledge can be represented in a certain language or code. Coded knowledge contains all types of signs or symbols either in text form, drawing form, or expressed in mathematical formulae. It can be passed on to others without your presence. Coded knowledge can be weakly coded (e.g. drawings) or strongly coded (e.g. formulae)
Theoretical knowledge Concrete ↔ Abstract	Theoretical knowledge concerns abstract formulae, models, diagrams and logical reasoning. You possess this kind of knowledge if you can answer why-questions and you can derive structural and causal relations (e.g. if–then relations). The interpretation of a mathematical formula is an example of this kind of knowledge. The more complicated the relations, the more abstract the theoretical knowledge; low complexity is concrete

TABLE 5.3 Definitions of knowledge types following the definitions given in Cijsouw and Jorna 2003 (see also Chapter 6)

6
Knowledge as a basis for innovation
MANAGEMENT AND CREATION

*René J. Jorna**

In the management literature, which is highly susceptible to trends, the attention paid to knowledge seems to have reached a peak. This does not alter the fact that management could ever do without knowledge. However, at the moment, terms such as 'competence' (Billet 2001) and 'learning' require attention, despite the fact that both have been around for some time. Too little attention is paid to the fact that competence and learning are based on some interpretation of knowledge. Competence starts from the capability of people to execute (entirely) new courses of action while learning, creation and, therefore, innovation, have knowledge as both the starting point and the ultimate goal (see also Chapter 2).

This chapter will deal with the subject of knowledge in a systematic way. Our point of departure is that knowledge exists within the minds of people, and also that collaboration with others creates new knowledge. The knowledge of people is rooted in their cognition, with the brain providing the physiological–neurological basis. In line with the work of Simon, Newell, March and many others in the fields of cognitive science and organisation studies, we see people as information-processing systems. Processing information requires cognition and generates knowledge. This knowledge is used in performing tasks, and results in actions and activities. We will discuss this in detail.

Knowledge is not the same as information. There are many definitions of knowledge. All discussions about knowledge recognise a distinction between the content of knowledge and how this knowledge is expressed: that is to say, its form or type. Content of

---

* With due thanks to Henk Hadders and Jo van Engelen for their comments on earlier versions of this chapter.

knowledge can refer to, for example, the construction of houses or the working of computers, but can also relate to sustainability. Knowledge according to form or type is our denomination of how this substantive knowledge is presented. We will deal with this issue thoroughly later in this chapter. The management and control of knowledge is something else than allowing new or renewed knowledge to develop.

Renewing knowledge or allowing new knowledge to develop involves knowledge creation. Allowing knowledge to develop is directly related to learning and developing. Here, too, we see the significance of competencies. In this respect an important distinction can be made. If knowledge exists principally in the minds of people, it is difficult to manage the development of the content of knowledge directly. One way of dealing with this from the perspective of organisations is to create favourable conditions under which new knowledge can develop and to choose proper organisational forms. In this way we provide an adequate interpretation of the sustainability of knowledge (SoK) issue, which also includes the design of a knowledge infrastructure.

The purpose of this chapter is twofold. First, we want to give an overview of the current subdivisions made with respect to the knowledge topic, although we cannot be exhaustive in this respect. Second, we want to create a framework for comparing the various organisational projects described in Part C in terms of knowledge.

Organisations, processes, tasks, people and knowledge

It is important to render explicitly the conceptual classification and (inter)relations of organisations, processes and knowledge. A first approach is to establish that an organisation consists of a range of processes (see also Chapter 5). In this respect, various aspects have been discussed by, among others, Thompson (1967) and Gazendam (1993). Processes can be investigated and treated as if they were pieces of a jigsaw puzzle that can be put together in various ways. However, processes cannot simply be divided (Simon 1969) and neither can they be (easily) approached empirically. If we really want to know what goes on in an organisation we have to go to a deeper level of aggregation in order to encounter the level of tasks.

An organisation can also be defined as 'the simultaneous functionalism and co-ordination of human interactions with respect to objective goals' (Van Dale 1996: 2,144). Actions are central in this description and can be structured according to tasks and processes. In addition, the description refers to 'goals' and 'co-ordination'. A goal is the answer to the question of why an organisation exists: a hospital (Chapter 16) exists to cure people; Grontmij (Chapter 17) is there to realise ground and harbour works while Philips (Chapter 13) aims to produce electronics. Co-ordination means there are entities that do not automatically form a unity, but which require cohesion. To which unity do we refer—that of processes, actions, tasks or people?

The unity of processes is, to a large degree, laid down in legal and financial constructions. In this way an organisation is ultimately a construct (a construction). To use drama terminology, an organisation is basically a unity of time, place and action. In the course of time this definition has changed considerably. The approach of 'action as a unity' has ceased to exist for a long time now. We now speak of a far-reaching division of labour and tasks. The unity of time and place at least guaranteed that, owing to physical presence and oral communication, one could maintain a coherent view of the daily affairs of an organisation or company. However, this unity is rapidly disappearing. Computers and certain ideological views, such as globalisation, play an important role in this.

Within organisations, co-ordination mechanisms as compensation for the loss of intrinsic unity almost always involve processes that play a role within an organisation in general (Van Dale 1996: 2378). A process can be looked on as 'an activity that is proceeding'. In the analysis of such processes the executing entity or carrier is mostly left out of consideration. A process concerns start, input, transfer, duration and end. However, a process should also have a material carrier as it must evolve from something. In production environments it quite often evolves from machines, tools, instruments and computers. In these environments, a process in all its characteristics can be very well investigated in an empirical way. In contrast with production, the carriers of processes in the field of service provision are mostly people, increasingly supported by computers.

A process is not isolated; it is embedded in a variety of processes with a mutual structure. Whether it concerns production, transport, service or other kinds of domain, it is always a natural tendency to consider organisations in terms of processes and structures. From this perspective an organisation is viewed from top to bottom. This is also called the **helicopter** (or **bird's-eye**) **view**.

However, if we consider organisations from bottom to top we need to place people and tasks (rather than processes and structures) in a central position as, fundamentally, it is about people who perform tasks within their functions and these tasks have their place within the organisation's primary and secondary processes (see also Chapter 5). In practice, people, usually in groups, perform tasks by interpreting these tasks and using their intelligence and knowledge. The co-ordination of these tasks is in the hands of the individuals themselves or is accorded to another person in a particular function. From this perspective an organisation can also be called a **multi-actor system**. This kind of perspective has many consequences for one's view of people, tasks, co-ordination and knowledge.

First, a **carrier** of processes and tasks is always required. It should be obvious that this is a person. In this way the **material carrier** of much that goes on within organisations becomes explicit. To give an example, it is management who makes the decisions, but making a particular decision for the organisation is the mutual decision of the board members. After consultation an agreement is reached and formulated as 'management has decided'.

Second, representations are central. At its heart an organisation is rooted in the individuals who are part of it or who think about it. In addition, it is embedded in (material) artefacts. The basic elements of an organisation are therefore always the intelligent people (actors) who co-operate within a multi-actor system. In this co-operation the actor executes tasks (Klos 2000; van den Broek 2001).

Third, an orientation on tasks and people leads to a more concrete and operational interpretation of knowledge management and knowledge creation whereby the starting point that knowledge exists in the minds of people is taken into account. Organisations are also cultural systems—the interaction among the actors is the result of their view on this interaction and how they act accordingly. The interaction among the participants, which enables them (and us as observers) to speak about an organisation, acquires meaning on the basis of more or less shared representations with respect to situations, events and actions. Organisations are also, according to Isenberg (1986), systems of shared knowledge and meaning, constructed from repertoires of schemes (Poole, Gioia and Gray 1989; Nooteboom 2000). These schemes are **cognitive undertakings** (Argyris and Schon 1978) or **interpretation systems** (Daft and Weick 1984).

A multi-actor perspective curtails a materialisation that is not justified. An organisation can be described by using metaphors, but so-called characteristics such as 'free will', 'cognition', 'memory' or 'the motives' of the organisation should not be taken literally. As metaphors they are enriching but deceiving. This at once settles the question of whether organisations possess knowledge, have a memory or can learn (Simon 1945, 1969). These expressions only have value in the figurative sense. Literally or, as one may prefer, materially, an organisation has no memory, no knowledge and no learning capabilities.

In brief, we state that organisations are (meaningful) constructions within, among others, the perceptions (representations) of actors (people) which enable them to structure their interaction with the social and physical environment. So, an organisation always constitutes a collection of actors within a specific historical context. These actors are intelligent and try to act as rationally as they can. Within such a multi-actor structure tasks are executed that are combined into processes. The intelligence of the actors and the execution of the tasks come together in the knowledge possessed by the actors required to execute the tasks. Knowledge is essential in innovation, to execute tasks and within the perspective that humans are cognitive information processing systems. But what, then, are we actually talking about? What is knowledge?

Data, information and knowledge

Data, information and knowledge can be considered as the parts of a three-stage rocket (Jorna and Simons 1992). Knowledge assumes information and information in turn assumes data. The bottom layer is formed by data. Data actually consist of information (facts). Data are the facts of reality. If data are interpreted in an explicit way we speak of information. If this information is used by people in reasoning or in performing actions (i.e. if it is interpreted) one can speak of knowledge. The line of thought that knowledge involves reasoning and making adaptations of interpretations of data also means that in the chain from data to knowledge the degrees of freedom increase. Data or facts can be interpreted in many different ways to serve as information. In a similar way, information can be interpreted in many different ways to serve as knowledge. When looking at it in terms of a dynamic process, the relations among data, information and knowledge can be considered as follows. Someone receives data and information and, with the aid of the knowledge this person already possesses, these data and information become knowledge which, in turn, can complement or change the person's existing knowledge.

Thus, the crucial distinction between information and knowledge is interpretation. This activity is carried out by people as information-processing systems. This implies a cognitive perspective on knowledge, both in its use and its creation. People are the ultimate carriers of knowledge and they themselves are sign- or symbol-processing systems (Jorna 1990).

In classical cognitive science, the (information) units within the cognitive system are also called symbols or signs. They are the embodiment of knowledge. In general, the collective name of the (information) units (mental or otherwise) is the term **representation**. The meaning of representation is 'something that stands for something else' (*aliquid stat pro aliquo*). So one speaks of a representation when someone (i.e. the sign user) refers with something (e.g. a form) to something else (e.g. the financial situation of a company) on the basis of a particular state or characteristic (i.e. a symbolic relation or supposed structural similarity). People form and have representations and these can be both internal (mental representations) and external (e.g. words, images, diagrams, mathematical formulas) (Goodman 1968; Jorna 1990). From now on, we will start from the view that people possess knowledge that manifests itself in the form of representations. We will return to this aspect of knowledge and representations later.

Knowledge: content and knowledge types

It is interesting to see how remote old views on knowledge have become. For example, Plato stated that knowledge is about truth. According to him it meant knowledge about the world of (unchangeable) ideas. Plato distinguished between knowledge (*epistèmè*) and opinion (*doxa*). The first is absolute—unchangeable in time and place—as a consequence it is directly connected to truth. The second is relative—changeable and tentative—susceptible to time as well as place. The difference has remained relevant to modern-day philosophy. However, in psychological, organisational and ICT environments knowledge can be created mentally by a person's cognitive processes in combination with data and information, resulting in an increase or change in a person's existing knowledge. This view differs enormously from Plato's notion of a stable unchangeable objective truth. In his view, knowledge does not depend on people while the current view on knowledge is pre-eminently connected with people.

The classical logical definition of knowledge is **justified true belief** (Edwards 1967). This knowledge view is not the same as the one central to the development of knowledge technology and knowledge management. Here, knowledge concerns a system of statements about facts, rules, opinions and findings. This system is based on a statement of truth which can be connected with the logical/analytical tradition of knowledge as truth (justified true belief). However, it is not, as in the Platonic sense, absolute, unchangeable and detached from people. Nowadays, knowledge is much more strongly linked to what people know and hardly to abstract structures beyond empirical reality: a world of forms, as Plato called them.

Knowledge categorisations in general

With respect to knowledge various divisions can be made. In this context, the most important is the distinction between knowledge content and knowledge type or form.

Knowledge content concerns what knowledge is about; domains, fields and disciplines are examples of knowledge content. Postrel (2002) calls a knowledge domain or discipline a **singularly linked cluster**. Scientific fields are good examples of knowledge domains: for example, medical science, economics or sociology. Within medical science there are specialisms: for example, orthopaedics. Postrel (2002) uses the degree to which knowledge shapes such a singularly linked cluster as the measure to determine the degree of specialisation.

Knowledge according to content can often easily be covered by the question 'what' and, in some cases, 'how' (i.e. 'knowing that' and 'knowing how'). We will not go into these and other distinctions here. As opposed to the development of knowledge systems, knowledge creation and knowledge management do not initially deal with this. It must be noted, however, that every analysis and support of knowledge begins with determining the knowledge content. In the remainder of this chapter the various types of knowledge mentioned in connection with the subjects of knowledge management and knowledge creation are especially important. First, we will present a number of classical bipartite divisions (Polanyi 1967; Pylyshyn 1984; Boisot 1995; Cijsouw and Jorna 2003). The types mentioned are:

- Declarative and procedural
- Abstract and concrete
- Tacit and explicit
- Coded and uncoded
- Dispersed and personal

Sometimes a transition is possible from one knowledge type to another. After a brief discussion of these bipartite divisions we will proceed with our own proposition concerning a division in three types of knowledge—**sensory**, **coded** and **theoretical**.

Declarative and procedural

In cognitive science, among others, the distinction between declarative and procedural was introduced by Pylyshyn (1984). Procedural knowledge is often represented as a production system. A production system is a complex 'if–then' structure within an activity of reasoning (see Chapter 9). The contents of the 'if' and 'then' clauses are considered as declarations (Anderson 1983). For example, if (procedural part) it rains (declaration) then (procedural part) the streets become wet (declaration). Procedures concern the ongoing and 'occurring' aspect of knowledge. Declarations are static. If procedures are often practised they can be thronged together or automated (compiled) to function as a declaration. The mutual interaction of declarations and procedures is a continuing process that shapes the knowledge increase and accumulation with the aid of different levels of aggregation as within a spiral.

Coded and uncoded

This distinction has been presented by, among others, Boisot (1995) to refer to structures of elements. A code assumes that units involved can become a composition via rules of amalgamation. In general we speak of applying syntax and semantics. Uncoded means that possibilities of structuring are absent. In the discussion about coded Boisot is somewhat incomplete. The distinction between coded and uncoded can be more refined by considering a code as a collection of elements accompanied by formation rules. So, given the elements and the rules, different kinds of codes can be constructed.

Goodman (1968) has divided codes in a different way. He speaks of collections of symbols or signs (elements) which have particular syntactical and semantic characteristics. Examples of such collections of symbols are pictures and icons, diagrams and schemes, texts and formulae. If we take pictures and formulae as an example, it can be stated that pictures have no elements that can syntactically, let alone semantically, be distinguished while formulae with both syntax and semantics are the most explicit. In brief, pictures form a weak code, formulae a very strong one. This has at least three important consequences:

- Pictures are subject to a large degree of ambiguity while formulae are, in principle, unambiguous. In general, it can be said that a set of signs is 'better' the more it reduces ambiguity. This means that the transfer of information via pictures will pose problems while this is not the case with formulae

- The learning time for understanding pictures is very short while that for mastering and applying formulae is very long

- Pictures are concrete and formulae are abstract (Jorna 1990). The possibilities of use are easier but more limited with respect to the first; with regard to the second they are more difficult but also much more extensive

Tacit and explicit

In the knowledge creation and knowledge management environment the distinction between tacit and explicit has been extensively used to distinguish between words and behaviour. Words are explicit and behaviour is tacit. According to Polanyi (1967), tacit knowledge is knowledge without speech; it is purely doing things (i.e. undertaking actions) while explicit knowledge is expressed or shown within structural forms.

A good example of the confusion about tacit (we prefer to speak of sensory knowledge and theoretical knowledge) is given by Linschoten (1964: 356) when quoting from Polanyi's work:

> Does someone know what he is doing when riding a bicycle? Hardly ever from his own experience. If he would know, it is probably because someone has told him. Ask a cyclist how he makes a turn to the right. He will say: by turning my steer to the right. This is not true. If one turns the handlebars to the right, the centrifugal power will push the cyclist away and he will fall, unless he adjusts his position, and bends over to the left to make a left turn. To make a right turn he first has to make a slanting movement to the right by turning the handlebars to the left. Polanyi found that neither physicists nor engineers nor cycle manufacturers questioned by him were familiar with this phenomenon. Even parents are not familiar with it when teaching their children to cycle. Obviously, such elementary knowledge is not required in order to practise cycling or manufacture bicycles: the goal of the execution is achieved by obeying a system of rules of which the person who follows it is not aware.

In this case the cyclist has tacit (sensory) knowledge. Another issue Linschoten (1964) brings up in the quoted passage is that, insofar as the cyclist possesses theoretical knowledge, this knowledge does not necessarily have to be penetrable cognitively. This aspect is ignored by Polanyi. With respect to normal (often automatically executed) actions, the proper reason 'why' cannot always be given. For the sake of completeness we have to mention that Linschoten quotes Polanyi, but as regards the physical principle both are completely wrong. Because what is important here is the gyroscopical moment of both wheels. The example reflects the principle correctly, but it is incorrect with respect to its content.

From the above it follows that the meaning of tacit is not simple. Three interpretations can be given. First, tacit could imply that people possess large quantities of knowledge that are not directly relevant. 'We know more than we can say' is the appropriate expression in this context. The quantity is there, but content slumbers and waits for a good opportunity to be retrieved in practice. This interpretation is closely in line with Polanyi's use of the term. Second, tacit knowledge can refer to impenetrable knowledge. With this interpretation, Pylyshyn (1984) wants to make clear that we are very limited in our ability to report on what happens within our cognitive system. In processes of problem-solving, decision-making and retrieving memories, cognitive activities take place that we cannot grasp, even if we try really hard. In cognitive science the expression **cognitively impenetrable** is used for this phenomenon. The third interpretation of tacit knowledge partly links up with what Polanyi meant. With regard to cognitive processes, tacit knowledge is automated or compiled knowledge. This means that for practical reasons we can limit cognitive processing because knowledge is thronged together (compiled). The advantages of this are that less memory space is required, no attention needs to be allocated and it can be carried out more quickly. However, it is also less accessible. Automated knowledge is in general also knowledge of or, rather, *in* skills. If I have learned to cycle, it is almost impossible to capture this skill in declarative terms; in other words, it has become tacit. In this respect, knowledge expresses itself in behaviour. Here the views deviate. Some say that knowledge of this nature can, by definition, be expressed only through behaviour; others follow the more basic compilation approach which states that compiled knowledge can be unpacked. This will take a great deal of effort and, in the process of making it explicit, some knowledge will be lost.

Unfortunately, with regard to clarity, the three interpretations do not exclude one another. The exception is that, according to the first interpretation, tacit knowledge as a large reservoir is, in principle, not coded (although it could become coded) while the second and third interpretations (i.e. impenetrable or automated) indicate that it once was a code and that it can again become a code. We are of the opinion that tacit knowledge can be translated into a weak or strong coded form. In this respect we realise that a certain amount of knowledge will be lost. In cognitive science, Reber (1993) has argued that there is something mysterious in the discussions about tacit knowledge. Being tacit cannot be observed as such. It can be deduced only from declarative and explicit knowledge or from overt behaviour. This means that the essential characteristics of tacit knowledge can be formulated only by the following dilemma—if you don't ask me anything about tacit knowledge, I know what it is, but if you ask me something about tacit knowledge, I don't know how to express it. This means that it is extremely difficult to make tacit knowledge operational.

From a cognitive perspective Reber shows that, of all the things we know, only a small part is available to direct introspection. The greater, invisible, part is not simply a mish-mash. Tacit knowledge, irrespective of the form in which it manifests itself, is internally connected with structure in the cognitive system and externally with the outside world. However, what is unpredictable is the way in which tacit knowledge crystallises itself in overt behaviour.

Abstract and concrete

The distinction between abstract and concrete has been presented by many to indicate that some knowledge can exist without being directly linked to empirical reality. A concept such as 'the chair' does not involve empirical reality and is, therefore, abstract while 'a chair' refers to something that actually exists in reality and is concrete. In this way, Boisot (1995) indicates that the application of knowledge coding involves different gradations. The larger the number of possibilities the more abstract the coded unit. In line with this reasoning one can say that 'the furniture' is more abstract than 'the chair'. The degree of abstraction will also play a role in theoretical knowledge, to be dealt with later.

Dispersed and not dispersed

This distinction has been introduced by Boisot (1995) to indicate that some knowledge can be dispersed but other knowledge cannot. This distinction is highly dependent on the process of knowledge coding. A code allows dispersion across greater distances and time. The absence of a code makes dispersion almost impossible. It should, however, be noted that tacit knowledge can be dispersed and shared by, for instance, examples and imitation. Tacit knowledge can be shown. As a result, it can generate knowledge accumulation on the part of the observers, and thus be dispersed and shared. Coded knowledge can, of course, realise this more easily, but it requires the observers to have knowledge of the code and thus a shorter or longer training time.

The five bipartite divisions make it clear that there is no unity in the description of knowledge types. Because we want to avoid the fact that within the organisational projects of Part C differences keep occurring in the interpretations of knowledge types, such as coded, tacit and dispersed, we apply a tripartite division: sensory, coded and theoretical. In Part D we will use this tripartite division to compare knowledge in the various business projects. Again, this involves types of knowledge connected with a particular content. This division has been inspired by the field of semiotics (Michon, Jackson and Jorna 2003) and the science of cognition (Jorna 1990). In the tripartite division into sensory, coded and theoretical knowledge, we will also discuss how the other types are connected with our division.

Sensory knowledge

We start with sensory or perceptive knowledge which we call **one-dimensional knowledge**. The knowledge we possess is just as concrete as the perceptions we interpret with this knowledge (not just visually, but with all our senses). So there is one dimension: namely, that of the concrete event. The only abstraction is the fact that the representation has abandoned the 'now' and forms part of our memory. This knowledge cannot be put into words. In this case the process of representation consists of both our memory of a concrete situation and our recognition of a new situation on the basis of similarity or analogy. Many of our daily activities are based on such sensory knowledge, just as is our capability to recognise places and faces. Therefore, with respect to memory, a new situation occurs as a transformation. This sensory knowledge is pointedly linked to context, with diffusion (dispersion) taking place only by imitation. Sensory knowledge partly coincides with tacit knowledge. We say *partly* because what is excluded is that tacit knowledge can also be automated knowledge. Consider, for example, the master–apprentice relationship. Let us assume that this relationship involves the transfer of knowledge. This transfer partly takes place via imitation and examples, and partly by translating the automated knowledge of the master. In this example, tacit knowledge is more than sensory knowledge. Quantification of sensory knowledge is possible by determining the degree of detail of the knowledge. Sensory knowledge is more detailed insofar as the perception consists of various partial perceptions on which a richer repertoire of actions (or schemes) is based. Research on sensory knowledge presupposes an analysis of the perceptions and actions of actors, especially the images the actors have at their disposal (not just visually, but with respect to all the senses).

Coded knowledge

Coded knowledge is **two-dimensional knowledge**. It is two-dimensional because next to the concrete image a second dimension emerges: namely, that of the code. A code links a concrete event (e.g. a sound or gesture) to a group, a category or images. The concrete event becomes a sign, and the category of images forms the meaning of that sign (e.g. a word). With respect to the first dimension the representation has changed. A situation is not only recognised as an image but is also categorised in terms of a general concept. In this way, the event or action is given meaning. Words and gestures have meaning thanks to codes (e.g. Morse, language, jargon, sign language). It is only because of coded signs that categories can emerge. This also clarifies how conventional (because of the codes) the world of our categories is. When we take a small step aside we have grasped part of the issue of innovation as knowledge creation. Often the big problem with both service as well as product innovations is finding terms for new artefacts and, if these are found, getting these terms accepted by other people.

Coded knowledge is tied to context to a lesser extent than is sensory knowledge (Boisot 1995). It is linked to the context of a code, of a language or of a collection of pictograms. In this way the dispersion of coded knowledge takes place much more quickly and easily than that of sensory knowledge. Thanks to shared codes this knowledge can be transferred quite easily within a community with the one who knows the code (or who can decipher it) sharing this knowledge. A change occurs when an event can be placed within different categories, possibly even contradictory categories. This forces sign users to reconsider the ways in which they have classified their world. Quantification of this coded knowledge is possible by analysing the characteristics of the codes—the number of elements and rules, and, possibly, the freedom of the sign user to ascribe meaning to them (Goodman 1968). The more freedom the user has, the 'weaker' the code and the larger the degree of ambiguity.

This can be illustrated by an example. Take a collection of pictures (e.g. the icons on a computer desktop), a text in the Dutch language and a mathematical proof. In all three cases signs are used. In the case of the pictures it is unclear how they are selected, whether more pictures will follow and, if this is the case, according to which design criteria. Also, the interpretation of a picture differs from person to person. Each picture is, in fact, unique. So there is ambiguity in the size of the collection of signs, in concatenation rules and in their interpretation. A text in Dutch consists of letters of the alphabet which are clearly defined. It can be determined whether the words and sentences are composed according to the rules of Dutch grammar. However, the interpretations evoked by reading a text differ per reader. This means that compared to the pictures the ambiguity in the construction of the signs has disappeared, but that interpreting (understanding) the text still involves ambiguity. In the case of a mathematical notation in a proof both the ambiguity regarding which signs take part and how these signs are interpreted have disappeared. If we put the pictures, the letters and the mathematical signs in a row, ambiguity decreases. This means that the codes used increase in 'strength': from pictures via text to a mathematical formulation.

Theoretical knowledge

Theoretical knowledge is **three-dimensional**. The third dimension that can be added to the other two other of perception (sensory) and conventional depiction (encoding) is the dimension of the structural identity. This third dimension emerges when it appears to be possible to depict relations by means of particular signs identical to the relations in the reality of events. Thanks to this third dimension it becomes possible to refer to the structure of our (constructed) realities, and to reason about and reflect on these realities. Theoretical knowledge, largely dependent on graphic (drawn and written) signs is, according to some (e.g. Donald 1991), the basis of the development of modern science. Changes in theoretical knowledge result from faults, incorrect predictions, contradictory hypotheses and facts that do not correspond with the theory. Learning processes take place by abduction (generating new hypotheses), induction (generalising on the basis of characteristics that repeat themselves) and deduction (on the basis of combining expressions leading to conclusions).

Some caution is required with respect to the meaning of theoretical knowledge as it is not only science that falls under theoretical knowledge. All knowledge reflecting a structure, systematicity or pattern can be called theoretical. Science is the obvious example in this respect, but in fact all knowledge that surfaces from an (extensive) 'why' question is theoretical knowledge. Explanations and predictions are in this respect the way in which knowledge manifests itself theoretically. So, in addition to science, religious, ideological and metaphysical knowledge can be denominated as theoretical.

The dispersion of theoretical knowledge is easier than the dispersion of coded knowledge because this knowledge should in principle be universal and so is not culture- or language-bound. At the same time this knowledge is so abstract that it is, for the most part, restricted to a (small) group of well-educated people. So what is gained by abstraction is lost by dispersion. Quantification of theoretical knowledge is possible by analysing the generality in terms of the reach or domain of the representations used. The larger the number of situations falling under the 'rule', the more abstract the knowledge is. Thus, the more a piece of knowledge is coherent the more abstract it is or, in a different formulation, the more extensive the 'why-chain' (*a* is so and so because of what *b* is and this is the case because of *c*) the more abstract the knowledge.

Figure 6.1 depicts these knowledge types.

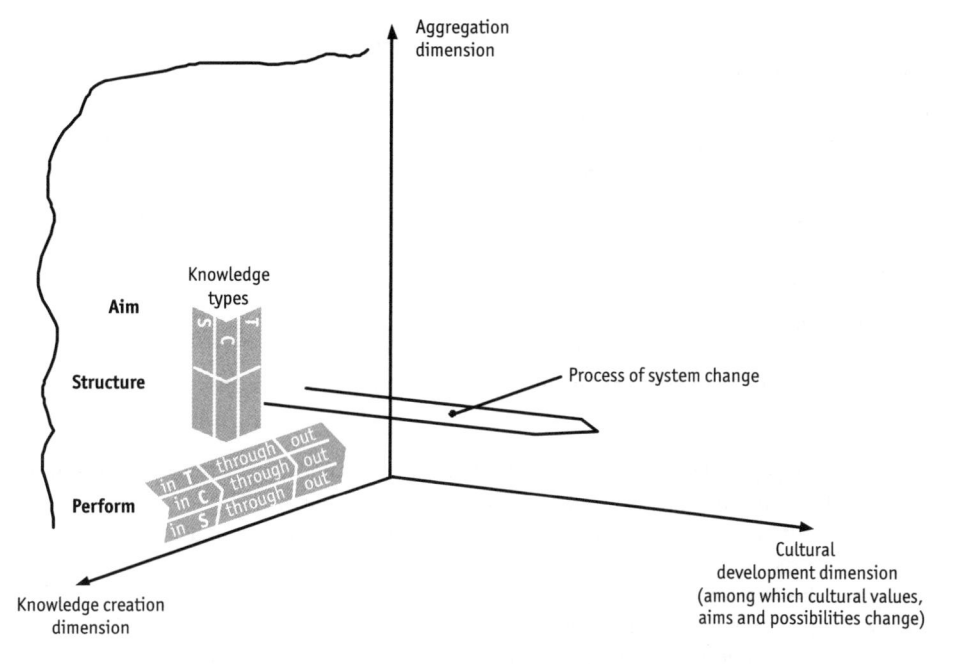

Key: T = theoretical; C = coded; S = sensory

Figure 6.1 The z axis: the dimension of knowledge types within primary and secondary processes

Figure 6.1 illustrates two things. First, with respect to people and organisations, knowledge content as well as knowledge types always play a role. We thereby make a division into sensory, coded and theoretical knowledge. Second, an organisation involves primary and secondary processes. Within these processes tasks can be distinguished for which knowledge is important; the three knowledge types can be distinguished in both processes. We discussed the primary and secondary processes in Chapter 5. Aim and structures relate to the secondary processes, perform to the primary processes.

Classification of knowledge types

The different knowledge types seem to exclude each other on the one hand while on the other they appear to deal with the same issues. On the basis of the frame of reference of sensory, coded and theoretical knowledge, we have classified all the knowledge types we have discussed (see Table 6.1). The columns represent sensory, coded and the-

	Sensory knowledge	Coded knowledge	Theoretical knowledge
Coded knowledge	No	Yes	Yes
Not coded knowledge	Yes	No	No
Declarative knowledge	No	Yes	Yes
Procedural knowledge	Yes	No	No
Abstract knowledge	No	Yes	Yes
Concrete knowledge	Yes	No	No
Tacit knowledge	Yes	No	Yes
Explicit knowledge	No	Yes	Yes

TABLE 6.1 A conversion table of knowledge from one type into another type

oretical knowledge. The rows depicts whether the other knowledge types can be put on a par with them. The cells indicate whether this is possible or not.

Henceforth, we will stick to the knowledge types sensory, coded and theoretical wherever possible. We further assume that the three knowledge types are cumulative and that theoretical knowledge presupposes coded and coded presupposes sensory knowledge. However, the knowledge types do not occur all by themselves. Given certain knowledge contents, sensory, coded and theoretical knowledge occur in certain proportions, whereby sensory knowledge will predominate in one case while in another theoretical knowledge will predominate. It is highly unlikely that sensory knowledge is the sole knowledge type one possesses. Everybody uses signs (coded knowledge) and tries to give explanations and make predictions (theoretical knowledge).

Both the relations between the three knowledge types and the degree to which each of the dimensions of sensory, coded and theoretical can be accorded a particular value can be depicted graphically. The relations among the three knowledge types can be represented by a web of three axes whereby each axis depicts a total knowledge content of 100%, but the total of the three axes can never be more than 100%, Thus proportions of S = 20%, C = 30% and T = 50% can occur, as can S = 90%, C = 10% and T = 0% (see Fig. 6.2).

The second aspect—whether sensory knowledge is rough or detailed, coded knowledge weak or strong and theoretical knowledge concrete or abstract—can be represented in a so-called **knowledge space** (see Fig. 6.3). This space is a metaphor with which we can demonstrate that knowledge types can occur simultaneously. It is, of course, a fact that divisions differ and that in most cases there is one dominant knowledge type.

The knowledge space can be interpreted as follows. Take a member of an organisation's finance department who is engaged in auditing the budget: in particular, staff travel expenses. Theoretically, it can be assumed that financial people, especially if

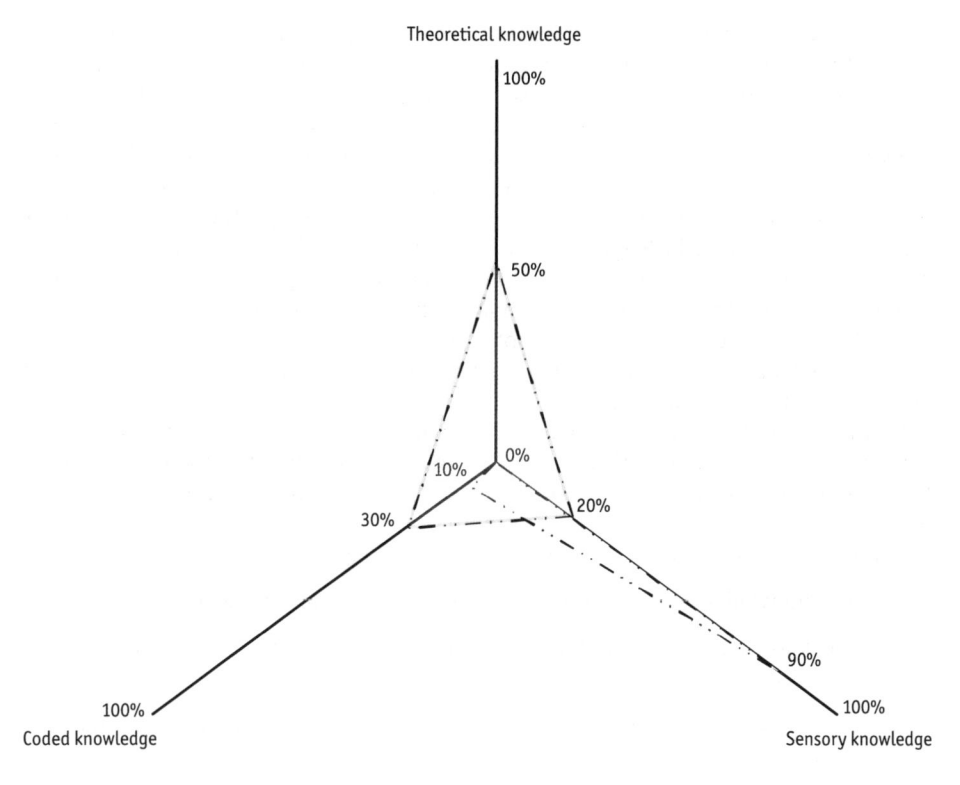

6. KNOWLEDGE AS A BASIS FOR INNOVATION: MANAGEMENT AND CREATION *Jorna* 87

FIGURE 6.2 Two representations of the relative weight of knowledge types

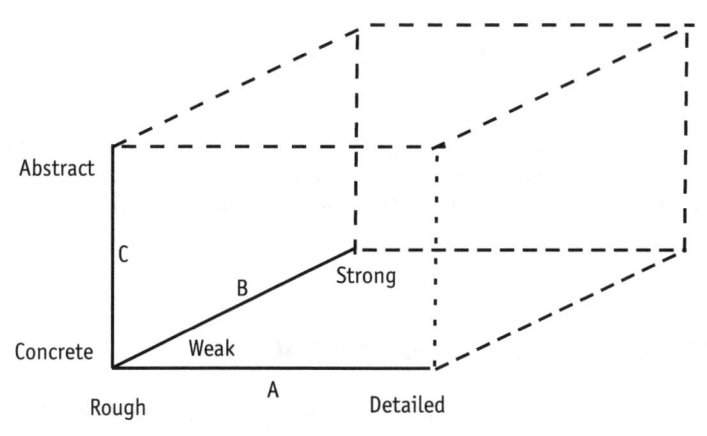

Knowledge space
  A: First knowledge axis: sensory knowledge: rough–detailed
  B: Second knowledge axis: coded knowledge: weak–strong
  C: Third knowledge axis: theoretical knowledge: concrete–abstract

FIGURE 6.3 The knowledge space: knowledge types belonging to a particular content, an individual or a team

they are involved in accounting activities, possess a great deal of coded but little sensory or theoretical knowledge. In empirical research the degree of this can be verified by means of questionnaires and score lists. When there are more people working in the finance department this can be mapped out for all of them. In this way, per task, per individual and per department the division of the knowledge types and the dominance of one particular knowledge type can be mapped out. Now suppose that the finance department never finishes its work on time, and that according to the knowledge types inventory there is very little coded knowledge present (and insofar as it does exist, is only weakly coded) while a great deal of co-operation is required. One can then conclude that the conditions for the dispersion of knowledge are not met.

The knowledge space can also be applied to innovations, especially in their implementation phase. In longitudinal research, determining the division and dominance of knowledge types per actor, task and department can take place more than once. The determination of points in a knowledge space will, at a particular point in time, lead to something we can metaphorically call a **knowledge snapshot**. Repetition of these through time will result in a series of knowledge snapshots that can provide an insight into the cognitive dynamics of an organisation.

In both Figures 6.2 and 6.3 four different levels of aggregation can be depicted:

- One knowledge content/domain for one individual for one task
- One knowledge content/domain for several individuals (a department or organisation)
- One knowledge content/domain for one individual carrying out several tasks (a role or a function)
- One knowledge content/domain for several individuals carrying out several tasks

Tasks cannot be separated from knowledge content. Nevertheless, this does not change the possibility of providing insight into knowledge types on the basis of each individual, task, department and organisation, as well as verifying whether conditions concerning the occurrence and division of knowledge are met.

The various knowledge types, resulting in non-content-based knowledge maps and in the knowledge space can now be rearranged into the building blocks of knowledge management and creation (i.e. the basis for sustainable innovation).

Management and creation of knowledge

There is a big difference between managing knowledge and creating knowledge. Managing knowledge concerns the management, administration, control, dispersion, sharing and updating of knowledge, and also information. This means two things; first, that knowledge and information must be present and available, and, second, that managing them has been taken care of: in other words, that there are arrangements, procedures, rules, habits and patterns in place to control, share and maintain the knowledge.

We will deal somewhat more thoroughly with both aspects here. After that, we will come back to the issue of knowledge creation.

Management of knowledge

The presence, accessibility and availability of knowledge or information concerns the people within the organisation as well as other knowledge and information carriers: that is to say, ICT. With respect to ICT we speak of databanks, management information systems, decision-making support systems, knowledge technology, intranet and the internet. Although ICT has become increasingly important to knowledge management, it has no meaning without people using and acting on it.

We will first go into the 'what' of knowledge management—the knowledge people possess. This knowledge occurs in sensory, coded or theoretical forms but is, in principle, only cognitive and thus, in the first instance, only indirectly accessible. As soon as people express this knowledge in terms of behaviour, words and other expressions, knowledge becomes information which in turn can be processed either directly or indirectly to become knowledge again. The good (but also awkward) aspect of knowledge is that it consists of ideas and images (also called representations) which individual actors within an organisation have with regard to their tasks and work. So the management of knowledge involves a focus on the representations of people (as information-processing systems). The methodological problem therefore is that mapping out representations mainly takes place indirectly (as there is, as yet, no reliable mind-reading equipment). In addition, it is not our intention here to consider the content of knowledge in detail. However, retrieving knowledge content occurs in other ways during the development of knowledge systems. Only after an expert has made his or her knowledge explicit can a system support others within the organisation.

Knowledge and other information systems can be involved in knowledge management, but managing knowledge is primarily about the types of knowledge relevant to the individuals involved in carrying out their (combined) tasks. Although beset by a considerable number of methodological problems, it is indirectly possible to map out the knowledge types. This can be done with the aid of questionnaires, knowledge maps and scoring systems (see also Chapters 7, 8 and 23).

Apart from the fact that in knowledge management there has to be something that can be managed (the 'what'), that is to say the knowledge and information, the way in which this happens is also important. We are then referring to the arrangements, procedures and behaviours associated with people. These have to be classified and a number of principles have been formulated for this purpose (Gazendam 1993; Nonaka and Takeuchi 1995; Sorge and Warner 2001):

- There has to be a concrete reward for people who place knowledge at the disposal of others, keep it up-to-date and share it

- The choice of not making knowledge available to others should *not* be punished. Although punishment may prevent undesirable behaviour for a short time, if it continues it will stifle creativity and encourage evasion. Rewards can be in various forms, such as promotion, public appreciation, money, task change or increase in status

- Awareness of the advantages of maintaining and sharing knowledge needs to be created. Creating awareness can be done in the form of representations, but can also be done behaviourally. Designing organisations in such a way that creativity, innovation, learning and curiosity are stimulated means implementing sustainable innovation

While the first two principles directly concern the influence of behaviour, the third also uses cognition. Awareness, recognising advantages and realising that knowledge does not just provide different and better possibilities individually, but also collectively, is important for its acceptance. The principles of behavioural and mental influence within organisations can be dealt with in numerous ways. That is why we are not really concerned with *how* they are dealt with, but more with the fact that they *are* dealt with (see also Chapter 5).

Creation of knowledge

Creating knowledge differs entirely from managing knowledge. Creating knowledge involves inventing either entirely or partly new products, services, production processes or organisational forms. This is only and pre-eminently an activity that people can perform, if necessary with the support of software. Often knowledge creation is considered equal to innovation, but this is only partly true. Innovation involves an inventive element and an implementation element (see also Chapter 2). Especially from a human information-processing perspective (psychological), knowledge creation coincides with invention, whereas implementation is realised by the larger group.

In the literature on knowledge creation (von Krogh, Nonaka and Kazuo 2000) it is argued that, because of the knowledge not yet present, knowledge creation especially involves tacit knowledge. The latter then concerns, in our terms, a combination of sensory and theoretical knowledge. These authors cite five steps in the process of knowledge creation:

- Sharing tacit knowledge
- Developing terminology
- Justifying the terminology
- Designing a prototype
- Dispersing the knowledge through all echelons

Sharing tacit knowledge (sensory knowledge) means that one tries to find a formulation of some vague notion, the detection of a problem or a possible new use of a material, a product or a service. With respect to this formulation one should not have too high expectations. It can take form as sketches or images, a few words or a multitude of vague words indicating that one is on to something new or renewing. This process can take a long time, it can emerge in a flash, and it can also take place through interaction with others. We refer here both to working with sensory knowledge and to a transition of sensory knowledge to coded knowledge. In this respect we are dealing with weak codes that are still highly ambiguous.

The development of terminology is important, especially here because codes of a stronger nature are being developed. Developing terminology goes much further than merely pictures and images; it means that a group of people knows what it is talking about and can make progress by using these terms. When people with different backgrounds work together on innovations (which is often the case in innovation or R&D departments) there can be a lack of co-operation, especially where one person thinks that the other person is talking about the same issue from a different content perspective. To give a trivial example, to a furniture development department the Dutch word *bank* (something to sit on) means something entirely different to a finance department. In this respect, we are especially referring to coded knowledge.

Justifying the terminology means that one checks whether a well-formulated first solution, a first effort or a first step corresponds with what is already known. On the one hand, this means that one looks at cohesion, eliminating contradictions and increasing coherence. On the other, it also means that one should try to gain a proper insight into why the innovation is as it is. Such a 'why' response can be very complicated. In terms of knowledge types we are dealing here with a transition of coded to theoretical knowledge and, especially, with the application of theoretical knowledge too.

Designing a prototype is the next phase within an innovation process. Naturally, this only holds for production and production process environments. With regard to service and organisation environments there is no prototype, but rather a construct or a test. In case of a test the processing may be tried out several times, possibly with the aid of a computer simulation. What also applies to service innovations is that the trajectory of sensory to coded and, subsequently, to theoretical knowledge has to be followed. The development of a prototype construct or test is required in order to consider the innovation in a critical and evaluative way.

Finally, there is the phase of knowledge dispersion: first through all the layers of the organisation and then in a broader sense through the local and, sometimes, even global environment. This is highly important because the knowledge created has to be transferred to others: for example, to the production department or to marketing and sales. Already during the process of knowledge creation this has to be taken into account. To do this, theoretical knowledge at all levels is not really an issue here. What is important is that the innovation can be properly explained in word (text), gesture (behaviour) and image (photograph).

The various phases of von Krogh *et al.* (2000) make three things clear:

- In the first place there is a continuous path leading through the particular knowledge types. From sensory to coded, from weakly to strongly coded, and from there to theoretical, but also back to coded knowledge

- Second, there is a continuous mutual interaction, exchange and trial and error taking place. Innovation is the work of people, be it through co-operation

- Third, processing is not linear but consists of feedback loops, going through the different phases in similar ways and also going back one step in order to go forward two steps. This also appears from the fact that after the phase in which the knowledge is widely propagated one simply returns to the first phase in which the sensory knowledge is shared (possibly within a new area of content)

In the second meaning of sustainable innovation, which concerns making the innovation process sustainable as well as the people within it, the five phases provide starting points to maintain this process and also to determine the sustainability of knowledge in moments of verification. In Chapter 23 we present an instrument—an extended, multi-layered questionnaire—that asks for aspects of knowledge, learning, organisational forms and the presence and opinions of a smaller and larger environment (stakeholders). The questionnaire is a list of questions to make an inventory of these aspects.

Learning, changing knowledge and conversion

Knowledge is strongly connected with learning. Nobody is born fully equipped with knowledge. So, for the larger part, knowledge has to be learned. Up to this point the different scientific disciplines dealing with learning agree with each other. After that, the differences between them lead to a number of different mainstreams. We focus on three important contrasts.

The first deals with knowledge present at birth. Rationalists say this is a considerable amount. Empiricists say there is only a small amount present. The second contrast concerns the course of the learning process. Some say it takes place in stages—one cannot be taught something if one is not yet ready for it. This is, among other ideas, the view of Piaget. Others claim that learning is a gradual process that goes on continuously. Many psychological behaviourists share this view. The third contrast concerns 'what' and 'who' learns. The behaviourists claim that learning is embedded in behaviour while cognitive psychologists are of the opinion that learning is a cognitive and mental affair. Irrespective of how much these views differ, both groups agree that only individuals have the capability to learn. In addition, there is an ever-increasing group of sociologists, business and management scholars and economists who advocate the view that it is not just individuals that learn, but also companies, groups of people and organisations. Sorting out and writing down all contrasts ever mentioned would take up an entire library. We will not give a complete overview here. Nevertheless, when dealing with knowledge creation and knowledge management a brief discussion about learning is important.

There are many definitions of learning. We will use a definition from a very well-known handbook in psychology as an example (Bower and Hilgard 1981: 11):

> Learning concerns the particular change in the behaviour or behavioural potential of an individual in a particular situation, produced by this individual's repetitive experiences in this situation, assuming that the behavioural changes cannot be explained on the basis of the individual's innate tendencies by maturation or temporary states, such as fatigue, drunkenness, tendencies etc.

The definition explicitly starts from the individual, is based on behaviour rather than knowledge, and advocates the assumption that matters that are innate are not related to learning. The important aspect of the definition is that it shows that the changes have to be permanent. The question is whether we can link this definition to knowledge (and especially also to knowledge types).

We will first look at what else could be meant by 'learning'. By learning we can indicate that behaviour or thinking is accelerated. One has learned to multiply, not only if one knows the rules, but also if one can use them very quickly. In addition, learning is regarded as expanding or increasing. This can be done in two ways. Expanding can imply that more of the same is added—I knew the multiplication tables up to and including 10, but now I know them up to and including 100. I have learned; my knowledge has expanded. Expanding can also mean that something of another nature is added. Next to learning multiplication tables I have also learned about division. The first type of enlargement can be called a quantitative expansion, the second a qualitative one. Especially with respect to a qualitative expansion the aspect of unlearning is also important. However, for the moment we will leave that aside.

What is clear in all cases of acceleration, enlargement and expansion, is that the basic issue is a change and increase in the *content* of knowledge. From the perspective of knowledge management and knowledge creation, changing or increasing the content of knowledge cannot be influenced. Learning in the sense of content is an activity to be carried out by the individuals themselves. In terms of content, knowledge is acquired via eyes, ears, mouth and the other senses of the individual. However, from the perspective of knowledge management and knowledge creation (i.e. beyond the individual) the presentation form of the knowledge, and whether and how knowledge types can be converted into each other, do matter. We have already explained various knowledge types and classified them into sensory, coded and theoretical knowledge. We will now successively deal with them in terms of transformation into one another (also known as conversion) (see Table 6.2). These conversions are not based on empirical research, but on theoretical considerations.

Conversion of . . . into . . .	Sensory	Coded	Theoretical
Sensory	Yes	Yes	No
Coded	Yes, other content	Yes, other content	Yes
Theoretical	No	No	Yes

TABLE 6.2 An overview of conversions of one knowledge type into another knowledge type

We can study the different conversions both on the individual and the higher aggregation levels. For now we will leave the individual level out of consideration because this would lead us into the domain of psychology. We will mainly elaborate on the advantages and disadvantages of these conversions of knowledge types on a level that goes beyond that of the individual. In this way we will enter the discussion about the knowledge infrastructure and thereby also about the subject of the SoK.

The conversions of sensory into sensory and coded are obvious. Sensory knowledge cannot be converted into theoretical knowledge without the transitional step of coded. Coded knowledge cannot simply be converted into sensory knowledge. This is only possible if, on the basis of the code, a new content is developed. The conversion from one code to another is possible whereby the preferred conversion will be from a weak to a strong code. The conversion of coded to theoretical knowledge is an obvious one. The conversion of theoretical to theoretical knowledge can be done very easily, and so can the conversion into coded knowledge. The path of theoretical to sensory knowledge does not apply here because from the perspective of a 'why-chain' one will not return to behaviour and skills without making a transitional step. All of the specific conversions deal with learning content. In this context we will leave content out of consideration.

Knowledge infrastructure

In the field of management and business studies, the knowledge infrastructure has been subject to a great deal of discussion. It is inadequate, it needs reinforcement, it has to be developed and it requires more attention. The important question is 'what is meant by infrastructure?' We will address some aspects with the aid of the aggregation levels of the individual, the team, the organisation, the network and society. The various aspects are psychological, economic, ICT, organisational and managerial.

To put it plainly, the debate on infrastructure is not about individuals and hardly focuses on psychology. Neither is the discussion relevant on the level of teams nor, in most cases, on the level of the organisation, except when it concerns ICT on an intra-organisational level. In this case it is mostly about the preconditions rather than the implementation of the knowledge infrastructure.

A knowledge infrastructure especially concerns the inter-organisational level. Organisations in the form of companies and institutions both in the public and the private sector are the junction nodes in a complicated network of connections and dependencies. Here, the economic and ICT aspects are often mentioned first. Economic means that one checks whether the network is suitable for business, employment as well as growth and profit in the middle and long term. ICT is mostly about a sufficient amount of hardware, cables, data junction points, speed and software for applications and data storage. The availability and accessibility of knowledge and information of and between organisations is a core theme here. In the debate on infrastructure, awareness increasingly grows that ICT is an important means or a precondition, but that a knowledge infrastructure is about both knowledge *and* the organisation, not as points of junction, but as a structuring principle. With respect to the structuring principle the question then becomes relevant which co-ordination mechanisms and organisation forms are the most suitable and when. And if these structures do not yet exist, the question is 'in what way and in what form can they be best designed and realised?'

In addition, it is important to be aware of the fact that the infrastructure is not about roads or water, but about knowledge. If we want to be precise, we ought to say 'information', because knowledge exists only in the minds of people, and the latter are not included in the knowledge infrastructure. As regards knowledge, we then return to our earlier mentioned distinction of knowledge content and knowledge type. An initial point of interest regarding the knowledge infrastructure is whether the content of knowledge that has been mapped up to a certain level of detail is also available to others outside the original organisation. Often, a great deal of work involving both descriptions and analyses is required to grasp the content of knowledge and make it available to others. Moreover, we know that when several companies work together on one and the same subject, there is still no guarantee that one company understands instantly what the other is doing. This is illustrated by the examples of the Synthetics House (Chapter 11) and the support of several carton and paper manufacturers (Chapter 12) in dealing with chemical substances. The discussion about this complicated subject matter of sharing and dispersing knowledge content and type has not yet been closed.

A second point of interest is that when knowledge content is actually available an organisation other than one's own should be allowed and enabled to make use of this knowledge. Even if this is allowed, there is still the well-known problem that knowledge is embedded in a context. While possessing all of the knowledge content, the first organisation implicitly takes so much for granted that the second organisation, even though it has a detailed insight into the knowledge, will still miss important parts of it. In the organisational domain this issue is known as **sense making** (Choo 1998).

A third point of interest deals with the form/type in which the knowledge is presented. The question connected with this issue is that, if the present form is not suitable, a conversion could be made into a form that is more suitable. For example, sensory knowledge cannot be transferred while coded and theoretical knowledge require a great deal of education and training. In the discussion about the knowledge infrastructure the subject of sense making and the importance of the different knowledge types is not at all, or hardly, recognised.

The availability and accessibility of content, 'making sense' adequately and the possibilities of knowledge type conversions are of the utmost importance not only in the management of knowledge but also in knowledge creation. Without an adequate description of knowledge on the levels of the individual, the unit or department and the organisation, the knowledge of sustainability (KoS) as well as the SoK cannot be properly structured, anchored and maintained.

Conclusions

It is possible to approach innovation (and thereby knowledge creation) within organisations and institutions from a macro-economic perspective. This is usually the case when talking about innovation. In this approach the preconditions and consequences of innovation are especially central. Economic, financial, and social aspects are dominant here. Mostly, this macro perspective does not initially start from the knowledge, insights and skills of the people in the organisation and the ways in which they mutually create knowledge, change it, give it form and share it. That is why research into innovation from a micro perspective is a crucial addition, especially when it is about SoK. Innovation on a micro level equals knowledge creation. It means that people work on knowledge and with knowledge.

We have also made clear that knowledge management has to be discussed on the level of actors and tasks, and that it has to be combined with ideas (concepts) and representations. In their capacity as information-processing systems people possess knowledge that they use to execute tasks and to learn. The same applies, to an even higher degree, to knowledge creation. The difference with knowledge management is that here one develops something new, and thus does not precisely know what one actually knows and what one does not know. In this sense knowledge creation, and thus also innovation, are unpredictable processes. Knowledge management is not the same as knowledge creation. The only thing both activities have in common is that they are directed towards knowledge. However, managing is maintenance and control, while creating implies renewal and partly also termination. The latter (creation) requires different organisational forms than the first.

Knowledge content has to be distinguished from knowledge type. The latter especially deals with how knowledge presents itself (i.e. which form it takes). The development of new knowledge content is reserved for individuals and, whether we like it or not, largely takes place outside our perception and the management of an organisation. The situation is more favourable with respect to the form/type in which knowledge manifests itself. These knowledge types and their mutual attuning can be structured and also influenced. Because each segment of knowledge content has to be given a form, one can indirectly acquire a view of the development of knowledge content.

Knowledge creation is related to learning. Not in the sense of acceleration, but in the sense of expanding and, especially, also in the form of renewal or the development of genuinely new products, services or knowledge. As regards the content of learning, an organisation can realise its conditions but, in the end, it has to be developed by individuals and almost always on a co-operative basis.

When connecting the knowledge debate with the principal theme of sustainability dealt with in this book, KoS is about the content of knowledge, especially in innovation trajectories. The central issues are, then, knowledge about 'planet', 'profit' and 'people' which can be increased, re-used, shared and maintained. Of course, regarding content, this differs per knowledge domain. However, SoK concerns the structure, the organisation model and the organisational form, all designed in such a way that they allow knowledge creation, and thus also innovation, to continue with the aid of knowledge management. In our view mapping out the different knowledge types is a suitable tool for this purpose.

When combining knowledge types and organisational forms, we can formulate the following assumptions. First, knowledge creation assumes an intensive perception. This generates sense-making problems which constitute the engine of cognitive change. A change in meaning also leads to a change of knowledge type. Second, innovation benefits from the dispersion of knowledge; a proper dispersion assumes codification. Third, in the more general sense, an organisation profits from a well-balanced and complex interplay of the various types of knowledge. Finally, it can be stated that information and communication technology stimulate codification, but impede perception (Sennett 1998) and, as a consequence, perhaps eventually also impede innovation.

Part B
Instruments and models

7
A method for the identification of stakeholders

Janita F.J. Vos and Marjolein C. Achterkamp

In the light of sustainability, organisational responsibilities increasingly tend to go beyond safeguarding financial returns. For example, from the triple-P perspective, responsibilities concerning the social (and ecological) environment are also important while from the perspective of 'reducing offload' it is important to reduce negative externalities (see Chapter 3; Achterkamp and Vos 2006). Because of this increase in responsibilities, stakeholders have become an indispensable element for organisations when it comes to giving meaning to sustainability. In addition, when sustainability becomes an issue in an innovation project, we assume that there is a crucial role for stakeholders too.

There are several reasons why we make this assumption. One is that stakeholders can be considered as representatives of the organisation's social (and ecological) environment. When, in the light of sustainable innovation, the organisation aims to reduce its negative externalities, stakeholders will certainly have an interest in this. Another reason is that stakeholders can help define criteria for sustainable innovation. Moreover, stakeholder involvement may lead to greater commitment to the sustainability of the innovation both within the organisation in general and the innovation team in particular, as well, perhaps, on the part of the stakeholders themselves.

These reasons explain some of the interests an organisation could have in involving stakeholders to improve sustainable innovation or to make sustainable innovation more concrete. Obviously, this raises questions about stakeholder management, such as 'who are those stakeholders?' and 'what should be their role within an innovation process?' However, dealing with these questions is not a straightforward matter. Of course, organisations may have certain ideas about who the stakeholders are or might be. Still, the question remains whether a possible stakeholder list is accurate or complete. Furthermore, in the case of a specific innovation project, other stakeholders might present themselves. So when aiming at sustainable innovation particular stakeholders might be (or become) relevant.

In order to resolve these kinds of issues, we have developed a stakeholder identification method. In this chapter we will describe the method, including its underlying foundations. In doing so, we will start by presenting the method, its building blocks and how they are to be used in practice. Having presented the method we will justify it. First, we discuss the current stakeholder literature and show that in this context the problem of stakeholder identification is considered mainly as a problem of classification. We then argue that the prevailing ideas fail to go beyond this classification of stakeholders; we believe that, in order to make the identification of real-world stakeholders a feasible task, a much broader approach is required. It should be noted that our analysis of stakeholder literature has been important in setting the requirements that the method must fulfil. Accordingly, stakeholder literature has influenced the basic format of the method. In the second round of justification we will show how critical systems thinking and innovation theory have led us to the two main points of the method (i.e. 'roles of involvement' and 'phasing this involvement'). The concluding section discusses to what extent the method contributes to solving the stakeholder identification problem. Parts of the method are included in a more general questionnaire (discussed in Chapter 23) which also involves aspects of knowledge, learning and organisational forms.

Describing the method: its building blocks and operating procedure

Building blocks of the method

The essence of the method is that it not only classifies the parties involved in an innovation project but also actually identifies these parties, designates roles to them and, as will be discussed further below, deals with the question 'at what point should the identified parties play these roles?' In doing so, the method uses a classification based on the activities at hand—meaning the activities within a particular innovation project. In such a project, there are several roles that should be fulfilled to make the project a success: the role of the client, the role of the decision-maker and the role of the designer. The parties who play these roles can affect the outcome of the innovation project. In addition to these so-called **actively involved** parties, there are others who are affected by the outcome of the project but who are not capable of influencing the results themselves. These parties are assigned the role of **passively involved**. In some cases these parties cannot be addressed directly. When this happens the notion of representation becomes relevant, whereby a certain party might act on behalf of a person or group that is passively involved. Examples are a union that represents (future) employees or a city council that represents a group of local residents.

Without getting too much ahead of the method's justification, it should be noted that the roles within the method are based on Ulrich's critical systems thinking (Ulrich 1983). However, our role labels are slightly different, as we will explain later. It should also be noted that in identifying the active and passive parties involved we take the perspective of the organisation concerned. Still, it can be expected that, in particular, the passively involved (or their representatives) will take the first step in making contact (in whatever way) with the organisation. Precisely for that reason, it is important that an organisation is aware of these types of parties involved. Table 7.1 gives an overview of the roles and their definitions as used in the method.

Role	Definition
Party involved, actively and passively	A *party involved* is any group or individual who can affect the achievement of the innovation's objectives or who is affected by the achievement of these objectives. The first category is labelled the *actively involved*; the second category the *passively involved*
Client	A *client* is the party whose purposes are being served through the innovation
Decision-maker	A *decision-maker* sets requirements regarding the innovation and evaluates whether the innovation meets these requirements
Designer	A *designer* contributes expertise to the innovation process and is responsible for the (interim) deliverables
Passively involved, representative	A *passively involved* party is affected by the outcome of the innovation project without being able to influence the outcome. A *representative* is a person who has been selected to act on behalf of the passively involved

TABLE 7.1 Definitions of the roles of involvement

Innovations are often developed within projects and consist of a starting-up phase, development phases and an end-point (see Chapter 2). These phases differ with respect to activities and goals. Therefore, it can be assumed that stakeholder involvement also differs with each phase. This notion of different, distinguishable phases within innovation processes has been integrated in the identification method. It makes it possible not only to deal with the issue of which parties should be involved but also in which phase of the innovation process this involvement should take place. We distinguish four phases: initiation, development, implementation and maintenance. Table 7.2 gives an overview of the phases and their definitions as used in the method (compare van de Ven *et al.* 1999).

Operating procedure of the method

The identification method uses the roles and phases to establish an overview of the parties involved which is as complete as possible. The method consists of four steps (see Fig. 7.1) that together facilitate a brainstorming session aimed at identifying the parties involved in a specific innovation project. The four steps will be discussed successively. Mainly for practical reasons, each of these steps involves two individuals who chair the discussion which is attended by a number of participants. It is required that the participants understand the innovation project at hand, preferably from different angles. Altogether, the four steps take approximately three hours to perform.

7. A METHOD FOR THE IDENTIFICATION OF STAKEHOLDERS *Vos and Achterkamp* 101

Phase	Definition
Initiation phase	This phase focuses on generating ideas as well as on defining the goal of the project
Development phase	This phase focuses on developing and performing activities to reach these goals
Implementation phase	This phase focuses on implementing the project outcomes
Maintenance phase	This phase focuses on applying, monitoring and evaluating the project's outcomes

TABLE 7.2 Definitions of the four phases in an innovation project

Four-step stakeholder identification procedure

Step 1. Defining (the goal) of the project

Step 2. Individual brainstorm: identification of the involved

Interlude. Explaining the stakeholder model

Step 3. Group brainstorm: identification of the involved based on roles

Step 4. Group brainstorm: phasing the involvement

Guiding questions

Stakeholder model: roles and phases

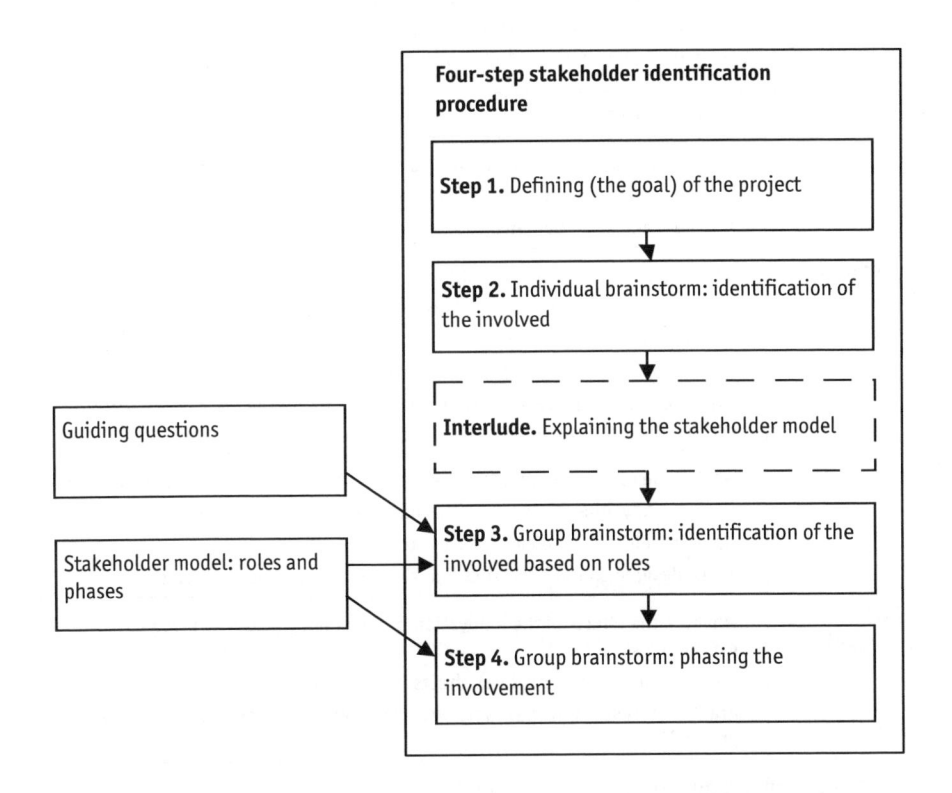

FIGURE 7.1 The identification method: building blocks and operating procedure

Step 1 concerns defining and delimiting the project. As mentioned before, the method is based on the idea that identifying the parties involved is useful only if it is clearly stated *what* parties are involved in. This means that stakeholder involvement should always—and not only in case of an innovation process—relate to a certain activity, a project or an item on the agenda. In step 2, the participants are asked to write down all the possible parties involved (people, groups of people, organisations) in the project. This exercise partly serves as a 'warm-up', but also offers the opportunity to compare these results with the information to be gathered in the group brainstorm later. Between steps 2 and 3 there is an interlude in which the stakeholder model (i.e. definitions of roles and phases) is presented and explained to the participants. In step 3, on the basis of the stakeholder model explained in the interlude, the participants are asked, as a group, to list all the parties who could fulfil the various roles in the project. In this respect, a party may play different roles. By posing specifically selected guiding questions (see Table 7.3), the chairing persons try to obtain an overview that is as complete as possible. In this way, the method aims to produce a list of parties involved which is both more extensive and more structured in comparison to the results of step 1. So, the guiding questions are designed to open up new directions in the discussion.

Role	Guiding question
Client	• What are the benefits of the innovation for the clients mentioned so far? • Are there any others who also benefit from these effects? • Are there any other benefits leading to different clients?
Decision-maker	• What are the power resources of the decision-makers mentioned so far? • Are there any other decision-makers with similar power resources? • Are there any other relevant resources; which decision makers use these? • What are the topics these decision-makers can decide on? • What are the topics these decision-makers cannot decide on; which decision-makers possess this ability?
Designer	• What is the relevant knowledge or expertise of the designers mentioned so far? • Are there any other designers with similar knowledge or expertise? • What are relevant problem areas and topics? • Which designers might contribute to these problem areas and topics?
Passively involved, representative	• What are the effects of the innovation project on the passively involved mentioned so far? • Are there any other (negative) effects, and who may be affected? • Are the interests of the passively affected taken into account in the innovation project? Why (not)?

TABLE 7.3 Identifying questions within the method

In step 4, regarding each party identified in step 3 as well as each phase in the project, the participants are asked to indicate whether this party should be involved in this phase. In doing so, a distinction is made between whether the party should *certainly* be involved, whether the party should *possibly* be involved or whether the party should *not* be involved at all in this phase of the project.

First round of justification: stakeholder literature and the basic format of the method

After its presentation, we will now justify the method. This section serves two purposes. The first is to explain the rationale behind the method by expounding why we believe that in the current stakeholder literature the identification problem has still not been solved. Second, we will explain how this analysis of stakeholder literature has led to the requirements of the method and, as a result, to its basic format.

As mentioned before, within an organisation there are normally various views on who the stakeholders might be. For an individual member of an organisation it is by no means a problem to produce a list of stakeholders. This seems to be a simple and straightforward way of solving the identification problem. During the application of the stakeholder identification method (step 2), five minutes were allocated for making such an individual stakeholder list. However, although the participants in the brainstorm sessions began writing immediately, they were unable to complete the exercise in just five minutes. There are a number of difficulties with this method of stakeholder identification. First, there is the question of when a stakeholder list may be considered complete. Second, it is not clear what it is exactly that makes a party a relevant stakeholder. For instance, is the stakeholder mentioned first on the list the most important one and the stakeholder mentioned last the least important? With these difficulties in mind, the question arises of how the process of identifying stakeholders can actually be accomplished.

In any case, identifying stakeholders comes down to the basic question 'who are they? (Frooman 1999). In the literature, dealing with this question has resulted in a variety of theoretical classifications (see Mitchell, Agle and Wood 1997). The question emerges to what extent classifications contribute to solving the identification problem in the context of management practice. An obvious starting point in the analysis of classifications is the definition of Freeman (1984: 46):

> a stakeholder in an organisation is (by definition) any group or individual who can affect or is affected by the achievement of the organisation's objectives

This definition takes a 'landmark' position in stakeholder theory (Wood 1991; Clarkson 1995; Rowley 1997; Andriof and Waddock 2002). In view of the identification problem, we consider three points relevant and will discuss them successively:

- The efficacy of the classification with respect to the actual identification of stakeholders
- The normative implications of using the classification
- The dynamics of the situation for which the classification is to be used

Regarding the efficacy of the classification, the Freeman definition clearly represents a very broad view on stakeholders which is, according to Mitchell *et al.* (1997: 857), based on the 'empirical reality that companies can indeed be vitally affected by, or can vitally affect, almost anyone'. This observation indicates the importance of setting boundaries when using a classification—what parties are to be included in or excluded from a list of stakeholders?

In the literature, the Freeman definition is usually cited as a starting point to give a more narrow view of stakeholders, in which finer-grained classifications than 'can affect' and 'affected' are described. Some examples of these classifications are 'primary and secondary' stakeholders (Clarkson 1995), 'voluntary and involuntary stakeholders' (Clarkson, cited in Mitchell *et al.* 1997), or 'fiduciary and non-fiduciary' stakeholders (Goodpaster 1991). Rowley (1997: 889) points out that:

> although debate continues over whether to broaden or narrow the definition, most researchers have utilised a variation of Freeman's concept.

However, what is more important is that these classifications (just as Freeman's definition) leave the issue of which specific stakeholder fits within a specific category unresolved. To managers who have to deal with the problem of identification, it is still a matter of drawing boundaries.

Let us now turn to one of the main classification models in the literature: the salience model of Mitchell *et al.* (1997). Salience is described as the degree to which managers give priority to competing stakeholder claims. Mitchell *et al.* try to answer the question of how managers choose their stakeholders and how they prioritise among competing stakeholder claims. Managers, they argue, perceive particular groups as stakeholder; they are inclined to give a high priority to a stakeholder if they believe that this stakeholder has a legitimate claim that calls for immediate (i.e. urgent) action and who possesses the power to influence the organisation's activities. The stakeholder who is believed to possess the attributes of legitimacy, urgency and power is called a definitive stakeholder. Likewise, a classification of seven stakeholder groups is developed, depending on the occurrence of one, two or three of the attributes in varying combinations.

Without discussing the salience classification of Mitchell *et al.* (1997) in further detail, we argue that the mere availability of a classification model is not sufficient to solve the identification problem within an organisation; this applies to both the salience model and to the other classifications. Mitchell *et al.* may explain the reason why managers pay attention to certain stakeholders, but they do not explain how to find these stakeholders to start with. As a result, they leave those who want to make practical use of their model for identifying stakeholders rather unprepared. From the perspective of this model, the first difficulty that remains unresolved is how to decide which specific stakeholders fit within the various categories. The second unresolved difficulty is how to decide when this task has been accomplished in a satisfactory way.

The first point of analysis to which the stakeholder literature was subjected led to the conclusion that an identification method should go beyond classifying stakeholders. The first and general requirement was that the method should be able to actually identify real-world stakeholders. To achieve this, we concluded that an additional identification procedure would be required. This conclusion has led to the basic format of the method: we made a distinction between the building blocks of the method (such as the stakeholder model and the guiding questions) and a procedure for using these building blocks.

The salience model of Mitchell *et al.* (1997) also brings to light the normative implications of the classification approach (i.e. our second point of analysis). In terms of Mitchell *et al.* (1997: 868), the model provides insights into the degree of salience of stakeholders in the view of the managers of an organisation and how they are, for that reason, able to influence that organisation's activities. Although some authors have a different opinion (see, for example, Wolfe and Putler 2002: 77), we argue that having these insights does not mean that the argument can be turned around; in other words, a manager may consider a particular party as a stakeholder but it still remains uncertain whether the manager's choices are legitimate or even sensible in that particular context. This brings us back to Freeman's basic distinction between 'can affect' and 'affected'. Although for the same reasons as the salience model this distinction should be considered not satisfactory for the purpose of identifying stakeholders, from a normative point of view it is nevertheless a crucial one. Also in the stakeholder literature this viewpoint is acknowledged and reflected by the position that organisations owe obligations to those whose freedom and well-being is affected by their activities (Goodpaster 1991; Donaldson and Preston 1995; Quinn and Jones 1995; Phillips 2003). This category of 'the affected' consists of persons and parties who are involuntary involved; they have interests in certain aspects of the organisational activities and are, for that reason, legitimate stakeholders (Goodpaster 1991).

The second focal point in the stakeholder literature analysis has led to the conclusion that the category of the affected should be regarded as a category of legitimate stakeholders. Although the acknowledgement of this category increases the risk that stakeholder identification becomes an endless undertaking, the method should still be suitable to facilitate the identification of this category. By means of the definitions and the guiding questions this issue has been taken into account.

The third point of analysis refers to the context of innovation in which stakeholders had to be identified. In fact, this has to be considered as a requirement of the method that had already been set beforehand (as explained before, the method had to be used in an innovation context). Our analysis of stakeholder literature in relation to this context entailed two aspects relevant to the identification of stakeholders and the introduction of a classification therein. First, we not only concluded that stakeholders are connected with particular issues, projects or 'items on the agenda' (also recognised by Mitchell *et al.* 1997), but we also found that this is helpful and even necessary in the process of identifying stakeholders. For that reason, we considered it important to make use of a classification model that is more closely based on the activity or issue at hand. As regards the method, this means that the activities within innovation projects (as performed or experienced by stakeholders) determine the classification of these stakeholders. This also means that the different phases of the innovation processes needed to be articulated properly. What distinguishes innovation processes from day-to-day routines, such as production or logistics, is that innovations are often developed within projects, with a starting-up phase, development phases, and an either clear or fuzzy end-point. In this respect, it is likely that stakeholder involvement differs over these phases. In sum, the dynamics of the process under consideration, particularly relevant in case of an innovation process, needed to be included in the method. And a classification of this kind was not available in the current stakeholder literature. Therefore, one of the building blocks has been designed to include the context of innovation projects (i.e. the nature of such projects including their dynamics).

Summarising, to make the actual identification of stakeholders in an innovation project an attainable goal, the stakeholder identification method had to fulfil three requirements. First, the method needed to facilitate the actual identification of stakeholders in an innovation project and thus go beyond a mere classification of stakeholders. Second, the method had to make the identification of 'the affected' possible, to be accomplished in such a way as to not become an endless exercise. Three, the method needed to be efficacious under the dynamic circumstances of an innovation project.

Second round of justification: further theoretical underpinning

Critical systems thinking: roles of involvement

In this second round of justification, we will underpin the elements of the method in more detail. There are two pillars underlying the method: critical systems thinking (CST) and the phases of an innovation project. This subsection explains the first while the next subsection will deal with the second. Regarding the requirements deduced from stakeholder theory, CST has been particularly relevant to 'real' stakeholder identification and to supporting the identification of the category of 'the affected' or, in our terms, the passively involved.

In fact, the choice of a systems perspective within the method seems rather obvious. After all, identifying stakeholders means that a line should be drawn between those involved and those not involved. It can therefore be considered as a boundary-drawing issue (Vos 2003). Dealing with boundary-drawing issues is typical of a systems approach.

Within systems thinking there are different perspectives on these boundary-drawing issues. These perspectives represent different strands in system theory. The so-called 'hard' systems approach proceeds from the assumption that boundaries are given and can be measured objectively (Schecter 1991). This assumption has been widely criticised in both the 'soft' (Checkland 1981) and the 'critical' (see, for example, Willmott 1989; Midgley 1996; Ulrich 2003) versions of system theory. Checkland (1981), in particular, has been an important advocate of the view, relevant in both soft and CST, that boundaries are social or personal constructs (see also Midgley 2000). In general, systems thinking can contribute in various ways to the analysis and solution of problems in order to improve the system concerned. However, as Checkland (1981) argues, problem assessment and, in particular, the problem solution are subjectively biased. An improvement for one person may not be an improvement for another. This means that a different system boundary may result in a different problem analysis and, accordingly, in different solutions.

In short, CST also underlines this subjectivity. However, in accordance with this approach, the normative aspect of system improvement together with the boundary issue are crucial. The basic assumption that drawing system boundaries is a matter of subjectivity makes it, at the same time, an ethical issue. In other words, drawing boundaries together with the resulting problem analysis and problem solution raise normative questions (see, for example, Churchman 1971; Ulrich 1983, 2003; Midgley 1996). After all, it is debatable whether a system change can be considered as an improvement

7. A METHOD FOR THE IDENTIFICATION OF STAKEHOLDERS *Vos and Achterkamp*

and whether this can be justified. It should be noted that this characteristic of CST fits in well with the normative stance we take within stakeholder thinking.

As mentioned previously, stakeholder identification can be viewed as a boundary-drawing issue (i.e. acknowledging who is involved). What is important in the identification of stakeholders is that expanding the boundaries of analysis or improvement could result in expanding the group of those who may be legitimately considered as stakeholders (Midgley 2000).

In the development of the method, particularly the ideas of Ulrich (1983, 1987, 1993, 2003) have been important. Ulrich not only deals with drawing boundaries in a critical way but also introduces a role perspective on stakeholders. The latter matches our conclusion that, if a classification model within the method is based on the activities in the project, it makes the identification of stakeholders an easier task to fulfil. The search for stakeholders can then be accomplished in a more focused manner. The role perspective means that stakeholders can be classified on the basis of the role(s) they are playing within a particular innovation project; a role has to be specified in a concrete case in order to decide which individuals or groups of individuals represent which roles. This is precisely what the method has been designed for—to support this aspect of decision-making.

Ulrich (1983: 248) acknowledges two reasons why anyone could claim to belong to a system or, in this case, to be a stakeholder. The first is that they have some kind of resource (expertise, political or financial, etc.) to contribute to the system. This reason relates to Ulrich's category of 'the involved', which we have labelled the actively involved. The second reason is that they are actually or potentially affected by the outcome of the system. This reason leads us to Ulrich's category of 'the affected', which we have labelled the passively involved. The distinction between these primary categories is based on two types of circumscriptions of innovation projects. Within a narrow circumscription those parties are situated who actively contribute to the outcome of the innovation project. A broader circumscription also includes those parties who are affected by its outcome (i.e. the passively involved) (see Fig. 7.2).

At first sight the similarity between Freeman's distinction of 'can affect' and 'affected' and Ulrich's distinction of 'involved' and 'affected' is striking. However, when considering the two basic groups in more detail, differences come to the fore. Let us begin by

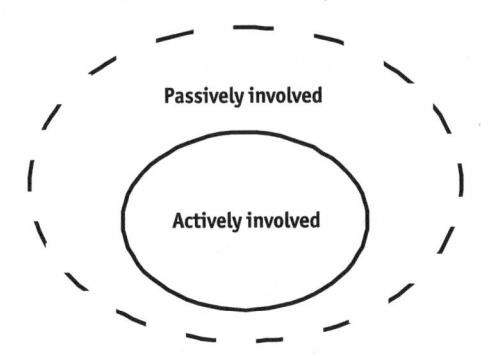

FIGURE 7.2 **Two types of involvement**

reflecting on the 'involved'. On the basis of three sources of influence Ulrich distinguishes three roles an actively involved party (in our terms) can play:

- The role of client (whose purposes are being served)
- The role of decision-maker (who has the power to decide)
- The role of designer (who contributes the necessary expertise)

The more precise role definitions (see Table 7.1) again differ from those of Ulrich (for comparison see Ulrich 1983: 252, 1987: 279f., 1993: 597). It is relevant that the circumscription of the actively involved is unambiguous, although this is no guarantee that the actual identification of, for example, all the clients is an easy matter.

Regarding the identification of the second basic group, the passively involved, there is a more fundamental problem. The question remains whether this group has been identified completely. For that reason, Ulrich (1983) states that this group (in his terms 'the affected') can only be bounded by means of representation. Furthermore, he argues that only 'the affected' themselves should determine their representatives. Although our method does support the identification of this particular group (i.e. from the perspective of the organisation), the notion of representation is also important. The circumscription of the passively involved is more ambiguous compared to that of the actively involved which is, for this reason, depicted by the broken line in Figure 7.2. The question of who is or who is not assigned to this group is also, as discussed earlier, a normative matter. From the perspective of sustainability, especially with respect to 'reducing offload', there is an important argument for expanding the group of the passively involved (including their interests) as widely as possible.

Finally, what remains to be addressed are our reasons for relabelling the main categories of stakeholders as used in the method. A language problem was the immediate reason for using different labels. Since the method had to be used within Dutch organisations, we needed to translate the word 'affected' into Dutch, which is by no means an easy matter. The Dutch words that come close to the English word 'affected' (*geraakte* or *getroffene*) have a different connotation, meaning 'injured', 'impaired' or 'victimised'. These difficulties were confirmed in testing a prototype of the method. And, indeed, our initial concern appeared to be even more serious. In identifying this type of stakeholder, the term 'affected' turned out to be counterproductive; it provoked resistance. According to the brainstorm participants, this term questioned the relevance of this particular type of stakeholder. Therefore, we tried to find a more neutral term and so decided on 'passively involved'.

Phasing the involvement in an innovation project

Now that the various roles of involvement have been defined and justified, the question arises of when these roles should be played. This takes us to the second pillar underlying the model: the different phases of an innovation project. As early as the 1950s, Johnson and Jones (1957) described (product) innovation as a stage-gate process. The stages are phases in which the evolution of 'new things' takes place. The gates can be considered as decision points, where the results of the preceding stage are evaluated and where it is decided how to proceed in the following stage(s). Several authors use this idea of product development as a sequential step-by-step process, thereby arriving at a discursive approach (see Cooper and Kleinschmidt 1990; Pahl and Beitz 1995). More recently, the non-linearity of innovation has been underlined (see van de Ven *et al.* 1999; Janszen 2000). Van de Ven *et al.* (1999) state that the innovation process is neither sequential nor orderly, nor is it a matter of random trial and error. It is actually best characterised as a non-linear dynamic system. However, van de Ven *et al.* recognise three major phases in the innovation cycle: initiation, development and implementation. These three phases are used in the method described here, although it should be noted that we added a fourth phase: maintenance (see Table 7.2). Most innovation models do not distinguish a maintenance phase, although there are some, such as the curriculum innovation models of Mennin and Kalishman (1998) and Mowat and Mowat (2001), which do explicitly refer to this phase.

There are two reasons for adding this fourth phase to our method. First, in testing the concepts of the method, the significance of this phase to certain innovation projects became clear. Furthermore, paying attention to this phase pre-eminently suits the concept of sustainable innovation. Including this phase, in which the focus is on applying and evaluating the innovation, can further sustain the innovation and also preserve its sustainable characteristics.

Conclusion

This concluding section is confined to a general reflection on the method in the light of the three requirements that it had to fulfil (the more specific matters related to particular organisational circumstances are discussed in Part C, Chapters 10 and 15–17). First of all, the method had to be suitable to support the identification of stakeholders (i.e. as real-world parties) in a specific case. The various brainstorm sessions showed that the method could indeed be used to facilitate this identification. However, the question remains whether the resulting lists of parties involved are (or, indeed, can ever be) complete. On the other hand, we believe the method to be useful and efficacious in an even broader context than that of innovation only.

Second, the method had to take into account the stakeholder category of 'the affected' or, as we define it, the passively involved. The brainstorm sessions showed that a number of participants found it very difficult to identify this category. Some of them considered it hard to let go of the improvement perspective they had on the innovation in question. To some extent, they expected that the outcome of the innovation project would lead to improvements for everybody, if not immediately then after some adaptations. However, after thinking it through, it became clear that improvements for some may imply deterioration for others. During the brainstorm sessions it appeared in a number of cases that the role of the passively involved was temporary or transitional. When parties have been identified as passively involved management can choose to involve them in the innovation process and, by doing so, allow them to strive for their interests. In fact, parties are then designated new roles: that of a client if their wishes are taken into account; that of a decision-maker if they are given some sort of veto on parts of the project design; or that of a designer if their knowledge and expertise actually contributes to the innovation project.

Third, the method had to take into account the dynamic circumstances within an innovation process. To integrate these dynamics into the method, the role classification was connected to a four-phase model of innovation projects. A few observations are relevant here. In each of the brainstorm sessions, phasing the roles over the project proved to be a test of the identification that had previously taken place. Some of the identified parties were shifted to another role or were given an additional role. Furthermore, phasing the roles led to an ordering of the identified parties involved. Parties who should, according to the participants, play a role in all four phases were apparently of more importance than those with no or just one role. In this way, the identification method provided a basis for the next step: managing stakeholder involvement or, in terms of this method, managing stakeholder roles. Managing stakeholder roles involves several management questions, such as 'what will be the actual activities of the actively involved?' and, especially, 'which of the identified passively involved should actually become involved in the project?', 'when should this involvement take place?' and 'what should this involvement look like?' Finally, phasing the roles of involvement can, as part of the method, be considered as a direct way of coping with dynamics. However, the fact that the passively involved category is included indirectly stimulates the awareness that stakeholder roles might change during a project, particularly the role of this category. It might be helpful, at an early stage, to be watchful of signals indicating that a number of parties are becoming more important to an organisation.

As an overall conclusion we can state that the method has indeed fulfilled the requirements we set: lists of stakeholders were obtained although, as already mentioned, it is never certain whether they are complete; attention was drawn to the category of the passively involved; and the dynamics of the projects were dealt with. However, tests also showed that the operating instructions for using the method call for attention. The method is actually not fit to be used in all circumstances. First of all, the project and its goals need to be clearly defined and delineated. Furthermore, the time required for a full brainstorm session can be a hindrance in applying the method. A shorter version of the method (as suggested in the UMCG case; see Chapter 16) might then be a solution (see also Chapter 23 for a first trial for Optichem).

These points of attention might necessitate extra requirements with respect to the situations in which the method is to be used. It should be noted that they are requirements on the project level rather than on the organisational level. We consider the latter not relevant to the use of the method. Besides these extra requirements, the tests showed an unexpected merit of the method—it revealed itself as a diagnostic tool for project analysis. Questions such as: 'Are all roles fulfilled?', 'To what extent is the division of roles over the different parties clear?' or 'Is there a party that fulfils too many roles?' have provided insights into the overall effectiveness of the project.

We conclude this chapter with a note on sustainability in the sense of 'reducing offload'. From this perspective it is of course important to determine what precisely constitutes the offload that should be reduced, and which parties should be protected from it (see Chapters 3 and 22). Although not discussed in this chapter, this question was one of the reasons for developing the method (see Achterkamp and Vos 2006). Therefore, the identification of the category of the passively involved should be considered as a matter of crucial importance.

8
A cognitive map of sustainability
A METHOD FOR ASSESSING MENTAL IMAGES

Derk Jan Kiewiet

Which aspects do people have in mind when talking about sustainability? Within companies or organisations that think about sustainability, this concept is a common topic of discussion. But does everybody actually mean the same thing? Are people referring to different concepts, and do they interpret sustainability in different ways? If the latter is the case, it is important that a company or an organisation knows what images people have with respect to sustainability. Without this knowledge discussions about sustainability and the comparison of projects, products or processes in terms of sustainability remain unclear and, as a result, hardly productive.

The method described below is called **cognitive mapping**. Cognitive mapping makes it possible to assess within a company or organisation images of sustainability. In this chapter the description of the method is structured as follows: first, each step of the method will be generally described, then an example is given based on a research study conducted at Grontmij (one of the biggest engineering firms in the Netherlands). Its core activities are construction, industry, infrastructure, environment, traffic and planning. After describing the method and the Grontmij example, we will explain the theoretical background to the method.

Aim

The aim of the method of cognitive mapping is to find out which underlying sustainability dimensions people use when making decisions with respect to sustainability. The sustainability concept is an abstract and theoretical one. Thus, in order to give their opinion on sustainability people will, either consciously or unconsciously, try to give concrete form to this concept. This method offers the possibility to find out how they give form to particular aspects or dimensions.

> Grontmij Friesland carries out a large number of projects. Because it values sustainability so highly, the management wants to assess the company's projects according to their degree of sustainability. The management must therefore decide how this assessment is to take place.

Description of the method

Data collection

Two kinds of decisions are important to assess images of sustainability. The first relates to who should be chosen to provide the images. In other words, which members of an organisation does the researcher prefer to approach to retrieve the images of sustainability? These could, for example, be managers who have to make decisions about projects in terms of their degree of sustainability, but they could also be consultants or project members. It is important that those chosen deal with the concept of sustainability in their daily activities, so that the client of the research study can find out how they actually use the sustainability concept in these activities.

The second decision is associated with the context of the sustainability concept. When people within the organisation discuss sustainability, are they referring to products, projects or processes? To begin with, the researcher has to select 10–15 projects, products or processes within the organisation (henceforth to be indicated by the general term 'objects'). These objects will later be compared on the basis of their degree of sustainability. It is therefore important that there is some degree of variety. This can be determined by the researcher asking a number of people about the degree of variety in the sustainability of the objects. Apart from the need for variety, there is yet another requirement in the selection of the objects—all of those who are involved in comparing the objects have to know the objects.

Next, the name of each object is written on one side of a piece of card and a short description of the object is written on the other side, if necessary. The cards are shuffled and the resulting random order of the objects is written down. This is called the **object order**. Then, each member of the selected group is asked to arrange the cards starting with the 'most sustainable object' and ending with the 'least sustainable object'. This sequence is compared with the object order: the position of object 1 in a person's ranking list is determined, after which the ranking number of this position is assigned to object 1. In this way, all objects are given a ranking number; this sequence of numbers is called the preference order. In addition, other, potentially relevant characteristics of the group member are recorded, such as their department, function or experience.

In consultation with the manager of Grontmij, 26 people were selected who were involved in sustainability issues as part of their daily work activities. A list of 15 recent projects (i.e. objects) was made which, in the manager's view, differed in their degree of sustainability. All 26 participants were acquainted with all 15 projects. The names of the 15 projects were written on one side of separate cards and a short description of the project was written on the other side. After shuffling the cards and determining the object order, the participants were asked to arrange the object cards, starting with most sustainable and ending with least sustainable to determine the preference order. Information was collected about the department, the function, the number of years of experience, and the dimension ('people', 'profit', 'planet') of sustainability that was regarded as important by each of the participants. This information was obtained in order to check whether the dimensions as retrieved by the method resembled those regarded as important by the participants. Table 8.1 shows preference orders for four participants. We see that participant 17 has placed project 1 in 14th position, project 2 in 10th position, etc. As far as this participant was concerned, project 12 was the most sustainable, followed by project 14, project 15, project 6 and so on, with project 13 the least sustainable in 15th position.

Respondent	Project														
	1	2	3	4	5	6	7	8	9	10	11	12	13	14	15
17	14	10	8	9	11	4	6	7	13	5	12	1	15	2	3
18	14	7	11	6	12	2	1	3	13	5	15	8	9	10	4
20	5	9	13	10	8	1	2	14	4	3	11	7	15	12	6
23	12	6	7	9	4	1	3	2	11	5	14	8	10	13	15

TABLE 8.1 Preference orders for four Grontmij participant

Data preparation

The analysis of the data (i.e. the preference orders) is conducted with the aid of SPSS, a statistics software program. In this program, the PRINCALS module is used (see next section). In order to use this module the preference orders have to be transposed. This means that they have to be positioned in the columns and not in the rows. Within SPSS this can be achieved by using the TRANSPOSE function (to be found in the DATA menu).

By means of the TRANSPOSE function the 26 preference orders are transposed to 26 columns. These columns are regarded as variables by SPSS, so according to SPSS each preference order has become a variable that can be subjected to analysis. In addition, an extra case variable was made, consisting of a short description of each project.

Data analysis

The analyses are made by means of the PRINCALS module within SPSS. Within SPSS this module is not accessible via the menu, but via the syntax mode of SPSS.

In the Grontmij research study the following commands were used.* This example looks at four participants (respondents)—17, 18, 20 and 23—who all work in a department within Grontmij.

Row	SPSS command
1	PRINCALS VARIABLES case res17 res18 res20 res23 (15)
2	/ANALYSIS res17 res18 res20 res23 (ordinal)
3	/DIMENSION=2
4	/PRINT DEFAULT OBJECT
5	/PLOT DEFAULT LOADINGS OBJECT (case res17 res18 res20 res23)
6	QUANT (res17 res18 res20 res23).

Explanation of the commands:

Row 1. In this analysis the variables *case res17*, *res18*, *res20* and *res23* are used. The *case* variable describes the projects and is used to identify the projects in the analysis. The *res17* variable describes the preference order of respondent 17, the *res18* variable that of respondent 18, etc. So in this analysis only the preference orders of respondents 17, 18, 20, and 23 are considered. The notation *(15)* indicates that the preference order has been made for 15 projects.

Row 2. This part of the command indicates to which variables the preference orders really apply (*res17*, *res18*, *res20* and *res23*). The difference with the previous row is that that particular row has to contain all variables playing a role in the analysis, so includes label variables such as the *case* variable. Further, this row indicates that the numbers used in the preference orders have no other meaning than their ranking position (this is indicated by the word *ordinal*).

Row 3. This row shows that the number of underlying dimensions of the sustainability concept is two. This is a choice of the researcher. The advantage of the choice of two dimensions is that the output of SPSS contains a number of plots which are highly suitable to interpretation in two dimensions. The disadvantage is, of course, that others may consider the number of underlying sustainability dimensions to be more than two (as evidenced by the triple-P model of sustainability which has three dimensions comprising 'people', profit' and 'planet'). However, the researcher can vary the analysis, by carrying out one analysis using two dimensions and another using three (or more) dimensions, and then comparing the two outcomes.

* These commands can be given with the aid of the syntax editor.

Row 4. Indicates which output has to be provided by SPSS. In general, the *default output* (as indicated) is sufficient to make an adequate interpretation.

Row 5. Shows which plots SPSS has to add to the output. The commands given as formulated in row 5 are generally sufficient to make an adequate interpretation.

Row 6. Says that SPSS has to print the so-called 'quantifications' (*quant*) of the variables *res17, res18, res20* and *res23*. This term will be explained later. It is important to end the last row of the PRINCALS command (here row 6) with a dot.

Results

The output of SPSS is represented by a number of tables. These tables contain information from which the underlying dimensions can be derived, as well as information on how well this can be done:

- **Table of object scores.** This table contains the co-ordinates of the objects within the space that is being expanded by the underlying dimensions

- **Table of 'component loadings'.** This table contains the co-ordinates of the respondents within the space that is being expanded by the underlying dimensions. Arrows (vectors) drawn from the origin of the space in the direction of these co-ordinates indicates in which direction a respondent is situated within this space

- **Table of 'multiple-category co-ordinates'.** This table contains the co-ordinates of the ranking order positions. For each position in the ranking order the co-ordinates are given of the object that matches it. Within PRINCALS these positions are indicated by the term 'category object' (*cat*). *Cat 1* is the most sustainable project, *cat 2* the second sustainable object, etc. Since each person has made his/her own preference order of the objects, this means that for each person there is a multiple category co-ordinates table

- **Table of 'single-category co-ordinates'.** As is the case with the multiple category co-ordinates, this table can differ per person. This is because the table does not represent the objects themselves but only their position within the ranking order. And an object can be given two different positions within the ranking order by two different persons. The single category co-ordinates represent the co-ordinates of the projection of a category on a respondent vector (see Fig. 8.1). These projections can be compared with the preference order of the respondent. If the order of the projections of the objects on a respondent vector corresponds with the sequence of the objects in the preference order of this respondent, there is an appropriate match between the representation in the expanded space and the preference order (see also 'quantification' and 'single fit')

- **Table of 'quantifications'.** The quantifications are calculated on the basis of the single-category co-ordinates and indicate at what distance, as measured from the starting point, the projection of a category is positioned on the respondent vector (see Fig. 8.1)

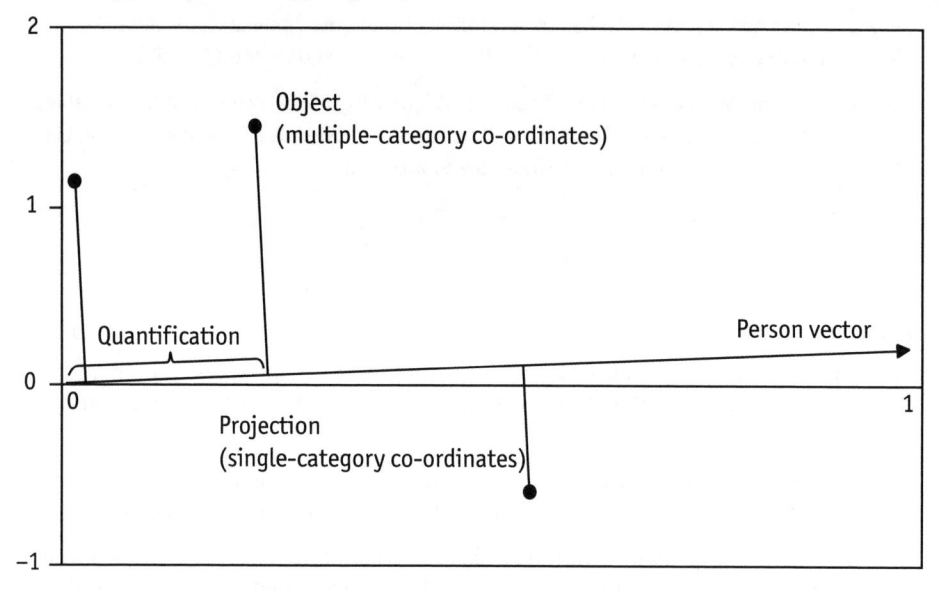

FIGURE 8.1 Graphical representation of a 'respondent vector', 'multiple-category co-ordinates', 'single-category co-ordinates' and 'quantification'

- **The 'single fit'.** This value indicates how well the sequence of quantifications (the projections of the categories on the respondent vectors) corresponds with the preference orders. In case of a perfect fit the order of the quantifications is exactly the same as the preference order. In this case the single fit equals 1. If the fit is lower, the positioning of the respondents and objects within the expanded space corresponds to a lesser extent with the preference orders. This means that the lower the value of the single fit the harder it is generally to interpret the underlying dimensions of the space

The above describes how cognitive mapping can be applied in retrieving images of sustainability. The description of the method is illustrated by applying it concretely within a research study on sustainability conducted at Grontmij. In the remainder of this chapter a brief description will be given of the theory behind the method.

Table 8.2 contains the object scores. From this table we can read the co-ordinates of the objects in the space, expanded by the underlying dimensions of sustainability that still have to be defined. For example, within this space object 1 has the co-ordinates (0.56, –0.56) and object 6 has the co-ordinates (–2.79, –0.62).

Object scores

Object	Dimension 1	Dimension 2
1	0.56	–0.56
2	0.52	–0.59
3	0.54	–0.58
4	0.53	–0.57
5	0.51	–0.63
6	–2.79	–0.62
7	–2.11	0.18
8	–0.27	–1.47
9	0.56	–0.56
10	0.01	1.47
11	0.67	–0.43
12	0.15	1.52
13	0.62	–0.56
14	0.24	1.63
15	0.24	1.69

TABLE 8.2 Table of object scores

Component loadings

Respondent	Dimensions 1	Dimensions 2
RES17	0.579	–0.812
RES18	0.982	0.117
RES20	0.975	0.044
RES23	0.909	0.344

TABLE 8.3 Table of component contents

Table 8.3 contains the co-ordinates of the respondents in the expanded space. We see that respondent 17 has the co-ordinates (0.579, –0.812) and respondent 20 the co-ordinates (0.975, 0.044). When we position the co-ordinates in a space, and then add the respondent vectors (see Fig. 8.2), we see that within this group of four people the underlying dimensions of sustainability have been used differently. We can see that respondent 18 and respondent 23 have highly similar images of sustainability (their vectors point in the same direction), whereas respondent 17 and respondent 20 differ. As regards the application of the sustainability concept, respondent 17 finds both underlying dimensions important, whereas respondent 20 finds only the first underlying dimension important. So, respondent 17 and respondent 20 have different interpretations of the concept of sustainability.

Table 8.4 indirectly contains the co-ordinates of the objects (the actual co-ordinates can be found in Table 8.2). These co-ordinates in fact represent the different positions of the preference order (the categories). We see that the most sustainable project as perceived by respondent 18 has the co-ordinates (–2.11, 0.18) (under multiple-category co-ordinates), the second most sustainable project the co-ordinates (–2.79, –0.52), etc. From Table 8.2 we can then derive the objects involved. In this table we see

Multiple-category co-ordinates (RES18)			Single-category co-ordinates (RES18)			Quantification (RES18)
Cat	Dimensions		Cat	Dimensions		
	1	2		1	2	
1	−2.11	0.18	1	−2.43	−0.29	−2.48
2	−2.79	−0.52	2	−2.43	−0.29	−2.48
3	−0.27	−1.47	3	−0.43	−0.05	−0.44
4	0.24	1.69	4	0.31	0.04	0.31
5	0.01	1.47	5	0.31	0.04	0.31
6	0.53	−0.57	6	0.41	0.05	0.42
7	0.52	−0.59	7	0.41	0.05	0.42
8	0.15	1.52	8	0.41	0.05	0.42
9	0.62	−0.56	9	0.47	0.06	0.48
10	0.24	1.63	10	0.47	0.06	0.48
11	0.54	−0.58	11	0.47	0.06	0.48
12	0.51	−0.63	12	0.47	0.06	0.48
13	0.56	−0.56	13	0.49	0.06	0.49
14	0.56	−0.56	14	0.49	0.06	0.49
15	0.67	−0.43	15	0.61	0.07	0.63

TABLE 8.4 Table of multiple- and single-category co-ordinates and quantifications

that object 7 has the co-ordinates (−2.11, 0.18) and object 6 the co-ordinates (−2.79, −0.62). So, in the preference order of respondent 18, object 7 has the ranking 1 and object 6 the ranking 2 (see Table 8.1).

The single-category co-ordinates columns of Table 8.4 contain the co-ordinates of the projections of the categories on the respondent vector for respondent 18. We see that the projection of the sustainable project (*cat 3*) of respondent 18 on their respondent vector results in the co-ordinates (−0.43, −0.05).*

These projections on the respondent vectors are used to calculate the 'quantifications' of a person. The quantifications are in fact scaled projections: with each projection, the distance towards the origin of the expanded space is determined and this distance is divided by the length of the respondent vector. In this way a scaled projection is

---

* However, when calculating the co-ordinates of the projections sometimes an extra transformation is executed. Through this transformation different projects, of which the co-ordinates vary in the expanded space, can obtain the same co-ordinates with respect to the projection on the respondent vector. This transformation will be explained in the appendix at the end of this chapter.

acquired. The projection of the most sustainable project, as perceived by respondent 18, is given the quantification −2.48, that of the second sustainable project is also given the quantification −2.48 while that of the third sustainable project is −0.44.*

Respondents' quantifications are now compared with their preference order. The correlation between them indicates their goodness of fit. At the same time, this correlation shows the adequacy of the representation of the preference order in the expanded space. A high correlation indicates that there is a good fit, a low correlation that there is a mediocre or bad fit. Where the fit is good, the expanded space can be used to find an interpretation of the dimensions. After all, the analyses themselves do not directly provide an interpretation of the dimensions; that interpretation still has to be made by the researcher. A good fit makes it easier to find interpretations, making it possible to determine the underlying aspects of sustainability.

In the case of the Grontmij research study the correlation between the quantifications and the preference order of respondent 18 is high: 0.977. In other words, there is a good fit. Also for the other persons in this analysis the correlation is high (0.944 minimally, 0.994 maximally), so the whole representation in the extended space fits in appropriately with the preference orders of the four respondents.

Figure 8.2 illustrates this representation. This figure makes clear that within this department the views on sustainability vary (at least with respect to the 15 projects studied), as the respondent vectors point in different directions with three distinct groups emerging. This means that some projects are more different with respect to dimension 1, and other projects differ more with respect to dimension 2. The next step is to describe the dimensions in comprehensible terms (i.e. to interpret them). Because we have not discussed the projects in this chapter, these interpretations will not be dealt with here.

---

* In the calculation of the co-ordinates of the projections sometimes an extra transformation is carried out. Object 7 (the most sustainable project according to respondent 18) has the co-ordinates (−2.11, 0.18) in the space expanded by the underlying dimensions. When this point is projected on the respondent vector of respondent 18, the projection has the co-ordinates (−2.06, −0.24) (in this case these co-ordinates of the projection on the respondent vector of respondent 18 are not indicated in the SPSS output and therefore neither in Table 8.4). Object 6 (the second sustainable project according to respondent 18; see Table 8.1) has the co-ordinates (−2.79, −0.52) in the expanded space. The projection of this point on the respondent vector of respondent 18 has the co-ordinates (−2.81, −0.34) (these are also not listed in Table 8.4). It now appears that this projection is positioned farther from the origin of the space than the projection of object 6, while according to the preference order object 6 (as most sustainable project) should have been located farther from the origin than object 7 (as second sustainable project). In that case the co-ordinates of the projections of object 6 and object 7 are averaged: in this case both objects are given the co-ordinates (−2.43, 0.29).

120 SUSTAINABLE INNOVATION

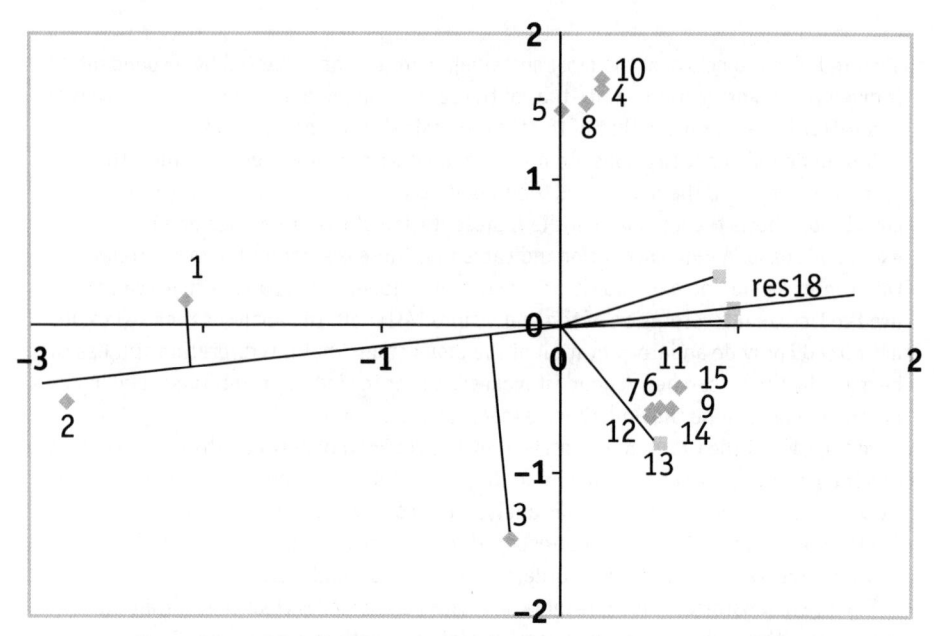

FIGURE 8.2 Expanded space of the Grontmij research study on sustainability. In the space three projections are drawn on the respondent vector of person no. 18 (of the most sustainable project, the second sustainable project and the third sustainable project)

Theoretical background of the method used

Finding ways to measure the concept of sustainability plays a major role in the research conducted in the overall NIDO programme. One of the problems of this approach is that sustainability is a multi-dimensional concept (i.e. it contains several aspects dimensions). Research into sustainability has in fact shown that sustainability can be considered from different perspectives—'people', 'planet', 'profit', 'reduction in offload', etc. These perspectives can, in turn, also be made operational in different ways. In addition, a project can be sustainable from one particular perspective, but does not necessarily have to be sustainable from another perspective. This makes it rather difficult to compare research results that are addressed in terms of sustainability.

One solution is to ask the assessor of the project for one or more aspects of sustainability that have been thoroughly described. Then, the researcher actually determines what is sustainable. Which aspects are included and how they are compared to each other is the researcher's choice rather than that of the evaluator of sustainability (here the assumption is that there are so many aspects mentioned in the literature that it is impossible to include them all). This may lead to a validity problem. The meaning of sustainability from the perspective of evaluators/organisations may differ from that of the researchers. So, we should in fact measure sustainability without determining in advance the aspects we wish to consider. This chapter presents and illustrates such a method whereby the aspects of sustainability can be determined that are relevant to the assessor, without providing a framework beforehand in which several aspects are mentioned.

This method is illustrated by describing how it has been applied within Grontmij. The first step in the method is to compare projects in terms of sustainability, without an interpretation of the sustainability concept given by the researcher. A number of Grontmij employees were asked to compare 15 projects, and to indicate their preference orders with respect to sustainability. The respondents could decide for themselves how they wished to make sustainability operational. After that, these preference orders were transformed into points within a multi-dimensional space by means of a multi-dimensional scaling analysis (PRINCALS) in which the points representing the products and the dimensions of the space show the respondent's cognitive (mental) images with respect to sustainability. In this way a cognitive map of sustainability was obtained. This map can be considered as a valid representation of sustainability.

Multi-dimensional scaling analysis

Multi-dimensional scaling analysis (MDSA) is a collection of analytical techniques which are able to compare objects and transform them into representations within a multi-dimensional space. This transformation takes place in such a way that objects, considered highly identical in the comparison, lie in close proximity to one another in the multi-dimensional space. And objects that, according to the comparison, do not resemble one another at all are remotely positioned from one another. The degree to which the comparisons correspond with the distances in the multi-dimensional space is called the 'fit of the solution'. The better the fit, the better the representation in the multi-dimensional space can be interpreted. The advantage of the representation is that the dimensions expanding the multi-dimensional space are supposed to tell us something about the considerations made in the process of making comparisons. Through the dimensions of the multi-dimensional space we can thus gain insight into the considerations (images) people had when comparing the objects.

There are a large number of different MDSA techniques. They differ, among other things, in the input (how exactly are the comparisons made between the objects) and in the type of relation allowed to exist between the observed comparisons and the distances (monotone, linear).

In the method described above, an analytical technique is used by which not only the objects (in the case of Grontmij they were the projects) were represented in a multi-dimensional space, but also the persons who made the comparisons (the respondents). By depicting the objects and the respondents together, differences among the latter can be detected. Thus, if the respondent vectors point in the same direction in the multi-dimensional space, then these respondents have used the same underlying dimensions when comparing the objects.

Conclusions

In this chapter a method has been described by which the cognitive images people have of sustainability can be mapped out. The advantage of this method is that there is no need to come up with all kinds of images in advance, which subsequently have to be checked for validity, but that the images are the result of the method. It should be added that, although the method does indicate the existence of different images, it does not directly interpret them. On the basis of substantial knowledge of the objects compared in terms of sustainability, the images can be given a valid interpretation.

Although in this chapter the method has been illustrated by an example of Grontmij, it can be easily applied to other companies or organisations. The only requirement is that there are 10–15 projects that can be compared in terms of sustainability. These objects can be projects, processes or products, depending on the situation. What is important, though, is that people who are well acquainted with *all* objects carry out the comparison in terms of sustainability. This makes a reliable assessment of sustainability possible. If this important precondition is met, it is relatively easy to acquire comparisons. In the case of the Grontmij research it took participants on average about five minutes.

It may be difficult to give SPSS the proper commands. However, by using the commands as given in this chapter, and adjusting them to one's individual situation, it is relatively easy to make an SPSS analysis.

9
Knowledge systems and reasoning with cases (and rules)*

Henk Hadders and René J. Jorna

Knowledge acquisition or elicitation plays a central role in developing knowledge systems. In an increasing number of cases knowledge is implemented by software systems. These systems are called knowledge-based decision-support systems (KB-DSS) or just knowledge systems (KS). Knowledge of sustainability (KoS) as well as sustainability of knowledge (SoK) can be enhanced by the support of these kinds of systems. Parsaye *et al.* (1989: 162; see also Jorna and Simons 1992) give the following definition of a KS or, as it is also called, an expert system:

> A knowledge system is a computer program that relies on knowledge and reasoning to perform a difficult task usually performed only by a human expert. A human expert reasons and arrives at conclusions based on personal knowledge. In a similar fashion, an expert system reasons and arrives at conclusions based on the knowledge it possesses.

In three business projects of the NIDO programme, the development and implementation of KS or decision(-making) support systems (DSS) played a central role. Within the project Optichem Infonet (see Chapter 12) a rule-based system was developed for technical service operators and workers within the Dutch paper and cardboard industry. Within the business project of AVEBE a DSS was developed for potato farmers in the northern part of the Netherlands (see Chapter 14), and within the mental healthcare project (see Chapter 15) a knowledge management system (KMS) was developed which incorporates case-based reasoning (CBR) for professionals.

---

* We would like to thank Yvonne Hoogendoorn (1996). We rephrased parts of her master's thesis in this chapter.

The methodology used in developing these systems consisted of CommonKADS (Chapters 12 and 14) and MiniKADS (Chapter 15). Both methodologies show great overlap and similarities. The CommonKADS methodology is described and explained in Chapter 12. KADS stands for knowledge acquisition and documentation system (Breuker and Van de Velde 1994).

KS can be distinguished by the way knowledge is represented within the system and by the way the system reasons with knowledge. We discussed knowledge representation in Chapter 6. The classical method to reason with knowledge in a knowledge system is rule-based reasoning (RBR). In a rule-based system, knowledge to solve a problem is available in 'if–then' rules. With the input specification—the current problem—appropriate rules are 'chained' together to arrive at a solution.

It is often very difficult to transform all knowledge into explicit rules. This is especially true for weak and unstructured domains, such as those in mental healthcare (see Chapter 15). In these weak and unstructured domains people tend to operate in a different way; this is illustrated by the following discussion. Why is it that when choosing a doctor we often prefer older and more experienced practitioners? A newly qualified doctor has the latest knowledge about diagnoses and treatments. Yet we feel more comfortable with older doctors because they are more likely to have seen and treated more patients with illnesses similar to our own. In essence, we value doctors more for the number of cases they have handled than for their knowledge (Barletta 1991).

This example exemplifies CBR. It is a rapidly emerging, although somewhat older, artificial intelligence (AI) technology that can use past experiences (cases) to solve current problems (Kolodner 1991, 1993; Riesbeck and Schank 1989; Hoogendoorn 1996). Especially in the medical domain, various examples of KS working with CBR exist (Gierl, Bull and Schmidt 1998; Armengol and Plaza 2003; Pantazi, Arocha and Moehr 2004; Nilsson and Sollenborn 2004).

In a KS, CBR is different from RBR. In the former all previous solutions are described and a novel problem is compared with those that have already been solved and that are part of the case base. Next, the most similar old cases and their solutions are presented as (possible) solutions for the new problem. The advantage of this method is that it is far simpler to describe the old solutions in terms of cases than to explicate the knowledge in terms of the rules necessary to reach a solution. Basic research has been done with this method, mainly in the US and within the academic medical world. However, there are few examples of the method being applied in practice, and it remains unclear whether CBR can deliver practical benefits. On the other hand, with the increasing complexity of multi-layered problems and with increasingly well demarcated fields (especially the case in medicine, but also in the domain of sustainability), reasoning with cases seems to be an acceptable complement to rule-based knowledge systems technology.

Because we want to show the relevance of knowledge support, especially modelled with CBR, in this chapter we will give a general description of CBR, outline the elements of a CBR system and provide an example. Furthermore, a short overview will be presented on the advantages and disadvantages of CBR and RBR. An extended example of the use of CBR in practice will be discussed in Chapter 15. There, CBR enhances the knowledge system CasusConsult.

Case-based reasoning and problem-solving

What is CBR? Kolodner (1991: 53) defines it as follows:

> Case-based reasoning is an AI-based, problem-solving approach that relies on past, similar cases to find solutions, to modify and critique existing solutions, and to explain anomalous situations.

Schank (1982: 25) defines CBR as:

> CBR is a rich and knowledge-intensive method for capturing past experiences, enhancing existing problem-solving methods, and improving the overall learning capabilities of machines.

Both these descriptions show that CBR is a problem-solving method that uses known solutions to arrive at new solutions. And it does this by using experience. This method of problem-solving is quite similar to the human way of solving problems. When a human being has to solve a problem, solutions from the past (i.e. 'things that worked') are remembered and applied as solutions to a new problem.

It is easier to adapt old solutions from our memory than find entirely novel solutions. Remembering old solutions can be compared with remembering cases in a case base. Regarding those who have knowledge, often a distinction is made between experts and novices. The former are people who have the knowledge to think of solutions for problems within a certain domain and also have the skills to solve these problems. The latter are people who have the basic knowledge to solve a problem, but don't have the skill to do so; they lack experience. Both have the rules to find a solution, but only an expert also has memories about solutions from the past. Generally, experts come to better solutions and much quicker then novices. This indicates that knowledge of experience is important for solving problems. More elaboration on differences between experts and novices regarding CBR can be found in Alexander 1992 and, to a lesser degree, in Kolodner 1993.

Knowledge engineers discover (or elicit) knowledge by way of experts. They try to structure and formalise the knowledge of experts in such a way that a KS can reason with this knowledge and hence can come to the same solutions for problems as did the expert. Research shows that the way the expert taps into his knowledge of experience is mostly based on analogous reasoning. This implies that they use old solutions to come to new ones.

Elements of a CBR system

What are the parts of a CBR system? As mentioned above, a CBR system is a problem-solving system which finds solutions for new problems by comparing them with existing solutions. The existing solutions are the so-called cases. These cases have certain features which can be described using keywords. The keywords are used by an indexing and selection mechanism to search the case memory for an existing case that matches the input problem and to select it as a possible solution for the new case.

The cases

Cases are descriptions of problems with their solutions. What cases look like depends on the problem domain for which the system is designed. A case is a list of features that leads to a particular outcome: for example, the design of a building or the treatment of a patient. The cases are stored in a case base and the knowledge with which the system works is in the case base. The cases therefore determine the quality of the knowledge the system works with. It is very important to select cases carefully when installing a case base. When the system is used, it will add the new case with the solution to the case base after a check for correctness and validity in relation to existing cases. The case base is therefore constantly changing as new knowledge is being added. While in use, the system is building up more and more 'experience'.

A case consists of three elements: the description of the problem; the solution; and the outcome of the solution. The outcome of (i.e. the execution of) the solution describes what consequences the solution had on the situation in which the problem was formulated. Actually, this can be seen as an evaluation of the complete case. It is important to provide this information, in order for the user to get a good understanding of the possible consequences of the suggested solution.

Two aspects of the case are important: the lessons learned from a case and the circumstances in which these lessons can be learned. In the case representation it is necessary that all features are described. This makes one case different from another. All features that determine the result and outcome of the case have to be part of the case description. These features often are the most important (key)words or concepts. The circumstances when these lessons are learned are described by the keywords connected to the case.

Keywords and the selection mechanism

With each new problem, CBR tries to search for a case that matches the problem situation as best as possible. In doing so, keywords are used as mentioned above. By using keywords for the case description the system is able to compare cases. The application of keywords is called indexing. The most important thing about indexing is to ensure that the right number of cases is selected. When the keywords chosen are not specific enough too many cases may be selected and when the keywords are too specific too few cases may be selected. Kolodner (1991) calls this the 'indexing problem'. With regard to the usefulness of keywords, it is important to look at the goals of the system.

Many problems have to be solved in the realisation of a case-based system. Cases can be used for providing a solution, for an evaluation or to explain errors. If cases are being used to find a solution, the index will have to contain the features (words) that predict the solution. If cases are used for evaluation, it is important that the consequences (i.e. the outcome of the solution) are part of the index. If cases are used to explain errors and to restore them, the index needs the source of the error to be part of it.

A CBR system needs the ability and a mechanism to retrieve relevant cases quickly and accurately from its memory (i.e. the case base). Several mechanisms and approaches are developed, all using case keywords to retrieve and return the most appropriate case. Barletta (1991) identifies the following kinds of case indexing processes or approaches: **nearest neighbour process, inductive process** and **knowledge-guided**

processes. These processes are also often combined. We will describe the different processes and their advantages and disadvantages.

Nearest neighbour approach

In this approach all the words used in case indexing are put into a list of words or index. After that, it is determined which cases have the most similar words as in the input case and these cases are retrieved from the case base. This approach looks at which cases are the closest to each other, based on the number of similar words in the index.

Inductive approach

This approach is used to induce a general rule from specific cases. The classic example is someone who has only ever seen white swans and who then concludes that all swans are white. In order for a computer to be able to induce general rules from specific cases many algorithms have been developed. Induction looks at which features or words determine a specific solution or outcome. These words are then used as predictors for that specific solution or outcome. New cases containing a number of these words will retrieve cases with that solution, based on a combination of these words. In short, compared to the nearest neighbour approach, an extra step is made. Not only does the inductive approach look at the similarity of keywords describing the problem, but it also looks at the possible solution or case outcome in order to retrieve the most useful cases.

Knowledge-guided approaches

Knowledge-guided approaches also try to use existing domain knowledge, but this is possible only if this kind of knowledge is available and can be represented. A particular way of adding knowledge to the system is by using a thesaurus. A thesaurus is a hierarchic structure of keywords and concepts of a knowledge domain, illustrating their relationships and describing the meaning of the words themselves. The thesaurus itself is not an indexing approach. It supports 'natural language' and is mostly used to refine an inductive indexing and selection process. It is therefore possible within the field of mental healthcare to recognise words such as 'fear' and 'anxiety' as one and the same concept, belonging to a specific disorder and related to a particular diagnosis. By using a thesaurus, the indexing process is capable of using the mutual relationship of the different disorders in the selection process. The advantages of a thesaurus and other knowledge-guided techniques lie in using domain knowledge. In this way the selection mechanism is able to select and retrieve cases based on relationships and which have been proven correct within a certain domain. The disadvantage of knowledge-guided techniques is that it is very hard to capture and codify this knowledge. This is particularly true when the choice is made to use CBR because a domain (such as mental healthcare) is rich in experience but poor in knowledge. Therefore, it will be very hard to make the necessary knowledge explicit for the use of these knowledge-guided techniques. Thus, the central underlying question when designing a CBR system in mental healthcare (see Chapter 15) is whether it is possible for a rather weak domain to develop good knowledge-guided mechanisms.

Organising the index

After the cases are indexed, the index will be organised and the cases from the case base will be ordered and grouped in clusters of similar cases. This can vary from a hierarchical order (and from general to very specific keywords) to an index with no order in which all the keywords of the cases just stand next to each other. With the nearest neighbour approach the keywords in the index are in no specific order. All the keywords of the new input case are matched and, based on similarity, the most appropriate cases are retrieved. When inductive approaches are used it is possible to generate a hierarchical order, often in the form of a cluster or decision tree. Knowledge-guided techniques are nearly always used in combination with the other approaches.

An example illustrating CBR in healthcare

We will give a concrete example from healthcare in order to show the way CBR works. The healthcare process of diagnosis, risk evaluation and treatment is measured by its cost and evaluated post-treatment by the patient with regard to their quality of life. At present, there are hardly any systems that are capable of combining all five parts of the healthcare process and understanding or measuring how they concurrently impact on each other. As a knowledge-based system, CBR can support the requirement of measuring the healthcare process for performance, appropriateness and, ultimately, cost effectiveness.

The application of CBR in the healthcare industry may look as follows. After finishing the treatment, professionals reconstruct the case and add this to the case base (even when the results of the treatment were poor). The case description has therefore to contain (beside demographic and problem features of the client) information about diagnosis (and associated tests), severity, treatment, cost and a quality judgement (as the final total outcome of the case). Structured and unstructured information such as this will be extracted from existing software systems (preferable automatically). In order to share and learn from cases in healthcare, it is necessary to make the case descriptions anonymous since it is not allowed (due to confidentiality rules) to give others access to client information. Each case has a title, contains a verbal description and uses structured fields with a series of questions and answers. Structured and unstructured fields can be used for indexing.

The use of CBR applied to each of the five steps in the healthcare process can offer the ability to evaluate the combination and impact of these steps concurrently as well as separately (Cognitive Systems 1993):

1. The patient's illness would be considered as the current case and would be compared to cases of similar diagnosis. The qualitative and quantitative factors associated with the patient's present condition would be identified by the doctor and used to retrieve a case with similar features. Induction retrieval would be used for providing suggested diagnosis for the patient's condition. The constant values are the factors associated with the patient and the variable (or outcome value) is a suggested diagnosis

2. Severity for a given illness could be a specific feature, but CBR systems also have the capacity to calculate this severity for cases based on a (domain) model and the factors associated with the patient and the final diagnosis. This severity could then be stored as a feature of each case and potentially adjusted whenever a new case is added to the library

3. The treatment outcome variable would be determined based on the diagnosis and the severity features for cases in the case base. The diagnosis could be generated by the system or specifically stated by medical personnel. The treatment would then be retrieved from the case base using induction, followed by a nearest neighbour match

4. The cost value seems to become the most important outcome from the system due to present government policies. The cost value of the care provided would be the variable outcome, where the diagnosis, severity and treatment values would be constant values used for inductive case retrieval

5. Measuring client satisfaction and quality of life is an attempt to quantify the quality of the outcome (quality index). Linking this to cases in the case base makes analysis possible regarding how 'good' the diagnosis and treatment were for a given patient. It is then also possible to retrieve cases in which the outcomes were desirable from both the patient's and the provider's perspective

For the patient, provider and funding body(ies) several potential applications can be developed. For patients, a system giving performance ratings when selecting healthcare providers could be developed, while for the provider, applications could be developed to support clinical diagnosis and treatment, to use the system for medical training or to provide economic credentials and support a rationing of care decisions. Finally, an application might, for example, allow the funding organisation to evaluate performance and compare providers with regard to appropriateness and consistency of treatment and cost-effectiveness.

Case-based versus rule-based reasoning

In order to be able to compare CBR with RBR, in this section we discuss various aspects concerning the development of a KS and we also compare the advantages and disadvantages of CBR and RBR (see Table 9.1).

Knowledge acquisition for CBR systems consists, for the most part, of collecting cases. Knowledge acquisition is hereby limited to identifying, storing and indexing cases. Cases are often written in natural language. Therefore, the knowledge can be presented in a much more rich and dynamic way than just by using if-then rules. Even when there is no actual reasoning by the system, the user can still interpret and apply this knowledge. This makes CBR better suitable to use theoretical knowledge (see Chapter 6). This is knowledge of 'why something works' or 'why a relationship exists between certain features'. In CBR therefore, knowledge is captured within the cases. If

Aspects	CBR	RBR
1. Knowledge acquisition	Cases and selection mechanism. Easy to acquire	Rules and inference mechanism. Domain model has to be made complete. Difficult to acquire
2. Development	Easy and fast to develop	Slow and difficult to develop
3. Validation	Hard, often impossible	Hard, but can be done
4. Knowledge	Knowledge of experience, deep and rich knowledge. Useful for experience-rich domain	Knowledge of rules. Useful for knowledge-rich domain
5. Solutions	Most similar cases. Comes up fast with solution. Solution is good, but not the best. Can present new solution by adding new cases. Can handle missing data very well	Solution is an answer with probability. Solution is always the best. Presenting a solution may take a long time. Cannot present new solutions outside the domain model. Cannot handle missing data
6. Explanation	By cases, easy to understand by user	By rules, hard to understand by user
7. Maintenance	By adding new cases. Easy. Can be done by users themselves. Often automated and continuous	By adding and changing rules. Hard. Is done by knowledge engineer. By hand and mostly not frequent
8. Learning	Learns by adding new cases. Continuous. System presents new solutions and learns from mistakes	Cannot learn

TABLE 9.1 Summary of various aspects of CBR and RBR

there are cases present in a domain, the knowledge engineer needs to determine the main features and present his or her representation to the computer, to index the cases and to develop a selection mechanism. For a RBR system the knowledge engineer has to extract the knowledge from experts and model this in rule-like structures (this is the most time-consuming part of rule-based knowledge engineering). If there are only a few or no cases available, we have a knowledge-poor domain. CBR is not suited here. If the expertise of a domain consists of applying rules instead of exceptions, then the domain is knowledge-rich and RBR will, in both circumstances, provide better results than a CBR system. Finally, it can be stated that experts themselves very often reason with cases. This makes it much easier to capture cases from experts and to describe the knowledge within a domain, than to extract and capture if–then rules. This is a consequence of imitating human problem-solving. Under these circumstances the knowledge acquisition is easier for CBR than it is for RBR.

The development of a knowledge system (development and validation in Table 9.1) is not only determined by the knowledge acquisition and its ease, speed and costs. In developing such a system one also has to consider the validity of the system. It is important that the way the system reasons is correct and that the solutions provided are also correct. With regard to validation it can be stated that CBR starts from implicit assumptions. It is therefore not possible to guarantee that the knowledge used can be applied correctly in a new situation. Most of the time a CBR system can be developed much faster and more cheaply where there are already cases in place and where developing a selection mechanism will not cause too many problems. A CBR system is, however, very hard to validate. That is why a RBR system is to be preferred, especially if it is to play a far-reaching role in decision-making.

The knowledge that is used in a CBR system differs by nature from knowledge storage in rule systems. CBR often describes the cases in natural language. Therefore, there are more possibilities to use specific knowledge. Case descriptions can accommodate richer descriptions and deeper knowledge. Although the selection mechanism often cannot reason with this, the knowledge does arrive at the user. The user can apply this knowledge in judging the proposed solution. RBR uses a full domain model, by which all the problems within a domain can be solved. For CBR this means that these problems will first have to be added to the case base.

Concerning solutions, a RBR system will always present the best solution because all the possibilities in the problem space of the domain are examined. With CBR it is not possible to determine whether a better solution exists since that solution should then already be present in the case base. CBR is therefore not able to come up with a solution that is not already part of the system (case base). It does not create new solutions. For domains where there are many good solutions, CBR can be used if those solutions are stored in the case base. For domains where there are only few or no good solutions for a problem, RBR is far more equipped to come up with the best solution. CBR presents solutions as one or more (retrieved) cases while RBR deduces the solution from its rules.

CBR can handle missing data very well. Even if certain information is missing to describe a new problem, CBR is still able to present some solutions based on the information that is available. If the system does not have good cases for the input problem in its case base, it will present a more general case or report that it has no solution available. Mostly, CBR finds a solution very rapidly because the selection mechanism has created the index. Comparing cases is therefore not a time-consuming search process. Indexing will have to been done on a regular basis in order that the latest new cases are also indexed. For RBR systems missing data are a great problem because then the rules cannot take a decision and cannot come up with a solution. And if the problem lies outside the domain boundaries, RBR has no solution. A new kind of problem with its solutions can, however, easily be added within CBR in order to extend the domain. A RBR system is capable of reaching every solution that is possible within explicit knowledge, but a CBR system is capable of coming up only with a solution that is already in its case base. If a RBR system has to process a lot of rules to find a solution, then a lot of possible pathways and branches have to be searched and this can take time.

The explanation aspect is very important. Users expect that a knowledge system can explain why it proposes a certain solution. CBR systems explain this by presenting the user cases from the past that used the same solution. Explanations are often clear for users to understand because the cases are presented in natural language. CBR thus gives better explanations than RBR systems. Very often RBR systems explain the presented solution only by showing the rules they have used. Often these rules are hard to read for average users.

Maintenance influences the duration and use of a system. If knowledge in a certain domain changes, or there are some new experiences, systems need to be updated. The maintenance of CBR systems in which new experiences are used takes place by adding new cases. New relationships between the features of the problem and solutions will be automatically installed by the selection mechanism. When the selection mechanism has been developed with a knowledge-guided approach, this will have to be adjusted if there is a change in the existing (domain) knowledge. The users themselves can easily do maintenance of a CBR system. Often they can maintain cases in the case base. Because cases and their knowledge claims are judged, criticised and validated with regard to their outcome before they are added to the case base, a routine may emerge from within the organisation 'to learn from its experiences'. Therefore, knowledge acquisition and knowledge creation can become a daily routine within the organisation. A RBR system needs to have its rules adjusted whenever knowledge changes. In order to realise this, the knowledge must first be described in rules whereby most rules influence each other. Especially with large RBR systems it is very hard to see all the consequences when changing the rules. It can be stated that the maintenance of a CBR system is much easier than that of a RBR system.

Finally, learning is important in every knowledge situation. It is essential for human experts to learn, but it is still very difficult to create KS that actually learn. The main cause is the fact that learning mostly happens by using new experiences when solving problems. CBR adds every new case with its result or outcome to the case base and from that moment on that case will be considered when solving new cases. By constantly adding new cases to the system, new experiences are archived and, therefore, the system can produce new solutions through time. RBR gives nearly always the same solution for the same situation. The rules are less frequently adjusted and also more difficult to adapt. As far as learning is possible, CBR is better capable of realising this. For RBR, if new knowledge is created within the domain or something else changes, it is necessary to describe all these new developments in rules and to add them to the rule base. This causes much work, mainly because rules relate to one another or influence each other. If a rule has to be changed, this change may have great consequences for other rules. The more complex the rule base, the more difficult it is to see the consequences of changes and additions. This is why RBR systems are not very flexible in general and why new rules are changed or added as little as possible. For a CBR system the conclusion is that new cases are added continuously, so enabling the system to show learning behaviour. The advice given by a CBR system improves over time because new experiences are taken into account. A RBR system shows virtually no learning behaviour since the rule base is not continuously updated with new experiences.

Conclusion

A CBR system is especially useful for problem domains where a lot of experience is available and, at the same time, little explicit knowledge. Within these domains there are often many documented and codified examples of solutions, but it is hard to formulate clear decision rules on how to solve a problem. The main advantage of CBR is the fact that the rules do not have to be described clearly; for the most part, this helps to overcome the problem of knowledge acquisition. But then the problem arises of how to create a good case index. CBR focuses on cases and therefore aligns very well with case-based learning (Visser 2003) as a developing method in (scientific) education. Besides using cases for daily problem-solving in business processes, CBR tools also have the potential to create new (scientific) knowledge and to search for new patterns, through data and text mining. They are therefore a promising future technology for the enhancement of SoK.

Part C
The organisational (business) projects

10
Biosoil
SUSTAINABLE REMEDIATION

Else J.M. Boutkan* and René J. Jorna

Biosoil is an innovative soil remediation company located in the western Netherlands. It is innovative because it remediates soil using new biological techniques which are developed and tested in-house. At first glance the association between soil remediation and sustainability seems obvious, for soil remediation aims to achieve a cleaner and safer environment. However, in practice, the remediation process itself may pose sustainability challenges. By 'reducing offload' and engaging with stakeholders these challenges can be addressed. This chapter looks at how Biosoil established the knowledge of sustainability (KoS) necessary for sustainable innovation in the soil remediation industry.

Soil is a vital environmental medium, but it has not always been treated with sufficient care. According to preliminary estimates, more than 600,000 sites in the Netherlands are classed as potentially contaminated[1] of which around 10% need remediation. Examples include former gas plants, chemical works, oil depots and petrol stations. The situation in other parts of Europe is unlikely to be any better.

Various soil remediation companies are actively involved in dealing with this historic contamination, as well as with contamination caused by new sources of pollution on a case-by-case basis. The majority of these companies make use of conventional methods

---

* Thanks are due to Jeroen Wierenga, a student at the Rijksuniversiteit Groningen, and Arnout van Diem, managing director of Biosoil. Within the frame of the work for his master's thesis Jeroen Wierenga has made an important contribution to the Biosoil project (Wierenga 2004). When writing this chapter we gratefully drew on various reports written by him. We thank Arnout van Diem of Biosoil because he initiated the project and delivered some valuable contributions with respect to content, often in the form of inspiring discussions.

1 See www.skbodem.nl/upload/documents/persbericht%2020%20april.pdf, accessed 20 April 2004.

such as: contaminated soil removal (digging out); applying a layer of clean topsoil; building bunds (dam walls) to isolate the contamination; and treating polluted groundwater.

Biosoil makes use of non-conventional methods such as biological *in situ* soil remediation techniques. It believes that these offer an environmentally friendly and more sustainable alternative to conventional methods. Biosoil strives to minimise any environmental damage from its remediation activities. Among other approaches, this is achieved by carrying out the remediation by means of a closed soil and groundwater balance. Moreover, compared to conventional methods, *in situ* techniques require fewer transport movements. This decreases the burden on the environment (i.e. it reduces the offload) caused by lorries as well as reducing risks to employees and those living nearby. In addition, there is no need to import clean soil from elsewhere. Another advantage with *in situ* remediation is that the contamination is not simply diverted elsewhere.

During the tender process, Biosoil emphasises these aspects of sustainability. However, unfortunately, clients tend to choose remediation contractors on the basis of cost rather than environmental or safety standards. As a result, Biosoil decided to look in depth at how aspects of sustainability can be properly integrated into remediation choices. It asked:

- How can sustainability be raised up the agenda of those involved in deciding which remediation contractor to use?
- Who are these stakeholders and decision-makers?
- How should sustainability be discussed with them?

In other words, how can proper KoS be transferred to the relevant stakeholders to ensure that sustainability becomes part of the decision-making process? In order to find some answers, Biosoil participated in the Knowledge Creation for Sustainable Innovation (NIDO) programme.

This chapter outlines how these questions were addressed by the research project. First, however, we set the framework by describing Biosoil and its remediation projects and then explain the role of government and legislation in regulating the remediation industry.

Biosoil and soil remediation

Biosoil's core activity is developing, designing and carrying out biological *in situ* soil remediation. The company's aim is to remediate soil contamination by stimulating and optimising the natural biological degradation of soil contamination by, for example, readjusting soil conditions. Biosoil is a relatively small organisation consisting of 50 employees. Its main office is in Hendrik Ido Ambacht near Rotterdam. Biosoil is an independent commercial organisation consisting of several subsidiaries—Biosoil B.V. is involved in the acquisition and execution of remediation activities in the Netherlands and in Germany and Chile, while Biosoil R&D provides R&D capacity for both Biosoil B.V. and external clients.

In the Netherlands, *in situ* remediation represents 20% of the total remediation market, of which Biosoil's market share is around 15% (i.e. 3–4% of the total). Biosoil focuses on large, difficult and complex projects at the upper end of the market. Internally the company strives for continuous improvement in project delivery and it does this by providing information and training for its employees. The aim is to foster the Biosoil culture with its focus on service, self-learning, relationships and group loyalty. For example, employees are encouraged to solve problems by themselves; although management may set out certain conditions within which the solution should be framed, it does not interfere with the actual content of the solution. This forms the basis for creativity and innovation.

There are two types of *in situ* techniques: biological and physical. The former involves adding air and nutrients to the soil in order to activate existing soil bacteria. The latter includes dividing the soil into fractions. The basis for this process lies in the fact that soil contamination is often linked to clay particles and organic material. Biosoil makes use of physical techniques it has developed itself such as the Biosoil Behandeling Installatie (Biosoil Treatment Installation), a mobile soil cleaning facility for sandy types of soil and almost all types of pollution and online monitoring (OLM).

Examples of Biosoil projects

Soil remediation work is project-based and often forms part of a larger construction project. Typical soil remediation consists of the following steps:

- Preliminary research into the severity of the contamination
- Drawing up a remediation plan
- Substantiating the choice of remediation methods
- Remediation, including aftercare
- After-care and evaluation

Many parties are involved in projects of this kind, either directly or indirectly (e.g. local and regional government [the client], consultancy firms and local community groups).

To provide a better idea of the meaning of sustainability in relation to soil remediation projects, we will give two examples of projects in which Biosoil was involved: a former fire service training facility at Schiphol and a former gas plant in Oud Beijerland (near Rotterdam).

Fire training facility

Initially, a specification for this project was drawn up by a consultancy firm. This acted both as a formulation of the contamination problem and as an invitation to tender for the project. The original specification was based on conventional techniques, such as digging out and external cleaning. The consultancy firm was asked, however, to indicate whether there could possibly be an alternative solution. In response, Biosoil offered a biological on-site cleaning technique. This type of cleaning does not require the removal of soil from the location nor the supply of clean soil from elsewhere, hence reducing transport movements. Instead, the contaminated silt was dredged from a polluted pond, thickened *in situ* and transported afterwards to a safe nearby location. In this manner 70% was saved in weight due to the thickening process in addition to the collateral savings in transport movements.

The biological *in situ* variant leaves behind soil that is full of bacteria and nutrients. This creates a self-cleaning effect, resulting in a soil with high 'potency'. After remediation Biosoil planted grass to minimise pollutant dispersion and to make the site more aesthetically pleasing.

Gas plant

The case of the former gas plant in Oud Beijerland demonstrates how environmental aspects can play a role in the decision-making process in a soil remediation project. Ultimately, the site was intended for a housing development. The first suggested approach was to cover the contaminated area with a 1 m layer of clean topsoil. However, this failed to address the ongoing future risks associated with the contamination remaining in place, both for the future occupants and the environment. Of interest here is the way that Biosoil became involved in the project. Some of the future occupants of the proposed housing development became concerned about the suggested approach and sought an alternative through Biosoil who offered a solution similar to that carried out at Schiphol. This illustrates how the interests of a key group, the future occupants, had not been sufficiently taken into account in the early stages of the decision-making process.

The role of legislation and the government

In the Netherlands, controls on soil remediation activities are set out in the Soil Protection Act (1980). This also lays down the authorities and agencies involved in enforcing soil remediation standards and procedures.

The issue first came to public attention in the 1970s after contamination was found at Lekkerkerk, a small town near Rotterdam, where houses were built on soil that was subsequently found to be contaminated. Because of the potential health risks there was a lot of media attention and the national government was obliged, at enormous cost, to remove the contaminated soil from under the houses. This led to a new legislative regime in the Netherlands. From this incident until the present day remediation policies have undergone some important developments,[2] changing from a rigid framework to one in which the local situation as well as local interests are taken into account wherever possible. Compared to existing practices, however, the legislation, of over ten years in age, is still lagging behind.

As a result of the Lekkerkerk case two conventional remediation options became of interest: digging out and covering up. After remediation, the soil had to be suitable for any type of use. This approach was too intensive and too expensive to be suitable for all

2 See www.geodelft.nl/files/geo_jaarverslag%20binw%20jv%202.pdf, accessed 9 June 2004.

potentially contaminated sites, however. In the years that followed remediation, policies started to take into consideration aspects such as functionality and cost-effectiveness. In addition, discussions were started on the pros and cons of different soil remediation options and on how to establish a remediation goal.

Recently, a readjustment in policies has been announced in order to make remediation more sustainable and simpler. In this context 'more sustainable' means that the potential soil users' options have to be guaranteed for the future. 'Simpler' means that a better evaluation should take place with respect to the way in which the soil is dealt with and the risks associated with it. Therefore, new structures and remediation criteria have to be developed that take into account communal and environmental aspects.

In the adjusted remediation policies cost-effectiveness is also crucial, simply because of the fact that remediation of all polluted areas in the Netherlands is not financially feasible. Therefore, choices have to be made. The difficulty is that remediation projects are delayed in anticipation of a more unequivocal policy.[3] It is also expected that in this line of business (even) more cost-effective remediation methods will be developed, stimulated by government support.

The Biosoil research project: research question and approach

Biosoil initiated contact with the NIDO programme Knowledge Creation for Sustainable Innovation. Biosoil's first question concerned the degree of sustainability of the remediation methods that it had developed itself. The company was looking for a way to demonstrate the sustainability of its methods in order to integrate aspects of sustainability into a particular method.

Motivation

During the first meetings of Biosoil and NIDO, Biosoil's principal motivation—to link sustainability parameters to its remediation processes—was discussed. Biosoil's motivation was twofold. First, sustainability or, rather, the environmental advantages of the Biosoil remediation process, was considered as a unique characteristic of its activities. Apart from that, there was a more general concern with respect to the fact that in various locations in the Netherlands, in projects in which Biosoil had no involvement, there was a tendency to choose remediation variants that were not really sustainable. Biosoil wanted to give the concept of sustainability, as well as the entire biological *in situ* remediation industry, a higher profile. In collaboration with NIDO it was Biosoil's wish to be the front-runner, and it was not afraid to show its vulnerability with regard to its own expertise in this field.

---

3 See www.skbodem.nl/upload/documents/persbericht%2020%20april.pdf, accessed 20 April 2004.

The importance of stakeholders

During the first explorative stage it was obvious that sustainability parameters of soil remediation processes needed to be accepted by the various directly interested stakeholders, such as public bodies (local, regional and national government), private clients (developers) and consultancy firms. One of Biosoil's goals was for aspects of sustainability to be consistently included in soil remediation plans that had previously been drawn up. However, the case of Oud Beijerland had shown that even those who are only passively involved, such as future occupants, can play a role in the choice of a soil remediation method and that, therefore, the role of those involved can change from a passive to an active one. Due to these insights the research question was extended. It was determined that stakeholders, and therefore stakeholder analyses, should be included in the project.

What are the aspects of sustainability?

The start of the project was officially announced both within and outside the remediation industry (Boutkan et al. 2004). A project plan was drawn up and this accelerated the explorative stage.

First, an explorative study within the Biosoil organisation showed that the concept of sustainability is mainly associated with the 'planet' aspects. Projects such as those described in this chapter at Schiphol and Oud Beijerland affirmed this.

Within the soil remediation industry, the foundation Kennisontwikkeling en Kennisoverdracht Bodem (Knowledge Development and Knowledge Transfer Concerning Soil [SKBodem]) had taken initiatives to assess aspects of sustainability (be it under another name) by means of a risk, environment and costs (REC) model. This model emphasises the risk and safety aspects as major components of sustainability.

Sustainability parameters as applied by various institutions such as the Global Reporting Initiative (see also Chapters 3 and 23) are divided into 'people', 'profit' and 'planet'—or social, economic and environmental aspects. These aspects may refer to an organisation's production process (in this case the soil remediation process itself), the final product (in this case the remediated soil) or it may be considered from an even broader perspective of overall soil conditions. These models of sustainability consist of many parameters that are not (or cannot be) directly linked to soil remediation processes.

The explorative study showed that sustainability parameters for soil remediation processes mainly fell into one of three groups:

- Burden on the environment (water, energy, air, demand on primary materials and biodiversity)
- Safety in the form of risk reduction (for occupants, employees, other individuals or groups and future generations)
- Costs (for those who are directly involved, other individuals or groups and future generations)

This first explorative study shed new light on the sustainability parameter concept. In this stage of the research it was decided not to strive for an ultimate list of sustainability parameters relevant to the soil remediation industry, but to ask what sustainability means for the various stakeholders. In order to make this step, the stakeholders in soil remediation projects had to be identified.

Who are the stakeholders in soil remediation projects?

Before determining the actual stakeholders, a functional characterisation (a typology) of stakeholders for Biosoil was investigated. The outcome was that it was important to characterise the stakeholders according to the role they play rather than according to the organisation to which they belong. For example, the government can have the role of both client and supervising body. A remediation company can have both an advisory role and the role of executor.

The instrument for the identification of those involved (see Chapters 7 and 23) has been used to make up a stakeholders list, based on concrete projects, by means of interviews with Biosoil employees. In this way, 16 types of stakeholder (who had been directly related to one of the projects) were identified. These people included: members of the regulatory authorities, in the role of client as well as that of supervising body; employees of consultancy firms; developers; representatives of authorities, such as environmental services; and representatives of occupants.

To get a clearer view of the various roles of the stakeholders in a soil remediation project, a workshop with Biosoil employees was organised and representatives of these groups of stakeholders were interviewed. The most important finding was that a good insight into the roles of those stakeholders who are actively involved in the various stages of a project is essential for a proper demarcation of the project tasks. Another important finding was that little attention had been paid to those who were passively involved in a project, such as future occupants of a housing development. Ways of involving such stakeholders in the decision-making process and other stages of the soil remediation process need to be found.

What do stakeholders say and think about sustainability?

As already mentioned, a number of selected stakeholders (mainly those who had been actively involved in a project) were interviewed to ascertain answers to the following questions:

- What are the roles, the influence and the significance of the stakeholder?
- What indicators are used in a remediation project during the decision-making process?
- What is the vision regarding sustainability, both in general and in relation to the project itself?

The interviewers elaborated on sustainability parameters and the reducing offload model (see Chapters 3 and 23).

In studying the findings on how involved stakeholders interpreted sustainability, it appeared that there are many approaches to this concept. We will give some examples.

Some parties related sustainability to the amount of aftercare necessary once a soil remediation project had been finished. The less aftercare required, the more the project could be considered sustainable. So here sustainability is connected with the final situation after the remediation rather than with the remediation process itself. Another view was that soil remediation is inherently sustainable as its goal is to eliminate or minimise existing contamination. The questions asked in relation to this perspective were:

- When is remediation necessary and when is it not necessary?
- Up to what final value (minimum concentration) of pollution does the remediation have to be carried out?
- Who determines this value?
- Is it sustainable purely because the law prescribes it?
- How can we make sure that remediation of locations is continued?
- Does it help to conceptualise sustainability as 'a reduction in offload'?

On a number of occasions sustainability was linked to the operational management of the stakeholders themselves. For example, one customer mentioned that choosing a sustainable remediation variant might avoid negative publicity for his company. A member of an executive public body remarked that better knowledge transfer within the sector would help to generate a greater number of sustainable remediation techniques. A consultant said that, for her firm, sustainability meant investing a portion of profits in innovation projects related to sustainability.

The predominant findings of the interview session were as follows (the outcomes should not be generalised, considering the small number of projects studied and the number of interviewees):

- Although the concept of sustainability is often cited by the soil sector, there appears to be little consensus about what it means. Common ground regarding knowledge of sustainability does not exist
- Whenever sustainability was referred to, the focus was on the final result of the soil remediation project, and the soil remediation approach 'as part of the larger spectrum' rather than on the process within the soil remediation project or the soil remediation location
- Determining sustainability parameters of soil remediation processes was not seen as the only way to introduce a common 'language' for sustainability in the soil sector. It was concluded that concrete parameters as well as the degree of completeness of the list of parameters would always lead to discussions
- The presented 'reduction in offload' model, or the underlying notion of the concept of offload, was considered as a workable concept for the soil sector only by parties who possessed a high degree of knowledge about sustainability. However, the interviews did show that the offload model is a useful instrument to initiate a discussion about sustainability with the stakeholders, and that it creates new perspectives for sustainability in relation to soil remediation

- More clarity regarding the question of whether or not the soil remediation processes of Biosoil were sustainable was not considered an advantage. This was a key issue for Biosoil. Unfamiliarity with the relatively new *in situ* remediation techniques appeared to be more important to potential clients than the issue of sustainability. Regulating authorities, in particular, preferred tried and tested techniques. Thus, for these parties, certainty in attaining the remediation goal of the project was more important than the sustainability of the process itself

Surprisingly, the interviewees often expressed doubts about the relevance of the sustainability concept to soil remediation and, therefore, of the offload model. The importance of sustainability was not considered sufficiently crucial for it to be taken into account in daily practice.

The next step toward sustainable remediation

In the introduction the central question was formulated as follows: 'How could the proper knowledge about sustainability be distributed among the relevant stakeholders to accomplish that sustainability becomes part of the decision-making process in soil remediation projects?' The findings of the stakeholder interviews combined with the offload concept provided useful tools to continue formulating hypotheses around this question. However, there was also some disappointment that KoS was not advocated overall.

Offload in soil remediation

In this book the concept of offload has been introduced to make the notion of sustainability more operational (see Chapters 3 and 22). During the process of offload the environment is burdened, harmed, destroyed or exploited. In analysing the process of offload it is necessary to assess the 'who' and 'what' of offloading, and in what period of time. Once this has been done, achieving a reduction in offload can be determined.

In this approach, assessing the environment is an important factor. The results of the interviews indicated that soil remediation can be viewed in two ways: the system of the remediation project (we will call this system one) and the system of soil remediation and soil conditions in society (system two). In the following section, the offload concept will be applied to these systems to explain the concepts of sustainability and the relevant stakeholders within each system.

System one: the remediation project

In the past, and this can be long before the execution of a remediation project, contamination was 'offloaded' onto the remediation location by a particular party, and thus onto the current owner of the location. The contamination also caused the offload of other risks: for example, health risks related to the contamination. Depending on the choice of the remediation method, the contamination is either offloaded to another location (as is the case with digging out) or cleaned up on the spot (as is the case with *in situ* remediation). Apart from the actual contamination, environmental effects and safety aspects related to the remediation method itself also cause offload. For example, in the case of digging out there is offload in the sense of emissions caused by lorry movements and the removal of primary materials (i.e. clean soil) from a different location. *In situ* remediation may also affect the environment in some ways; however, this effect is less than in conventional remediation methods and is largely restricted to the remediation location itself.

An inverse relation exists between the gravity or scope of the process of offload and the closeness (both geographically and in terms of involvement) of the stakeholder who is exposed to the effects of offload. Both a large number of lorry movements and the demand for primary materials from elsewhere have a considerable impact on the environment. However, these factors do not impact the stakeholders in the system who are actively and directly involved, such as the owner of the location, the client or those who live in the surrounding area. When choosing a remediation method, cost-effectiveness as well as reducing any negative impacts on themselves will be the major motives of these stakeholders. In the decision-making process the degree to which there is offload elsewhere will play little, if any, role. Also, the executive local public authorities seem to benefit from as little local inconvenience as possible, therefore incentivising offloading to more distant areas.

During *in situ* remediation, however, actively involved stakeholders may experience a certain degree of offload, such as an uncertain end situation (unlike digging-out which guarantees the removal of the contamination) and an unknown remediation method. There is a sense that those directly involved are subjected to a larger degree of offload during *in situ* remediation even though, overall, there is actually less offload.

In practice it appears that in the current decision-making model the stakeholders who are actively and directly involved have a bigger say than those who are passively and indirectly involved. The decision-making model is based on interests that play a role within the system of the remediation project. That is why offloading outside the system is rarely, if ever, taken into account.

System two: conditions in society

Often a soil contamination is connected with both the piece of land where the pollution has been localised and the owner of that land. Nevertheless, soil contamination is society's problem; it is not restricted to the boundaries of contaminated land. In the period between the contamination and the final remediation the soil may already have exchanged owners a number of times. And, although nowadays owners are held accountable for the contamination, they are at the same time exposed to uncertainties, such as whether the pollution has entered groundwater. Such factors support the application of a system that is more extensive than the present soil remediation project alone.

Current remediation policies strengthen the relationship between soil remediation and sustainability. Due to financial constraints, choices must be made about which locations are given priority in the process of remediation. And also the aim to establish a future in which safe options of soil exploitation are provided shows the broad social interest regarding soil remediation in relation to sustainability. Offloading can then be minimised.

Ever since the start of intensive remediation after Lekkerkerk in 1976, the soil remediation industry and the government have gained a great deal of experience with respect to the phenomena mentioned above. This took place during a process of cleaning up contamination that had been offloaded onto society by perpetrators who could no longer be traced.

A system definition such as 'soil conditions within society' seems appropriate here. However, when considering such a broad system one would expect that the amount of offload is restricted to a minimum.

Within the current decision-making procedures the stakeholders who represent this system—such as government policy-makers, environmental protection groups and occupants—are not clearly visible.

KoS for sustainable remediation

In the following analysis, our point of departure will be 'soil conditions in society'; this includes the concomitant collective interest and the underlying individual interests of all those who are both actively and passively involved. So the emphasis is on those playing a role associated with the soil remediation location and the interests of society. Thus, the focus is on establishing 'safe' soil and sustainable soil usage, as well as carrying out soil remediation in a way that is maximally sustainable.

Offload as a concept seems a good starting point for the various views, lines of approach and interests of those involved with respect to sustainability, and it has the potential to serve as a basic principle that is generally accepted by all parties. It fits in with the decision-making process at both the strategic and the project level. Therefore, it is potentially a suitable concept in the discussion about sustainability in the soil remediation industry.

When thinking about what kind of KoS should be used in addressing the relevant stakeholders in order to include sustainability in the decision-making process, an initial response is to use the concept of a reduction in offload in conjunction with a systems approach.

Because those who are passively involved in a remediation project are the most obvious parties to take a stand with respect to reducing offload, it is particularly important that these stakeholders possess a good knowledge of the principles of offload. The findings of this research are therefore presented to this group of stakeholders, including government policy-makers, environmental protection organisations, financiers and policy-makers in consultancy firms.

Only when the offload principle has become an established concept can well-founded specific sustainability parameters of, for example, the environmental effects of remediation methods, begin to play a role in the decision-making process around the choice of a remediation method. These sustainability parameters or indicators belong therefore to the relevant KoS. It is essential to link these sustainability parameters to both the system in which they are relevant and the group of stakeholders on which they have an effect. The parameters should be aimed at both the (reduction in) offload, taking place within the system of the remediation location and the offload outside the system. The indicators should stimulate decision-making towards sustainability rather than evoke discussion. So, they should ultimately aim at the collective interest and, in doing so, combine individual interests to a maximum.

Sustainable innovation within Biosoil and the soil remediation industry

The guidelines mentioned above regarding KoS in the soil remediation industry serve as important preconditions to continuously stimulate organisations such as Biosoil to practise sustainable innovation. In the case of Biosoil, a good distribution of this KoS among all stakeholders is a stimulus to continue the ongoing innovation of *in situ* techniques. Furthermore, the industry as a whole, as well as society, will benefit from innovations of this kind. Biosoil's idea to develop sustainability indicators for soil remediation has been a step in the right direction, with its most important finding being that within the soil remediation industry sustainable innovation starts by aiming at a reduction in offloading.

11
KunstStoffenHuis and synthetics innovation within the small business sector

Cees van Dijk, Koos Zagema and Han van Kasteren

For many small businesses in the synthetic materials sector, sustainable innovation is critical. But for many it is difficult to achieve, especially when the innovation has to be realised by the companies themselves. By presenting four case studies, this chapter will show how a number of small businesses, in co-operation with KunstStoffenHuis (KSH) (Synthetics House), formed separate innovation clusters to develop product innovations in a structured way. KSH is associated with the Technical University Eindhoven, but is an independent company. At the end of 2004 KSH was renamed the Polymer Technology Group Eindhoven B.V., but this chapter will refer to KSH throughout. The aim of KSH is to commercialise innovations in chemical applications, especially those related to plastics production in small and medium-sized enterprises (SMEs). Although very much technically oriented, the development of this innovation project illustrates the importance of organisational and knowledge aspects—what we call the sustainability of knowledge (SoK). This chapter describes the ways in which KSH catalyses innovation.

The need for innovation within small businesses

Since the Second World War the use of synthetic polymers has increased almost exponentially to more than 150 million tonnes per year worldwide in 2002. Currently, the European sector provides more than 30% of world demand and employs more than 650,000 people. In the past few years the sector has seen rapid change. Product locations of bulk polymer production (polyethylene, polypropylene) have moved to oil-producing countries such as Iran and Canada to decrease the transport costs of raw materials. In addition, facilities have started to relocate to low-wage economies with large consuming markets, such as China.

A similar trend threatens to take place with respect to the processing of polymers (synthetics). This indicates that as long as labour costs remain the determining competitive factor, most of the polymer processing industry will disappear from the Netherlands. Synthetics processing in the Netherlands is dominated by small businesses. The sector consists of some 1,200 companies employing a total of 22,500 workers. The view that the main objective should be the full deployment of machines and the production of large volumes is no longer realistic. Instead, the sustainability of a small business can be increased by continuously innovating its own supply.

Successful innovations can lead to higher turnover and profits, provided they are sustainable. But translating new ideas into concrete products is difficult. Cooper (1998; see also Muller 1999) reveals that out of every 11 new ideas only three develop into prototypes and of these only one is commercially successful. Many SME entrepreneurs find this success rate too low to justify investing time and resources into new ideas.

Small businesses tend to fulfil merely a supply function. Their renewals are often limited to participating in collecting ideas about a desired innovation for a large organisation. As a result, they run the risk of encountering sales problems within a foreseeable period. As soon as demand for a specific semi-manufactured product decreases, the business's survival is threatened.

This situation forces many synthetics-producing small businesses to innovate products and production processes. Most small businesses aim at reducing costs and improving the efficiency of their production processes. The majority of SMEs employ fewer than 100 people, and few of these spend any of their time on innovation. Furthermore, any time spent on innovation is mostly labelled as a cost rather than an investment. In most cases the SME lacks the means (knowledge and financial resources) to introduce innovations on its own.

This KSH research project aimed to set up and realise four clusters of innovative small businesses. Through sharing knowledge these clusters developed an innovative product and preserved the lessons learned, thus embedding the innovation process within the sector.

This chapter describes the realisation of the clusters, the role of KSH, participants' learning experiences, the steps that still lie ahead and, finally, how the sustainability of these innovation processes can be guaranteed.

KSH as intermediary between the small business sector and knowledge institutes

KSH was established in 1999 as a collaboration between the Technical University Eindhoven, TNO Industry, Fontys Higher Vocational Education and the Dutch Polymer Institute. Since September 2002, KSH has been operating as a foundation. The aim of KSH is to stimulate and help small businesses pursue future success by abandoning short-term thinking and being open to renewal. In this respect, making entrepreneurship more professional is essential so that it can lead to a situation where entrepreneurs go along with developments in a proactive, timely and ongoing manner. It is about acquiring a view of the market, applying new principles, adjusting the organisation and financing this process.

To achieve innovation, knowledge is required over an increasingly broader field. Moreover, the developments within these knowledge fields are moving swiftly. It has become an impossible task for organisations to keep up; they have to specialise. As a consequence, expertise is dispersed throughout several small businesses and knowledge institutes, and translating an idea into one or more marketable products requires a multitude of experts. Therefore, co-operation with other small businesses and with knowledge institutes is increasingly required.

In the meantime, KSH has carried out activities in co-operation with more than 100 Dutch and foreign small businesses within the framework of entrepreneurship and innovation in the field of synthetics technology. The first experiences have revealed a number of bottlenecks that threaten structural knowledge development within small business clusters. These are:

- Shielding knowledge from potential partners; distrust dominates
- Indistinctness with respect to common advantages
- Non-communicative specialisms which have grown apart
- Prejudices and diverging views

Thanks to some large multinational companies (DSM and AKZO Nobel), the Netherlands is an important European centre for innovations in the synthetics processing sector. The success of these large companies is realised through close co-operation with universities and knowledge institutes that are being paid for contriving new principles. As far as knowledge institutes are concerned, small businesses often present no intellectual challenge. A knowledge institute prefers to deal with fundamental questions which are time-consuming and suitable for publication. A small business player prefers quick and profitable applications. As a result, the current ways of knowledge dispersal are ad hoc, fragmented and slow (Tweede Kamer [Parliament] 2000).

Knowledge institutes and small businesses are not convinced of the need to establish a relationship. For the latter, co-operation in product development must lead, in a short period of time, to concrete products that are commercially viable. However, successful co-operation requires patience, and 'cross-pollination' between organisations can develop only if there is mutual trust. To nurture this, involvement in the initial stage is crucial, as is the identification of individual and common advantages. Only then can small-scale systematic co-operation take place. The successes achieved need to be made explicit and described in further plans, so that credibility increases and trust grows. Where co-operation is satisfactory, it can be deepened and anchored, depending on what is being aspired to.

The ambition of KSH was to act as a catalyst to establish and maintain innovations in synthetics processing SMEs. It aimed to become an expert in finding companies with innovative ideas, suitable partners, knowledge institutes and financiers as well as guiding the innovation processes. The leap project Synthetics Innovation Small Businesses described below examines how an intermediary organisation can teach a small business to co-operate in a sustainable way with partners in a cluster.

Synthetics Innovation Small Businesses

Objective

The objective of the business project Synthetics Innovation Small Businesses is to form a number of clusters in order to:

> Learn how practical knowledge acquired in the corporate life and specialised knowledge of knowledge institutes can be combined and made into new products for the market, produced by small businesses in the synthetics processing industry.

In the project both the participating small businesses and KSH are objects of study and change. In this context KSH has the role of cluster catalyst and functions as a knowledge broker between the participants and the knowledge institutes. The concrete results to be achieved during the whole project have been stipulated as follows:

1. Setting off and realising four clusters of innovative small businesses, aimed at the development of an innovative product through sharing knowledge

2. Preserving the learning experience obtained in co-operation with KSH in order to continue the innovation process within the small business synthetics processing sector

3. By setting up, supporting and evaluating the four clusters of innovating small businesses the various innovation trajectories will provide answers to the following questions:
    - How can small businesses benefit in the best way possible from their own knowledge, the knowledge of other small businesses and that of knowledge institutes?
    - How can innovation trajectories be given shape in such a way that they can be started and maintained by KSH without external support?
    - Which interventions and instruments could support a trajectory of this kind?
    - What lessons can be learned from the actual cases in view of new innovation trajectories within the small businesses in the synthetics processing industry?
    - What lessons can be learned from the actual cases in view of innovation trajectories carried out by small businesses in other sectors?

Selection of small businesses

We know from experience that small businesses are, overall, businesslike enough to be aware of opportunities for new products in the market, but they lack the capability to take advantage of these opportunities. Launching new product lines onto the market requires more than an innovative idea. During a 2003 symposium organised by KSH, Innovations in the Land of Synthetics, 110 participants were asked how they felt about starting an innovation trajectory around one of the following four themes: synthetics processing; coatings; composites; or recycling. Based on this inquiry a list was made of 20 small businesses that were interested. They formed the basis for the selection of companies that might be able to fulfil the role of pioneers in an innovation cluster. The starting point here is that the chance of a cluster's success will be increased if companies show a certain degree of willingness and capability to initiate the process. Potentially suitable companies were selected on the basis of their responses to the following questions:

- With which industrial partners do you regularly co-operate?
- What does this co-operation consist of?
- What efforts have you made to come into contact with knowledge institutes?
- Are you a member of any trade or professional associations; if so, which ones and why?
- Why did you participate in the Innovations in the Land of Synthetics symposium?
- Do you employ developers and, if so, how many? How many employees are involved in marketing and are they in contact with the developers on a regular basis?
- How much money is available/reserved for innovation (i.e. the R&D budget)?
- Do you consider yourself innovative; how is this shown?
- Have you at any point:
  - Published?
  - Attended conferences?
  - Received visitors at your business location?
- What concrete plans have you made (last year, the last three years, more than three years)?
- How does your business see its future?

Out of the group of 20 companies that expressed interest by filling in the questionnaire, four were selected as initiators (these were termed 'jewels') to lead a particular cluster to develop their innovative idea. A number of companies indicated that they did not consider themselves as initiators, but would be willing to participate at a later stage. A precondition in the final selection of the four jewels was that they were not engaged in competing activities. This ensured they could participate fully in the development of another company's idea and share their experiences of the innovation process. Moreover, the chances of mutual (substantial) co-operation were small, and it could be assumed that in a sequential phase each jewel would have to look elsewhere for additional competences, rather than addressing the other three jewels. It was not the intention to encourage co-operation of these small firms, but to realise a platform for the exchange of innovation ideas.

Phasing the search for certainty

The **innovation trajectory**, in which an idea leads to the creation of one or more successful products suitable for the market, is subject to many uncertainties. Questions that need to be asked include:

- Could the idea really be successful?
- How do I convince my organisation?
- How can we acquire a position in the market?
- Can we do this alone? If not, who is suitable and can be trusted to participate?
- How will we co-operate?

Answering these questions is a quest for certainty. At each stage of this quest it is important to know the next step. In this project five phases have been defined to help each jewel firm form a cluster with partners who will eventually benefit from the commercial realisation of the idea (see Table 11.1).

Phase 1

In the first phase of the innovation project, the jewel firm's contact person (in co-operation with the consultants of KSH) explored the idea and acquired approval within his or her own organisation. Although the jewel was enthusiastic about the innovative idea, it was looking for more certainty regarding the chances of success. This would depend on market demand and the feasibility of manufacturing the new products. To identify suitable market segments some market research is required. In order to manufacture a product line for a market segment, an analysis is required of the production line or the system to be designed. To conduct this analysis, the functions are identified and their realisation is verified along general lines. We know from experience that as a result two cardinal questions will emerge; these require further research. If the jewel's management has a good feeling with regard to the practicality of the function and the opportunities in the market, it will, if necessary, adjust its organisational goals.

Phase 2

The second phase concerns finding suitable partners to develop a product line for a market segment. Partners of the cluster to be formed operate as both the first customer ('launching customer') and as the organisation possessing the essential additional knowledge. From previous cases we know that involving a first customer in the cluster in an early stage results in a better understanding of the product to be developed (Muller 1999). Partners are selected on the basis of their strategic position and innov-

154 SUSTAINABLE INNOVATION

Phase 1	Phase 2	Phase 3	Phase 4	Phase 5
I have a brilliant idea!	I need partners in this	We want to start planning	We want to start the development process	Customers want to start using the product
Which potential markets are there?	What is their strategic position?	What new results do we want to achieve?	How do we specify user requirements and functions?	How do we train the sales department in the (im)possibilities of the product?
Which production lines are suitable in this respect?	What is their capability to innovate?	Which existing products are we going to improve?	How do we design modules?	How do we train the production department in the construction and assembling process?
What are the implications for our organisational ambitions?	What do we include in the declaration of intent?	What are the expected costs, revenues and throughput times?	How do we construct a prototype? How do we execute experiments with the prototype?	How do we train the service department in dealing with defects?
Idea accepted	Intention accepted	Route map delineated	Prototype realised	Product in use

TABLE 11.1 Phasing of the innovation process

ative power. The strategic position tells us something about the core competence of a partner. Is this core competence complementary to the competencies of others in the cluster or is there some degree of overlap? The partner's innovative power indicates whether they are capable of adding ideas and participating fully in the realisation process (the first customer in the product requirements and the knowledge partner in inventing creative solutions). The next step can be taken when both the jewel and the partner have good feelings about the declarations of intent. These declarations constitute the general agreements about, among other things, the distribution of the costs and revenues.

Phase 3
By depicting in the third phase the results to be achieved, a better view is developed of the necessary budgets. The development of a new product requires, among other things, specification, design, construction and experimentation. If the innovation concerns a change in an existing product, it will involve investment. This phase determines whether it is still cost-effective to improve the product, given its life-cycle. The process as a whole results in a roadmap consisting of steps to be taken, results, expected costs, revenues and throughput times. If necessary, financiers can be approached who are

prepared to invest. Once the budget has been agreed, the project's realisation can be started in phase 4.

Phase 4

The fourth phase results in a prototype design. The knowledge partners and the first customer will get to work by starting with the specification for user requirements and the necessary functionalities, developing the concepts and designing the modules. After the design stage, the prototype is made, with which the first customer can start experimenting. The knowledge partners can then determine where the prototype could still be improved. In order to satisfy the customer, iterations will take place, as necessary. The stronger the knowledge partners are challenged by the first customer, the more they are stimulated to find the optimum solution to each problem. During this phase the knowledge partners dealing with the production, sales and service of the product will begin to participate in the process.

Phase 5

In the fifth phase, all participants start to make money on the (product) idea and a large number of customers start to use the product. The knowledge partners, who participated in the thinking process during phase 4, train their employees to ensure proper sales, production and service transfer.

Uncertainty reduction

During the five phases, KSH fulfils different roles: catalyst, knowledge broker and knowledge supplier. In the first two phases, the role of catalyst is fulfilled proactively so that a cluster can be formed. In the last three phases KSH participates in the innovation clusters on the basis of the arrangements made in the roadmap, which is adjusted regularly. At the time of writing, some phases had not yet been achieved. The project results described in this chapter deal with the first and second phases which establish the basics of the clusters. In these phases any uncertainties that the participants might have regarding the success of the product have been largely removed, without much initial cost. By structuring the innovation issue and subdividing it into smaller questions (Goodwin and Wright 2003), insight is obtained into matters that have already been sufficiently examined as well as into questions that still have to be answered. By answering questions about market potential, knowledge partners and technical attainability, uncertainty is reduced.

The decision whether to stop or to continue towards phase 3 is taken as soon as the cluster is happy about the risk in relation to the expected outcome. Participants are more inclined to strive for a solution that is satisfactory than to find an optimum one (Simon 1969). In structuring the innovation issue the **object model for product development** has been applied. In the next sections, this model is explained and the results achieved by the four innovation clusters during the first two phases are described.

Project results

Object model for product development

During the innovation trajectory, the object model for product development supports the search for certainty. This model (see Fig 11.1) was developed by the consultancy firm Pernosco in co-operation with ALSI (a company in the semiconductor industry) to map out the discussion topics relevant in product development. The model is object-oriented and starts from a logical order of objects (Coad and Yourdon 1991). The same model is useful in the development of products in synthetics. By structuring the innovation issue and subdividing it into smaller questions insight is obtained into matters that already have been sufficiently investigated as well as questions that still have to be answered.

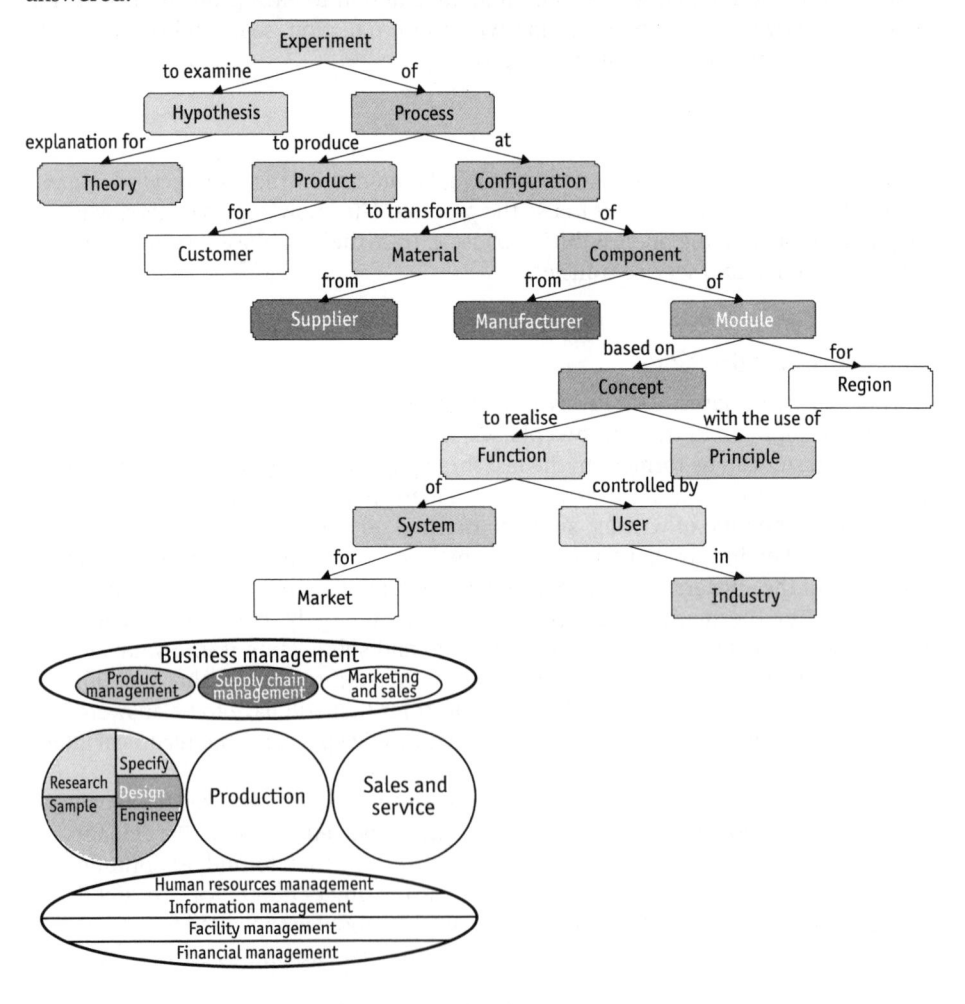

FIGURE 11.1 The object model for product development

The discussion about the integration or elaboration of a new idea can be initiated with every object (an element in the knowledge domain) and can take place both from bottom to top and from top to bottom. For example, one could begin with the object 'concept'. A new concept may create a unique function by making use of a principle which may or may not be patented. In some cases this function may improve an existing system (or product line) in such a way that it can fulfil the needs of new markets.

Wheelwright and Clark (1992) indicate the importance of mapping at an early stage of the innovation project. The object model enables the small business entrepreneur to make a map, in co-operation with a KSH consultant, which includes the functional areas of marketing, product development and production. With each phase of the innovation trajectory an analysis can be made of which topics cause the most uncertainty. The uncertainty in phase 1 concerns the market and the functions of the system. A combination of functions and market has to be found which can be realised and is commercially interesting as well. On the one hand, a market has to have enough potential but, on the other, the costs of the required adjustment or realisation of a system should not exceed expected revenues. Phase 2 deals with uncertainty in the choice of partners. A suitable first customer has to be found, and the degree to which the necessary materials and components are innovative needs to be confirmed. For these materials and components a supplier and a manufacturer have to be found who are able to participate in the thinking process as knowledge partners. Sometimes it is desirable and possible to outsource an entire business process to a knowledge partner: for example, R&D. The next sub-sections will describe the results of the four participating small companies.

Polux

Polux produces façade components of polyester, for which dozens of alternatives are available. As a result, the price is continuously under pressure. Polux's strategy is to develop new products for markets where the competition is less severe. The company developed an idea that took off in New Zealand—an animal cleaning device comprising a polyester bathtub manufactured by Polux. A modular approach makes it possible to provide different tubs for different animals and users, from chickens to cows and from farmers to pet owners. The object model is used to identify the necessary functions and concepts, and then to consider the modules and components. The most crucial research questions were to do with the function of adding a well-balanced amount of shampoo to water and mixing the shampoo with the water. A manufacturer from Israel has combined these two functions into one component—the shampet.

LWB Eindhoven Ltd

A system can also be a production line. For years now, the production line of LWB Eindhoven Ltd has manufactured fluorescent powders for television screens. The market for these powders is characterised by stagnation and, recently, has seen a sharp decline with the replacement of conventional screens with LCD and plasma. In reaction to this trend LWB Eindhoven Ltd has designed an innovative product—nano-powders with two unique qualities, transparency and conduction. The market for this combination of qualities seems to be related to the materials which are made of synthetics. Phase 1 suggested there was too little certainty with respect to the expected market demand, but market research showed that the demand is sufficient for LWB Eindhoven Ltd to seriously consider the required adjustments to the production line. The company is already capable of manufacturing nano-powders in a water solution. However, the result does not stick to synthetics. For this reason, two extra functions appeared to be necessary, dispersal and modification. With the aid of a subsidy, Technical University Eindhoven was approached to conduct research into principles that could realise these functions. As soon as the principles have been substantiated and proven, it should not be difficult in the light of the realisation of the two functions to design concepts and modules to extend the production line. On the basis of insights into the market and the production process, the business development manager of LWB Eindhoven Ltd (who was also the KSH contact person) was able to convince the organisation to reconsider its existing organisational goals.

It did not take LWB Eindhoven Ltd long to realise that the results from phase 1 were convincing enough to start looking for a creative and co-operative first customer in a market with a great deal of potential. After a number of talks a first customer was eventually selected as the purchaser of the nano-powder for the two markets. The two first customers had the opportunity and were prepared to prove, in co-operation with LWB Eindhoven Ltd, the applicability of the necessary principles in actual practice. Moreover, they had the same vision and enjoyed a good market image. On this basis, LWB Eindhoven Ltd was confident to build a long-lasting relationship. As a knowledge partner Technical University Eindhoven will continue to play a role in the research. The next stage is to find a strategic supplier.

Boekelo Decor

Boekelo Decor manufactures decoration foil for the DIY (do-it yourself) market. The product has a somewhat traditional image, and is often used to decorate kitchens and windows. Based on the current production line, Boekelo is considering developing new products. An idea has been put forward for a foil that can serve a variety of functions for the customer. With regard to this new approach, the research question concerns two functions. The question is to determine on the basis of which principles these functions can be realised. To make research in this field possible, the development manager of Boekelo Decor (who is also the KSH contact person) has initiated an internal discussion with the marketing department and management. They also see a bright future for the new application. In 2004 the renewal of existing products was given first priority. In the meantime, the realisation of this new idea as a project has been realised in 2006.

Flowlight

Flowlight manufactures synthetic transparent sandwich panels for flat roofs to create more light in working spaces. Customers regularly ask for improved lighting facilities with better thermal insulation. Flowlight concluded that thermal isolation could be achieved by applying a honeycomb structure between the two synthetic plates of the sandwich panel. Surprisingly, this idea appeared to increase the amount of light. Flowlight has purchased a machine in Germany to manufacture honeycomb plates at low cost. As well as profiting from the innovation, Flowlight hopes to develop new products for new markets. For example, including PUR or PIR (synthetic materials) in the honeycomb structure reduces transparency and increases thermal insulation, making the product suitable for use as lightweight wall panels for boats, caravans and cars. The most important research question is how to fill the honeycomb structure with PUR or PIR, and a subsidy to conduct further research has been applied for.

Lessons learned

All four cases have shown that small businesses do have a sufficient amount of entrepreneurial spirit and sense of the market to assess the chances of an idea and be aware of the research questions. However, they may not have considered all the necessary questions or sufficiently reflected on all the alternative solutions. The lesson that can be learned from phase 1 is that a great deal of uncertainty can be removed with the aid of the object model. An overview of the research questions can be developed when all the functions required to manufacture the desired product are identified. Often, it appears that there is uncertainty only for one or two functions related to the chosen concept. Further research into these functions and the market potential often provides the entrepreneur with sufficient trust to continue with the idea and move on to phase 2. In phase 2, the object model provides a structured approach to the selection of partners. Partners are the first customers but may also be material suppliers, component manufacturers or, even, managers of the entire business process.

The effects achieved

Small businesses

On 30 October 2003, the intermediaries (i.e. contacts) of the four selected jewels were invited to a meeting in order to identify and give concrete form to their ideas for sustainable innovation. This meeting resulted in each jewel taking away a concrete idea. The companies present were by no means in competition with each other and operated in different markets within the sector. In spite of their different backgrounds and partly with the aid of the object model, the intermediaries were able to ask each other critical questions and give tips on, for example, the possibilities with respect to applying an idea.

After the meeting, the intermediaries started individually to work out some of the unanswered questions, under the supervision of KSH and the consultants of Pernosco. Where necessary, support for the ideas was acquired internally. Support on behalf of the top level of a small business appears to be an absolute prerequisite. For this reason, a realistic view must be established as early as possible of the attainability of the project and the expected financial returns. Two of the participating companies were part of a larger international holding. Here, gaining support for the innovation project proved difficult, especially with respect to resource allocation. In the case of the other companies the entrepreneurs themselves were present, and this considerably quickened the decision-making process. After the first phase, one of the companies proceeded at a great pace on its own with the actual product innovation.

Most small businesses that were approached indicated that innovation is of vital importance for their survival over the next one to two years. However, the means for innovation are often limited, and investment costs need to be recouped rapidly. Therefore, methods and initiatives that clearly increase the likelihood of success, decrease the chance of making a wrong decision and shorten 'time to market' are of importance. In this respect the object model for product development provides a sound basis, widening the scope of discussions, producing insights, resolving dilemmas, creating opportunities, stimulating questions and structuring information.

Two of the original four selected jewels have continued with phase 2 and, partly, with phase 3. In the meantime, new jewels are presenting themselves as participants in a second trajectory set up by KSH which deals with innovation within clusters and is based on the experiences with the first four jewels.

KSH

At present, small businesses can turn to KSH for answers to technical questions. In most cases, these questions concern specific problems relating to the processing of synthetics in the manufacturing processes of products. KSH already works by means of a demand-oriented organisational structure in which its consultants maintain contact with small businesses. In addition, KSH aims to make knowledge about new and existing technological developments accessible to the small business sector. The results of scientific research often contain good ideas and provide contributions to product innovations. However, these publications are often unreadable for the average small business entrepreneur. KSH has started translating the most promising research studies into more accessible prose.

In the process of initiating and guiding innovation clusters, consultants have found that the research questions are often poorly structured. Moreover, small business entrepreneurs often have still to be convinced of the necessity to start the innovation process together with KSH and other companies. For a consultant to operate successfully in a context of this kind, he or she should possess managerial knowledge as well as advisory skills. In this respect we should, together with the entrepreneur, think about asking questions, asking more questions, listening well, summarising a problem, structuring the information, indicating sequential steps and providing solutions to the missing pieces of the jigsaw.

Initiated by this NIDO business project, KSH started to make a map of the small business market. Organising theme meetings and seminars is a good way of getting to know companies (and entrepreneurs) while at the same time highlighting the potential contribution of KSH. In this way, contacts are established with people who have good ideas about innovation within their own organisation but who do not know how to transform that idea into a new product. These contact persons are helped by the ideas developed in the phases 1 and 2.

Expanding and structuring a problem area (and using the object model) resulted in questions that neither the small business entrepreneur nor the KSH consultant (who is actually more focused on the technical content) would have thought of spontaneously. In this case, the questions were mostly of a managerial nature, such as:

- What does the potential market look like?

- What function could my solution fulfil in the products portfolio or processes of my intended customers or in those of my current customer?
- What are the possible consequences of this innovation to other products or components?
- What is my role in the supply chain?
- How can I involve my suppliers in this innovation?
- Are there any subsidies available?

The small size of innovation projects within the small business sector and the limited amount of available resources in most cases require a combination of the aforementioned competences within one consultant. In this project, attention has been paid to transferring advisory skills and knowledge in the field of business administration to the staff of KSH by training and guiding them. As a result, KSH has developed into an organisation that operates more actively in the area of small businesses. This process is ongoing, with technical knowledge being complemented with organisational and managerial knowledge.

Business results in terms of innovation and the sustainability framework

Initially, the emphasis in the Synthetics Innovation Small Businesses project was on structuring and organising innovation processes (within the synthetics processing small businesses sector). Four companies actually started the process of realising innovation in a structured manner. Although the content of the innovations differs, all those involved applied the same method. Experiences are exchanged via the project as well as via KSH and are used in subsequent innovations stimulated and supervised by KSH within the small businesses sector. By working in a highly structured manner with the aid of the object model, the knowledge content of the innovation is represented in conceptual maps. By now the innovations of three of the four jewels have entered a more advanced stage.

In this NIDO business project the sustainability aspect comes across in three ways. First, in the form of re-use of the acquired knowledge of the innovation processes, preserved within KSH. Second, by enhancing the chance of successful sustainable innovations. Third, the sustainability of KSH as an organisation is increased. By operating actively in the market in a broader area (not only by means of technical advice and research but also by advice about and supervision of innovation processes), KSH has expanded its added value within the synthetics processing small businesses sector.

In this project, the creation, dispersal and preservation of knowledge (as described in Chapters 2, 3, 4 and 6) take place within parts of the three aforementioned dimensions. The project is aimed at system changes on the level of the individual as well as that of the group, the organisation and the network. In the spiral of knowledge creation several processes take place simultaneously. Existing coded and theoretical knowledge is transferred via KSH to the small businesses sector by translating it into comprehensible language, and by selecting directly applicable knowledge elements which are passed on to the small businesses. Within the sector, learning processes take place both on the level of individual employees who acquire new knowledge and on the level of the group and the company. The way in which this process takes place within small businesses in detail has not been an object of study in the framework of this project. However, knowledge is shared and developed on the level of the network by exchange within the clusters. At the same time, knowledge creation takes place within the innovation processes of the clusters. The experience gained within the clusters is preserved within KSH. Most of this knowledge is of a sensory (tacit) nature and, as far as it is coded, it is partly preserved with the aid of fixed methods such as the object model, course documentation and case descriptions.

The experiences acquired in this business project with respect to knowledge creation and knowledge distribution are limited in an absolute sense because of the fact that the number of clusters and steps to be taken by the clusters is still small. However, the first signs and experiences are encouraging in the sense that it can be expected that the situation will lead to a sustainable development of knowledge. It appears that even with limited resources small businesses are able to innovate in a structured way with the help of colleagues and the support of KSH. Several companies are capable of doing this on their own, and actually do so. Innovation as such is a precondition for sustainable innovation of small businesses, but also for the sustainable development of KSH as an institute within the synthetics processing industry. By combining the knowledge and resources of small businesses and knowledge institutes, a situation develops in which the value of KSH increases. The extent to which this added value corresponds with how the sector perceives value remains to be seen, but the signs are favourable. It appears that small businesses are indeed prepared to pay for support in the form of clusters to guide their innovation processes and they will not leave it at one consultation only.

Conclusions

On the basis of our first innovation experiences, carried out with the aid of innovation clusters within the small businesses sector, several lessons can be learned and conclusions drawn with respect to the internal process within KSH and the external process within the small businesses involved. These are:

- The difficulty of the entire innovation process requires the participation of a large number of organisations from the start. The approach of selecting in advance potential candidates on the basis of a limited number of characteristics in order to subsequently start exploratory discussions with a select group has worked well. Three of the four companies selected have actually immediately continued the intended innovation. It was expected though that at the end of phase 1 we would meet again with more jewels than the current two (up to three). Although the sample survey is too limited to draw conclusions from it, we can prudently start from the basic rule that minimally five to seven times more preselected organisations are ultimately required to enter a subsequent phase. When we apply this rule of thumb to KSH, it means that, if it intends to play a central catalytic role within the synthetics processing small business sector and wants to make a sustainable living out of doing so, the innovative power and requirements of at least a few hundred small businesses will have to be mapped out

- Structuring with the aid of the object model results in an overview and increases insights into and control over the innovation process. In most cases, the enterprises in this sector are too small to have all the technical and managerial disciplines at their disposal. Often there is a strong emphasis on a specific technology or a particular product or market segment. As a result, small businesses often do not possess sufficient insight into how their own activities fit into a broader perspective (e.g. developments in the market, suppliers, product families, adjoining technologies, possible partners). Innovating small businesses runs the risk of being dragged into a promising but impracticable idea. The consequence is that energy and resources are spent on an idea that is unattainable; resources that could have been deployed in a more cost-effective way. Analysing the idea and offering an overview at an early stage in the production development process increases the chance of success

- First customer in a market offers focus and certainty. During the elaboration of the market exploration on behalf of LWB a market strategy emerged showing a strong link with the systematic approach of the object model. The focus in this approach is on finding a first customer to conquer their own market at a later stage. Of course, the size of the potential market is a determining factor here, but the enthusiasm of the first customer is certainly important. In this process the first customer provides, in a critical way, all the information a developer needs to tune the product specifications and establish a suitable production line or system. On this basis the other customers are subsequently served in this market. The advantage to first customers is that they are served on the basis of their own particular needs, possibly at a reduced price

- One captain on the ship. Although it is still too early to be entirely certain, the concept of the 'jewel' surrounded by other small businesses appears to be working well. The jewel is the entrepreneur who came up with the idea and who has the potential to market the resulting product (with the help of others within the cluster). The jewel is committed and often makes the heaviest investment. In this context all participants are required to sign a declaration of intent with the jewel

- Support within the organisation is a precondition to move on to phase 3. With the exception of sole traders such as Flowlight, the 'visionaries' within an organisation do not necessarily have sufficient authority over the innovation. By combining the processes of product development and marketing and sales, those responsible were better able to assess the impact of the desired innovation. However, to what extent the obtained insights can be sold to management (i.e. those who make the decision on whether to invest or not) depends on the intermediary's competencies. A KSH consultant can help gain internal support and so contribute to the launch of the innovation trajectory. Knowledge transfer from the consultant to the contact person appears to work best in brief meetings with knowledge transferred verbally so it can quickly be translated into action. In this way the contact person acquires extra support to start looking for answers to the unanswered questions

Recommendations, discussion and future research

Co-operation is not just a matter of offering and following the proper approach and supervision; it is also a matter of good will and attitude. A reliable research instrument to determine whether a good basis for innovation exists within clusters—also with respect to the more intangible aspects of the firms—would be a welcome addition to the method presented here, but would need to be developed.

Subsidies and (partly) free consultancy could make innovation stimulation easier. A sustainable form of innovation on a mutual basis can develop only if all parties are convinced of the added value of co-operating with others and with the cluster. In that case there will also be partners' money available for guidance. In order to establish clusters, it is necessary that institutions playing the role of catalyst (such as KSH in this project) make investments in advance in order to unlock scientific knowledge, map out the small businesses sector and form innovation clusters. Not all activities result in clusters. However, investments of this kind have to be financed one way or another.

In many other branches of industry comparable issues play a role and institutions such as KSH are active here. A comparison of the problems within different branches, the role of a branch association and/or knowledge institute and the way in which the innovation process is dealt with may lead to more effective ways to increase innovative skills within the small businesses sector.

Anchoring and further development on the part of KSH requires the structural organisation of an ever-progressing framework of discussions, existing *within* differing disciplines as well as *among* them. This framework of separate discussions is called the **discourse**. Discourse management co-ordinates this framework of discussions by providing an agenda and appointing specialists to cover various items on the agenda, thereby placing all these discussions within a knowledge development and knowledge diffusion process. In this respect attention is paid to both constraining and stimulating factors within the knowledge exchange whereby the focus has to be on communication within the group of collaborating specialists, both with respect to each separate network partner to the relations among the partners.

A precondition for the success of innovation clusters is initially formed by the practical knowledge of the small businesses and the specialised knowledge of knowledge institutes. They should be connected with one another optimally (i.e. in a win–win situation). In addition, the accessibility of the knowledge suppliers (Technical University Eindhoven, Fontys Higher Vocational Education and the Dutch Polymer Institute) is an important condition. The knowledge carriers and the mediating contact persons must be market-oriented; how this is achieved needs further research. KSH consultants should be able to advise and support interactive knowledge development in a way that suits the objectives and participants. The object model appears to be a suitable method for achieving this.

12
Know what you're blending!
A TOOL FOR A SUSTAINABLE PAPER INDUSTRY

Niels Faber and Kristian Peters

This chapter covers the Optichem Infonet project—an innovation in paper production in the Netherlands. The project introduces decision-support software (DSS) to interconnect the different knowledge domains that lie at the heart of paper production. The introduction of DSS serves two objectives: first, to improve personal safety surrounding the use of chemicals; and, second, to reduce chemical spills. Together, these objectives aim to contribute to an improvement in the overall sustainability of the **value chain of paper production**.

Besides the paper mills that actually produce paper, paper production involves many other organisations, such as chemical suppliers and installation builders. The set of organisations involved in paper production, from raw material to final product, is termed the value chain of paper production. For brevity, we use the term **paper production** to refer to the complete value chain of paper production.

Despite several initiatives to improve the sustainability of paper production, the use of chemicals within the production process hampers further progress towards sustainability. Chemicals have gradually entered paper production, enabling the production of a large portfolio of products. Currently, chemicals are a necessity to paper production. In spite of their advantages, the use of chemicals in paper production has also introduced a number of problems which stand in the way of the industry's pursuit of sustainability.

Improving paper production's sustainability is difficult because the knowledge necessary for these improvements stems from multiple knowledge domains that are separated from each other. First, knowledge about chemicals is scarce in paper production, mainly residing with chemical suppliers. Second, knowledge about paper-making, engineering, electronics and organising is also important in paper production, with the integration of the different knowledge domains playing an important role in the targeted improvement of sustainability. Problems related to chemicals within paper production are not restricted to the chemical domain. A lack of co-ordination between tasks that use the different knowledge domains is identified as a cause for these problems.

In general, correct handling is crucial within any type of production process in which chemicals are of secondary importance, especially processes such as paper production. The Optichem Infonet project attempts to support employees in their execution of different tasks in paper production, providing them with relevant knowledge about chemicals. We argue that employees are able to co-ordinate their individual actions within paper production regarding personal safety only when they have appropriate knowledge about chemicals.

Organisation

Value chain of paper production

Paper production consists of several processes which we divide into a main process and several secondary processes (see Fig. 12.1). The main process of paper production concerns the transformation of wood fibres into sheets of paper. Here, a process structure is used that has been the same for centuries. In short, paper is produced at the mill in seven phases—grinding wood into small fibres; bleaching; adding water to turn the bleached fibres into paper pulp; sorting and diluting the pulp; forming sheets; pressing; and thermal drying.

Chemicals are added at various places in the paper production process. For instance, during the bleaching phase bleach is added to whiten the paper. Other chemicals are added at different places during the production process: for example, to enhance the paper surface or texture (see Bos *et al.* 1995 for an overview of the different chemical treatments).

Several secondary processes complement the main process of paper production. As stated before, the focus of this study is on the use of chemicals within paper production. We identify three secondary processes in which chemicals play a part. First, the process that delivers chemicals to the actual paper production process consists of two tasks: producing chemicals and transporting them to the mill. The parties involved in the delivery of chemicals are the producer of the chemicals and the transport company. The next secondary process is the delivery of the installations that are used within the main process. Installation builders and fitters execute tasks within this process. The installation builder constructs the necessary installations whereas the fitter installs the installation on the paper mill's production floor. Third, we recognise the service process. In this study, the two service tasks of cleaning and transportation are identified. Other tasks in the service process are, for instance, maintenance, purchasing, etc. The cleaning task refers to the cleaning of the mill's production floor and its installations; professional cleaners execute this task. Maintenance organisations perform the task of maintaining the different installations of a paper mill.

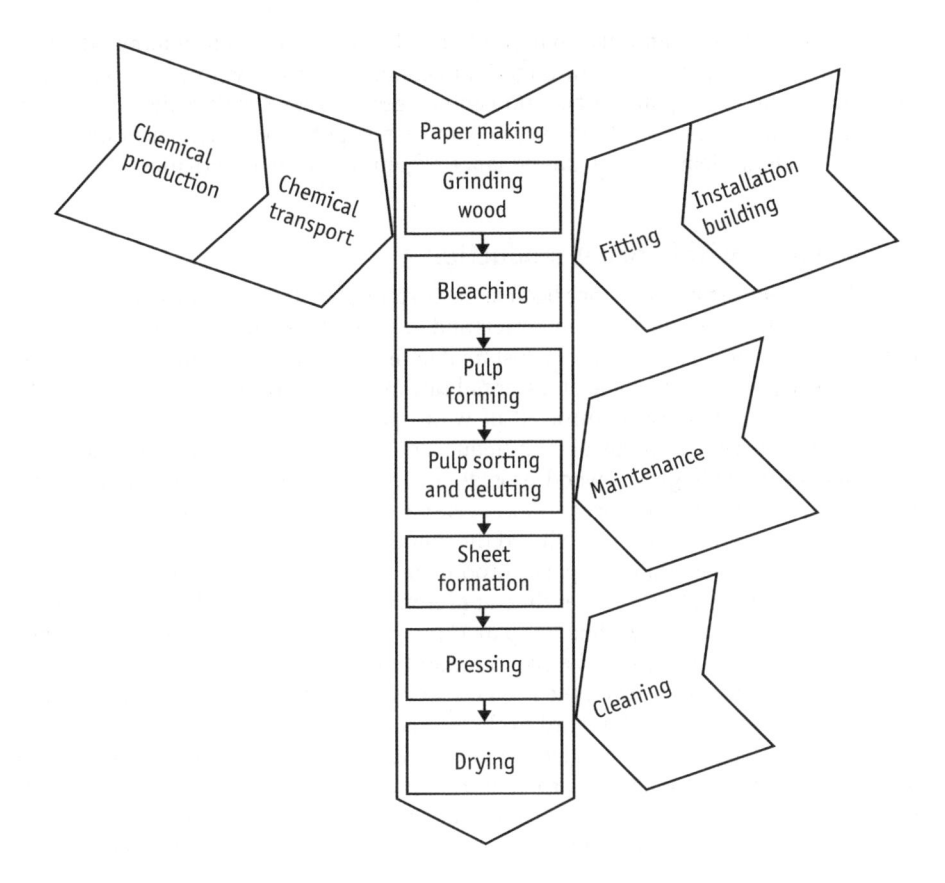

FIGURE 12.1 Value chain of paper production

Optichem Infonet

The Optichem Infonet project is executed within the value chain of paper production in the Netherlands. Participants in the project are: a producer of chemicals; a transportation organisation; an industrial cleaner; a machine builder; and five paper mills. Big River Innovation, an organisation that advises industrial parties and governmental institutions in improving their performance, initiated the project. Big River Innovation also initiated the Optichem platform, a discussion panel consisting of several chemists from different Dutch paper mills. During the meetings of the Optichem platform, the need was expressed to enhance the knowledge of chemicals within paper production in the paper industry.

The Optichem Infonet foundation co-ordinates the project. The foundation's mission is to enhance knowledge on chemicals within the value chain of paper production and its objective is to become the knowledge centre of chemical usage in practice through the creation, collection and distribution of knowledge. It intends to improve the sustainability of paper production through innovation. The primary group on which the foundation focuses are paper production employees whose work directly or indirectly involves chemicals. The foundation actively involves paper-makers, chemical suppliers, machine builders, cleaning and maintenance organisations in its activities.

Sustainability within paper production

Since the 1960s, sustainability has been an important issue for paper production in the Netherlands. Due to a lack of raw materials and increasing demand for paper, the paper industry needed to search for more sustainable methods and materials. As indicated before, waste paper has become an essential raw material within paper production. In 2000, 75% of raw materials consisted of waste paper. In addition, wood fibres are increasingly sourced from sustainably managed forests. Together, the use of waste paper and sustainably grown wood provide a constant flow of sustainable materials into the paper production process. Moreover, chemicals are now recycled within the production process and this has reduced the amount of polluting discharges.

However, the sustainability of paper production is not only determined by the environmental dimension. We consider that, at present and within boundaries, the ecological optimum has been reached in paper production. Consequently, any further improvements need to focus on the economic and social aspects of sustainability. Thus, in the Optichem Infonet project, the primary focus is on improving the social aspect of sustainability, especially with regard to chemicals.

Earlier, it was suggested that a lack of integration between the different knowledge domains was a possible cause for problems relating to chemicals use within paper production. Improving the exchange of knowledge might prevent such problems from occurring in the future. Innovating paper production could resolve these knowledge dispersal problems.

One attempt to overcome knowledge dispersal throughout paper production is the aforementioned Optichem platform. This provides a forum for technologists from different paper mills to discuss problems relating to, among other things, chemicals. However, the Optichem platform's reach is limited. Only individuals that work at paper mills participate in the discussions. The platform identified that not all problems that are encountered at a paper mill can be resolved internally. Having recognised its limitations, the Optichem platform initiated the start of the Optichem Infonet project.

The Optichem Infonet project attempts to extend the integration of knowledge domains that are relevant within the context of paper production, using a DSS to realise this integration. On the one hand, the integration of knowledge domains is meant to resolve direct problems surrounding the use of chemicals. On the other, this innovation removes barriers for further improving paper production's sustainability. The next section discusses the business project in which this innovation is realised.

The business project: realising a DSS

Problem statement and cognitive starting points

Currently, employees within paper production do not fully understand chemical interactions. This poses a risk to chemical delivery personnel who may need to rely on paper mill employees for help during unloading: for example, to tell them where to deposit the chemicals. A similar problem relates to cleaners who may not know what chemicals are used in the production process or how they react with water or detergents.

The chemical knowledge domain is therefore a complex one. An obvious solution is to give employees training on chemicals and their dangers. However, this is time-consuming and expensive. Furthermore, the effectiveness of such training is difficult to measure. Another solution is to apply expertise from outside the firm. This solution is also costly and, in many cases, is unlikely to fit the specific context of the company. Therefore, we chose another solution: using ICT to bridge the knowledge gap between the knowledge domain of certain task performers and that of chemicals.

It should be possible to reduce the gap between the chemical and the other domains in paper production using a computer system to store and analyse chemical data and information, and then present it in an understandable way. DSSs have demonstrated their success in bridging knowledge gaps in other situations (Keen and Scott-Morton 1978; Klein and Methlie 1995; Turban, Aronson and Bolloju 2001). We therefore identify the application of a DSS as a solution for the knowledge dispersal problems associated with paper production. The corresponding research question is how to interconnect the chemical domain with the paper production domain using a DSS in order to improve personal safety in paper production.

A DSS aims to support and improve decision-making (Turban *et al.* 2001) by coupling the intellectual resources of individuals with the capabilities of a computer (Keen and Scott-Morton 1978). Figure 12.2 presents the coupling between an individual and a DSS in a two-layered model. The bottom layer is the architecture layer and the top is the application layer. The former is of a technical nature and the latter of a conceptual nature. The coupling of the individual and the DSS application layers takes place through the architecture layer of this model, as indicated by the thick arrow in Figure 12.2.

The DSS application supports the human being during a decision-making process. We use the decision-making model of Simon (1977) with the phases of intelligence (I), design (D) and choice (C), discussed in more detail later. Underlying the decision-making process is the cognitive architecture (Card, Moran and Newell 1983) which demarcates and enables the human problem-solving process. The DSS architecture, on the other hand, underlies the DSS application (Holsapple and Whinston 1996). Similar to the cognitive architecture, the DSS application is associated with and influenced by the characteristics of the architecture. For the design and construction of a DSS, all levels and both the individual's and DSS's sides of Figure 12.2 must be taken into account.

The terms 'decision-making', 'planning' and 'problem-solving' are often used interchangeably to denote human cognitive activity (Turban *et al.* 2001). Wilson and Keil (1999: 220) define decision-making as 'the process of choosing a preferred option or course of action from among a set of alternatives'. Problem-solving is explained as the transformation of an encountered state of affairs into a situation that is desired. Plan-

170 SUSTAINABLE INNOVATION

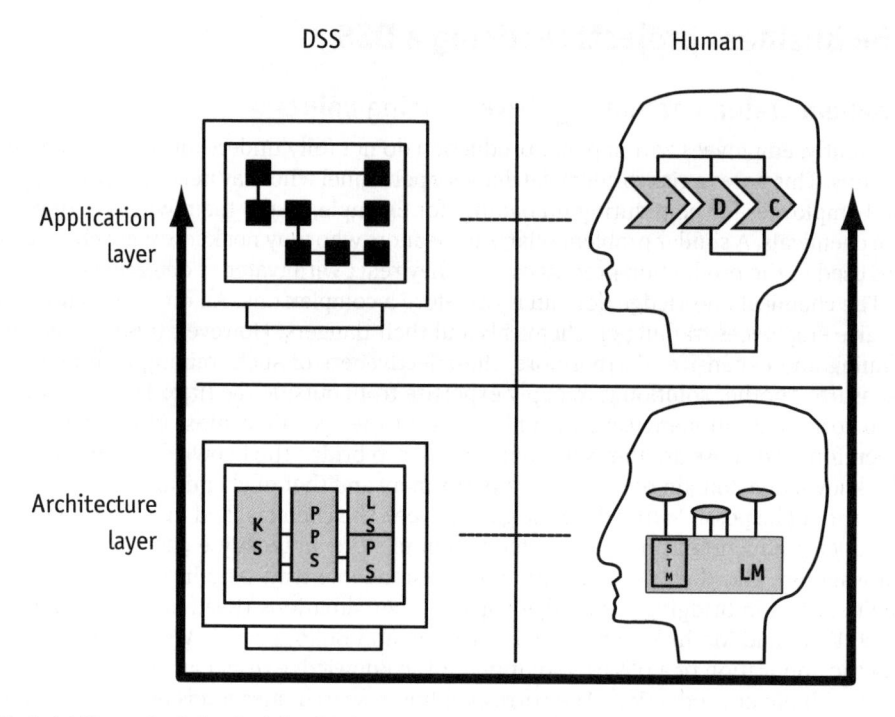

Key: I = intelligence; D = design; C = choice; LM = long-term memory; STM = short-term memory

FIGURE 12.2 Cognitive versus decision-support system architecture

ning concerns 'the process of generating representations of future behaviour, prior to the use of such plans to constrain or control that behaviour' (Wilson and Keil 1999: 652).

Despite the different definitions, we argue that the processes of decision-making, planning and problem-solving are varieties of one underlying generic process. All the processes mentioned centre on the notion of **problem**. A problem is the perceived difference between the current situation and a desired situation (Newell and Simon 1972: 72). Starting with a problem, the processes of decision-making, planning and problem-solving are explained as the construction of a representation of the problem, the plotting of multiple approaches to overcome it and, finally, selecting the approach to which the individual commits his or her actions. Because of the existence of this generic underlying process, we treat the concepts of decision-making, planning and problem-solving as similar. For clarity, the term 'decision-making' is used in this research.

Simon (1977) constructed a model of the decision-making process identifying three phases (see Fig. 12.3):[1]

---

1 Simon's decision-making model is one of many models about decision-making (e.g. Andriole and Adelman 1995; Jorna 2001b; Turban *et al.* 2001), but according to Turban *et al.* (2001: 41): 'Simon's model is the most concise and yet complete characterisation of rational decision-making.'

1. Intelligence phase (I)
2. Design phase (D)
3. Choice phase (C)

In the intelligence phase, the problem is formulated. Data and information are gathered and problems are identified, classified and assigned to problem holders. A mental model of the situation is created whereby interpretation and meaning assignment are important processes (Jorna 2001b). The mental model the individual constructs is generally referred to as the **problem space** (Newell and Simon 1972; Simon 1977). In the design phase dimensions, variables, parameters and alternatives are found using models and criteria based on the information gathered and organised in the intelligence phase. In addition, probabilities and chances of occurrence are calculated in this phase. In the choice phase, one of the alternatives is selected. In addition, the implementation and realisation of alternatives are taken into account.

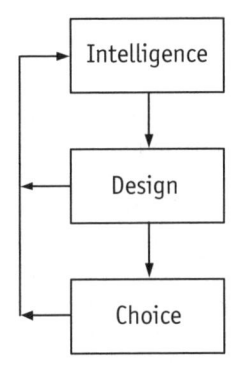

FIGURE 12.3 Simon's model of human decision-making

Source: Simon 1977

Simon's (1977) decision-making model is iterative. It is very likely that an individual needs more information when new (unforeseen) problems are discovered during the design phase, resulting in a new intelligence phase. The same is true for the choice phase. Another important characteristic of this model is the **decomposition of problems**. Complex problems are decomposed into a set of subproblems. Problem decomposition stops when the decision-maker encounters a subproblem he or she is able to solve immediately. The decision-making model is the same for these subproblems.

The DSS supports parts of the human decision-making process. Hence, the decision-making model of the DSS should mimic the parts that it intends to support (see Fig. 12.2). However, DSSs and human beings have different architectures. To fit the DSS application to the human decision-making process, an understanding of the cognitive architecture is required.

Card et al. (1983) made a simplified model of the cognitive architecture (the model human processor [MHP]; see Fig. 12.4) based on the human information-processing system of Newell and Simon (1972). Originating from the context of human–computer interaction, the model shows only relevant parts of the human in the interaction.

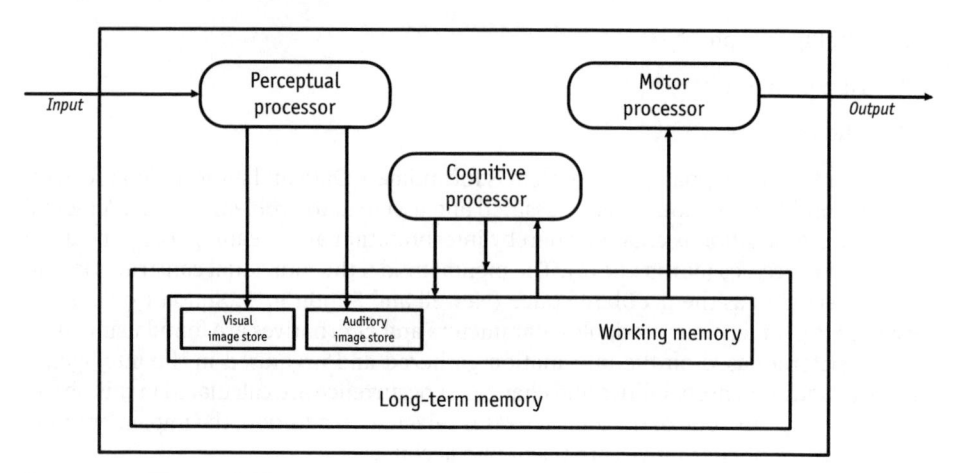

FIGURE 12.4 The model human processor
Source: Card, Moran and Newell 1983

Hence, the only human inputs of the MHP are visual and auditory senses. Similar reasons limit the MHP outputs to the hands and mouth. Meyer and Kieras (1997a, 1997b) and Wilson and Keil (1999) provide a more extensive model incorporating other senses.

The MHP (see Fig. 12.4) consists of three related subsystems. Each subsystem has its own processor. First, the perceptual system consists of sensors and buffers to store the raw signals of the sensors. The perceptual processor encodes the raw signals from the sensors and stores it into the visual or auditory image store. Second, the cognitive system stores the symbolically coded information from visual and auditory image buffers into working memory. Working memory is described as short-term memory and has a limited capacity. The cognitive system uses information from long-term memory in combination with information of working memory during the decision-making process. The cognitive processor plays a central role in this process. Lastly, the motor system and motor processor transform the outcome of a decision into physical behaviour by means of hand movements or speech. The **recognise–act** principle is the basic procedure of cognitive processing (Card *et al.* 1983: 41).

> On each cycle, the contents of working memory initiate associatively-linked actions in long-term memory ('recognise') which in turn modify the contents of working memory ('act') . . . Plans, procedures and other forms of extended organised behaviour are built up out of an organised set of recognise–act cycles.

However, what happens if no recognition takes place? Then, an individual cannot act in response to the situation by retrieving and constructing a plan or certain behaviour from memory. In other words, one lacks the knowledge to act. This is an important situation for a DSS and its user. A DSS aims to fill up this knowledge gap, enabling a user to act. Furthermore, there is a second consequence associated with the recognise–act principle related to learning theory.

We define the learning process in terms of the constructivist's view of learning: in order to learn, an individual has to incrementally and actively assimilate and accommodate knowledge (Rajlich 2003; Savery and Duffy 2001; von Glaserveld 1989). The process of assimilation denotes that learners process new facts and fit them into the existing knowledge in the form of schemata. The construction of schemata consists of three parts (von Glaserveld 1989: 127):

- Recognition of a certain situation ('recognise')
- Association of a specific activity ('act') within the situation
- Expectation of a certain result

When the expectation has not been met (resulting in the generation of a **perturbation**, a condition for cognitive change), the learner has to reorganise ('act') his or her existing knowledge so that new schemata can be constructed. This process is called **accommodation** (Rajlich 2003; von Glaserveld 1989). It is clear that, from a constructivist perspective, prior knowledge is an important factor in the learning process. Besides, there is ample evidence for this statement in literature from other fields (Beier and Ackerman 2005; Greene 1995; Hinds, Patterson and Pfeffer 2001). When information and facts from a DSS (after several accommodation trials) still fit imperfectly into a user's prior knowledge, the user modifies the facts to make them fit. However, when the difference between the individual's prior knowledge and the information provided by the DSS is too large, no assimilation or accommodation will take place at all (i.e. all the new facts are rejected; this is formally exemplified in Valiant's (1984) **theory of the learnable**). When a user rejects or improperly modifies information, no effective decision support can take place because critical information is altered incorrectly or ignored.

What is mentioned above is especially important for a DSS that aims to offer knowledge crossover between different knowledge domains. We define knowledge crossover as mapping two knowledge domains whereby a person is familiar with one domain and unfamiliar with the other. Here, it is insufficient to offer solely chemical expertise via a DSS because the users (from paper production) lack the knowledge to process the information properly. To bridge two different knowledge domains the DSS design should incorporate features that enhance the processes of accommodation and assimilation. This has consequences for knowledge elicitation and the human–computer interface.

Knowledge elicitation

All data and rules in a DSS are elicited from chemical and safety experts. Important choices are made with respect to what information is taken into account in the assessment of the safety risks and the associated countermeasures. Yet another important aspect regarding the focus on knowledge crossover is the involvement of practitioners. These individuals are engaged in day-to-day decision-making in a particular domain (Schreiber et al. 1999). We assume that knowledge from a practitioner can enhance knowledge crossover because they are able to link explicitly the (same) knowledge domain from field A to application B.

Practitioners are those employees with exposure to and experience in the domain. However, they master the concepts and theories in the domain to a lesser extent (Hinds et al. 2001). Research by Hinds et al. (2001) showed that novice task performers instructed by practitioners performed better in the execution of a new task than novice task performers instructed by experts. In comparison to experts, practitioners use more concrete statements and basic concepts during instruction (instead of abstract statements and advanced concepts). In contrast, instructions by experts lead to better results when the learned task was slightly changed. Hence, the abstract statements and advanced concepts provided by experts were more generally applicable. We expect that the combination of the two will contribute to knowledge crossover.

The human–computer interface

Structuring is about how organised, how much, what kind of and in what form information should be presented to the user. Should a DSS offer only a minimal information structure needed for a specific situation or should it offer a broader view of the situation at hand. The human–computer interface is about how all the information is presented.

The structure trade-offs can be described by four principles extracted from instructional hypertext theory (Fastrez 2001, 2002). The four principles are opposed two by two: the rationality versus functionality dimension and the simplicity versus deliberate complexity dimension. We discuss both, starting with rationality versus functionality.

Functional structures can be described in two ways (Fastrez 2002: 12):

> [First], functional structure is the type of structure that is specific to the organisation of knowledge in memory [and, second,] the term 'functional knowledge' describes the knowledge activated by an individual in a specific context.

Hence, two important aspects of functional knowledge are that it differs depending on the context and the subject who activates it. The design of a structure suitable for multiple (or an infinite number of) contexts is the ideal situation for knowledge transfer. Therefore, some authors argue that a good structure is not structured functionally but rationally (Tricot and Bastien 1996, as reported in Fastrez 2002). A rational structure is a logical structure, independent from the content of the document and from the context in which the knowledge will be used.

We choose a functional structure because a DSS offers task-specific information depending on the context and on the task performer. A rational structure collides with this philosophy behind DSSs. Therefore, a rational structure is not considered in this study.

With a functional structure, task-specific knowledge is presented in an orderly way suitable for optimal task performance. The structure of the DSS should 'mimic that of the task to be achieved, rather than follow a logical classification which is specific to the information' (Fastrez 2002: 13). In this way, task performers using DSS learn through a guided process closely related to concrete tasks from their familiar domain, so minimising learning problems.

The second dimension concerns simplicity versus deliberate complexity. This is about the difference between how the DSS relieves the burden on the user associated with the navigation of complex structures and introduces the user to the complexity of the domain as soon as possible. Deliberate complexity is based on cognitive flexibility theory (CFT) (see Fastrez 2002) whereas, according to Fastrez (2002), again, simplicity is highly related to usability (a term to address the extent to which a computer or DSS is easy and enjoyable to use). We argue that the concept of usability is applicable to both the simple as well as the complex structure; thus, usability is subject to the navigation tool rather than to a specific structure.

According to Norman (1989: 188), design should:

> (1) make it easy to determine what actions are possible at any moment (make use of constraints), (2) make things visible, including the conceptual model of the system, the alternative actions, and the results of actions, (3) make it easy to evaluate the current state of the system and (4) follow natural mappings between intentions and the required actions; between actions and the resulting effect; and between information that is visible and the interpretation of the system state.

The needs of users are incorporated into the design; they should be able to see where they are and what they can do. The DSS should be easy to learn and predictable in how it behaves. The structure of information should be based on usability principles. CFT emphasises the opposite, considering oversimplification as a threat to learning. One of the most important aspects of CFT is the combination of multiple concrete examples and abstract concepts.

We chose to use both the simplicity and the complexity structures as design principles for the DSS's human–computer interface. We performed several tests to determine the most suitable structure with respect to effective decision support and learning. The expected results are discussed later.

We argue that the two structures need different navigation tools. The simplicity approach denotes the extent to which a DSS is simple and easy to use. Furthermore, we couple the functional structure to simple structures. Simple structures need little navigation effort or tools to navigate (Puntambekar, Stylianou and Hübscher 2003). For instance, one can easily follow the paths of a hierarchical structure to find the right information suitable for the task (e.g. a website sitemap). Instead of discussing navigation within simple structures in detail, we argue that 'standard' interface design guidelines cover this appropriately (see, among others, Norman 1989; Wright, Fields and Harrison 2000).

We linked the navigation tool by Puntambekar et al. (2003) to the deliberate complexity principles. Their navigation tool—navigable concept maps—seems suitable for the complexity structure because its foundations lie in constructivism and CFT. The main assumption of Puntambekar et al. (2003: 397) is that 'if navigational aids can be designed to reflect the conceptual structure of the domain, both navigation and learning can be supported'. The concept maps introduced in their COMPASS project (Concept Mapped Project-based Activity Scaffolding System) externalise the relations between concepts so that users can see the interconnections between the concepts and are able to navigate through the concept structure. The theory is based on the strength of visual representations during learning and the importance of presenting a context. Puntambekar et al. (2003) show that navigable concept maps are suitable to provide information from the knowledge domain of physics. Based on their findings, we assume similar results when we apply navigable concept maps for the chemical knowledge domain.

The structure of the domain is presented by fish-eye views (Puntambekar et al. 2003: 401):

> In fish-eye views, concepts that are spatially close . . . to the focus appear bigger than those on the outer (peripheral) levels.

The stronger the relation, the closer they spatially are in the concept map. The maps are constructed together with experts and practitioners. The most important task is to get consensus on how they see the relation strengths between concepts.

Objective and targeted users

The goal of the DSS is to improve the personal safety of employees executing a variety of tasks in paper production by reducing the knowledge gap between the chemical domain and other knowledge domains that are used in their tasks.

Phase one of the Optichem Infonet initiative resulted in a first DSS prototype. This prototype supported the tasks of the dosage unit operator and the dosage unit mechanic. The prototype shows the feasibility of task-specific support (Jorna, Van Engelen and Hadders 2004). The second phase of the project resulted in a new design and corresponding prototype. The new prototype can be seen as the second test and feasibility study for the overall project. We treat only the elements that are relevant for the design of the DSS here. This section discusses the CommonKADS concept level models (Schreiber *et al.* 1999).

The new prototype is meant to provide decision support regarding the tasks of cleaning and unloading. Figure 12.5 shows the different steps of the cleaning task. We chose not to discuss the cleaning task with respect to content because this is context-specific. Instead, we are interested in the preparation of each task with an emphasis on safety. We can distinguish two parties that are involved in the cleaning task. The primary party consists of the team of cleaners and their project manager. The cleaners execute the cleaning tasks; the project manager is responsible for the preparation and overall quality of the cleaning task. The secondary party consists of the production manager of the paper mill who is responsible for the machines and its environment.

The project manager starts a cleaning task with a project preparation. He or she visits the factory site and investigates the task environment together with the local production manager. During this phase, issues associated with chemicals and safety are discussed and documented. After the preparation phase, the actual cleaning task starts with a work briefing and safety briefing of the cleaning team by the project manager. Standard procedures (work instructions) and the documented project preparation are combined here. When the cleaning team has been informed about the task at hand, the project manager secures the targeted machine and its environment, and the cleaning team installs the required detergents, tools and equipment. Before the cleaning team starts cleaning, a last authorisation call from the production manager is needed. Depending on the situation, the cleaning task is performed mechanically or chemically. Inspection takes place during the actual cleaning of the machine and afterwards. When all equipment has been put away safely, responsibility regarding the machine is reassigned to the production manager.

The unloading task refers to the unloading of a truck by its driver into some storage facility. With respect to the unloading task, we can again distinguish two parties. The primary party consists of the truck driver and the secondary party is the responsible employee of the paper mill. The truck driver is responsible for the transport of the

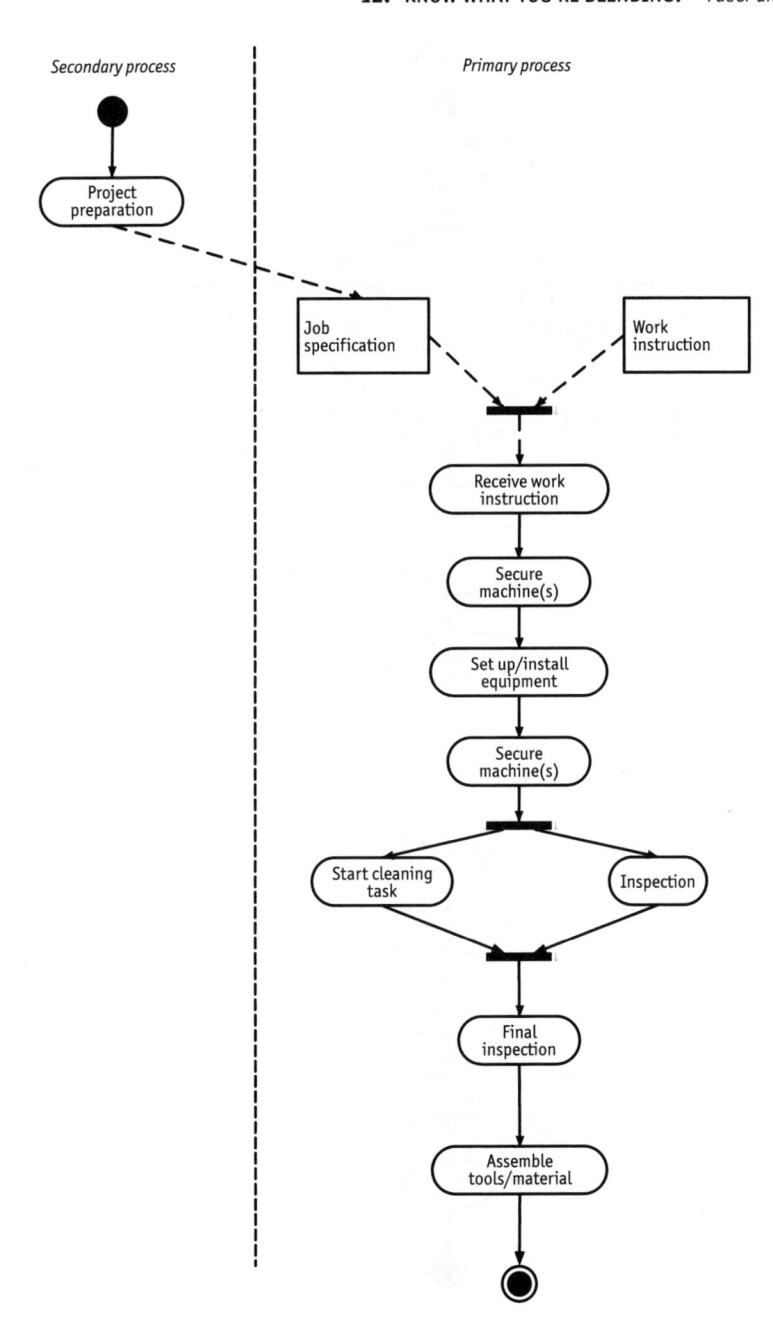

FIGURE 12.5 Activity diagram: cleaning task

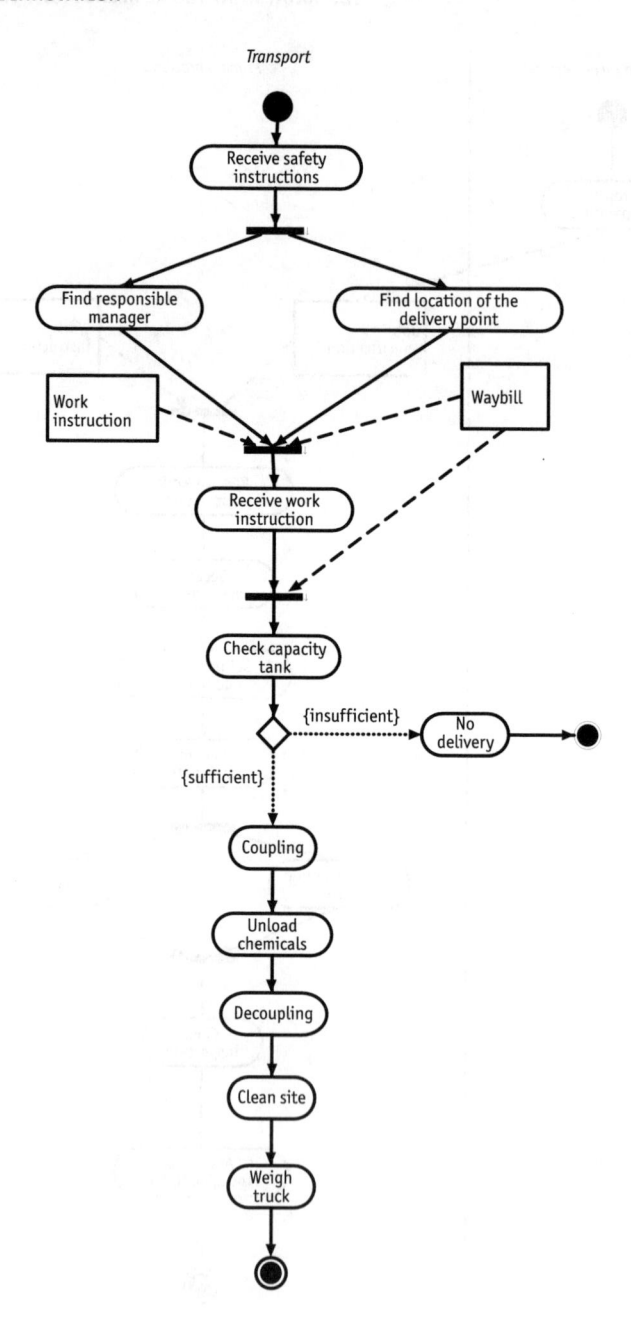

FIGURE 12.6 Activity diagram: unloading task

chemical load and the truck, with responsibility for the load ending at the coupling point where it is transferred to the mill employee.

Figure 12.6 shows the decomposition of the unloading task of the transport agency. Having received local safety instructions, the driver has to find the corresponding site manager for the delivery of the chemicals as well the proper location for delivery. There are usually multiple delivery locations at a paper mill. When at the right location, the driver receives local work instructions and checks whether the capacity of the storage tank corresponds with the truck load. When the storage tank capacity is insufficient, no delivery takes place. After the capacity check, the truck is coupled to the proper coupling point and the unloading of chemicals starts. When the tank truck is empty the truck decouples from the coupling point and both driver and local personnel clean the delivery site with water. The last action is the weighing of the truck, to check whether the right amount of chemicals has been delivered.

Method/methodology

Design

The design and implementation of knowledge-oriented DSS is covered by the field of knowledge engineering. The Optichem Infonet project uses the CommonKADS methodology (Schreiber *et al.* 1999). This is a methodology for knowledge design and knowledge engineering. CommonKADS is an extension of the KADS methodology (e.g. Tansley and Hayball 1993). KADS stands for Knowledge Acquisition and Documentation System.

CommonKADS is developed as a method for the design and implementation of knowledge systems that supports people executing their tasks within organisations. To achieve this, it distinguishes agents, processes and knowledge elements. Agents can be either humans or intelligent machines. Knowledge elements are elementary parts of a knowledge domain. CommonKADS defines a knowledge domain as a set of knowledge elements that is necessary to execute a certain task (Schreiber *et al.* 1999: 22). Agents possess the knowledge elements, but one agent does not necessarily possesses all the knowledge elements of one knowledge domain. Finally, CommonKADS assumes that knowledge elements comprising one knowledge domain can be distributed among multiple agents.

The CommonKADS methodology distinguishes three levels of design: the context, the concept and the artefact level. At context modelling level organisation, task and agent models describe the context in which the targeted DSS will function. The organisation model describes important characteristics of the organisation. The task model presents different tasks within the organisational process for which decision support is created. The agent model describes the agents involved in these tasks.

The concept level of the design consists of two models: the knowledge model and the communication model. The knowledge model shows all concepts and their relationships that are relevant within the knowledge domain under investigation. The unified modelling language[2] is used to represent the knowledge model. Because multiple agents can perform a specific task, the communication model describes how these

---

2 www.uml.org, accessed 13 June 2003.

agents communicate. Both knowledge and communication model are independent of the computer platform that is used for implementation.

Based on the context and concept level models, the translation into the actual DSS is made at the artefact level of design. Context and concept level models express the specifications that the DSS has to meet. Hardware and software choices are subsequently expressed in the design model. The DSS is constructed when final choices are specified within the design model.

Testing protocol

Currently, the development of the DSS is in progress. Therefore, we report the test protocol we intend to use for testing the two human–computer interfaces A and B of the DSS. Following Robson (2002) we use a mixed design. In the first test, we consider only employees from the transport agency. We use a random sample of 20 employees who are involved in the unloading task at different paper mills. The sample is randomly divided into two groups.

All participants are instructed to assess their personal safety, using the DSS, concerning a predefined work context in which they presumably will execute their unloading task. Beforehand, the DSS is initialised with a limited set of characteristics of this work context. For this, experts are asked to specify which factors are of relevance regarding the personal safety of the participants. This concerns information regarding safety in relation to chemicals that are present in the work context. In order to assess their personal safety within the work context, participants first need to collect information regarding their safety. Second, they need to retrieve information concerning the precautions they can take before entering the work context.

Subsequently, group 1 is asked to use the human–computer interfaces A and B. To control for order effects, group 2 uses the human–computer interfaces in the order B and A. Next to controlling for order effects, a mixed design also enables us to gather between subjects data and repeated measures data (Robson 2002: 131).

The time a participant spends retrieving the information is recorded. A maximum of 10 minutes is spent. After using a human–computer interface, participants are asked to fill out the Dutch version of the Software Usability Measurement Inventory (SUMI) (Kirakowski 1994). The SUMI is used to measure the individual interfaces' usability. Additionally, we record the factors participants are able to retrieve from the DSS that relate to their personal safety while using the specific human–computer interface. After receiving both interventions, a participant is asked to specify his or her experiences regarding both human–computer interfaces, expressing their strong and weak points and indicating which interface best serves the purpose of providing decision support regarding their task. For this we used a structured interview.

Results of testing the DSS

The design

This section consists of two parts. First, we deal with the knowledge and communication models and, second, the implementation model is addressed. We classify both tasks as 'assessment' tasks. The assessment task template's objective is to categorise a specific situation based on a set of domain-specific norms (Schreiber *et al.* 1999). The inference structure of the safety assessment is shown in Figure 12.7.

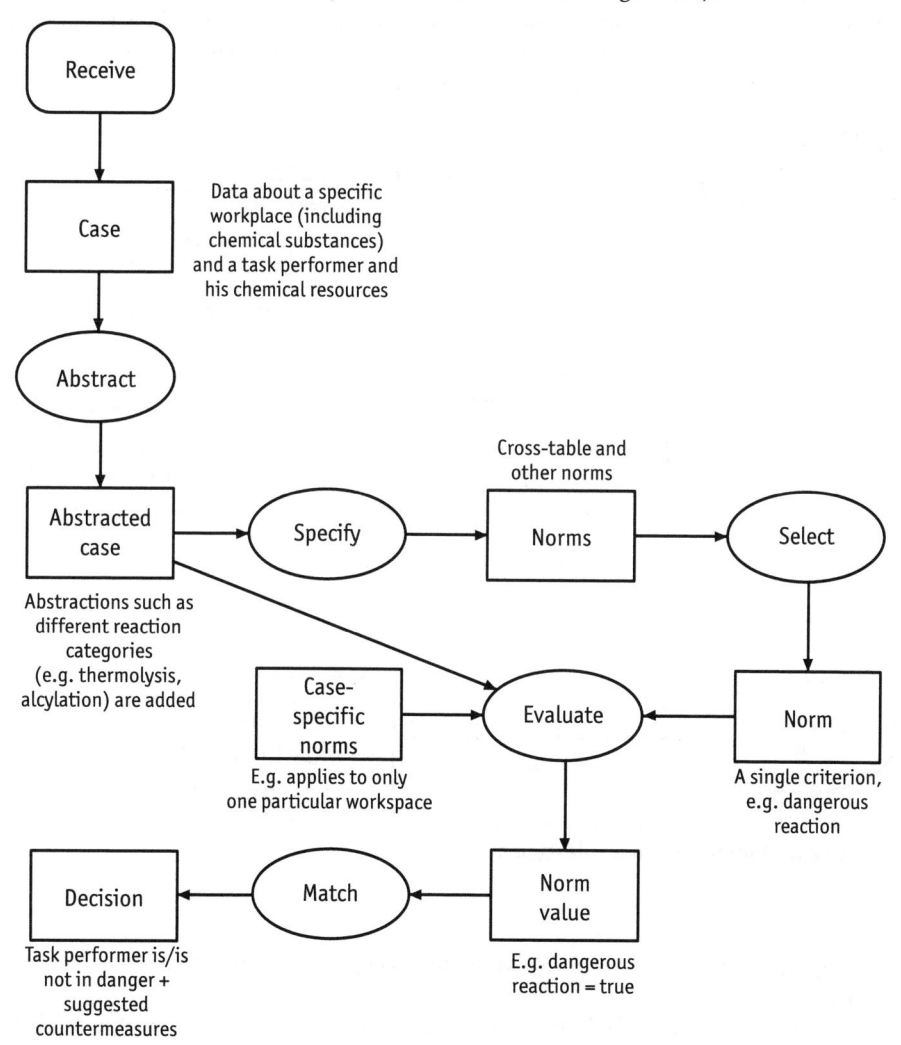

FIGURE 12.7 Inference structure cleaning and unloading tasks

182 SUSTAINABLE INNOVATION

The system receives data about the task performer and the task to be performed (i.e. information about a cleaner and his cleaning task, or a truck driver and his unloading task). Together with data from the system about the workplace (for instance, a dosage unit or a delivery site) they form a case. To work with the case, some data need to be abstracted. For example, the temperature of a machine needs to be categorised in classes to assess reaction specifications. Specific norms are used to make an assessment: for example, 'correct cleaning method' or 'reactions between chemical substances' (with a chemical cross-table). First, the norms should be specified and then selected for evaluation with case data. Every workplace has some situation-specific norms which are also used to evaluate the case data. A set of norm values is matched after the evaluation to make a decision regarding countermeasures to prevent accidents. A part of the domain schema is shown in Figure 12.8.

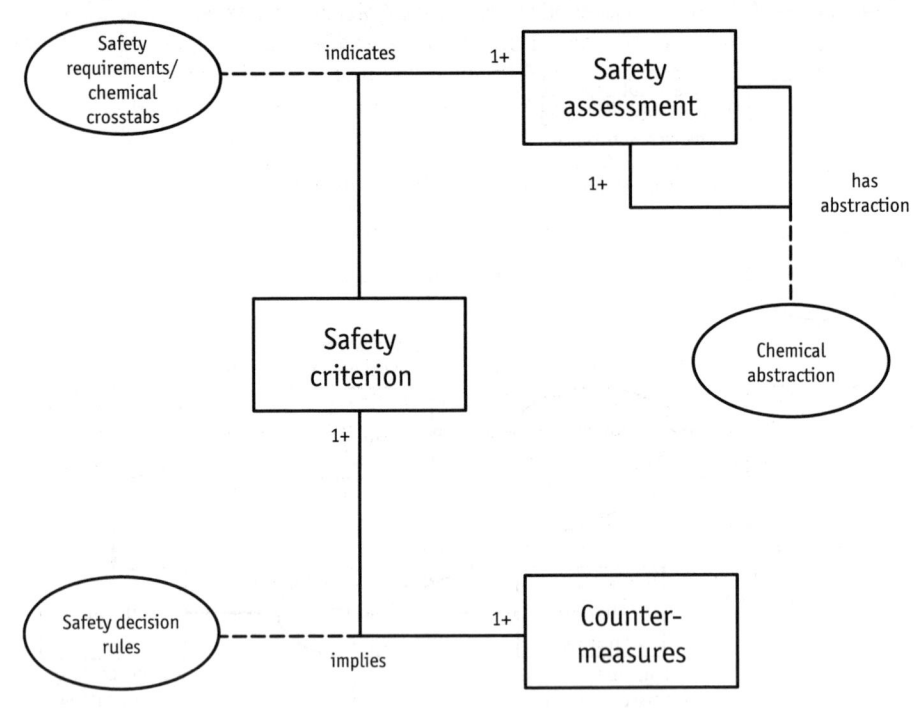

FIGURE 12.8 Domain schema rule-types

A simplification of the two central domain concepts in the safety assessment is represented in Figure 12.9.

Both concepts are specified with a set of attributes. For clarity, we suppressed the attribute types. A workplace is situated in a factory, and houses machines and chemical substances. A machine can be a dosage unit or a coupling point for unloading chemicals. A workplace also has a location at a factory site. Lastly, a workplace has a number of safety regulations, often captured in work safety documents. A task performer

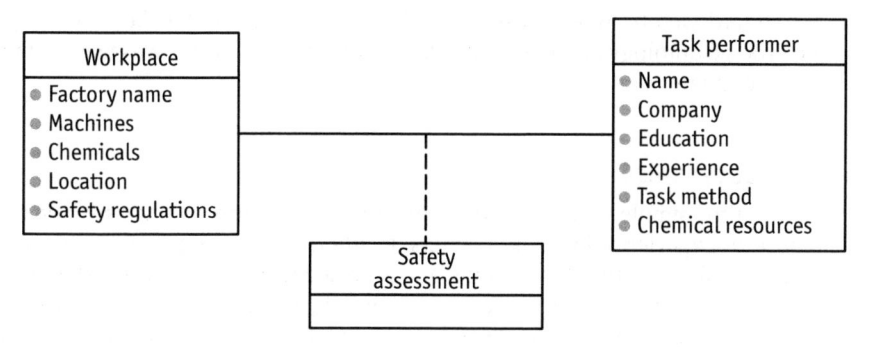

FIGURE 12.9 Domain schema concepts

has a certain level of experience and education. Next to that, he or she follows a certain task method and uses certain chemical resources to accomplish a task.

Looking at the safety criterion we can make a subtype hierarchy. 'Safety criterion' is the supertype and its subtypes are 'correct cleaning method', 'reactions between chemicals', 'reactions between chemical substances and machine parts', 'reactions between chemical substances and the human body', 'workplace-specific constraints' and so on. A similar hierarchy is used to model countermeasures. For example, 'personal protection countermeasures', 'securing machine', 'fire precautions', 'environmental constraints', etc.

The communication model for this prototype is simple; there is only one transfer function in the knowledge model. A transfer function is a function that transfers an information item between the DSS and the outside world (Schreiber *et al.* 1999). The 'receive' transfer function is used at the start of the inference structure. At this point, the task performer has to supply the system with data and information about his task and his workplace.[3] When the system has received all required data, no further interactions between user and DSS take place; only the final results are displayed.

Concerning prototype implementation, we chose a functional structure regarding the human–computer interface. We will vary on the simplicity versus complexity dimension to determine a suitable structure for decision support and learning. We have chosen to build the simple structure using a simple navigation structure and the complexity structure using fish-eye views from the navigable concept maps concept.

The prototype

A web-based, three-tier (a database logic, business logic and presentation logic layer) DSS prototype is used. A Microsoft Access database implements the database logic layer.[4] An Algernon rule-base[5] that controls database access combined with a Tomcat JavaServer page server[6] form the prototype's business logic and presentation logic

3 This depends on whether all data about the workspace are already captured in the system or not.
4 office.microsoft.com/en-us/FX010857911033.aspx, accessed 2 September 2004.
5 algernon-j.sourceforge.net, accessed 2 September 2004.
6 jakarta.apache.org/tomcat/index.html, accessed 2 September 2004.

layer. A standard web browser is used as a client. The database has been developed using the Protégé ontology and knowledge base editor.[7] A text editor was used to build the JavaServer pages.

Expected test results

We expect that the simple structure is the most suitable structure for task-specific decision support for experienced task performers. Furthermore, we expect that this structure is not a suitable solution for learning and knowledge crossover for inexperienced task performers (i.e. those with little experience in, or exposure to, the chemical domain). To learn the complex chemical domain, inexperienced task performers need more information about the concepts than shown in the simplicity structure. They need explicit links between concrete and simple cases from their familiar domain, and more abstract and advanced concepts from the unfamiliar chemical domain. Therefore, we expect that results of the tests will show differences between experienced and inexperienced task performers in relation to the tested human–computer interfaces.

The relation of this DSS project with innovation and sustainability

We want to come back to the main theme of this book with regard to innovation and sustainability. The current dispersion of knowledge within the value chain of paper production is classified as a barrier to the improvement of the industry's sustainability. A thriftier use of chemicals and improving personal safety are proving challenging. This is especially the case when we consider the disconnectedness of the different knowledge domains within the sector.

The innovation realised by the Optichem Infonet project brought together different knowledge domains relating to paper production. The DSS realises this innovation. It is important to note that this is not a technological innovation but, rather, a knowledge or an organisational innovation. The DSS provides task-specific support to individuals performing their tasks within the paper production process, such that an improvement of in sustainability occurs. The primary aim is to increase personal safety surrounding the handling of chemicals. A reduction in the use of chemicals is the secondary aim.

Because problems relating to paper production originate from the level of the involved industries, the Optichem Infonet project targets the entire value chain of paper production. These problems concern a lack of organisation and knowledge exchange. The parties involved are individual parties from separated industries. For instance, paper mills produce only paper. Chemical suppliers produce chemicals. Machine builders build and install machines within multiple production process and differently each time. The earlier discussed problems show that the co-ordination of activities, machines and chemicals relating to paper production falls short.

7   protege.stanford.edu, accessed 2 September 2004.

From a sustainability perspective, lack of co-ordination and knowledge exchange shows issues of undesired devolvement in a variety of ways. Lack of knowledge concerning effects of certain chemicals causes unnecessary pollution. Carelessness or thoughtlessness regarding chemicals leads to material damage or personal injury. These examples show that lack of co-ordination and knowledge exchange have effects at the societal as well as the individual level. Additionally, Dutch environmental and labour legislation attribute liability to paper mills. Furthermore, an individual cannot resolve organisational devolvement (i.e. 'offload') because its origin lies at the industry level.

The Optichem Infonet project identifies current knowledge exchange and co-ordination as problems standing in the way of a further improvement in the sustainability of the paper industry. Paper production is characterised by a wide variety of parties residing in separate industries, and hardly exchanging knowledge. The Optichem Infonet project strongly focuses on the knowledge exchange necessary for a more sustainable paper industry (i.e. KoS).

The chosen solution of a DSS can also be perceived as an instrument that fits a knowledge management strategy. This DSS realises the desired co-ordination and knowledge exchange. In addition, a storage facility is created that contains KoS for the paper industry. Embedding the DSS within the Optichem Infonet foundation ensures its long-term use. Both the technical realisation of the DSS and the organisational embedding guarantee the sustainability of the collected knowledge.

Conclusions

The next step in improving the paper industry's sustainability concerns its social aspect (the people dimension). Until now, this industry mainly focused on the environmental aspect (the planet dimension). However, these initiatives did not entirely cover the idea of sustainability. Improving the paper industry's sustainability also has implications for the use of chemicals. This is true for the handling of chemicals as well as for the quantity of chemicals used.

Improving the sustainability of the paper industry is highly complex because of the number of parties involved in paper production and the multiplicity of knowledge domains that need to come together. In addition, no structure exists to control communication between the parties. Furthermore, the paper industry lacks the instruments to bring together the different knowledge domains. The integration of knowledge domains is necessary to realise the intended improvement of the industry's sustainability, and to enable communication between the parties involved.

The DSS that the Optichem Infonet project implements is an attempt to resolve some of the problems obstructing the industry's transition to a more sustainable future. This DSS intends to integrate different knowledge domains. The system unites knowledge domains and translates these into a task-specific landscape that different users are able to understand, by providing them with task-specific safety information about chemicals.

The first prototype showed that it is possible to capture and incorporate different knowledge domains that are involved within paper production into a functional artefact (i.e. a DSS). The second prototype provides an indication of how the system's design can be altered to bridge the gap between different knowledge domains.

Recommendations

Using a DSS for the use of chemicals within paper production is not the end but, rather, the next step towards a sustainable paper industry. As a technical solution, a DSS always targets a specific problem that exists at a specific moment. Furthermore, and as explained elsewhere in this book (see Chapters 3, 22 and 23), sustainability does not denote a final situation. Instead, it expresses a process of identifying problems. From a sustainability perspective, problems are perceived from an ecological, a social and an economic point of view. Finally, we do not claim to have captured the paper industry's entire domain within the models presented here. However, we have shown that it is possible to model different knowledge domains, to translate these into a technical tool and to bridge gaps between different knowledge domains within a DSS.

13
Philips and the long road towards social sustainability

Floortje Smit and Niels R. Faber

In the field of social sustainability, Philips is still developing new ideas. As well as measuring the extent to which its products are environmentally friendly (the 'planet' dimension of sustainability), Philips also wants to measure social sustainability (the 'people' dimension) on the product level. An initial research study has determined those who play a role in social sustainability. In a second research study, assessment criteria have been established to measure social sustainability on the product innovation level.

The founders of Royal Philips Electronics Ltd, Anton and Gerard Philips, advocated a socially oriented company. From its establishment in 1891 care for the employee as well as the local community has been given a prominent place in the management of the business. And it was participation in the Club of Rome in 1970 that initiated the company's proactive approach to environmental management. Since then, the company has sought to play a leading role in the field of sustainable development. This chapter will describe two preliminary studies conducted at the request of NIDO and Philips[1] to examine what is possible in the area of the social sustainability of products (we use the term **social sustainability** to refer to the people dimension of the sustainability concept). The data and results referred to here are taken from the reports of the research study (Asper *et al.* 2003; Hermans *et al.* 2003).

In addition to the economic aspects (the 'profit' dimension of sustainability), Philips takes full account of a number of environmental aspects in developmental and realisation trajectories, expressed in its five Green Focal Areas. However, there is as yet no structured approach that incorporates the social consequences of the company's products. Indeed, one could ask whether this is necessarily desirable, given the complexity

1   With due thanks to Dr Chris Sherwin.

and qualitative nature of such an approach. In this respect the social aspects of product manufacturing have to be separated from the consequences of the intrinsic aspects of the product. With regard to the production process, Philips has a strong tradition of social responsibility. As it is, increasingly, manufacturing fewer products itself, the company is now spreading this tradition to its supply chain. Suppliers have to meet a minimum number of obligations in the fields of the environment, human rights, working conditions and ethical behaviour.

One reason to subject the social consequences of their products to further research is partly fostered by the company's innovative character. Apart from being a responsible organisation, Philips wants to be a company that, through innovation, improves the quality of life of its employees and that of society more generally, so strengthening its contribution to sustainable development. As far as the company is concerned these two aspects co-exist very well, and can perhaps be used to tap new markets or business models.

Within the framework of this basic idea, two research studies were conducted. In the first, an inventory was made of Philips' 'stakeholders'—all those who are directly or indirectly involved in the company or its products. In addition, representatives of one particular group—consumers—were asked to identify what was, in their view, the most important aspect of social sustainability. In the second study, an initial list of indicators was drawn up, enabling Philips to measure its progress in the field of social sustainability.

Philips plans to use the findings from these two studies to focus further on two key areas:

- How to deal with the specific social aspect of 'a sustainable product'
- To what extent can this aspect be integrated into the development and realisation trajectory of its product portfolio?

The Philips organisation

Royal Philips Electronics' philosophy is summarised in the slogan 'Let's make things better'. Here, 'better' not only refers to the various products, systems and services but also to quality of life issues.[2] This is also implicitly formulated in the company's new slogan 'Sense and Simplicity'. It is considered important that everyone can benefit from the company's actions and that future generations will not suffer from today's developments.

Since 1891 Philips has grown from a small Dutch enterprise, established with the objective of 'manufacturing electric light bulbs and other electrotechnical devices',[3] to the biggest electronics manufacturer in Europe. With a turnover of €32.3 billion Philips

2 www.philips.nl/InformationCenter/NO/FArticleSummary.asp?lNodeId= 530&channel=530&channelId=N530A1632, accessed 7 May 2004.
3 www.philips.nl/InformationCenter/NO/FArticleSummary.asp?lNodeId= 384&channel=384&channelId=N384A971, accessed 7 May 2004.

is one of the world's top ten electronics companies, employing some 164,500 people in more than 60 countries.[4]

No unambiguous primary process can be identified within Philips. Its core competencies exist within various domains: namely, personal care, healthcare and technology. Its activities are divided into five sectors:

- Consumer electronics
- Lighting
- Personal care and domestic appliances
- Medical systems
- Semiconductors

Philip's home base is in the Netherlands. The head office is in Amsterdam and most product divisions are managed from the Netherlands (consumer electronics from Amsterdam, lighting and semiconductors from Eindhoven and personal care and domestic appliances from Amersfoort). Medical systems has head offices at two locations—Best near Eindhoven and Andover, MA in the US. Philips has research centres in a range of countries, with Philips Research in Eindhoven being one of the largest private research institutes in the world. Out of the 160 plants worldwide 25 are located in the Netherlands.[5]

Philips and sustainability

Sustainability is a theme that suits the culture of Philips. For decades now, economic prosperity, environmental technical quality and social equality have gone hand in hand as far as the company is concerned. It is aware of its responsibility in these three areas. Thirty years ago Philips was one of the first companies to establish procedures to minimise the adverse effects of its activities on the environment and local community. In 1993 these were translated into a company-wide programme called the Environmental Opportunity Programme, later renamed EcoVision.

The objectives of EcoVision, drawn up in 1994, have evolved over the years. EcoVision was one of the first programmes in the framework of Philips' current sustainability policy. In the 1990s the company introduced the principle of **ecodesign**, incorporating environmental aspects right at the start of the design process. This way of designing involves five focal points known as the Green Focal Areas. This means that a designer has to be aware of weight, dangerous substances, energy consumption, waste disposal and packaging. A product receives Green Flagship status when it performs better than earlier Philips' products or similar competitors' products in two or more of these focal areas. Philips observes a growing market interest in its Green Flagship standard.

---

4 www.philips.nl/InformationCenter/NO/FArticleSummary.asp?INodeId= 308&channel=308&channelId=N308A869, accessed 7 May 2004.

5 www.philips.nl/InformationCenter/NO/FArticleSummary.asp?INodeId= 574&channel=574&channelId=N574A1721, accessed 7 May 2004.

To assess the progress of the EcoVision programme on the company at division and business level, the Corporate Sustainability Office (CSO) collects twice-yearly data from the entire organisation by means of a central database. Apart from product innovations, such as ecodesign, this programme stimulates and assesses improvements in the production process, such as better energy, waste and water management.

The CSO advises the board on matters associated with the environment, health, safety and effects on society. The different divisions have similar structures consisting of a sustainability champion in the different management teams and a sustainability support manager who supports the divisions in co-operation with the CSO. In order to advise and support the various divisions in the field of corporate sustainability, Philips has set up the Philips Environmental Services Knowledge Centre (PES). PES has played a crucial role in realising co-operation with NIDO.

Ethics forms an important part, and is the basis, of Philips' sustainability programme. The company is also actively engaged in a dialogue with its stakeholders. The outcome is integrated into the company's business management in a structured way via the quality approach and a programme named BEST (Business Excellence through Speed and Teamwork). In addition, Philips is part of the World Business Council for Sustainable Development (WBCSD), a coalition of 170 international organisations dedicated to sustainable development.[6]

The Philips business project in general

Given Philips' culture and approach, it should not be surprising that NIDO decided to approach the company in connection with the 'people' side of sustainable products. A preliminary research study was carried out by Philips' employees, with additional support from experts within the company and NIDO. The aim of the study was to map out the possibilities pertaining to the social aspects of a sustainable product. This instantly generated two important questions:

- Which groups are affected, directly or indirectly, by the company's activities?
- How may this social aspect be transformed into qualitative and/or quantitative indicator(s)?

The research team was split into two groups. The task of group A was to identify the key stakeholders and determine the best way to start a dialogue with them. Group A also investigated which social sustainability aspects were considered the most important by stakeholders, focusing initially on consumers. Several methods were used to collect this data. Following a literature search, group A gathered information from consumer organisations, via questionnaires, on what consumers see as the most important social aspects of Philips' products. Information was also obtained from focus groups. The focus groups' findings were used to test a different kind of dialogue and to check and compare the results from the questionnaires.

6   www.wbcsd.org, accessed 7 May 2004.

The task of group B was to establish a set of indicators to measure both qualitative and quantitative factors, with the aim of determining whether a product can or cannot be labelled as sustainable. The group first drew up an inventory of existing social indicators used by institutions and companies, and then customised it to apply to the specific situation of Philips.

The projects: approach and execution

Stakeholders (group A)

The first objective of group A was to identify the stakeholder groups involved and investigate their importance. After an extensive literature review it was concluded that four questions were required to identify those involved and determine their position:

- Who are they?
- How interested are they?
- How much influence do they have?
- What do they expect from the company?

A stakeholder is a person or group that represents a particular social or ecological environment and who has rights or interests in the corporation and its activities in the present, past or future.

The literature describes six ways in which those involved can have an interest in an organisation (Freeman and Reed 1983):

- **Material interest:** stakeholders who are dependent on the company for their income. However, an interest can also be non-financial, such as access to healthcare or occupational safety

- **Political interest:** how power and influence are divided. This has a bearing on policy within the organisation; but it is also about the external influences on the organisation (e.g. legislation and government policy) and the way the organisation manipulates or engages with these influences

- **Interest of membership:** a stakeholder belongs to a particular group and asserts the interests of this group. Factors playing a role are, for example, how the organisation fits in with the values and norms of the local community or the degree to which it enables its employees to engage with the local community

- **Interest of being informed:** a stakeholder requires a certain amount of information in order to make decisions. An organisation is judged according to its ability to provide useful information

- **Symbolic interest:** the impression that a stakeholder has of the organisation. Does the organisation behave well? Does it guarantee the safety and well-being of its employees? Does it respect the local community?

- **Spiritual interest:** ethical factors that a stakeholder believes to be important. These are determined by religious and philosophical values, a belief in the divine and a connection with nature

Those involved can exert influence in different ways. Shareholders have voting rights, employees will impact on an organisation's costs and benefits by virtue of their productivity, while campaigning groups will exert pressure via political channels.

In the study of interest and influence, a distinction can be made between those who are actively and those who are passively involved, as discussed in Chapter 7. The former will be intimately involved in the activities of the organisation. As a minimum this group consists of owners, employees, customers[7] and suppliers. The latter is not directly involved in the activities of the organisation, but can exert influence on it or be affected by it. Examples include environmental activists, the media and financial analysts.

Customers will let the organisation know if their expectations are not met. In this case, an organisation is forced to be reactive. It is better, however, to be proactive. Thus, the organisation needs to know its customers' expectations. A dialogue with those involved is therefore essential, and this was at the heart of the second part of group A's remit.

The group wanted to determine the degree to which customers perceived certain social sustainability aspects as important. In co-operation with NIDO, the researchers made use of a combination of questionnaires and focus groups to gather data from consumer organisations in the US, Europe and Asia. The questionnaires were divided into two sections—the first focused on sustainability aspects within the electronics sector while the second dealt with sustainability aspects of electrical and electronic products. Respondents were asked to rate, on a scale of 1 to 5, various aspects of sustainability for these two sections. They were also asked to list what they considered to be the three most important subjects with regard to sustainability.

With regard to Europe, group A wrote to one consumer organisation in six European countries and to two organisations in total specifically aimed at social sustainability. The response rate was 40%. In the US ten of the 22 organisations approached responded (45%) while in Asia 35% of the organisations approached replied.

Using focus groups makes it possible to let the consumer speak for him- or herself, and an open discussion can sometimes lead to new insights. In Europe a focus group of five people was formed. The focus group in the US also consisted of five people. In Asia, four larger focus groups (two in Taiwan with two individuals each; one in Thailand with three individuals; and one in Indonesia with four individuals) were formed because consumer organisations in Asia have less power than those in Europe or the US.

Finally, group A also decided to question Philips employees working in customer services and on sustainability issues. This provided extra insight into the views of Philips consumers and employees.

---

7   Philips uses the term 'consumer'. In this book, however, we use 'customer'. The term includes both consumers (or end users) and buyers. In this way we can cover organisation-to-organisation relations as well as organisation-to-consumer relations.

Indicators (group B)

The second research group (group B) was assigned to establish a set of indicators enabling Philips to focus on social sustainability aspects within the process of product creation. First, the researchers distilled a group of 198 indicators from different sources. They started with established sources such as the Organisation for Economic Co-operation and Development's (OECD)'s Guidelines for Multinational Enterprises,[8] the Global Reporting Initiative (GRI),[9] and the Dow Jones Sustainability Index (DJSI).[10] Next, group B addressed the social indicators used by the top ten electronics companies. Philips also advised the group to look at the top ten European companies on the DJSI and the top ten companies worldwide. The organisations which, according to SustainAbility,[11] produce the best sustainability reports and the European organisations which, according to *Fortune*, are the best employers, were also studied (*Fortune* 2003).

Not all indicators found were of use to Philips. The list was therefore filtered in two steps. The indicators were first divided into three groups. The first group consisted of 25 indicators referring to the products themselves, such as material composition, the product's impact on the customer, innovation and technical composition. The second group of 113 indicators concerned the production process, such as the techniques applied in the manufacturing process, the plant's status with respect to human rights and the way in which the production is organised. The 54 indicators that could be placed under both product and production characteristics formed the third group. With the aid of two experts within Philips these indicators were revisited and subsequently added to the two other categories.

Eventually 26 indicators referring to the product itself remained. The indicators used by most organisations are:

- Suppliers adhere to guidelines (eight companies, including Sony and Ericsson)
- Observing human rights in connection with employees and other parties (five companies, including Sony and Ericsson)
- Satisfaction of customers (five companies, including Sony and Ericsson)
- Suppliers, stakeholders and partners are screened for whether they observe human rights (five companies, including Ericsson)

Applying an amorphous group of 26 indicators was not simple. The researchers therefore focused the indicators on the basis of recommendations made by Sustainable Measures[12] and divided them according to the priorities of the stakeholders involved.

---

8   www.oecd.org/dataoecd/12/21/1903291.pdf, accessed 7 May 2004.
9   www.globalreporting.org/guidelines/archives/2000/June2000GuidelinesA4.pdf, accessed 19 March 2003.
10 www.sustainability-indexes.com/pdf/DJSI_World_Guidebook_40.pdf, accessed 29 April 2003.
11 www.sustainability.com/philosophy/triple-bottom/tbl-intro.asp *and* www.sustainability.com/services/tools-social-kpi.asp, accessed 7 May 2004.
12 Sustainable Measures (2002) Organising indicators, www.sustainablemeasures.com/Indicators/Organize.html, accessed 7 May 2004.

Results and bottlenecks

Stakeholders (group A)

The actively involved who, according to group A, are capable of exerting the most influence on Philips are: trade unions; employees; suppliers; competitive companies; local and national authorities; society; management; customers; and non-governmental organisations (NGOs).

The groups involved tend to fluctuate regarding their composition. In identifying stakeholders it is therefore important not to focus too much on fixed structures.

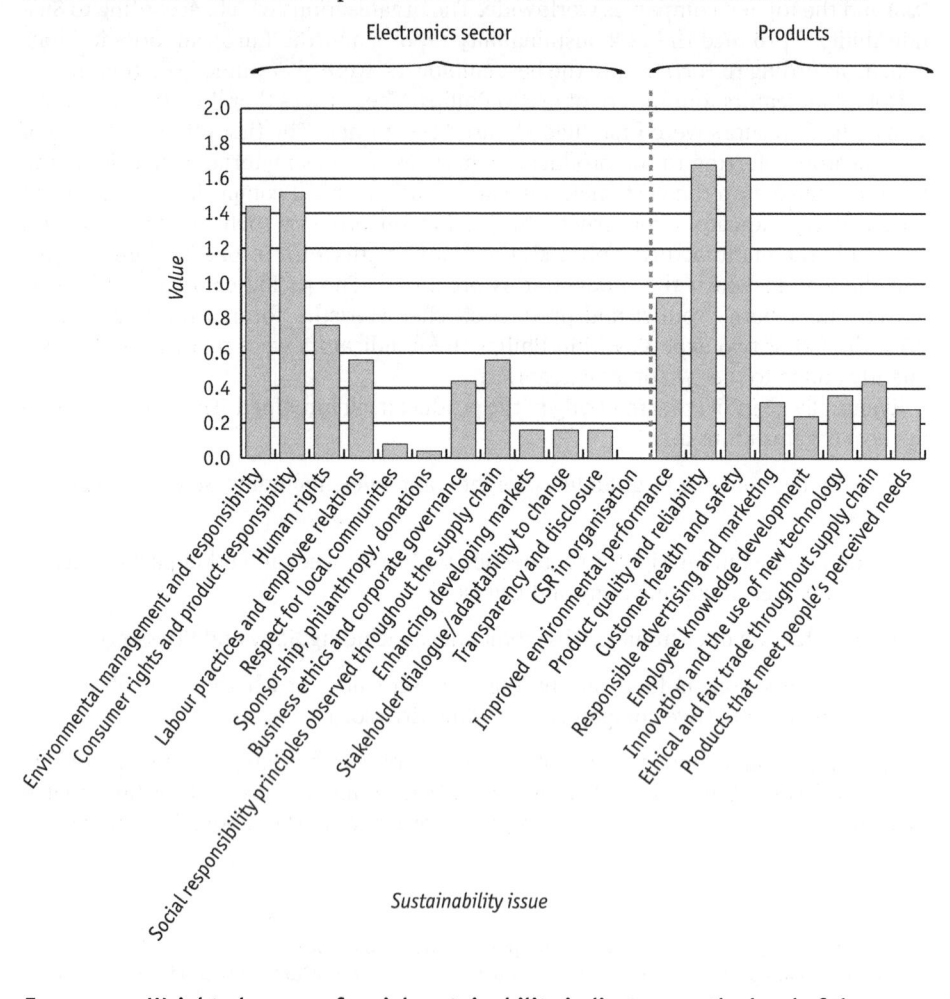

FIGURE 13.1 Weighted scores of social sustainability indicators on the level of the entire electronics sector and its products

Source: Hermans *et al.* 2003

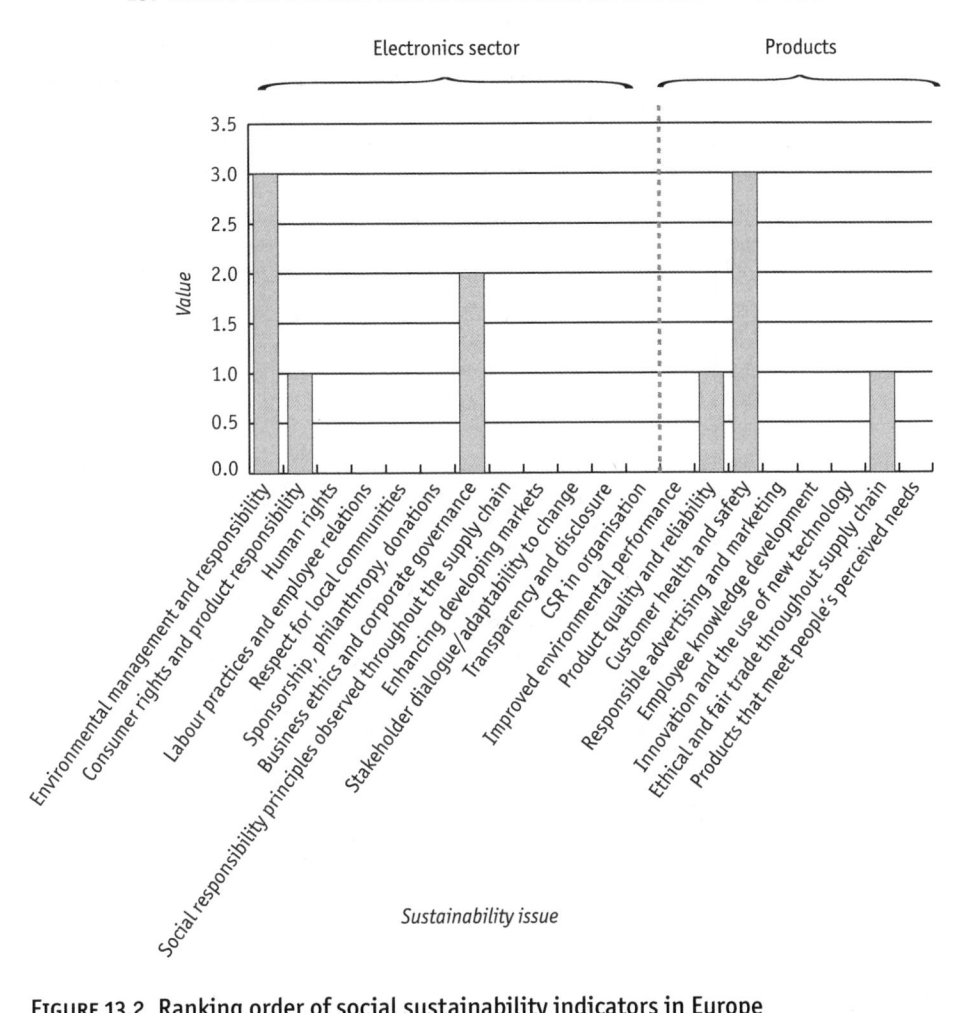

13. **PHILIPS AND THE LONG ROAD TOWARDS SOCIAL SUSTAINABILITY** *Smit and Faber* 195

FIGURE 13.2 **Ranking order of social sustainability indicators in Europe**
Source: Hermans *et al.* 2003

With regard to priorities, after the questionnaires and focus group discussions had been analysed, the researchers came to the conclusion that with respect to each level to be distinguished, there are in fact two matters that all nationalities consider important (see Fig. 13.1). With regard to all the figures shown here, the x axis consists of various sustainability indicators and the y axis indicates the weighted importance given to each indicator by the different stakeholder groups. The first 12 indicators concern the electronics sector; the eight remaining relate to social sustainability at the level of its products. This weighted evaluation is based on the degree of importance and the appointed ranking order of the various sustainability indicators applied within all areas studied. Figure 13.1 shows that, at sector level, consumer rights and product responsibility are initially considered as most important. The second issue on this level concerns the environmental management and the environmental responsibility of organisations

196 SUSTAINABLE INNOVATION

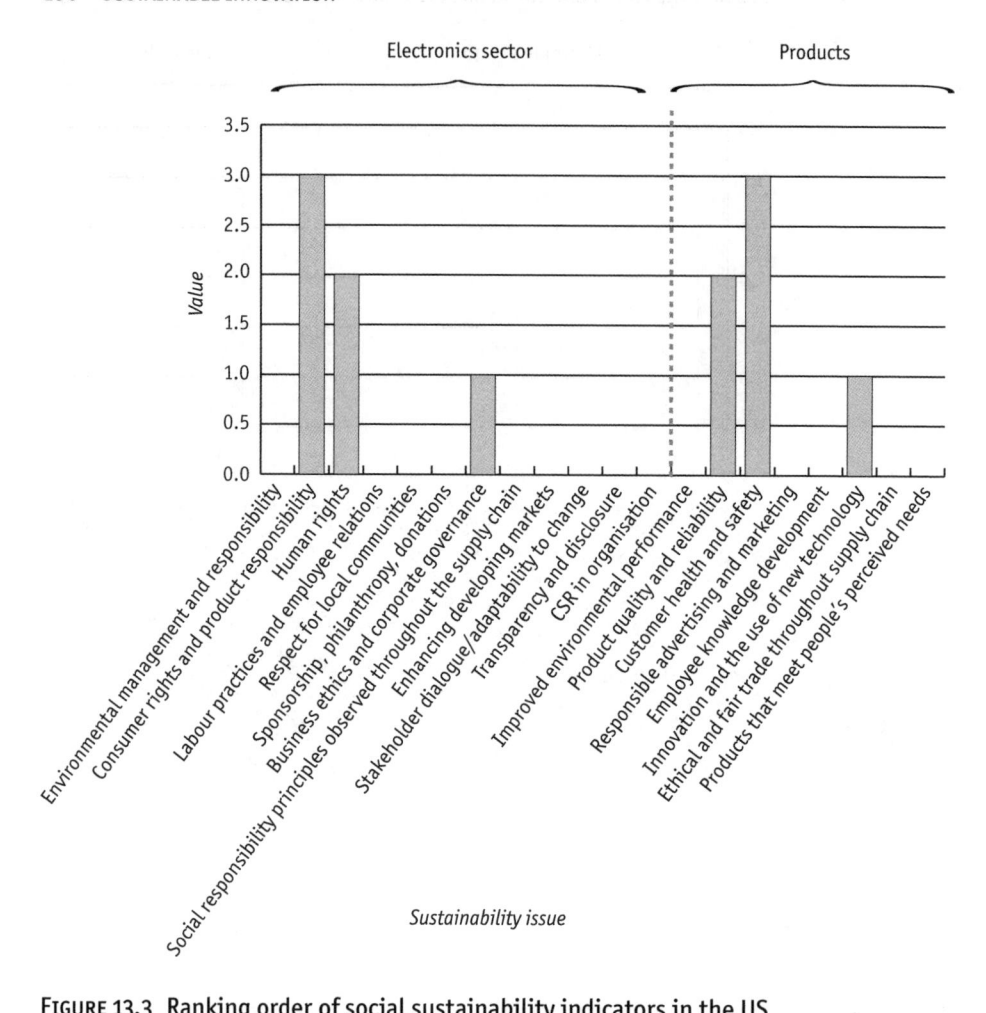

FIGURE 13.3 Ranking order of social sustainability indicators in the US

Source: Hermans et al. 2003

in the electronics sector. On the product level, both the safety and health of the customer and the quality and reliability of the product are regarded as the most important.

As Figures 13.2 and 13.3 show, the way in which the interviewees graded the aspects differed per continent and per research method. We will give only the most relevant outcomes. Further details are provided in Asper et al. (2003) and Hermans et al. (2003). For example, the European focus groups in the electronics sector find transparency and openness the most important whereas the focus groups give priority to customers' rights. With regard to products, the consumers in the focus groups demand quality and reliability. Consumers' safety and health are placed second on the list. The focus groups in the two continents both give equal weighting to customers' health and safety; the big difference is that the US groups give equal weighting to consumer rights and product responsibility (and no rank at all to environmental management and

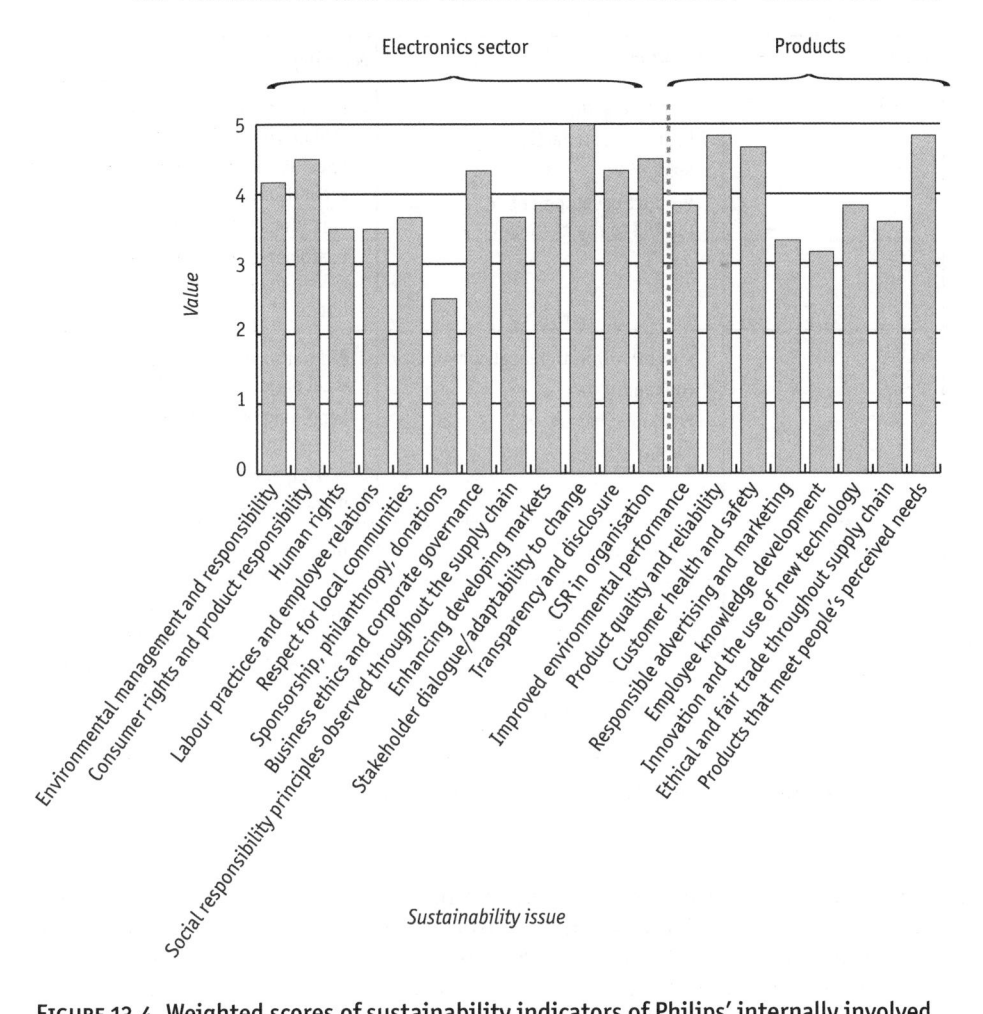

FIGURE 13.4 Weighted scores of sustainability indicators of Philips' internally involved

Source: Hermans et al. 2003

responsibility) whereas the European groups give equal weighting to environmental management, with a significantly lower weighting to consumer rights and product responsibility.

The focus groups in the US assign the highest scores to consumer rights and environmental management and responsibility. As regards products, as far as the organisations and the focus groups are concerned the two important aspects are the same as those in Europe (see Fig. 13.3). Also in the US, quality and reliability take the first place. Safety and health take a second place.

In Asia consumer rights scores the highest in the first section. Second are environmental management and responsibility. In the section on products consumer organisations argue that health and safety of the customer are the most important, followed by quality and reliability of the product. The focus groups show the same picture.

Group	Indicator	Meaning
Customer	• Customers' rights • Customer satisfaction • Marketing • Product development (directly related to the customer)	• Privacy, health and safety (composition of the product) • Loyalty, service, number of reparations • Labelling and advertising • Customer-oriented research and development, attuned to particular needs
Society	• Charity within the local community • Human rights • Economic impact	• Aid to those in need, support of local projects and initiatives • Screening of suppliers, financiers and partners • Making purchases on the local market, creating jobs
Organisation	• Making reports • Product development in general	• Developing ethical policies in which customers participate • Designing products that add something to society as well as general research and development
Employees	• No indicators on the production level	

TABLE 13.1 Classification of social sustainability indicators

Source: Asper *et al.* 2003

The research conducted among those internally involved revealed a different picture. As can be seen in Figure 13.4, they consider the category 'Products that meet people's needs' as considerably more important than the externally involved do.

These results need careful interpretation. Group A chose to focus mainly on the consumer, accessed by means of the focus groups. However, group members were not representative of the population as they all belonged to the same age category and were all highly educated. Additionally, only one group of five people was used to represent the whole of Europe. The same applies to the US. However, the outcomes are indicative.

Another problem was the language barrier. For example, none of the companies in southern Europe returned the questionnaire and the response in Asia was also low. In addition, a large number of Asian respondents reported that they did not understand what the questions meant—they had never heard of social sustainability or the social dimension of sustainability.

When using questionnaires of this kind, there is the risk that the respondents give socially desirable answers. US participants in particular were unwilling to label an issue as less important than another and expressed feelings of 'guilt' when they did so, although this problem was partly removed by asking them to identify their top three priorities. However, few participants provided additional comments or observations,

Indicator	Category	Type	Measurement suggestion
Any upheld non-compliances with domestic human rights legislation	Boolean		
Complaints about products and services	Quantitative	Ratio	No. of complaints/year
Compliance with the UK Human Rights Act and international human rights standards with regard to employees and other stakeholders and absence of upheld cases against the company	Boolean		
Concerned about the aesthetics of the product	Boolean		
Customer loyalty measures	Quantitative	Percentage	% of customers sustained from year to year
Customer retention	Quantitative	Percentage	% of customers retained
Customer satisfaction levels	Quantitative	Percentage	% of customers dissatisfied
Direct local purchases	Quantitative	Percentage	% of product using supplies from local purchases
Evidence of consideration of human rights impacts as part of investment and procurement decisions	Qualitative		
Initiating a repair and service system	Boolean		
Measurement for number of inventions	Quantitative	Absolute	No. of new inventions/year
Measurement for patent applications	Quantitative	Absolute	No. of patent applications/year
Measurement for speed with which new products meet the marketplace	Quantitative	Percentage	% of revenues generated from products less than five years old
Measurement of repairs	Quantitative	Ratio	No. of repairs per product/year
Number advertising/marketing complaints/number of complaints upheld	Quantitative	Ratio	No. of complaints/year
Number and type of instances of non-compliance with regulations concerning customer health and safety	Quantitative	Ratio	No. of non-compliance cases/year
Number and type of instances of non-compliance with regulations concerning product information and labelling, including any penalties or fines assessed for these breaches	Quantitative	Ratio	No. of non-compliance cases/year

TABLE 13.2 Possible measuring methods (continued over)

Source: Asper *et al.* 2003

200 SUSTAINABLE INNOVATION

Indicator	Category	Type	Measurement suggestion
Number of complaints upheld by regulatory or similar official bodies to oversee or regulate the health and safety of products and services	Quantitative	Ratio	No. of non-compliance cases/year
Proportion of suppliers and partners meeting the company's expected standards on human rights	Quantitative	Percentage	% of suppliers meeting the company's expected standards
Proportion of suppliers, investors and partners screened for human rights compliance	Quantitative	Percentage	% of suppliers, investors and partners complying to human rights standards
Provisions for customers with special needs	Quantitative	Ratio	No. of products made for people with special needs per year
R&D costs per product	Quantitative	Absolute	Costs per product
R&D policies that focus less on new technology developments	Qualitative		
Recognising and catering for diversity in advertising and product labelling	Qualitative		
Suppliers screened by certification/guidelines (ISO)	Boolean		
Total contribution to economy	Quantitative	Ratio	Total value of community impact (job creation, local investment, etc.)/total company profit in that geographical area

TABLE 13.2 (from previous page)

so the research did not provide the extra qualitative information that had been hoped for.

Indicators (group B)

Group B selected aspects of social sustainability occurring in the relevant literature and in the reports of leading companies.[13] These are classified in Table 13.1. From these the group generated a system of possible measuring methods for each indicator (see Table 13.2), making a distinction between qualitative and quantitative methods. Quantitative methods can be expressed in three ways: Boolean, absolute or ratio. A Boolean value can only be 'true' or 'not true'. Indicators with an absolute value indicate the size of the measured quantity. Ratio indicators are used to indicate the relation between two or

---

13 See footnotes 8, 9 and 10 on page 193.

more absolute indicators. In the measurement of sustainability the use of both absolute and ratio indicators is generally recommended (see Bossel 1999).

The Philips business case in terms of innovation and sustainability

With the aid of the projects described in this chapter, we tried to provide Philips with some insight into how the company can be more focused on social sustainability in the innovation and product creation process. In the light of this objective, the two sub-projects should therefore be considered as a whole. Philips can use the research conducted on those involved in determining the priorities of this group. The list of indicators composed will help them to establish usable social sustainability indicators. This research study forms the beginning of a possible extension of the Green Flagships concept which has been used by Philips for several years now to determine the sustainability of its products. The interplay of the two research studies discussed will help Philips make use of a set of instruments leading to greater insight into both objectives and providing a basis for further action.

From the very beginning, the Philips chain as a whole served as the system level on which this project has been based. On this level the instruments created can realise reductions in offload in the social sphere. This does not only apply to a reduction in offload with respect to the individuals involved, such as Philips' customers or employees. It also holds for those in the value chain, such as suppliers, purchasers and society as a whole. For example, if the company ignores consumer rights and renounces responsibility for its products it will alienate its customers, will attract a reputation for poor corporate social responsibility and may end up in court. In other words, such an approach not only offloads onto customers but onto social institutions too. So, a reduction in offload with regard to these aspects will have far-reaching benefits.

When we subsequently look at the key social sustainability indicators on the product level, offload behaviour appears to result in offload onto the customers of Philips. If the customer's safety and health or the quality and reliability of Philips' products are ignored, the customer's dissatisfaction with respect to these products will increase. Where safety and health risks are offloaded onto the customer they will also pose a burden on the healthcare sector. Furthermore, if a product's quality and reliability is below par, the is are more likely to dispose of it, creating unnecessary waste. The product must then be replaced, so consuming more resources. Thus, offload occurs both at the level of the individual and of society.

Through this project Philips has acquired access to a tool to measure the social sustainability of its products. The tool enables Philips to determine which social sustainability criteria are perceived as important by its stakeholders and whether its current products meet these criteria.

As well as indicating the current status of Philip's products, insight into the social impacts of products raises possible new directions for the company to explore. Further research, based on the work presented here, could therefore develop a company guide in the knowledge domain of the social dimension of sustainable products for the benefit of future innovations. Primarily, the result of this project is therefore connected with knowledge of sustainability (KoS).

However, the project results are also applicable to the sustainability of knowledge (SoK) concept. Knowledge management can be guided in new directions by the instrument. When an organisation lacks particular knowledge in the field of social sustainability, the instrument indicates the direction in which it could focus its knowledge-creating activities. Innovation is a process of elaborating knowledge in order to create new knowledge. In this respect, sustainability is a requirement that has to be increasingly fulfilled in the creation of new, innovative products.

Conclusions, recommendations, discussion and future research

The research studies described here show that it is indeed possible to set up a programme to determine the social sustainability of products and services. Thus, an organisation can develop its own theory on the social sustainability of its products. In this way, the organisation is capable not only of making its products socially sustainable, but also its production and management. The company can continue its leading role and can express its ambition to make a substantial contribution to the broader view on sustainable development.

Group A made an inventory of Philips' stakeholders and assessed different approaches to initiating a dialogue, through questionnaires and focus groups. The group found that both approaches have advantages as well as disadvantages.

Group B developed a collection of social indicators. From this work, it advised Philips to add a social variant to the ecodesign programme so that products can be assigned the status of Social Flagship. (In addition to the Green Flagship, indicating a product's environmental-friendliness, the Social Flagship indicates its social-friendliness.) The organisation can then specify how many of these products should be brought on the market each year.

Although this research has shed some light on the subject of social sustainability, it also shows that further research is needed. For example, the classification of those involved needs further elaboration. It is wise not to demarcate the different stakeholder groups too rigidly as they are diverse and fluid. Also, the dialogue with those involved is far from complete. Group A has only spoken to one group: consumers. It is a first step, but Philips will also have to approach other groups. Moreover, from Philips' point of view, a more open dialogue seems more productive than questionnaires, because it provides more qualitative data. Therefore, in the future Philips should seek closer contact with its stakeholders. To this end it needs to start an open dialogue providing the stakeholders with information concerning its products and listening to their demands and wishes. The indicators themselves also require extra testing and elaboration, and new ones need to be identified (for example, the percentage of production taking place in under-developed countries).

Two things emerge from these research studies: the importance of transparency and education. The research on the focus groups in Asia revealed that no participants understood what the social side of sustainable development means. If Philips wants to make itself more known in the field of sustainability, the challenge lies in addressing issues such as this. If customers are not aware of a company's initiatives in the area of sustainability, their buying behaviour will not be influenced.

Although Philips is already very open about its affairs via its website, further research into other ways of reaching customers is needed. These research studies have shown that people are interested in these issues, but that many do not yet possess sufficient knowledge of the possibilities and initiatives taking place.

14
Knowledge systems for sustainable innovation of starch potato production
ACHIEVING MORE WITH LESS

Niels R. Faber and Rob van Haren

This chapter discusses transforming knowledge into economic and ecological value as a way of improving the sustainability of the starch potato value chain in north-west Europe. The study particularly targets types of concentrated knowledge—decision-support systems (DSS)—regarding starch potato growth. As a participant in the Agrobiokon research programme (Agro-Biotechnological Carbohydrate Research Netherlands) the starch potato growers' co-operative AVEBE has developed DSSs to enable farmers to increase their yield without increasing resource consumption. However, so far, these systems have not had the intended effect. Improving sustainability requires the use and re-use of knowledge of sustainability (KoS). If farmers and the agricultural sector as a whole in the Netherlands are to survive in a globalised economy, it is imperative that they improve their KoS. However, some barriers stand in the way of the transfer of knowledge through DSSs. This study explores these barriers.

The starch potato growing region of the north east of the Netherlands and north-west of Germany (referred to as the Ems Dollar Region [EDR]) forms the base of a sustainable agricultural production chain for food and non-food applications. This growth is concentrated within Groningen and Drenthe within the Netherlands and Emsland within Germany. Approximately 70,000 hectares of starch potatoes are grown on about 5,000 farms. Within the last ten years both the area and total number of farms have decreased while the average size of individual farms has increased. On average, the region produces around 39 tonnes per hectare (field weight) representing a total value of approximately €170 million a year. But the added value of the potato starch industry, which directly and indirectly employs around 8,000 people in the region, is estimated at €700 million. Thus, the value chain of potato starch is an important factor in the EDR economy. This chapter addresses only the Dutch sector which covers some 45,000 hectares comprising 2,100 farms.

Societal, technological and climatologic changes are known to undermine the starch potato value chain. For example, changes to the EU's Common Agricultural Policy (CAP), in line with World Trade Organisation (WTO) agreements, will eventually stop current subsidies for potato starch production and will open the EU's borders to cheaper sources of starch. Technical trends influencing the value chain of potato starch include:

- Greater use of information
- Utilisation of green (genetic engineering) and white biotechnology (the use of biological means and techniques to optimise industrial processes)
- Further increases in scale

Adequate information, correctly applied and delivered through appropriate advice systems is assumed to increase yields by 20–30%. Green biotechnology (e.g. changing a plant's genetic make-up) and white biotechnology (e.g. the industrial application of genetically modified enzymes and bacteria for enzymatic and fermentation processes) influence the configuration of farmers' and processors' production processes. Green biotechnology enables the design of new potato cultivars with an estimated 20–30% yield increase. Combining green and white biotechnology enables the production of additional valuable components such as, for instance, aromas, medical ingredients or industrial chemicals. A further increase of scale results in either large-scale, capital-intensive farms, producing several agricultural raw materials or small multifunctional farms, profiting from a multitude of economic activities that are linked to plants, animals and land. The agri-industrial value chain benefits mostly from large-scale farms.

Climate change is already influencing starch potato growth; changing patterns of precipitation, more frequent periods of extreme weather and an increase in average temperatures all cause fluctuations in farmers' income and affect risk-prone capital-intensive farms in particular.

Being one of the few European large-scale value chains of potato starch, starch potato growth in the EDR has the innovation capacity to utilise changing circumstances to improve the value chain of potato starch in both the market and society. The strong Dutch knowledge position regarding agriculture and the food industry, as well as the professional knowledge of Dutch farmers, are particular strengths in this regard. Eight years ago the Agrobiokon platform was established to target innovation in carbohydrate value chains. Agrobiokon consists of knowledge institutions, growers, national and regional authorities, and the potato starch processing industry.

By participating in Agrobiokon, AVEBE signals its intention to meet the demands of the future. AVEBE estimates that, in order to withstand future challenges, an average-sized farm will have to realise a yield improvement of 25%. Such a huge increase implies the adaptation of every farm and farmer that is part of the AVEBE co-operative. Knowledge generated by the Agrobiokon programme has to be transferred to individual farmers and applied within their daily activities. To achieve this knowledge transfer, the Agrobiokon programme developed and applied different channels of knowledge transfer. However, the effect of the intended knowledge transfer on farmer and farm performance has been moderate up to now.

The AVEBE organisation

Background

The Dutch starch potato growers' co-operative, AVEBE, is a world leader in selling, marketing, developing and producing potato starch and custom-made potato starch products for use in other industrial sectors such as textiles and concrete. In order to strengthen its market position AVEBE actively participates in the ongoing liberalisation of global trade. Internally, the organisation implements its strategy of becoming the world leader in potato starch and the supplier of solutions to customers from other industrial specialties by increasing its knowledge of functional applications. Its divisions control the total value chain of potato starch production. In addition, AVEBE strives for sustainable development.

AVEBE is strongly connected with the history of the three northern provinces of the Netherlands (Friesland, Groningen and Drente). After the ice age, the Bourtanger Moor marshlands developed between the river Eems and the Hondsrug. From these marshlands, ten-metre-thick peat bog was laid down. From Roman times, peat has been extracted for fuel. However, the systematic extraction of peat within the former fen communities started only in the 17th century, later being transformed into farming land. As the soil was suitable for growing potatoes for consumption, in the 18th century the potato was introduced into the former fen communities (van Houten 1994). In the 19th century the potato was industrially processed, initially as part of alcohol and syrup production.

Around 1840, the first small-scale potato starch factories appeared in the area, running on horsepower. These factories innovated and quickly switched to steam power. This increase of capacity stimulated further growth of potato production, as did another innovation: fertiliser. As the potato starch industry grew, farmers united within agricultural unions and co-operated over the purchase of seed, fertilisers and tools. At the end of the 19th and the beginning of the 20th centuries, the starch industry produced a surplus. Potato starch industrialists organised themselves into purchasing cartels, to set a price. Farmers responded by building their own starch producing factories, in effect as extensions to their farms. This also preludes the second innovation at the farms: mechanisation in the form of ploughs, planting machines and fertiliser spreaders. Since 1875, the visionary organisation Veenkoloniale Boerenbond (a former fen farmers' union) offered rewards for the development of a harvester. After many prototypes, a suitable harvester was developed just after World War II.

Another stimulus for production was the introduction of new high-starch potato varieties. Coming to the market in 1893, the Eigenheimer is probably the best-known variety (Dendermonde and Sierman 1979). The co-operating potato starch factories united into the organisation AVB (Aardappelzetmeel Verkoop Bureau [Potato Starch Sales Agency]). AVB largely depended on the potato starch industrialists that sold chemically modified products such as dextrins as well as starch. After World War II, AVB changed its name to AVEBE and started producing chemically modified products too. By the end of the 1970s, AVEBE was the only manufacturer of potato starch products and derivatives in the Netherlands, and still is.

After World War II, the agricultural sector experienced an increase in scale, with the consolidation of land and the development of new crop-protection substances increasing production even more. However, the potato cyst nematode infested the potato crop of the former fen communities and proved impossible to eliminate. In 1949, potato farmers were forced to switch from two-year to three-year crop rotations because of this nematode. This regime changed in 1967 due to the introduction of new resistant varieties of potato and effective pesticides, although potato cyst nematode remains one of the potato farmer's biggest problems. Optimising nematode control is discussed later in this chapter. At present, farmers and the potato starch industry are challenged to transform current demands into a future strategy. Later in this chapter, we discuss the role of knowledge management within innovation and the transformation of the value chain of potato starch.

AVEBE's vision on sustainability

Sustainable development is one of AVEBE's core values, as evidenced by its credo 'achieving more with less'. Thus, AVEBE performs a balancing act between its economic, social and environmental responsibilities. These core values are also communicated to its stakeholders, among whom are the starch potato growers. Improving quality and decreasing resource use per unit of production is the objective. AVEBE attempts to achieve this by increasing the yield per hectare on the one hand and by decreasing the use of resources through the implementation of knowledge on the other.

Genetically modified organisms (GMOs) fit AVEBE's strategy. AVEBE develops GMOs exclusively for technical, non-food applications. GMOs potency is high and leads to improved product quality and a reduction of chemicals and energy use. GMOs can replace synthetic (oil-based) products with renewable resources, so reducing carbon dioxide emissions.

Agrobiokon

The Agrobiokon research programme co-ordinates research conducted by different knowledge and information agencies. Accessibility of existing knowledge prevails within the Agrobiokon and HPA (Hoofdproductschap Akkerbouw; the main agricultural agency) research programmes. Together they built the knowledge portal Kennisakker (Knowledge Field)[1] which provides access to all research collectively financed by the farmers. In order to communicate one clear message to farmers, results from research are offered through this website to all parties involved, including extension services.

Agrobiokon's research programme objectives are:

1. Reducing production costs and crop losses

---

1 optiras.kennisakker.nl.

2. Increasing yields through the increase of production per hectare within the limits of the available environmental, natural and societal resources

3. Developing new starch products and processes with high added values

Together, AVEBE and Agrobiokon offer a variety of solutions to overcome the bottlenecks that have been identified within starch potato growth. The portfolio of knowledge transfer consists of individual growth advice, study groups, demonstrations, Optimeel[2] study days, readings, the Kennisakker knowledge portal, growth manuals, magazines and, particularly, DSSs. In this way, support can be tailored to the needs of the individual farmer. The underlying assumption is that different farmers are identifiable in terms of economic performance. Different means of communication are required in order to address the individual attitudes of farmers. DSSs are considered here in more detail because they are regarded as condensed, interactive channels for knowledge transfer which can be tailored by farmers themselves.

Two DSSs are discussed briefly, each targeting a different segment of the AVEBE farmer population: TIPSTAR™ and OPTIras™. The first interactively advises farmers on irrigation, fertilisation, quality improvement, control of losses and optimisation of costs. It was designed to support high-yielding farmers. The TIPSTAR™ prototype generates area-specific advice, targeting the optimisation of starch and protein production per hectare, bounded by predetermined natural and environmental conditions. TIPSTAR™ supports tactical and operational decisions.

TIPSTAR™ is a DSS based on the paradigms and concepts of system theory. The crop, soil and climate are identified as the subsystems to be studied and understood, and can be described using mathematical functions. Knowledge from the domains of soil physics, soil chemistry, crop ecology, ecophysiology and meteorology are used. A simulation model formalises this knowledge, in which crop management, daily weather, physical and chemical soil data are inputs to the system.

Solar energy, temperature, water, fertilisation, and diseases and plagues determine growth and development of starch potatoes. The crop growth model assumes that solar energy transforms into assimilates (sugars) and subsequently divides among the processes of growth, maintenance and reproduction. These processes function well if enough nitrogen and water are present to produce protein and other structure and stock components. The plant absorbs nitrogen through its roots, after which nitrogen is transported towards the different organs for processes of biosynthesis. Water is required for uptake of nitrogen, for breathing and for cooling the plant. The processes mentioned describe growth and development of the different organs of the plant: leaves, stems, roots and tubers. Technically, this is called a **multi-compartment stochiometric dynamic crop growth model**.

The soil water system simulates the crop's daily availability of water. The farmer's irrigation data is used together with precipitation data from weather stations and groundwater data from the 1:50,000 territorial maps of the Netherlands. The soil is divided into 1 cm thick layers. The functional description of these layers is aggregated into soil profiles of 1.20 m depths. In this manner, water retention can be determined per layer of the soil profile. The simulation calculates the available water per 1 cm layer,

---

2 Optimeel is a management information system which allows individual benchmarking of farm performance.

using the difference between the soil's drainage and its capillarity. The crop growth model calculates total root depth and root density per 1 cm layer, summing up to the total water usage of the crop.

The soil organic substance and nitrogen system simulates the crop's daily availability of nutrients (nitrogen) for each separate layer of the soil. In this, the farmer's fertilising data are used. The soil is schematised similar to the soil water model. The crop's daily available amount of nitrogen per layer results from the processes of mineralisation, nitrification, de-nitrification, and drainage and uptake by the crop. Mineralisation is the process that transforms organic substances (such as green fertiliser, compost or crop residue) into carbon dioxide and nitrogen (ammonium/nitrate). It is one of the most important processes determining the soil's sustainability. The amount of organic substance in the soil determines its water retention and is the source of the saprophytic soil life.

The second DSS OPTIras™ is a DSS for cultivar selection that supports a farmer in selecting cultivars relative to cultivar characteristics. It is intended for low-yielding farmers. A variety of properties relating to yield, resistance against pests and diseases, and storage, characterises a potato cultivar. Personal preference, diseases present in the field and cultivar properties determine the farmer's choice. OPTIras™ assists the farmer in choosing the cultivar properties and sorting the cultivars based on priorities. Despite its long history and the fact that a lot is known about it, the potato cyst nematode still costs an average €150 per hectare per year in the starch potato industry. This is about 10–15% of a farmer's net income. Reducing the infestation to economically acceptable levels requires the right combination of cultivar, growth frequency, field choice and nematicide usage. Cultivars differ greatly with regard to resistance (the ability to reduce the infestation) and tolerance (the ability to resist the infestation), which are uncorrelated. A non-resistant and highly tolerant cultivar can multiply the existing nematode population by 30 times while a highly resistant and intolerant cultivar reduces the nematode population by two to three times. However, the intolerance indicates that the crop is highly affected by the nematode population, resulting in high losses of yield.

OPTIras™ combines information about the cultivars with the population dynamics of the nematode and the properties of available pesticides. The DSS ensures that the farmer gains insight into nematode damage levels and the financial consequences of a wrongly selected cultivar or incorrect application of pesticides. OPTIras™ thus contributes to sustainable soil management.

Short-term challenges

As indicated before, farmers will need to increase their yields by at least 25% to survive in an increasingly globalised economy. However, in the short term, farmers need to overcome several serious obstacles that stand in the way of the required changes. Research shows that a number of factors determine yield and efficiency (see Fig. 14.1); the top five are:

- Nematode contamination
- Storage losses due to harvest damage

210 SUSTAINABLE INNOVATION

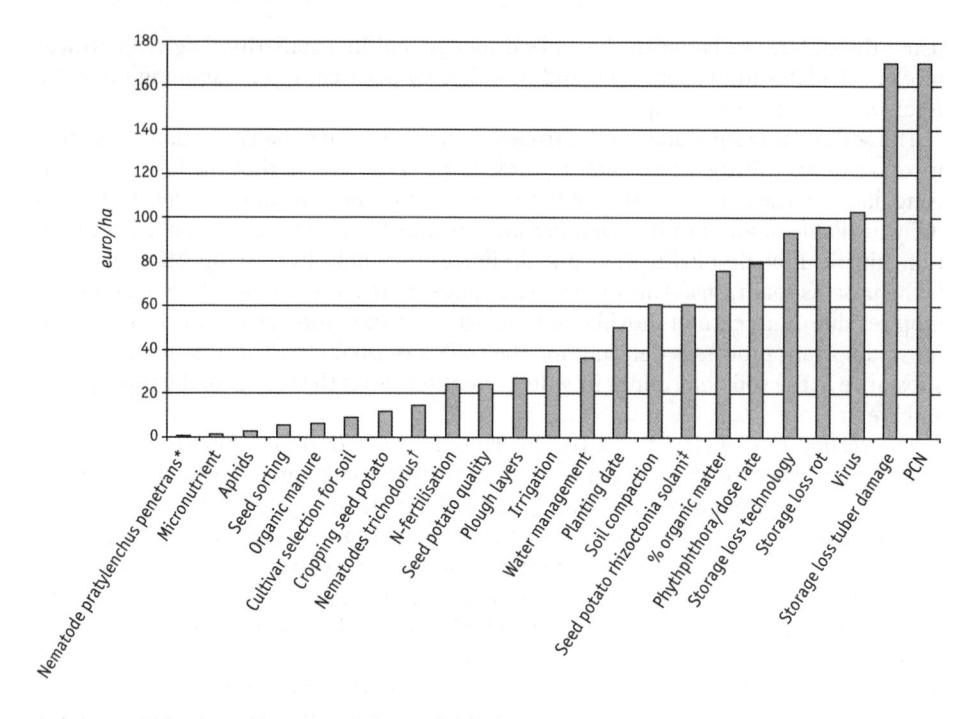

[Bar chart showing factors affecting yield (euro/ha), from lowest to highest: Nematode pratylenchus penetrans*, Micronutrient, Aphids, Seed sorting, Organic manure, Cultivar selection for soil, Cropping seed potato, Nematodes trichodorus†, N-fertilisation, Seed potato quality, Plough layers, Irrigation, Water management, Planting date, Soil compaction, Seed potato rhizoctonia solani‡, % organic matter, Phytophthora/dose rate, Storage loss technology, Storage loss rot, Virus, Storage loss tuber damage, PCN]

* a lesion nematode   † a stubby root nematode   ‡ a fungus

FIGURE 14.1 Factors affecting yield and production efficiency
Source: van Haren 2005

- Viruses
- Storage losses due to rot
- Storage losses due to inappropriate storing techniques

The knowledge required to remove these bottlenecks is available in the Netherlands. If these five factors were resolved, 80% of AVEBE farmers would increase their income by €500 per hectare per year.

Target groups of innovation

Approximately 2,100 Dutch starch potato farms started the 2004 growing season. Four different types of farmers are assumed to exist within this population, differing in their turnover, productivity and farming methods:

- Top
- Quantity
- Quality
- Normal

Cluster	N	Base weight (tonne/ha) μ	Base weight (tonne/ha) σ	Premium points μ	Premium points σ
Top farmers	512	54.78	4.46	87.18	3.30
Quantity farmers	585	45.41	3.21	82.05	2.88
Quality farmers	391	41.26	3.65	88.80	3.05
Normal farmers	412	32.84	4.44	80.99	4.30

TABLE 14.1 Clusters of farmers

Table 14.1 shows the differences between clusters regarding yield in tonnes per hectare (base weight) and potato quality in premium points. Figure 14.2 displays the same clusters graphically.

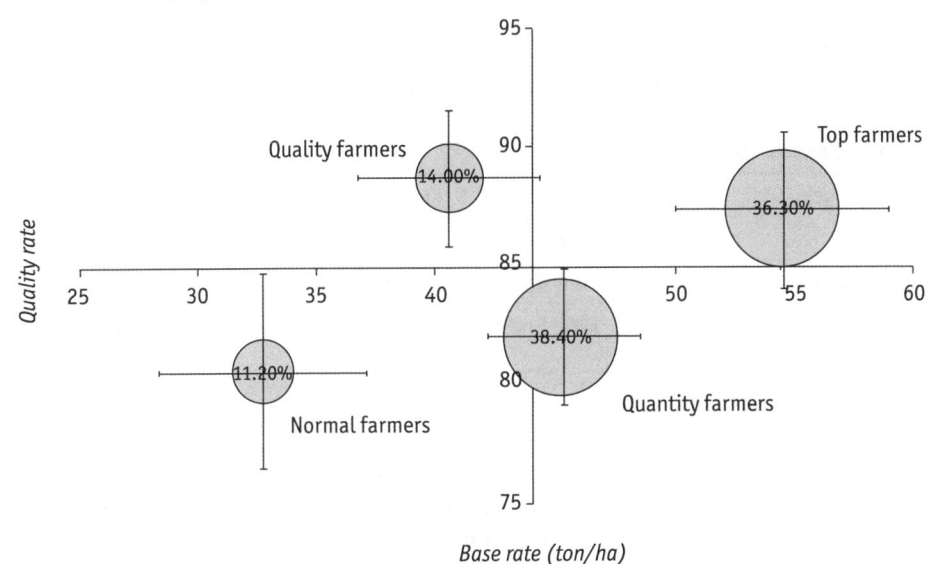

FIGURE 14.2 Farmer clusters

Table 14.2 displays cluster profiles, based on farm and farmer characteristics of the individual clusters. The clusters differ significantly with regard to farm size ($F(3,587) = 5.4$, $p < 0.01$) and area used for growing starch potatoes ($F(3,587) = 6.7$, $p < 0.01$). Quantity growers participate more in sugar beet growth whereas other farmers report growing other types of crops (Pearson $\chi^2 = 19.6$, $df = 3$, $p < 0.01$). Clusters also differ with regard to age ($F(3,588) = 2.908$, $p < 0.05$). Lastly, top farmers tend to be better educated (Pearson $\chi^2 = 33.58$, $df = 3$, $p < 0.01$) and are more likely to seek out information on starch potato growth (Pearson $\chi^2 = 13.86$, $df = 3$, $p < 0.01$). In relation to the top five problems, top farmers are considered to be the only group able to operate sustainably without additional measures.

212 SUSTAINABLE INNOVATION

Population characteristics	Cluster			
	Top	Quantity	Quality	Normal
No. of farmers	526	605	379	390
Percentage of population of Dutch potato farmers	27.7%	38.4%	19.9%	20.5%
Percentage of total production of Dutch starch potato industry	36.3%	36.3%	14.0%	11.2%
Farm characteristics				
Average farm area (hectare)	88.3	78.2	67.8	65.8
SD farm area	60.4	48.2	43.6	43.2
Average starch area (hectare)	34.1	32.1	23.6	23.6
SD starch area	29.2	22.1	23.5	23.3
High participation in growth of	Other crops	Sugar beets	Other crops	Other crops
Farmer characteristics				
Average age	48.4	46.5	47.9	50.3
SD age	10.9	10.7	11.3	12.1
Frequency of extra education	Every 6 months	Once a year	Once a year	Once a year
Frequency of information collection	Every 6 months	Once a year	Once a year	Once a year

TABLE 14.2 Cluster profiles

Quantity and quality of a farmer's yield are the dimensions used for cluster analysis, both averaged over the last three years. The quantity of a farmer's yield is measured in tonnes per hectare and corrected for its starch content (base weight). The quality of a farmer's yield equals the premium points AVEBE ascribes to the yield. These premium points are a quality measurement of the potatoes a farmer delivers to the factory gates. A sample of the delivery is valued on ten dimensions, graded on a scale from zero to ten. These include contamination (tare weight), amount of rot, heating and frost damage, and diseases. Additionally, defects due to dirt enclosure are judged. These defects include damage, growth cracks, the presence of diseases and rust. A farmer's premium points equal the sum of the ten dimensions. Subsequently, the premium points are used to determine the percentage of the premium the farmer will receive as bonus, on top of a weight-based fee.

In our cluster analysis, we used multiple clustering methods[3] to determine which clusters could be recognised based on farmers' yields and premium points. The differ-

3 Hierarchical cluster analysis based on Ward's method, k-means cluster analysis and a two-step cluster analysis were used to recognise the different farmer clusters within the Dutch AVEBE farmer population.

ent clustering methods were all initialised to find two to six clusters within the complete dataset of yields and premium points of the entire population of Dutch AVEBE farmers. The different methods converge at four clusters within the set, conforming to our assumption. The clustering appears to be insensitive to location and soil type. Table 14.3 presents the functions that linearly describe the different clusters found. These were determined using a discriminant function analysis using the two clustering variables (yield and premium points) and the found clusters as inputs.

Cluster	Constant	Base weight (tonne/ha)	Premium points
Top farmers	−443.7	3.82	7.74
Quantity farmers	−372.9	3.20	7.27
Quality farmers	−403.2	2.89	7.78
Normal farmers	−327.2	2.34	7.12

TABLE 14.3 Discriminant functions

The business project with AVEBE: achieving more with less

Use and implementation of DSSs

The Agrobiokon research programme has almost finished and, as mentioned earlier, although solutions for knowledge transfer have been implemented they have not yet realised the project's objectives. In particular, the developed DSSs often remain unused. In the NIDO project, the OPTIras™ system was examined in more detail. Originally, the OPTIras™ system was focused on low-yielding farmers (i.e. normal and quality farmers of the AVEBE farmer population) in an attempt to increase their yields. As stated earlier, the OPTIras™ DSS helps the farmers select the best cultivars for the next growing season.

This study explores what factors stand in the way of knowledge transfer using DSSs within the value chain of AVEBE's starch potato growth. Based on Waern (1989) we distinguish two sides to this issue. First, the user side refers to the motives of a user to use a DSS. Focusing on this side provides answers to the question of why a certain user is willing or unwilling to use a DSS for a certain task. Furthermore, the focus on the user side provides footholds for intervention at the level of the user. Second, the DSS side refers to the design decisions that are made during its development. A focus on this side provides an answer to the question of whether the DSS connects to the way that farmers make decisions and how they perceive the DSS as an effective tool. It also provides footholds to alter the design to improve this connection (Waern 1989: 124). In this research, we focus on the DSS side. Figure 14.3 displays our conceptual model.

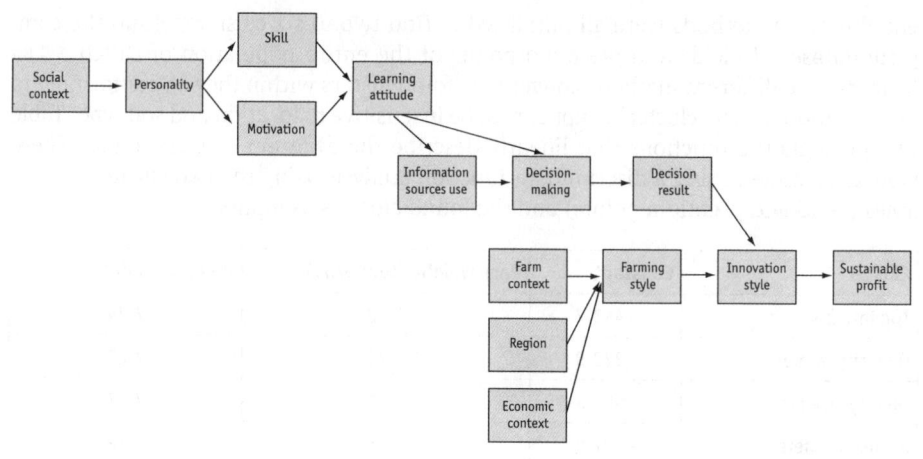

FIGURE 14.3 Conceptual model

Studies conducted in the Agrobiokon programme focusing on the different bottlenecks of the starch potato growth process form the basis of the developed DSSs. The outcomes of these studies tend to be mathematical models of, for example, potato cyst nematode population dynamics, weather dynamics or soil dynamics. Based on a fixed set of variables, these models compute how certain processes influencing starch potato growth behave over time, and calculate the implications for the growth itself. These mathematical models form the basis of the DSSs that have been developed within the Agrobiokon programme. However, whereas Agrobiokon researchers concentrated on building mathematical models to describe accurately different aspects of starch potato growth, farmers presumably use a different rationale, based on experience and rules of thumb. Therefore, providing support via DSSs based on scientifically constructed mathematical models might distance farmers from DSSs, right from the start.

As indicated, Agrobiokon's DSSs intend to provide decision support for different segments of the AVEBE farmer population (normal, quality, quantity and top). The TIP-STAR™ system targets the top farmers whereas the OPTIras™ system is aimed at normal and quality farmers. However useful, the subdivision into normal, quality, quantity and top farmers is arbitrary, for it was based entirely on quantitative and qualitative measures related to a farmer's yield. Additionally, these measures provide no footholds concerning the design of DSSs. Instead, the subdivision of the AVEBE farmer population needs to be related to farmer characteristics that can be used as input parameters for the DSS design trajectory.

In this study, a decision-making perspective is chosen, perceiving farmers as human decision-makers which in their turn are postulated as information-processing systems (Newell and Simon 1972). Based on Newell *et al.* (1972), we argue that human decision-making involves two components. First, the farmer with his personal characteristics and his personal decision-making behaviour and knowledge regarding his starch potato growth is of importance. The second factor of importance concerns the task environment in which the farmer makes his decisions (i.e. the farm). Before we can discuss design factors of DSSs, a clear view of both the farmer's decision-making and the farmer's task environment is needed. Therefore, we discuss both farmer decision-making and a farmer's task environment first.

Human decision-making

In decision theoretical terms, a farmer involved in decision-making relating his starch potato growth equals a human decision-maker or human problem-solver, a term that denotes humans involved in decision-making or problem-solving relating to a certain task environment in general (Newell and Simon 1972). Hereby, the human decision-maker is perceived as an information-processing system (Card, Moran and Newell 1983; Newell and Simon 1972). As an information-processing system, the human decision-maker exchanges information with his or her task environment. Through information exchange with the task environment, the human decision-maker creates mental representations of the task environment. These representations are knowledge about the task environment that helps the decision-maker accomplish certain objectives within the task environment.

Different orientations exist in relation to the manner in which human decision-making has been perceived (Simon 1977). These orientations roughly fall into two main streams. First, the normative or prescriptive stream focuses on how a decision should be made. Research fields comprising this stream are, for instance, operations research, management science and economics (Klein and Methlie 1995: 6). At the other end of the spectrum, the descriptive stream treats the decision process as the starting point for providing decision support. In this stream, decision theories concentrate on the actual processes of thought that underlie human decision-making. This stream encompasses research fields such as cognitive science, social psychology, artificial intelligence, etc. (Klein and Methlie 1995: 6).

A generic model originating from the descriptive stream and describing the phases of human decision-making stems from Simon (1977) who divided the decision process into the phases of intelligence, design and choice (see Fig. 14.4).[4] In the intelligence phase, an individual explores the problem at hand and determines relevant issues. Hereby, the individual constructs a mental model (a representation of the problem in

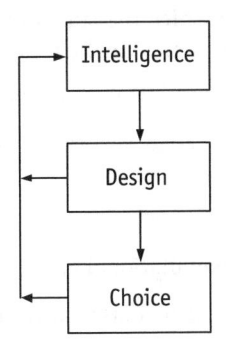

FIGURE 14.4 Simon's model of decision-making

Source: Simon 1977

---

4 Simon's decision-making model is one of many about decision-making, but according to Turban, Aronson and Bolloju (2001: 41): 'Simon's model is the most concise and yet complete characterisation of rational decision-making.'

the brain) of the perceived problem. A problem concerns the individual's perception of the present state of the environment and a future target state (Newell and Simon 1972: 72).

The mental model the individual constructs is generally referred to as the **problem space** (Newell and Simon 1972: 809). In this problem space, the individual can represent both the problem and the solution. The problem space is constructed through the breaking-up of the overall problem into smaller pieces (i.e. subproblems). Subsequently, the individual formulates one or more possible solutions to the recognised (sub)problems that are specified in the problem space; this process is termed the **design phase**. Eventually, a total solution is formed in the **choice phase**. In this final phase of decision-making, the different partial solutions are evaluated against the criteria that belong to the target state. Partial solutions that best meet these criteria are selected to solve the problem. The selected partial solutions are combined into the complete solution to the problem.

The three phases that comprise human decision-making do not follow linearly upon each other as neatly as might be concluded from the description above. Simon (1977) stipulated that the decision-making process must be iterative. He pointed out that each stage must be seen as a decision-making process in itself. That is to say, the phases of intelligence, design and choice can again be subdivided into the phases of intelligence, design and choice. In this way, the decision-making process becomes a cyclic multidimensional process.

The subdivision into intelligence, design and choice provides the skeleton for the problem-solving process. Generally, the distinction is made between well-structured and ill-structured problems (Newell and Simon 1972) to indicate the differences between problems and the processes required to solve them. Simon (1973) stipulated six criteria that characterise well-structured problems:

- They have a specific target criterion
- They have a problem space in which the state of the initial problem (i.e. the end state) and all intermediate states can be represented
- They have a problem space in which state transitions can be represented
- They have one or more knowledge spaces in which the decision-maker's knowledge can be represented
- They reflect the real world
- They require a minimum of computational effort to be solved

Simon (1973) defined ill-structured problems as those that do not meet one or more of the above criteria.

The amount of effort a decision-maker needs to exercise in order to resolve a problem is determined by the way the problem is structured and is heavily influenced by the decision-maker's current problem-related knowledge. If decision-makers possesses knowledge that is applicable to the problem at hand, then they are not expected to experience any difficulties in making decisions (i.e. they are able to create a suitable problem space). Within this problem space, initial, end or final, and intermediate states can be represented, as well as the appropriate state transitions. Regarding a decision-maker's current knowledge, the factors of importance are the number of years of their experience within a certain field and their educational level.

In contrast, decision-makers will fail to make effective decisions when they lack the required knowledge to do so. In this case, the decision-maker needs to learn and acquire additional knowledge. To acquire this knowledge, the decision-maker is assumed to use multiple information sources. Different types of information sources are distinguished based on the medium used. Table 14.4 shows the different information sources we identified. A distinction is made between paper-based, social and electronic sources of information. Concerning paper-based information sources, a distinction is made between magazines and newspapers that target the agricultural sector in general and those that specifically target potato growth. General magazines and newspapers about agriculture are *De Boerderij* (*The Farm*), *Oogst* (*Harvest*), *Het Landbouwblad* (*The Agricultural Gazette*), *Agrarisch Dagblad* (*Agriculture Daily*) and *Veldpost* (*Field Post*). Magazines specifically targeting potato growth are *Informa* (AVEBE's monthly magazine), *Aardappelwereld* (*Potato World*) and the Optimeel annual report. The Optimeel system is an electronic crop and paper-based registration system. Recorded data are stored and analysed in a central database. Annually, a report of the analysed results is issued to subscribers, enabling farmers to benchmark their own performance with average performance of similar farms and crops.

Paper		Social	Electronic
General agricultural	Starch potato growth		
De Boerderij	*Informa*	Starch potato study groups	Kennisakker knowledge portal
Oogst	*Aardappelwereld* magazine	Field gatherings electronic potato	Optimeel crop registration
Het Landbouwblad	Optimeel annual report	Harvest damage study groups	OPTIras™
Agrarisch Dagblad		Experimental farm demo days	OPTIrob™
Veldpost		AVEBE extension workers	

TABLE 14.4 Information sources

Social sources of information concern a variety of study groups, focusing on starch potato growth in general or, specifically, on harvest damage. At field gatherings, farmers' harvesters are assessed using an electronic, potato-like device. This device measures all the factors that are known to cause damage to potatoes during harvesting. Demonstration days at experimental farms inform farmers about new potato cultivars and crop management methods. AVEBE extension workers are advisors who provide personal advice to a farmer.

Electronic information sources that are currently available to farmers are the Kennisakker knowledge portal, Optimeel crop registration, OPTIras™[5] and OPTIrob™.[6] The

5 OPTIras: Rassenkeuze Adviessysteem voor Zetmeelaardappelen, optiras.kennisakker.nl, accessed 11 November 2005.
6 OPTIrob: Adviessysteem voor Rooibeschadiging en Bewaring Zetmeelaardappelen, optirob.kennisakker.nl, accessed 11 November 2005.

Kennisakker portal provides information about various topics relating to starch potato growth. In principle, the portal displays results from farmer-funded fundamental, strategic and applied agronomic research. Optimeel crop registration is an electronic channel farmers can use to record the crop management data they need to provide to different authorities. OPTIrob™ is a DSS that calculates a farmer's losses due to poor storage.

In addition to these different sources of information, the frequency of receiving extra training and the frequency by which decision-makers obtain information about a specific topic are recognised as important factors. Both factors provide an indication about the extent of knowledge renewal.

The task environment

In principle, decisions concerning starch potato growth centre on the three elements of field, cultivar and farmer. The field, which is either owned or leased by the farmer, is used to realise growth. Important factors are its nutrient status, water status and presence of pests and diseases. The cultivar's most critical factors are its potato cyst nematode resistance and tolerance. Other important factors are the storage period, the timing of deliveries of potatoes to AVEBE factories and the likelihood of pests and diseases occurring other than the potato cyst nematode. An example of another disease is late blight, which is caused by the Phytophthora fungus. These factors determine expected yields and costs.

A farmer's decision is based on a specific field–cultivar–objective combination per field, balancing individual factors relating to field, cultivar and economic objectives. Farmers are familiar with these types of decisions which involve considerable uncertainties (e.g. changing weather conditions, existing field variations, cultivars' biological variations and the occurrence of diseases).

Farmers' decisions take place at four different levels of aggregation: current growth, crop rotation, farm and society. Operational decisions concern the current cropping season. Tactical decisions relate to crop rotation, spanning two to three years. Decisions concerning crop rotation, determine what crops are grown on what fields and how these crop–field combinations alternate in the next growing period. For instance, a farmer might choose to grow potatoes in one year and sugar beet in the next.

At farm level, a farmer makes strategic decisions with a time horizon of four to ten years. Farm continuity and societal developments drive these strategic decisions. Factors influencing farm continuity are a farmer's economic circumstances and the farm's succession. Examples of societal developments, which may span more than ten years, include public opinions about farming, tightening up of legislation and rising land prices.

AVEBE actively gives advice and financial support in relation to farmers' decisions, at all four levels of aggregation. At growth and crop rotation level, AVEBE provides information on paper and through software systems. At farm and society level, AVEBE takes the role of contact person.

The complexity of decisions at an operational level becomes apparent when considering one growth in more detail. Potato growth is seasonal, implying that there is a small time-frame in which to realise the growth. The season starts in the spring when the potatoes are planted and lasts until harvesting in the autumn. Outside this time-frame, potatoes either are kept in storage or are delivered to the factory. In contrast to the limited time-frame of potato growth, decisions concerning one cropping season span almost three years, assuming farmers organise their own potato seed multiplication. If a farmer buys seed potatoes, the time-frame reduces to 18 months.

Growth decisions can be divided into two phases depending on whether farmers multiply their own potato seed or not. Preceding both phases, farmers select the cultivars they plan to use in the next growing season. In the first phase, farmers use one field to increase their stock of seed potatoes. The second phase denotes the actual growth phase whereby seed potatoes are planted in different fields. Once mature, the potatoes are harvested and either stored for later delivery or delivered directly to the factory.

To complicate matters, farmers usually grow more than just starch potatoes, meaning that they must allocate their land and resources accordingly. Most Dutch starch potato farmers combine their starch potato growth with sugar beets, grain or other crops. Essentially, crop growth involves crop-related and crop-independent risks. Growing a variety of crops enables farmers to reduce crop-specific risks and allows them to spread operational costs among different crops.

DSSs

The main aim of a DSS is to assist the decision-making process. However, the two streams of thought on which decision theory is based also determine the underlying assumptions of DSS design (Keen and Scott-Morton 1978; Klein and Methlie 1995). For a long time, solutions from the fields of operation research and management science dictated the design and application of DSSs (Keen and Scott-Morton 1978; Klein and Methlie 1995). In principle, these systems optimise decision-making. In contrast, recent approaches to design and application of DSSs, based on insights from the descriptive school of thought, connect more closely to the human decision-making process.

Positioned within the descriptive school of thought, Klein and Methlie (1995: 300) define a (knowledge-based) DSS as:

> A computer that provides information and methodological knowledge (domain knowledge and decision methodology) by means of analytical decision models (systems and users), and access to data bases and knowledge bases to support a decision-maker in making decisions effectively in complex and ill-structured tasks.

The DSS user's task relates to a specific knowledge domain (Schreiber et al. 1999). This knowledge domain is represented in information structures within the DSS. In this way, the DSS is able to reason regarding the knowledge domain, and gives as output a result that presumably aids its user.

Holsapple and Whinston (1996: 169) present a generic model of DSSs, consisting of a language system, presentation system, problem processing system and knowledge base. Together, language and presentation systems form the DSS's human–computer interface. The human–computer interface components and knowledge base are connected through the problem processing system. The language system accepts and processes a user's inputs. Next to navigational elements, the presentation system presents outcomes of the DSS's reasoning and, if desired, provides additional information explaining presented outcomes (Klein and Methlie 1995: 282). Based on a user's inputs and factual and inference rules from the knowledge base, the problem processing system is able to make inferences within a certain knowledge domain. Subsequently, outcomes of these inferences are transmitted back to the presentation system component of the human–computer interface. Different reasoning mechanisms can be used within the problem processing system (Luger and Stubblefield 1998). Finally, the knowledge base contains factual and inference rules information. Factual information concerns encoded declarative knowledge from a certain knowledge domain. Inference rules represent procedural knowledge from a certain knowledge domain.

In order to describe situations in which a human and a computer system interact to performing a certain task together, Waern's (1989: 124) framework is appropriate. She posits that the introduction of a computer system within a task environment transforms the task into a two-actor job. No longer does the human perform the task alone; the computer takes over those parts of the task that it can do better than the human actor (Waern 1989). Depending on where the border is drawn, the original task falls into two subtasks. One subtask remains the human's responsibility while the computer performs the other (Waern 1989).

Because the original task is split between two actors, the actors need to communicate in order to co-ordinate their individual actions. Waern (1989: 127) calls this split the 'division of labour' between the human and the computer. In order for both human and computer to perform their respective subtasks, both require a certain model representing their own task. In addition, both human and computer require a certain representation of the other. Waern emphasises that, in order to co-operate with another actor, it is not sufficient simply for each actor to have a representation of its own task (1989: 137):

> Users have to learn the system's model of the task before they can cope adequately with the task in the system.

For similar reasons, a model of the user must be embedded within the computer system. Depending on the designer's intentions, a computer system needs to be able to determine what information the human can and cannot understand and, consequently, adapt its information exchange. At present, such a user model is lacking from the DSS developed through the Agrobiokon programme. This is the main reason for the lack of knowledge transfer using DSS in the AVEBE context. The lack of user representation disrupts Agrobiokon's strategy for tailored knowledge transfers for different types of farmers. In order to rectify this, we posit a hypothesis that the four different clusters used to differentiate between farmers on economic grounds can also be equated to distinct decision-making and learning behaviours.

Method

Three different measurements were taken at three different points in time. The first was a questionnaire sent to AVEBE's entire Dutch farmer population in December 2004 (N ≅ 2,100). This asked about farmers' familiarity with and use of information sources, and their views on cultivar selection. With regard to information sources, farmers were asked to rate their applicability to starch potato growth. Farmers were also asked whether they use Optimeel crop registration and DSSs. On cultivar selection, farmers were asked to specify whether they took account of certain potato-related variables in making their decision and, if so, how important these variables were to the decision-making process.

In total, 720 farmers responded to the first questionnaire. Of these, 608 could be ascribed to a cluster as follows: 181 were top farmers (29.7% of 608); 218 quantity farmers (35,9% of 608); 122 quality farmers (20.1% of 608); and 87 normal farmers (14.3% of 608).

The respondents to this survey were then asked about their attitudes to learning and personality, again via a questionnaire. The learning questionnaire was inspired by the Motivated Strategies of Learning Questionnaire (MSLQ) (Pintrich and de Groot 1990) and adapted to a farming context (Pieters 2005). The personality questionnaire was inspired by the Five-Factor Personality Inventory (Hendriks 1997), a validated instrument for measuring five personality factors. In total, 359 farmers responded to the second measurement of which 119 were top farmers (33.2% of 359), 131 quantity farmers (36.5% of 359), 66 quality farmers (18.4% of 359) and 43 normal farmers (11.9% of 359).

The third measurement took place at the 2005 potato cyst nematode day, during which farmers received advice on nematode risks for their crops and countermeasures to take. Visitors to the potato cyst nematode day were asked to run a complete session of OPTIras™. These sessions were timed and the operator's behaviour was noted by the researchers. At the end of the sessions, participants were asked to fill out a questionnaire consisting of three constructs from the Software Usability Measurement Inventory (SUMI), a validated instrument for measuring the usability of software. The three constructs were helpfulness, control and learnability, each composed of ten indicators. Helpfulness refers to the extent to which the software is self-explanatory. The dimension of control denotes the degree to which the software can be controlled by the user. Finally, learnability is the extent to which a user understands the system and is able to learn the system's new features (Kirakowski 1994). Additionally, participants were asked to specify whether they experienced problems using OPTIras™. Because of the in-depth treatment, only 22 individuals participated in this third measurement activity. Of these 22, 17 were farmers. Of these 17, 11 farmers could be allocated to an appropriate cluster—five top farmers, four quantity farmers, one quality farmer and one normal farmer.

Results

Measurement 1

No significant differences exist between clusters with regard to the value of information sources ($\alpha = 0.05$). However, significant differences exist between clusters in relation to the use of social and electronic sources of information. Table 14.5 shows the Pearson χ^2 values for variables representing familiarity with social information sources that significantly differ between clusters. The cluster(s) that show significant differences from the other clusters are mentioned in the column 'Highest cluster(s)'.

Familiar with	Pearson χ^2	df	Highest cluster(s)	p
Starch potato study groups	27.1	6	1	<0.01
Field gatherings electronic potato	24.9	6	2	<0.01
Extension workers	27.0	6	1 and 2	<0.01
Experimental farm demo days	41.5	6	1 and 2	<0.01

TABLE 14.5 Familiarity with social information sources

Table 14.6 displays Pearson χ^2 values regarding significant differences between different types of farmers and their familiarity with electronic information sources. Tables 14.5 and 14.6 indicate that farmers from high-yielding clusters are more aware of different social and electronic sources of information. Additionally, top farmers are more familiar with study groups on starch potato growth in general whereas quantity farmers are more acquainted with field gatherings focusing on the electronic potato. Quality and normal farmers are largely unaware of the social and electronic sources of information. No differences are found in the appreciation of the different social and electronic sources of information ($\alpha = 0.05$). Additionally, types of farmers do not differ concerning their familiarity with OPTIras™ (Pearson $\chi^2 = 7.629$, df = 6, p = 0.267) and OPTIrob™ (Pearson $\chi^2 = 5.496$, df = 6, p = 0.482).

Familiar with	Pearson χ^2	df	Highest cluster(s)	p
Optimeel crop registration	27.1	6	1 and 2	<0.01
Kennisakker portal	24.9	6	1 and 2	<0.01

TABLE 14.6 Familiarity with electronic information sources

Table 14.7 shows Pearson χ^2 values for variables denoting use of different information sources by the farmer. Computer use and use of Optimeel crop registration during their last growth are significantly higher among top farmers. Additionally, use of DSSs is higher among top and quantity farmers.

Use of	Pearson χ^2	df	Highest cluster(s)	p
Computer	16.7	3	1	<0.01
Optimeel during last growth	13.8	3	1	<0.01
Decision-support systems	7.9	3	1 and 2	<0.05

TABLE 14.7 Use of electronic information sources

Regarding the value farmers ascribe to factors involved in cultivar selection decisions, differences are found regarding timing of delivery of starch potatoes to the AVEBE factories, base weight and protein content (see Table 14.8). Quality farmers ascribe

Factor of importance	Pearson χ^2	df	highest cluster(s)	p
Delivery moment	25.9	12	3	<0.01
Base weight	18.1	9	1 and 2	<0.05
Protein content	26.7	12	3 and 4	<0.01

TABLE 14.8 Important factors within cultivar selection

higher value to early delivery to the factory. Top and quantity farmers value base weight as being more important than do quality and normal farmers. Finally, quality and normal farmers ascribe more importance to protein content of potatoes. No differences exist regarding other factors of cultivar selection between types of farmers (α = 0.05).

Summarising the first questionnaire's findings, different types of farmers differ in the way they handle information. Electronic channels of communication seem more suitable for top farmers and quantity farmers even though OPTIras™ is intended for quality and normal farmers. And they are also more likely to attend conferences, advice days and other social gatherings regarding starch potato growth. Finally, top and quantity farmers seem more critical of the information they receive, and they appear better at determining relevant criteria to select cultivars (base weight) then normal and quality farmers (protein content).

Measurement 2[7]

Farmer learning styles and personalities differ between the four economic clusters. Farmer clusters differ significantly on the learning motivation scales of extrinsic value and self-efficacy and on the learning skills scales of peer learning and help seeking. Figure 14.5 shows the major findings while Figure 14.6 gives all the results of the inquiry. Top farmers appear to have better learning attitudes relative to other cluster types. Quality-oriented farmers seem to lag behind with respect to their learning skills. Normal farmers (cluster 4) rank very high on extroversion and openness. This suggests that this group may be less interested in improving starch potato cultivation and more interested in other aspects of farming and farm life. Learning styles and personality impact on farmers' use of DSSs; especially anxiety is one of the factors that impedes the use of DSSs.

Measurement 3

The average time all participants spent using OPTIras™ is 12.19 minutes (SD = 5.046). On average, farmers took 12.59 minutes (SD = 5.209, N = 17) while other participants on average used 10.50 minutes (SD = 4.509, N = 4). One participant did not finish his session.

7 This section summarises the research of Pieters (2005).

224 SUSTAINABLE INNOVATION

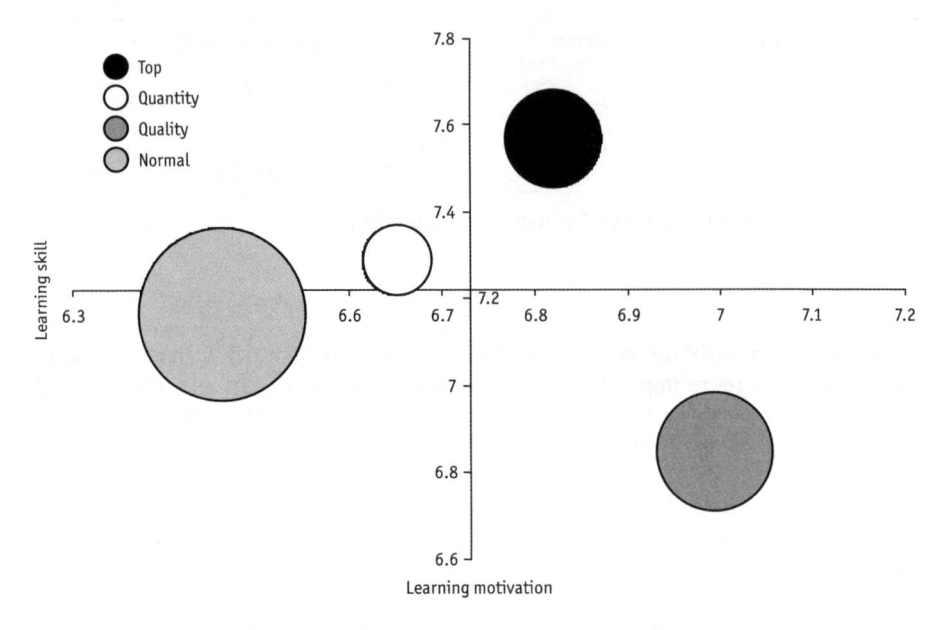

Note: The sizes of the circles correspond to the scales of openness and extroversion. The clusters conform to those in Figure 14.2.

FIGURE 14.5 Farmer clusters for learning motivation (extrinsic value and self-efficacy), learning skills (peer learning and help seeking) and personality

Table 14.9 reports the scores on SUMI constructs of helpfulness, control and learnability, whereby a distinction is made between farmers and other participants to OPTIras™ sessions. Both farmers and other participants report above-average scores on helpfulness and control. Similarly, learnability is reported just above average by both groups of participants. Most participants had no problems using OPTIras™, although one participant, who did not have computer experience, was unable to complete the task.

	Farmers (N = 17)		Other participants (N = 4)	
Construct	Average	SD	Average	SD
Helpfulness	23.50	1.592	21.25	4.272
Control	22.56	1.590	22.75	1.708
Learnability	16.19	3.600	15.75	1.258

TABLE 14.9 Scores on SUMI constructs of helpfulness, control and learnability

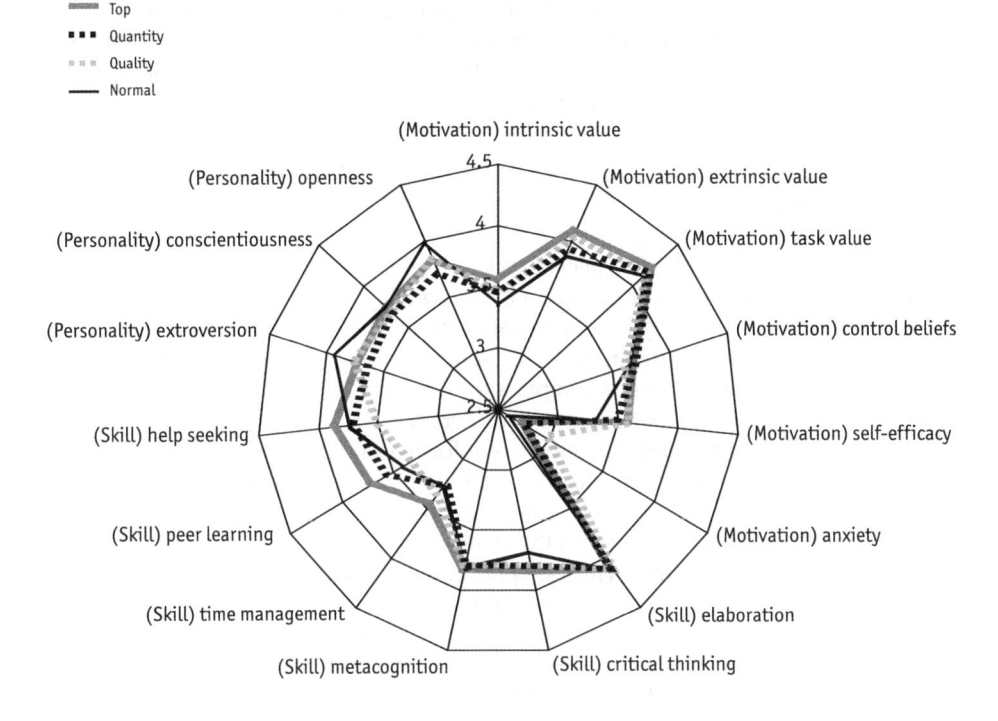

FIGURE 14.6 Radar plot for learning motivation and personality for farmer clusters

The AVEBE project in terms of innovation and sustainability

As mentioned previously, political, environmental, social and technical developments have forced the starch potato farmer to innovate in order to survive, not just in economic terms but also in terms of sustainability.

Farmers need KoS in order to take proper account of the social and ecological consequences of their decisions. Although this knowledge was generated in the Agrobiokon programme and made available to farmers in different ways, it did not prove useful.

The Agrobiokon programme focuses on the entire value chain from seed potatoes to final products in food, paper and industrial specialities. The farmer marks the beginning of this value chain, followed by AVEBE and, finally, the potato starch processing industry. Agrobiokon also involves other parties, as mentioned previously.

Agrobiokon activities are directed towards the generation of new knowledge to benefit starch potato farmers and help them improve their farms' sustainability. Thus, Agrobiokon activities have resulted in knowledge about a sustainable value chain of starch potato growth. Transferring this knowledge to farmers is a key Agrobiokon objective. DSSs are of particular importance because farmers rarely use them in making growth-related decisions. Agrobiokon hereby focuses on the transfer and embedding of knowledge in the existing starch potato growth process. In summary, Agrobiokon should lead to SoK as well as to KoS.

Conclusions

Farmers have their own ideas, especially when it comes to farming methods, and are often resistant to change. But innovation in the starch potato value chain is inevitable if it is to survive. In realising necessary innovations, AVEBE participates in the Agrobiokon programme, attempting to steer its members towards a more sustainable manner of farming. However, these attempts are blocked if farmer characteristics or the ways farmers interact with DSSs are not considered.

Different farmers use different sources of information and do so in different ways. This has implications for communicating with the farming community. High-yielding farmers use DSSs, the internet, study groups and other sources of information. In contrast, low-yielding farmers do not use these information sources and so cannot, therefore, be reached through them. Thus, it appears that the current approach to disseminating OPTIras™ does not meet Agrobiokon objectives. Furthermore, we find that information geared to low-yielding farmers should express farming-related topics much more carefully. Low-yield farmers are less critical of the information they receive and so may base their growth-related decisions on less relevant factors (e.g. protein content). Additionally, different types of farmers report different learning skills and motivations. Because top farmers possess the necessary skills and are more motivated to learn, they are more inclined to innovate. But for normal, quality and quantity farmers, the possibilities for innovation are considered low. Finally, if OPTIras™ is to be a means of realising innovation in the value chain of starch potatoes, its learnability needs to be improved. Systems, such as OPTI™ and OPTIrob™, which are perceived as simple by scientists, were frequently used by highly educated farm extension workers and top farmers. This implies that top farmers and extension workers probably understand these systems better than other farmers. In other words, these decision-support systems reflect the more complex decision process of top farmers and extension workers. The connection with the decision processes of the targeted farmer groups, i.e. quality and normal farmers, does not exist.

We explain the finding that farmers are not using DSSs for their growth-related decisions on the lack of user involvement in the design phase of a DSS. The Agrobiokon programme developed new insights into the value chain of starch potato growth including knowledge about the costs and benefits of farming and links to starch potato biology. To inform farmers, this new knowledge was encoded and made available through a variety of information channels. In addition to paper-based communication, several DSSs were realised either as prototypes (e.g. TIPSTAR™) or developed as operational systems (e.g. OPTIras™ and OPTIrob™).

However, the translation from scientific research into practical tools was hampered by the lack of user involvement at the design stage. While on the one hand the Agrobiokon programme succeeded in enhancing KoS of the value chain of potato starch potatoes, SoK was not assured. Enhancing the SoK within the Agrobiokon programme is necessary if the starch potato industry in the Netherlands is to survive.

15
Sustainability of knowledge within mental healthcare
KNOWLEDGE INFRASTRUCTURE,
KNOWLEDGE MANAGEMENT AND LEARNING

Henk Hadders and Derk Jan Kiewiet

What is the value of sustainable development without good health? Health can be considered as an important integrating index which reflects the current state and, in the long term, the sustainability of our ecological and our social–economic environment (Martens 2005). 'Steering' the health and healthcare transition demands a multi-level policy that comprises social, economic and environmental sectors. At the individual level, the social, cultural and behavioural aspects that determine health should be addressed, but this can be done in a sustainable manner only in combination with an organisational and societal approach. Our society faces structural, persistent and sometimes severe problems that cannot be solved by incremental changes alone. These problems occur not only in healthcare but also in the areas of agriculture, energy, water, transport and ageing (Rotmans 2003, 2005).

On the societal level we have no sustainable health systems that generate sustainable results, and from a social and economic perspective it has generally been agreed that the current systems for providing 'health' will not be sustainable in the future either. Daily, newspapers report the various symptoms of non-sustainable development in the healthcare context. Access to healthcare is limited. Costs are frequently higher than necessary and more extensive than societies can afford in the long term. In most OECD (Organisation for Economic Co-operation and Development) countries, expenditure on healthcare is outpacing economic growth, forcing governments to find new funds or to pass a larger share of the costs on to individuals (OECD 2003). Care provision by healthcare organisations is plagued with problems of timeliness, quality concerns and errors. In many developed countries serious chronic diseases are associated with lifestyle choices (e.g. obesity, heart disease) while in developing countries infectious diseases such as AIDS, poor sanitary conditions and malnutrition pose major health risks (WBCSD 2005).

Although a great deal has been written about the role of environmental factors in (public) health, policy-makers rarely recognise the dependence of healthcare services on the environment or the environmental impact of their activities. In addition, the numerous institutions and public–private partnerships in the healthcare sector consume huge quantities of water, energy and resources, and produce vast quantities of waste and pollution. Although the ecological and social (McElroy 2003) footprint of the Dutch healthcare system has not been analysed, it is clear that national healthcare systems depend on wealthy economies (which are themselves unsustainable) to sustain them. According to Jameton and Pierce (2001), governments in developed societies should start focusing on how to reduce the scale of healthcare to more modest, sustainable levels.

There is a great gap between healthcare as we know it and the healthcare we should receive. This also holds for the subdomain of the Dutch mental healthcare sector (known as GGZ in Dutch). How can we solve these problems? What is needed is more open knowledge management that is focused on sustainability at both an organisational and a societal level, combined with new governance structures and organisational and societal learning environments (Waddell 2002). In addition, we need a transition to a new system: for example, an 'open' healthcare enterprise, pursuing perfection and high performance.

According to Mark McElroy (2003), director of the Centre for Sustainable Innovation,[1] in order to be sustainable an organisation should possess two things: knowledge of its impact on the world and the ability to innovate or learn in response. But how does an organisation acquire knowledge? How does problem-solving and learning take place within the organisation and its teams? Are learning mechanisms helpful or maladaptive? When organisations continue to produce large-scale negative ecological or socioeconomic effects, their learning systems are maladaptive by definition (Doppelt 2003; McElroy 2003). Symptoms of unsustainable performance can be detected at the business process level of an organisation; on this level one can observe behaviour expressing 'existing knowledge in use'. Healthcare needs sustainable innovation (Jorna, van Engelen and Hadders 2004). Knowledge management has to play an important role here, enhancing knowledge processing to generate new knowledge, allowing organisations to adapt effectively to changes and realising sustainable competitive advantages (McElroy 2003). Knowledge processing within organisations consists of two major processes: knowledge production and knowledge integration (i.e. innovation). Plesk (2003) has added a third (sub)process for healthcare: the widespread adoption of innovative ideas across organisations. In the past a great deal of attention was paid to the dispersal, diffusion and sustainability of best practices, but this was mostly done from a mechanical top-down, command-and-control point of view. However, societal systems and organisations are complex adaptive systems and we should therefore make use of systems thinking and complexity science to try to influence the

---

[1] www.sustainableinnovation.org.

existing learning processes (Ravensbergen and Mik 2003; Gezondheidsraad 2000).

On a national level, we need a vision and policy programme to close the gap in the mental healthcare sector and to adopt a permanent path towards sustainability. An agenda for change should consist of five parts (IOM 2001; Schellekens 2003):

1. On the level of the individual patient (the ultimate healthcare experience) the focus has to be on systems/services that are safe, effective, patient-centred, timely, efficient and equitable

2. On the team and process level, new principles and rules for the design of care are required, including an understanding of complex adaptive systems and organisational learning based on commitment, evidence, customised care, a free flow of information and shared knowledge, transparency, safety as a system property, co-operation among clinicians (within the regional chain), anticipation of client needs and waste minimisation

3. On the organisational level there has to be support to redesign care processes, to invest in ICT and knowledge technology, to manage knowledge and skills, to develop effective multidisciplinary teams, to co-ordinate care and to measure and improve performance and results

4. On a societal level, 5–10 priority conditions should be identified (e.g. depression, anxiety, Alzheimer's, schizophrenia) and innovation should be funded

5. On the societal level there are four critical environmental factors that have to be aligned: ICT, payment, clinical knowledge and professional workforce (education)

In short, the new principles and rules for the design of care mentioned above are all aimed at establishing care that is evidence-based, patient-centred and systems-based. Critical success factors are the use of ICT and the recognition of the growing knowledge gap and ways to close this gap (Open Clinical 2000). Three business projects of the NIDO programme (see Chapter 1) focus on sustainable innovation within the mental healthcare sector and they have contributed at the organisational and national level to the issues mentioned above. This chapter describes the work of the Trimbos Institute (the Dutch mental healthcare knowledge institute) in developing a national knowledge infrastructure (i.e. clinical knowledge, education). We then describe the projects of GGZ Drenthe (a mental healthcare provider) to illustrate the development and testing of a methodology for formulating a knowledge strategy at an organisational level (knowledge and skills management, ICT). This is followed by a description of the projects of GGZ Drenthe and GGZ Netherlands (the Dutch organisation for mental healthcare) in which a functional design is presented of a knowledge portal to support care delivery, research and clinical education (ICT, knowledge technology and clinical knowledge).

Knowledge infrastructure, stakeholders and evaluation

Mental healthcare in the Netherlands consists of a large number of different parties. These parties do not, however, operate as individual non-communicating entities. Rather, they form clusters that overlap and share knowledge. Thus, Dutch mental healthcare is characterised by a large number and variety of knowledge flows. Each of these knowledge flows has a (knowledge) supplier and a (knowledge) receiver. The entirety of suppliers, receivers and flows is called the **knowledge infrastructure** within the mental healthcare system. In order to make sure that within this knowledge infrastructure the supply of and demand for knowledge are attuned efficiently and effectively, a **knowledge policy** is required. After a conference in 1998 a policy of this kind was established in 2000 for mental healthcare (Verburg 2001). Among other things, this policy laid down which fields required new knowledge, how co-operation in the development of knowledge could be initiated and facilitated, what roles the different parties should have in the knowledge infrastructure (for example, co-ordination, evaluation or technological support) and what requirements would have to be set for new knowledge to make it suitable for the development of care programmes within the mental healthcare system. The implementation of this knowledge policy will be evaluated in future research. Given the importance of the knowledge flows within the infrastructure, an evaluation of this kind will be aimed especially at the roles of the various parties within this infrastructure. To structure this evaluation, a theoretical framework is required. Here, we discuss such a framework in conjunction with additional research questions.

The knowledge policy is based on the **knowledge cycle**. This consists of five phases that describe the development of knowledge and how it may be applied. These phases are:

- Knowledge development
- Knowledge synthesis
- Knowledge translation
- Knowledge transfer and implementation
- Knowledge evaluation

In the knowledge development phase new knowledge is developed by means of scientific research. Universities and research institutions play an important role in this phase. This new knowledge has, however, not yet been dispersed or categorised, nor have its components been compared for consistency. The collection and comparison of this knowledge (as well as making it accessible) takes place in the knowledge synthesis phase. Knowledge synthesis is performed by, among others, the Trimbos Institute. Although after this phase reliable knowledge of a particular theme is available, this knowledge can often not immediately be used in practice. This translational step takes place in the knowledge translation phase by means of establishing directives and protocols. The Trimbos Institute as well as the national knowledge centre ZonMW-Geestkracht (part of the Dutch National Science Foundation) are, for example, parties engaged in knowledge translation. This translated knowledge then needs to be put into practice. Simply offering directives and protocols does not automatically mean that people will use them. In the knowledge transfer and implementation phase the translated knowledge is dispersed and its use ensured through continuing education. The national knowledge centres of the Dutch mental healthcare system, as well as training and post-educational institutes, are active during this phase. Finally, the concluding phase of the knowledge cycle determines to what extent the knowledge has actually proved usable in practice. The Trimbos Institute mainly carries out this knowledge evaluation.

Between two phases of the knowledge cycle knowledge transfer takes place. To study this transfer, a distinction is made between the knowledge **context** and the knowledge **outcome**. The knowledge outcome is the (desired) increase in the knowledge level of the knowledge receiver, while the knowledge context is formed by the knowledge management process and the co-operative culture of both the knowledge supplier and the knowledge receiver. In order to realise the desired increase in the knowledge level, the knowledge context has to adhere to certain standards (Duivenboden, Lips and Frissen 1999; Gold, Malhotra and Segars 2001).

Many authors emphasise the importance of **social capital** for knowledge accumulation. Some people, however, consider social capital merely as the structure of the network within which knowledge is realised (Baker 1990). Others also include the sources to which the network has access (Bourdieu 1986; Edelman *et al.* 2004). Nahapiet and Ghoshal (1998) indicate that, for an organisation, the availability of social capital is crucial in view of the development of **intellectual capital** (e.g. knowledge). This view suggests that knowledge accumulation can take place only within a network. Nijkamp, Bovenberg and Soete (2000) argue that going through the phases of a knowledge cycle is not an individual activity, but one that takes place within a network structure. Such a network can be defined on two aggregation levels. On the lowest aggregation level, the network is formed by individuals within an organisation who communicate by means of particular structures (formal and informal). On this level, knowledge accumulation is the result of this individual communication. Gupta and Govindarajan (2000) call this the 'system view' of the organisation. On the highest aggregation level, the network consists of various organisations; the organisations themselves form the nodes in the network and the structure of the network determines the way in which communication takes place, resulting in knowledge accumulation. Gupta and Govindarajan (2000) call this the 'nodal perspective' on an organisation.

Choosing a particular aggregation level when studying a knowledge network has consequences for the conditions that the knowledge context has to fulfil in order to achieve a particular knowledge outcome. With respect to the higher aggregation level, these conditions will have a bearing on the network of organisations while at the lower level they will affect the network of individuals within an organisation. The GGZ approaches the knowledge cycle from a nodal perspective—there are a large number of organisations connected with each other via the knowledge cycle (Verburg 2003). In this research study the organisations will therefore be considered as nodes within a network rather than as a group of individuals who are learning.

The knowledge context of an organisation within a network contains various dimensions (Gold, Malhotra and Segars 2001; Grant 1996a). The first dimension is the technological ability of an organisation to deal with a large variety of information and communication systems (Gold, Malhotra and Segars 2001) and knowledge media (Bhatt 2000). Since an effective and efficient use of these kinds of systems is dependent on the specific situation of the knowledge transfer in question (see, for example, Theunissen, Friele and Keijsers 2003), it is important that organisations are capable of using at least several of these systems. The second dimension of the knowledge context is the ability of organisations to design and implement an organisational structure that stimulates the access to, and transfer of, knowledge. The structure's flexibility is of particular importance here (Bhatt 2000; Hedlund 1994). According to Bhatt and Hedlund, the traditional 'control and authority' points of departure have to be abandoned because a structure based on these concepts hinders the organisation in its openness to new ideas, knowledge and innovations. The third dimension is the cultural one: what are the organisation's values and norms with respect to learning? If a knowledge accumulation is really to take place, the organisation should make clear that it values openness and trust (Nahapiet and Ghoshal 1998; Gold, Malhotra and Segars 2001), that the norm is to be open to criticism, that mistakes are not instantly reprimanded and that co-operation with others is sought (Starbuck 1992; Nahapiet and Ghoshal 1998). When looking at this cultural dimension from the nodal point of view, one issue that plays a role with respect to 'effective learning' is that the distance between two organisations in terms of norms and values should not be too large (Asakawa 1995; Nahapiet and Ghoshal 1998; Schlegelmilch and Chini 2003). The final dimension that plays a role is the process dimension. This dimension deals with the factual execution of the phases of the knowledge cycle. Grant (1996a) states that an organisation's place in this dimension is determined by three factors:

- **Efficiency:** the degree to which expert knowledge is sought from other parties during a particular phase in the knowledge cycle
- **Flexibility:** the degree to which an organisation is capable of interpreting new knowledge in such a way that it becomes usable for the organisation
- **Scope:** the breadth of knowledge used during the knowledge cycle process

The more efficiency, flexibility and scope, the better an organisation is capable of going through the knowledge cycle process in such a way that an accumulation of knowledge actually takes place. The above mentioned factors and relations can be depicted schematically in a conceptual model (see Fig. 15.1).

From this model the following research questions emerge:

- How is knowledge passed on?
- What organisational preconditions have to be met before knowledge can be passed on?
- On what criteria is the knowledge receiver selected?
- How is the search for new knowledge deemed successful?
- To what extent is new knowledge instantly ready for use, and what kind of activities does an organisation carry out to ensure that the usability of the new knowledge is increased?
- To what extent does the new knowledge fit in with the organisation's need for knowledge?

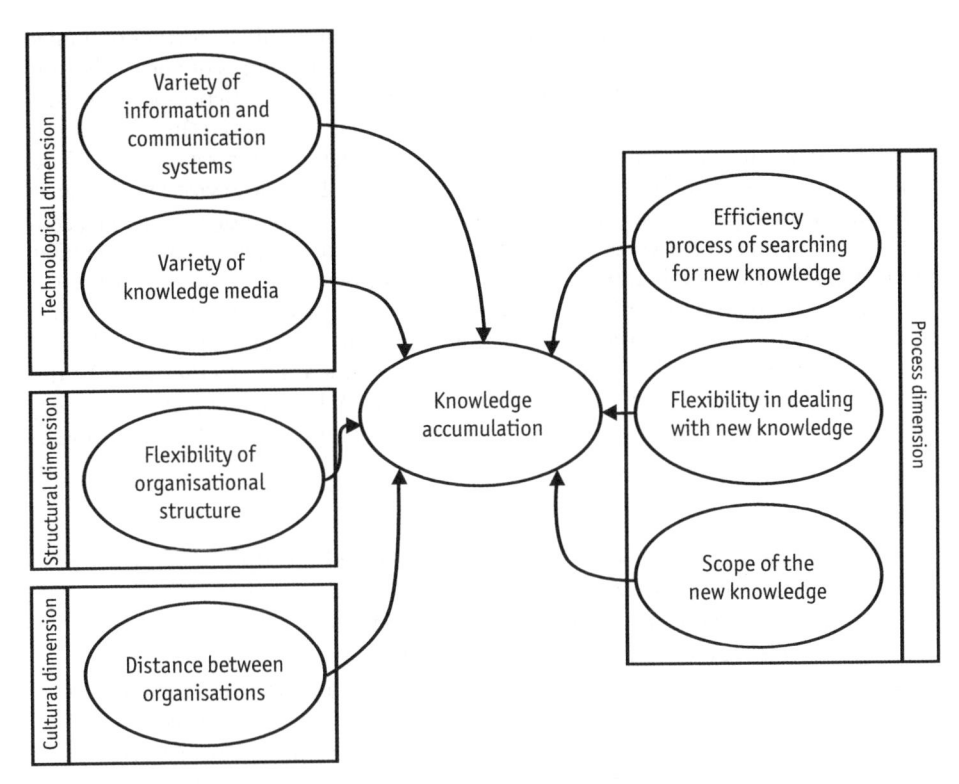

FIGURE 15.1 Conceptual model for the transfer of knowledge

A methodology for knowledge management

Mental healthcare is a knowledge-intensive sector, but most local organisations have no knowledge management strategy and neither do they have knowledge management functions at their disposal (such as a designated chief knowledge officer). Unfortunately, knowledge management initiatives are mainly ICT-related and deal with existing knowledge. What is really needed is new knowledge management (McElroy 2003; Firestone and McElroy 2003) with more attention to the production of new knowledge. Managers lack insight into how knowledge management can benefit their business operations, and they have no commitment to support initiatives on knowledge management. What is therefore required is new knowledge leadership at all organisational levels (Cavaleri and Seivert 2005). Evidence-based knowledge from outside the organisation is important, but managements should also focus on the **inside knowledge** of their workers by fostering a company-wide approach in which all people create pragmatic knowledge based on their own problem-solving experiences and openly interact with others in communities to validate new knowledge claims (Cavaleri and Fearon

2005). Practice-based research and operational innovation should be further promoted (van Yperen 2003), thereby striving to integrate the different kinds of knowledge and knowledge claims: evidence-based knowledge (researchers), practice-based knowledge (professionals) and experience-based knowledge (clients) (Hutschemaekers 2001). So, how can an enterprise become a knowledge-based organisation that is functional, adaptive, sustainable and timely? What are the roles of knowledge and knowledge management, and which knowledge management methodology should be used?

The development of a corporate strategy involves issues such as time-to-market, product and market combinations, image and so on. Besides time-to-market there is also a concept called **time-to-knowledge** which is the basis for the sustainable execution and implementation of a corporate strategy. This means that the necessary knowledge and experience are there, but that in order to realise a strategy they must be dispersed throughout the organisation or the network. A knowledge-focused strategy addresses the issue of time-to-knowledge within a strategic setting, aligning this issue

Background

GGZ Drenthe was established in 1999 after the merger of APZ Drenthe (APZ is the Dutch abbreviation for general psychiatric hospital) and RIAGG Drenthe (mental health centre). GGZ Drenthe offers many types of mental healthcare as well as care for the elderly. Its target region is the province of Drenthe in the northern part of the Netherlands. GGZ Drenthe employs more than 2,500 people (such as psychiatrists, psychologists, doctors and community psychiatric nurses). Within this framework, GGZ Drenthe treats, supports and protects people with serious psychiatric, psychosocial, forensic psychiatric, psychogeriatric or old-age problems to enable them to function autonomously to the best of their abilities. Based on the informal knowledge management initiatives taken at different levels within the organisation, a member of the board formulated a knowledge management initiative to develop a knowledge-focused strategy. Underlying questions were:

- Is knowledge management suitable for us?
- What should our strategy be?
- What are the value propositions?
- How and where should we start?

What methodology should we use? Can we use one of the current generic methods or do we need to develop our own methodology for mental healthcare?

GGZ Drenthe decided to send one of its staff members to the knowledge management masterclass of CIBIT (a leading knowledge management consultancy firm) to acquire the necessary information and to start a pilot with the support of the NIDO programme Knowledge Creation for Sustainable Innovation. The pilot had two aims: first, to formulate suggestions about how knowledge could be better shared to improve the quality of service delivery and, second, to develop and test a specific methodology to be used in a local mental healthcare organisation, in this case GGZ Drenthe (Joenje 2004; Lubbers 2004).

with other strategic aspects and translating (collective) ambition into concrete actions within relevant knowledge areas (van der Spek 2004).[2] CIBIT developed a knowledge strategy process in collaboration with partners such as ISVOR-FIAT and Siemens AG (van der Spek, Hofer-Alfeis and Kingma 2002). The main goal was to create more focused knowledge management programmes or initiatives and align them with company strategies and relevant business drivers. The knowledge strategy process is an iterative process to be integrated within the strategic management cycle. In this process, the separate steps are taken by means of workshops. ICT tools are available for assessment as well as gap analysis support, and techniques from other disciplines are used. However, applying this approach on a company level may result in rather general and high-level results, so it is more beneficial to focus the knowledge strategy process on specific departments, units or processes.

A knowledge management trajectory can be looked at from the **content** or the **process** point of view. From the content perspective there are six key elements of knowledge management: business results; people; organisational processes; knowledge (areas); knowledge processes; and the knowledge infrastructure (van der Spek and Spijkervet 1995). Knowledge management has to contribute to the results of the organisation, and people will make their contribution by performing activities that are part of the business processes. They will use existing knowledge from different knowledge areas and will learn and create new knowledge; this requires good organisation of the knowledge processes. In this context, the knowledge infrastructure (tasks, roles, ICT) supports the knowledge processes. From the process perspective, one can distinguish clear phases of activities in time during a knowledge management initiative, such as aiming, construction, implementation and communication towards the organisation as a parallel activity. The project and the pilot were especially focused on the first phase of aiming, which equates to the strategy phase. This first phase—the knowledge strategy process—consists of six basic steps and results in an important delivery document—a knowledge management action plan (see Fig. 15.2). We will give a brief description of these steps and an illustration of the results.

Step 1: Specification of the business case

This step aims at a clear description of the characteristics of the business case. It aims to establish boundaries and perspective (e.g. that of the business unit or of the process). For a proper understanding of the business case, information should be collected about, for example, the context and the strategic challenges the organisation is facing or what developments are expected within the next foreseeable future. Images of the future could be obtained through scenarios. If the overall strategy of the company is not clear, subsequent steps will be difficult to perform.

---

2   The relationship between strategy and knowledge management is fiercely debated. One school argues that knowledge management strategy should be aligned with organisational or corporate strategy (the management-based approach), whereas the other school opposes this view. The latter claims that the organisation's knowledge processing abilities should be enhanced, including the involvement of corporate strategies and the knowledge claim evaluation of these strategies (the governance-based approach) (Firestone and McElroy 2004).

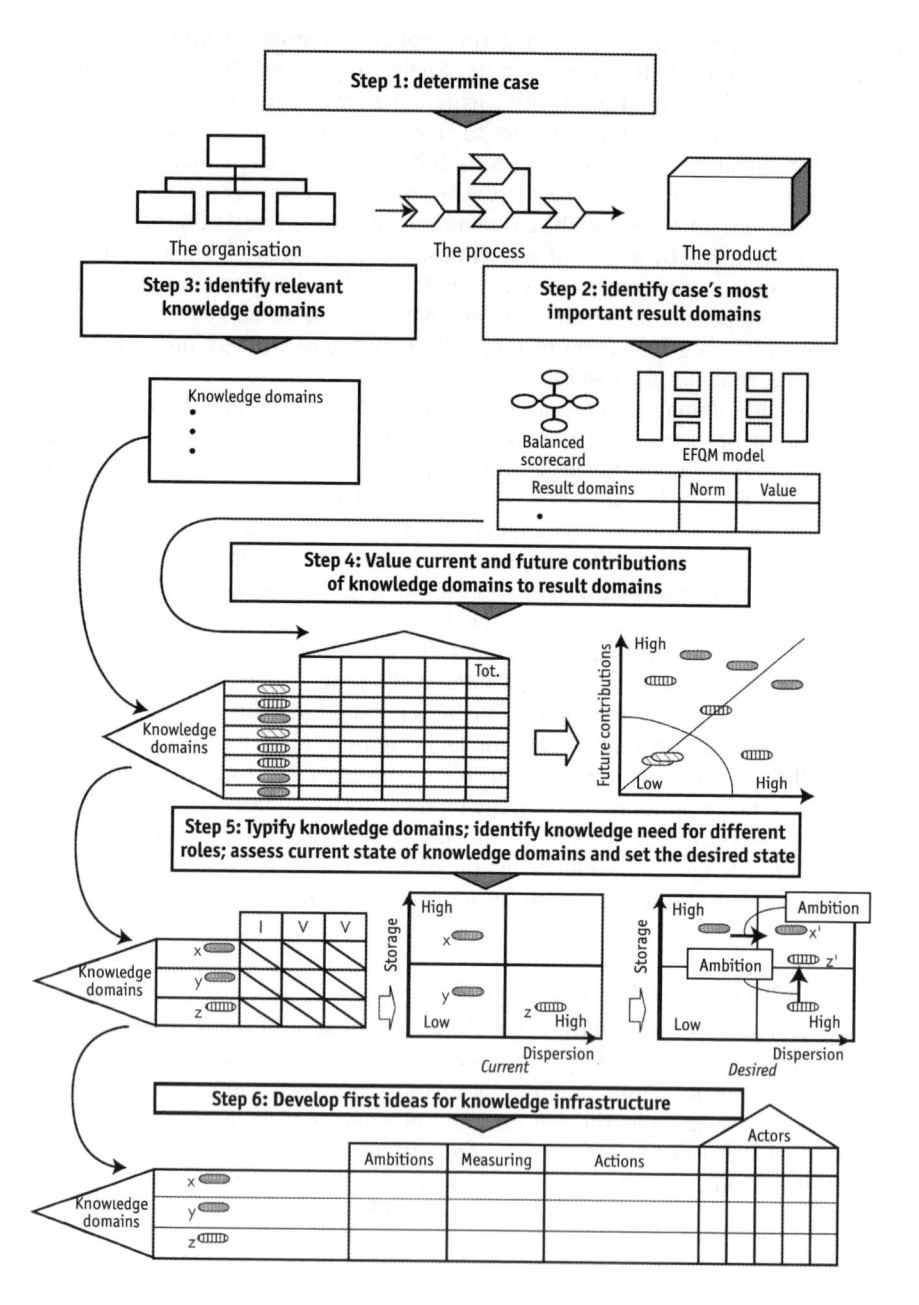

FIGURE 15.2 A knowledge management action plan

Sources: CIBIT; Kingma and Rienstra 2002

Step 1: business case
For the realisation of the pilot, GGZ Drenthe selected a (closed) unit of the forensic psychiatric clinic as the scope of the business case. The clinic offers both ambulant and clinical forms of treatment. It deals with clients who have psychiatric problems and have got into trouble with the law or are in danger of doing so. The clinic is basically the front line between the criminal justice system and healthcare. Professionals working in the unit are psychiatrists, social psychiatric nurses, psychologists and group leaders. During this step the aspect 'culture' was added and examined.

Step 2: Identification of the knowledge areas relevant within the context of the case

The result of this step is a high-level list of knowledge areas relevant for both the organisation and future scenarios. Knowledge areas are coherent clusters of experience, know-how and heuristics which are coupled to the relationship between the input and output of a process. Knowledge areas can be focused on customer groups, services, products, processes or technologies. It is important to determine the characteristics of the knowledge areas by asking questions such as:

- How dynamic is the knowledge area?
- Who are the internal and external actors within the area?
- What type of knowledge is involved?

During this step various techniques and tools from other disciplines are used.

Step 3: Identification of the most important key performance indicators in the context of the business case

This step aims at identifying the contribution of knowledge management to performance. The result is a list containing all the relevant key performance indicators (KPIs) as well as references to existing measurement methods and systems, current scores and targets. In this context it is important to relate as much as possible to systems (such as the **balanced scorecard**) and the indicators already in use.

Step 4: Analysis of the knowledge areas in terms of the current and future impact on KPIs

The main objectives of this step are to identify the relationship between performance and knowledge areas, and to assess whether the impact of these areas will increase or decrease in the future. The result is a prioritised list of knowledge areas. The assessment will be performed by applying relative scoring techniques and by depicting the

Strep 2: knowledge areas/clusters

Which knowledge areas are important for the pilot unit? In the workshops a large number of knowledge areas were identified and then clustered. The following five were chosen to elaborate on:

1. Psychiatric disorders
2. Treatment knowledge
3. Social and communication skills
4. Legal knowledge
5. Patient information

Jorna (2001a) makes a distinction between the top-down and the bottom-up knowledge management strategy. The top-down strategy starts with processes and structures. The (bottom-up) approach taken here starts from the tasks and activities individuals have to perform and the knowledge that is required (similar to taking a 'knowledge snapshot'). Three knowledge types were classified in the Castor project: sensory, codified and theoretical (see Chapters 6 and 23). Further research has indicated that the knowledge areas differ in the importance of knowledge types. The knowledge areas psychiatric disorders, treatment knowledge and legal knowledge mainly consist of theoretical knowledge. The area of social and communicative knowledge, however, involves mainly sensory knowledge. In general, codified knowledge scores the lowest.

Step 3: performance areas

There are performance indicators on different levels: national (the sector, GGZ Netherlands); organisational (GGZ Drenthe); and local (the pilot unit). A brainstorming session identified the following local indicators:

1. Prevention of recidivism
2. Optimal treatment offers
3. Optimal treatment setting
4. Abstinence (no access to alcohol and drugs)
5. Motivated patients taking responsibility for their treatment
6. Adequate referral to a subsequent setting
7. Employee satisfaction

results in a matrix that can be visualised in a knowledge portfolio. Scores can be analysed in various ways; one can focus on the impact of knowledge areas on each indicator or one can aggregate all KPIs. At this step the classification into four types of knowledge categories might be helpful: promising, key, basic or non-relevant (van der Spek and Spijkervet 1995). Or one could make use of the knowledge types described by Zuurbier (2004): exploration, exploitation, optimisation and acquirement.

Step 4: impact analysis
With respect to the current impact of the knowledge areas, the 18 participants in the pilot unit scored low on the performance indicators. Added to this step was a questionnaire which also focused on knowledge types and ways of learning (practice experience, communication and study). Experience in actual practice is generally considered by everyone as the best learning method.

Step 5: Assessment of the knowledge areas in terms of proficiency, codification and diffusion

The aim of this step is to determine more precisely the different ambitions and requirements with respect to the most important knowledge areas, so that a knowledge management action plan can be drawn up more efficiently. In addition, this step helps to determine the risks arising from *not* taking any action. To underpin their suitability, the knowledge areas are assessed in terms of three dimensions (each with a four-level scale from 1 for beginner to 4 for expert):

- Proficiency
- Diffusion among internal/external parties
- Codification (e.g. handbooks, training materials, intranet)

There are two assessments, one for the current situation ('as is') and one for the situation as desired ('to be') in one, two or three years. A gap analysis is performed on the results and a matrix and a graphical visualisation are produced. Another activity in this step could be the (high-level) identification of the knowledge requirements with respect to the different roles.

Step 6: Knowledge management action plan

The result of this step is a description of the appropriate actions necessary to support the development of the knowledge areas in accordance with the formulated ambitions, and to develop a first design of the knowledge infrastructure. Action planning should involve the use of traditional project management techniques and include standard risk assessment, project planning, staffing and cost–benefit accounting.

Step 5: assessment of the current and target state

In a workshop the levels of ambition regarding proficiency codification and diffusion were prioritised. Table 15.1 gives examples of three of the most important knowledge (sub)areas.

Knowledge subdomain	Knowledge type	Expertise/ competence	Registration	Diffusion
	Now → desired	Now → desired	Now → desired	Now → desired
Clinical syndromes (psychopathology)	ST → SCT	2.5 → 3	1 → 2	1.5 → 2.5
Treatment plan and offence/crime analysis	C → CT	3 → 3	2 → 3	2 → 3
Behaviour of patient	S → SC	2 → 2	1 → 2	1 → 2

Content	Registration	Diffusion
		Knowledge level stakeholders:
1. Moderate basic knowledge	1. Heads/minds of people	1. Moderate basic knowledge
2. Good basic knowledge	2. Descriptions, stories	2. Good basic knowledge
3. Specialist	3. Explanatory concepts	3. Specialist
4. Expert (within the Netherlands)	4. Best practices	4. Expert (within the Netherlands)

Knowledge types: S = Sensory; C = (En)coded; T = Theoretical

TABLE 15.1 Ambitions for three important knowledge areas/domains

Learning by cases: the case-based approach especially aimed at mental healthcare

The objective of this third project was to develop a functional design of a knowledge management system for organisations operating in the mental healthcare sector (Joenje 2004; van der Putten 2005). The questions GGZ Netherlands and GGZ Drenthe posed were:

- What should this knowledge management system look like?
- What functionalities should it have, using the learning experiences with the CBR (case-based reasoning) prototype of CasusConsult (see also Chapter 9)?
- How does the system fit in with the aforementioned pilot unit?

In this section we will address three parts of the project: the study of the operational business processes in the mental healthcare sector, the analysis of the experiences with the CBR prototype and the functional design of a knowledge management system in which the focus lies on the use of ICT tools (Firestone 2003; de Hoog and Wielinga 2003).

At the business process level, professionals and knowledge workers, such as psychiatrists, psychologists and community psychiatric nurses, work together in multidisciplinary teams to treat psychiatric patients (also referred to as 'cases'). Each has to fulfil a specific role and undertake various tasks within the main subprocesses of registration, intake, treatment and referral. One of the core information systems in this primary process is the patient's health record which contains structured data/information and a large number of unstructured documents, such as transcripts of therapy sessions, letters from general practitioners and so on. Most organisations still have no electronic health record system at their disposal. Structured anonymous information about individual clients is electronically fed from the health records into regional systems, such as the case register used by the province of Drenthe (Giel and Sturmans 1996) and the national Zorgis system of GGZ Netherlands. These systems with data warehouse capabilities are used for policy-making by managers and by epidemiologists for research purposes. They are, however, little used by professionals in problem-solving.

At the business process level, the professionals use information and existing knowledge to perform their roles and tasks. In the case of an operational gap (i.e. a treatment problem), they use single-loop learning to find the solution (i.e. the acquired existing knowledge). When combining information, knowledge and learning by means of the two main strategies distinguished in knowledge management (Hansen, Nohria and Tierney 1999)—the **personalisation** strategy and the **codification** strategy—the following conceptual model of knowledge use management within mental healthcare can be presented (see Fig. 15.3).

At times professionals may encounter a knowledge (or epistemic) gap when treating a case that triggers a process of double-loop learning (or knowledge-processing) based on a problem claim formulation. This process then leads to (new) knowledge production involving knowledge claim formulation, knowledge acquisition and individual as well as group learning. In this secondary knowledge processing mode the professional and mono- or multidisciplinary communities come together to test and evaluate the knowledge claim. And this is exactly what knowledge management is all about. The process of knowledge claim evaluation distinguishes knowledge production from information production and, ultimately, knowledge management from information management. When claims are not falsified but survive, the surviving knowledge claim is fed back to the organisation through knowledge integration (involving activities such as sharing, broadcasting, searching or teaching).

The main idea behind the CBR prototype of CasusConsult is to reconstruct cases and to learn from them (van der Laan 2001, 2002a, 2002b; Joenje 2004). Within the areas of education and practice **case storytelling** plays an important role in terms of teaching and learning. The main objective of CasusConsult is to capture, codify, distribute and re-use cases as 'lessons learned', and combine them with other knowledge (objects). Important issues are: how to make CBR cases and how to re-use them (see also Chapter 9).

242   SUSTAINABLE INNOVATION

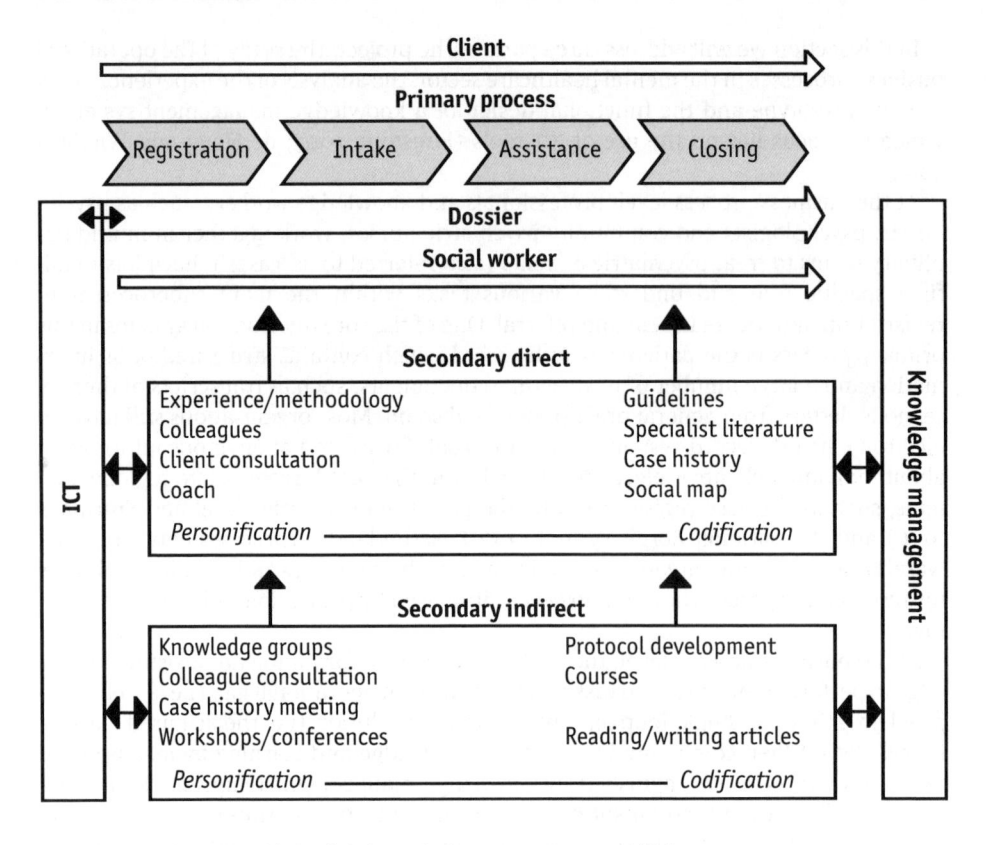

FIGURE 15.3 Conceptual model: knowledge management MHC

But what is a case? The concept has different meanings. First, there is the 'current case' which refers to the patient who has been treated during the business process by the professional team members. The information and knowledge claims are fed into the business process core ICT tool (i.e. the electronic health record of the patient). In our view, all other ICT tools should be linked to this core tool and used in combination with it. The patient's actual healthcare record should be the 'driver' of other ICT support tools, containing push and pull information flows. Due to privacy reasons, only the professionals directly involved in the treatment process are allowed to see the personal data record in its entirety. Within their team meetings these professionals discuss the problems and monitor the progress of the (case) treatment. But they may also formulate a problem claim and anonymously reveal part of the healthcare record (similar to a 'CBR case' in the making; see below) to a community of practice or inquiry within the organisation or to outside groups or experts, and ask for their reflection, advice and suggestions. This requires a knowledge management organisation consisting of moderators, experts, librarians and professionals to support these processes. The resulting discussions, knowledge claims and the scientific literature are then linked to the patient health record.

The CBR case is the electronic representation of a patient's health record which is stored in a case base and contains an anonymous summary of the completed treatment. The representation constitutes the health record's main subjects, such as demographic data, problems, intake, diagnosis, treatment, costs and results (e.g. client satisfaction, quality of life, clinical outcome, etc.). The CBR case makes use of structured and unstructured fields of the client's record and is elaborated with discussion links (containing knowledge claims by clients, professionals, team members and external actors) as well as links to articles and scientific knowledge claims provided by librarians. One of the problems encountered in the CasusConsult pilots was that professionals were supposed to write and publish their own cases (as a kind of 'after action review') and add them to the CBR case base. In the pilots too few cases were added, mainly due to the fact that in the business process environment there was hardly any time for reflection because of the high production pressures. In addition, the absence of an electronic patient health record made reconstruction quite time-consuming, having to retype (or copy and paste) all the information from the different document sources.

There is also the 'retrieved, similar case'. During the different treatment phases, as professionals make notes in the electronic patient health record these are constantly analysed with the aid of a thesaurus offering them (anonymous) cases from the case base that are similar to the one they are treating at that particular moment. If the problem is similar in the sense of solutions, tests and treatments used, costs of treatment and outcomes, the main advice will be to consider and discuss these issues with other team members in order to learn from them. This function of CasusConsult could not, however, be properly tested because too few relevant cases were coded and added to the case base. Nevertheless, research has indicated that CBR is a useful tool in mental healthcare (Bakkenist Management Consultants 1997; Verburg 2001, 2003; van der Putten 2005). In fact, the idea of an active 'corporate memory' may lead to the next or third generation of knowledge management, embedding knowledge in workplace and business work processes, and combining the competence of the individual with the work style of the collective (group, team, network or community) by means of the required ICT and KT (knowledge technology) support tools (Lekanne Deprez 2003; Berg 2000; Davenport and Glaser 2002). At present, the pilots of CasusConsult are still being carried out at the organisational level, but just consider the possibilities if CBR cases could be re-used by professionals at the regional or national level. Epidemiologists, for example, could have access to a robust non-structured (anonymous) treatment data resource. The core knowledge management tools to analyse the different knowledge claims (by clients, professionals and scientists) already exist (e.g. GreenForrest combines data and text mining to discover and produce new (scientific) patterns and knowledge.

CasusConsult is familiar with a large number of pilots within the field of education in which the case-based learning approach is taken (Visser and Gaarthuis 2003). This approach teaches students systematically to analyse a case and compare the results electronically with similar cases. If the fields of research and education would also contribute their cases (by, for example, translating the latest evidence-based results into random clinical trials and new protocols), the gaps in theory, practice and education could be further closed.

Finally, how should a knowledge management system for mental healthcare be given form at an organisational level? First, a set of functionalities suitable for the system would have to be determined, then their function in a mental healthcare setting should be described as follows:

- Electronic patient health records
- Portal
- Communities of practice
- Discussion forums
- Digital knowledge maps
- Protocol databases
- An electronic library and literature, intelligent search systems and agents
- CBR systems

The functionalities would have to be used in the functional design. Figure 15.4 illustrates the position of these components and how they are integrated.

Figure 15.4 shows that the anonymous case, the patient health record and the different ICT tools are combined into an integrated system model. Most tools will have their place on the intranet, which is to be used as the underlying system structure. The patient health record systems of ICT providers are mostly stand-alone applications. Enhancing them and linking them with other ICT tools onto the intranet will make them suitable for new case functionalities. In the outer ring of Figure 15.4 are the main requirements, such as user interface(s), content management, database management, authorisation, taxonomies/thesaurus, system interfaces and technical maintenance. Furthermore, a distinction has been made between users within the primary business process (the professionals) and users within the secondary processes (such as coach, expert and ICT personnel).

The second question of this project ('does it fit?') has been answered by conducting an empirical study within the pilot unit. Based on an analysis of the information and knowledge processes, and with the aid of dataflow diagrams, the knowledge management functionalities were tested to determine whether they had to be altered or expanded to provide the proper support in actual practice. The testing of the model proved that practically no other functionalities were required.

Final remarks

When several parties have to share knowledge with each other to attain common goals, it is crucial that the knowledge transfer is as efficient as possible. It is therefore important that the factors influencing the knowledge transfer are identified so they can be taken into account. Here, a conceptual model has been designed on the basis of a literature search in which such factors are discussed. In total seven factors have been found, subdivided into four dimensions, which play a role in knowledge transfer among parties in various organisations. The validity of this model could be assessed in future research.

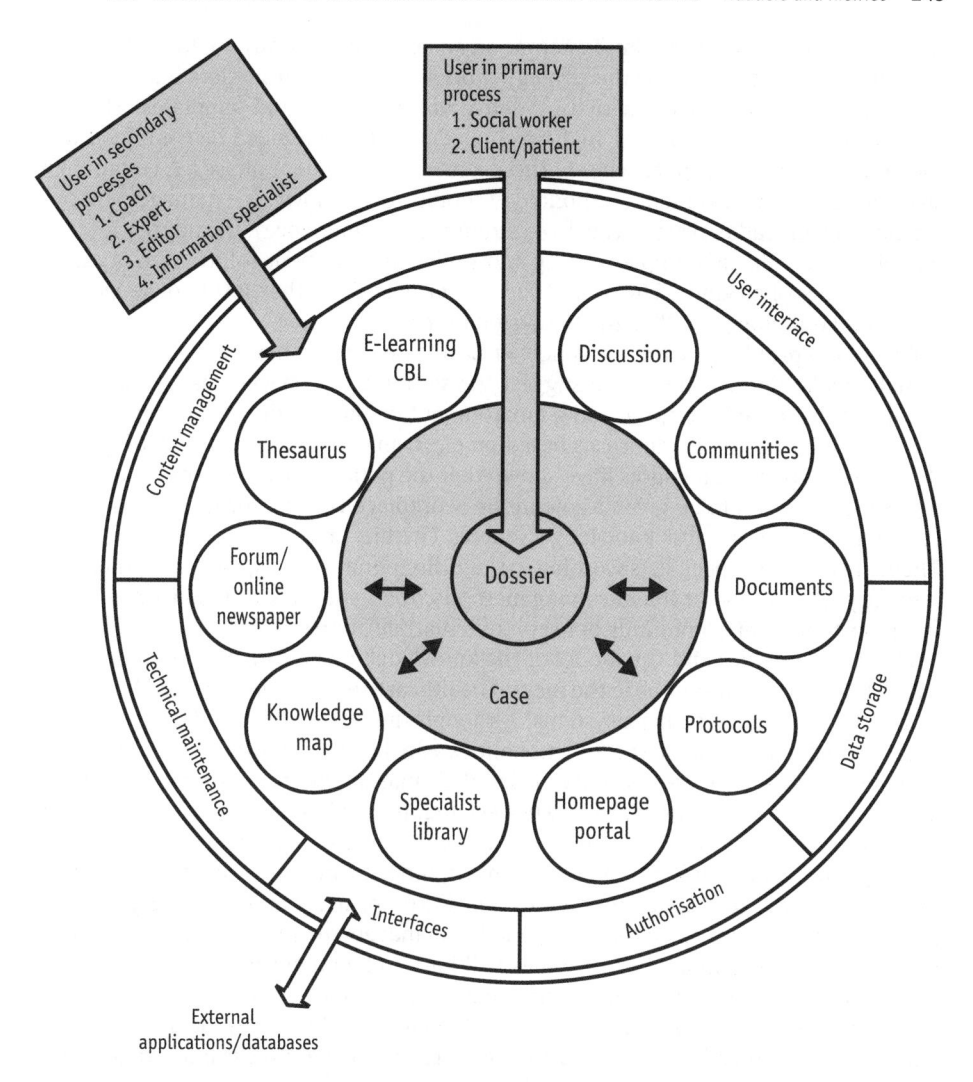

FIGURE 15.4 Integrated model: MHC knowledge system

CIBIT's knowledge strategy process worked well in a mental healthcare setting such as GGZ Drenthe. It has many good and interesting aspects. The distinction of knowledge ambitions (proficiency, codification and diffusion) has made fruitful discussions possible, even about the knowledge levels of colleagues within certain knowledge areas. The two main features added to the methodology were the introduction of three types of knowledge and three types of learning, which proved to be very useful. By these small modifications the knowledge strategy process can now be used by GGZ Drenthe within the first phase of a knowledge management initiative—the strategy and assessment phase—to formulate a knowledge-focused strategy. The other phases of the CIBIT methodology (construction, implementation and communication) are to be dealt with at a high level and do not (as the strategy process does) constitute detailed key attributes, such as descriptions of activities, deliverables, formats and templates. The next challenge is to explore how the high-level results of this phase can be combined with the mid- and low-level approaches to these issues in subsequent phases. A comprehensive knowledge management methodology should cover knowledge management programmes from cradle to grave (i.e. from strategy to maintenance), including aspects of planning, designing and implementing knowledge management solutions in organisational settings of all kinds. The overall comprehensiveness of the CIBIT knowledge management methodology will be further tested in the future.

One of the problems within the pilots of CasusConsult was having the professionals actually make the CBR cases. We suggest the setting-up of special case development groups in the knowledge processing environment or the creation (electronically and automatically) of simple CBR cases based on electronic patient health records (where these are available). The pilots have shown that the patient's health record is the starting point and it has to be given a role in the 'workplace cockpit', providing fast access to other information and knowledge sources (within or outside the organisation). There are different specialists working in multidisciplinary teams, each with their own specific problems and problem-solving methods. Tools such as CasusConsult will have to support these different kinds of users (psychiatrists, nurses, etc.).

The functionalities and the model of the knowledge management system provide a useful basis for organisations in the mental healthcare sector to develop and build their own knowledge management systems. Although the test conducted during the pilot unit showed that most of the functionalities can be used without modification, it remains necessary to always make a detailed analysis of the information and the knowledge flows in order to achieve a perfect alignment of the system with actual practice. Other recommendations are to use the electronic patient health record as the starting point and to link it to other systems in order to stimulate the development of interesting cases, to embed these cases within the primary and secondary business processes and to make sure that a knowledge management strategy and organisation are realised. Furthermore, professionals will have to be taught how to deal with profound knowledge to improve their performance, and managers will have to be trained to become knowledge leaders in an era in which high performance, operational innovation and sustainability in (mental) healthcare are of the utmost importance. Only then can SoK (sustainability of knowledge) be guaranteed.

16
The University Medical Centre Groningen
SUSTAINABLE INNOVATION IN POSTGRADUATE MEDICAL EDUCATION: A KNOWLEDGE AND LEARNING APPROACH

*Marjolein C. Achterkamp and Jan Pols**

The University Medical Centre Groningen (UMCG) offers postgraduate training in 28 different medical specialties, with the programmes organised on the basis of speciality. The specialities function as independent institutions and each individual specialty is therefore engaged in developing its own training programme.

Several developments in the healthcare sector, as well as in society, have resulted in a need for changes in medical education. There are plenty of reasons for reconsidering undergraduate, graduate and continuous medical education: for example, increasing demand for care; the long duration of the current educational trajectories; increasing shortage of specialists; restrictions with respect to the working hours due to the working time directive; and the increasing number of part-timers. To accomplish the necessary revisions, proposals have been introduced at national level, giving rise to a multitude of activities in the programmes for (under)graduate medical education.

---

* Part of the research in this project has been conducted by Wouter Scheper (University of Groningen), supervised on behalf of the UMCG by Pine Remmelts (subproject 1), Janita Vos (University of Groningen) and Marjolein Achterkamp (University of Groningen) (subproject 2) and Erik Jippes (University of Groningen), supervised on behalf of the UMCG by Ruud Veenekamp and Jan Pols (subproject 3). In the process of writing this chapter we have gratefully made use of their reports and graduation theses.

On the initiative of the University Medial Centre Groningen, the Innovation of (post)Graduate Medical Education project group (IpGME) has been set up. Its task is to support and structure innovations in postgraduate medical education in the education and training region in the northern and eastern parts of the Netherlands (ETR NE-Netherlands). The project group is supported by the Organisation and Development staff group (O&D) of the UMCG. Several O&D staff members contribute to the innovation trajectories initiated by the various programme directors.

The NIDO/UMCG project has been used to facilitate the first phase of the IpGME project. The NIDO/UMCG project was not intended to focus on all parts of the project group's assignment; it merely aimed at the innovations in the area of SoK (sustainability of knowledge) within postgraduate training programmes. These could entail educational innovations and models as well as methods for curriculum innovation. Apart from studying innovations within the curricula of specific specialities, the project has also assessed to what extent these innovations are useful for the curricula of other specialities.

The project has resulted in three subprojects which have each developed an instrument to be used by members of the staff group in innovation projects within the different specialties, namely:

- A scenario for curriculum innovations
- An instrument for making a stakeholder analysis
- An instrument for testing the organisational attainability of innovations in the area of education

This chapter outlines the role of the UMCG O&D staff group, which can play an important role in UMCG's pursuit of sustainable innovation, and describes the three subprojects finally executed in the NIDO/UMCG project.

Background

UMCG and postgraduate medical training

Employing more than 7,500 people, the UMCG is one of the largest teaching hospitals in the Netherlands. Approximately 1,000 patients are admitted every day, and there are more than 28,000 admissions to the various departments each year. Annually, accident and emergency treats 28,000 people and outpatients handles 465,000 patient contacts. The hospital has three core tasks: patient care, education and training, and research. Although these tasks are not easily separated, the NIDO/UMCG project focuses on just one: postgraduate medical education.

The current continuum of undergraduate, postgraduate and continuous medical education consists of three relatively independent parts (see Fig. 16.1). In the Netherlands, undergraduate medical education is the responsibility of the Faculty of Medicine. After a six-year programme, students are licensed to work under supervision and to enter into postgraduate medical education. The Royal Netherlands Medical Association is in charge of postgraduate medical training. It is responsible for making

1	Undergraduate medical education		
2	Postgraduate medical education for medical specialties	Postgraduate medical education for family medicines	Postgraduate medical education for social medicine
3	Continuous medical education		

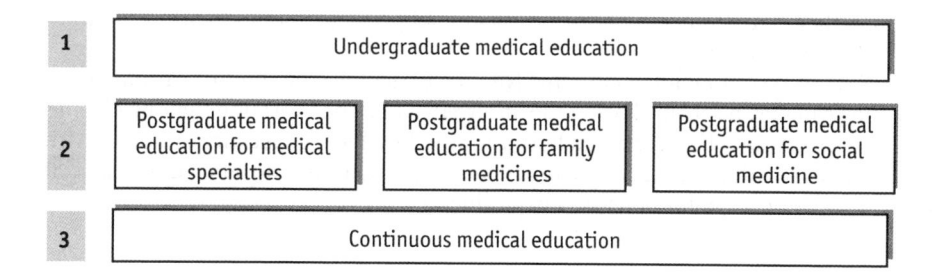

FIGURE 16.1 The current training continuum
Source: KNMG 2002

arrangements for the training programmes and the registration of medial specialists, general practitioners and physicians for public and occupational health.

At present, there are training programmes for 28 medical specialties at UMCG, ranging from surgery to neurology and paediatrics. The individual scientific associations of these specialties set the requirements for the training programmes. The Central Board for Medical Specialties (CBMS) subsequently determines the requirements. Individual specialties are responsible for structuring and executing their own training courses. The scientific associations themselves appoint programme directors in various hospitals. With respect to the content of the courses, these directors are therefore accountable, not to the hospital in which they provide the training but to the national association of the specialty in question.

The UMCG offers postgraduate training in all 28 medical specialties. In most cases, the UMCG departments provide a curriculum in co-operation with the departments of hospitals in the region, such as the Medical Spectrum Twente in Enschede and the Isala Clinics in Zwolle. In these hospitals, medical student education involves on-the-job training.

So the postgraduate training programmes do not function as one large stand-alone training institute but as 28 separate, independent organisations. This has consequences for the sharing of knowledge among the various programmes.

Staff group O&D

As already mentioned, the individual specialties are themselves responsible for the structure and execution of their training programmes. This means that they tend to carry out curriculum revisions on an individual basis. The mutual exchange of knowledge and experience largely takes place at national level within specialties, with little knowledge transfer between the specialties.

Within the UMCG, programme directors can make use of the support of the professional development group of the O&D staff group. In the past few years, the O&D group has developed a considerable degree of educational expertise which, as a result of new developments, will require further expansion.

250 SUSTAINABLE INNOVATION

One of the staff members of O&D fulfils the task of secretary to the IpGME project group. Other O&D members perform tasks in subprojects initiated within the framework of the IpGME project.

Because O&D staff members are involved in curriculum revisions of various specialties, they can play a role in sharing the knowledge obtained through their involvement in those specialties. This concerns both the way in which a specialty has dealt with a particular curriculum revision (the process) and the solutions developed by a specialty for specific educational problems (the products).

The business project: sustainable innovation in the curriculum revisions of the UMCG

Developing and sharing knowledge

The task of the IpGME project group is to develop proposals to restructure postgraduate medical training programmes, including adjustments to the curriculum. Innovations such as new modular structures and other improvements need to be developed and implemented. The NIDO/UMCG project seeks to contribute to this process by asking some key questions:

- Which innovations are successful in a curriculum revision of a medical continuation course?
- Which innovation processes lead to successful innovations?
- To what extent and in what way are these innovations applicable to other specialties?

In order for these innovations to be sustainable, knowledge must be developed in a sustainable manner and must then be shared.

The NIDO/UMCG project can be divided into three subprojects. The aim of each of these is to offer instruments to the IpGME project group and the O&D department that can be used within the innovation projects of several departments. The first project examined the extent to which the management literature dealing with successful innovation processes can be applied in the context of curriculum innovations of postgraduate training programmes for medical specialists. This has resulted in a scenario for curriculum innovations. In the second subproject, one aspect of innovation projects was studied in more detail: the identification of stakeholders. The stakeholder identification method described in Chapter 7 has partly been developed here and applied subsequently. The third subproject focuses on a specific curriculum innovation—the 'ideal way to learn'—within the surgical training programme. Among other elements this features modular education and the use of a skills laboratory. This research has resulted in an instrument for testing the organisational attainability of an educational innovation of this kind. In all subprojects co-operation took place with O&D staff members. In the remainder of this section the three subprojects will be discussed in more detail.

Subproject 1: a model for sustainable innovation within the UMCG[1]

Management literature has produced a considerable number of theories and models dealing with innovations, project teams and the development of new products or services. Many of these models have been developed in the context of for-profit organisations. This project has focused on the extent to which these theories and models can provide insight into the curriculum innovation projects at the UMCG. This led to a scenario for these projects. Figure 16.2 depicts the model on which the scenario has been based.

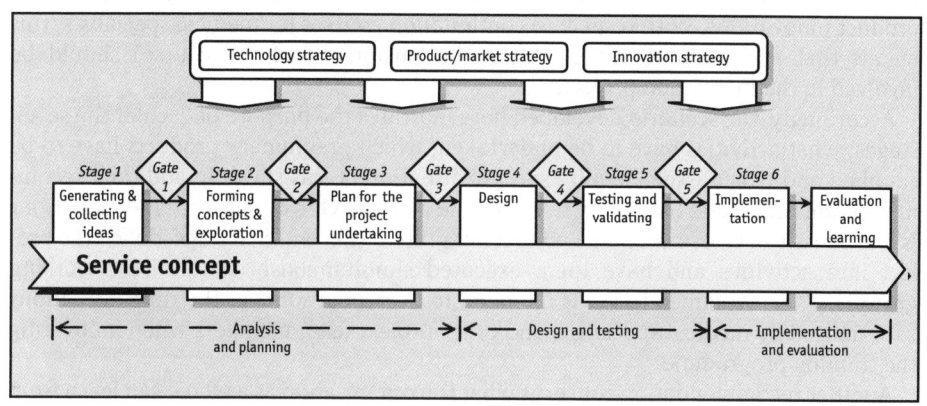

FIGURE 16.2 Model for curriculum innovation
Source: Scheper 2004

According to the model of Scheper (2004), the scenario rests on three pillars. The first links the technology strategy, the product/market strategy and the innovation strategy. This linkage leads to an umbrella project plan for the innovation project. This pillar is based on the idea that an innovation trajectory should never be detached from the other activities of the organisation (here, the medical department in question). Organisational-level strategies should indicate the goal of the innovation.

The second pillar is phasing the innovation trajectory. Analogous to the well-known innovation model of Cooper (2001), Scheper's model has a seven-stage structure. These seven stages can be joined within three umbrella stages (see Fig. 16.2). The umbrella stages (with their substages in brackets) are:

1. Analysis and planning (generating and collecting ideas; forming concepts and exploration; plan for the project undertaking)

2. Designing and testing (design; testing and validating)

3. Introduction and evaluation (implementation; evaluating and learning)

The innovation project has been structured through the demarcated stages, bounded by the 'gates' in which reports on progress achieved are tested against criteria already

---

1 For a detailed description of this subproject we refer to the master's thesis of Wouter Scheper (Scheper 2004).

made explicit. The recent literature shows that in a large number of organisations innovation processes do not take place linearly (see, for example, van de Ven et al. 1999). However, in an organisation such as the UMCG, where the development of curriculum innovation is not a core task, it is important to pursue a step-by step approach.

The third pillar is the insight that education is not a product but a service. Services differ from products in several ways. For example, an important characteristic of services is that they are produced and consumed simultaneously. The degree of customer contact is usually higher for services than for products. This has an influence on the innovation of services where the role of the customer will be more important than in product innovations. With respect to continuation courses for medical specialists, this means that postgraduate students (i.e. the 'customers' of the course) should be involved in the innovation projects.

Accordingly, the scenario developed here indicates the purpose of each of the seven stages, what activities have to be undertaken, which preliminary products have to be supplied and which issues require specific attention at this stage. In addition, recommendations are made that apply to the whole process. One of these recommendations is to make use of cross-functional project integration (i.e. within a stage, divide the project into activities and have them executed simultaneously by different working groups). This recommendation is intended to overcome some of the time limitations experienced by medical specialists and other project team members when innovating the training programme.

Another recommendation concerns what the organisation as a whole can learn from the innovation projects, so that future projects can proceed more effectively and efficiently. It is not enough simply to acquire experience; rather, the experience needs to be evaluated both explicitly and systematically. This evaluation does not just take place at the end of the project; it is crucial throughout the entire project. The gates between the stages are the appropriate points for evaluation. In this way, feedback loops are kept short, enabling mistakes to be identified and dealt with immediately. An explicit systematic framework for learning and sharing these lessons guarantees that the expertise obtained is preserved and that it will become common property throughout the whole organisation.

The recommendations are based on literature research and interviews with staff members of the O&D. The scenario does not just pay attention to the improvement of the individual innovation trajectories. A number of recommendations are also made on the way in which the O&D staff group can learn in a more sustainable manner, thus enabling the group to contribute to sharing the knowledge among the trajectories. An important recommendation here is that one has to look for ways in which knowledge can be shared, in particular within the O&D staff group. This is because there is little structured knowledge sharing either within departments or in the staff group.

Subproject 2: stakeholders in a curriculum revision process

Apart from the subproject dealing with a general model for curriculum innovations, one form of process innovation has been studied in greater detail: namely, stakeholder involvement in curriculum development. Subproject 2 used the stakeholder identification method discussed in Chapter 7. This chapter will focus on the specific requirements set by the UMCG with respect to the use of this method. The method was partly developed in this subproject and was subsequently applied by members of the O&D staff group when analysing one of the curriculum revision trajectories, that of dermatology.

Results achieved in dermatology

As stated in Chapter 7, the goal of the stakeholder identification method is to provide a complete list of stakeholders. The method structures the identification on the basis of four roles stakeholders can play in an innovation project: client, decision-maker, designer, and passively involved. In this result section, we will not give a complete overview of the obtained stakeholder list, but rather focus on interesting outcomes. For the identification of the clients of the curriculum revision in dermatology, the choice was made to view an educational course as a service, instead of as a product. Based on this choice, the course attendees (i.e. postgraduate students) emerged as the main clients. If the approach was taken that medical education courses deliver 'products' (i.e. doctors), the clients of these 'products' would be future patients, employers and colleagues. These different approaches lead to different types of demands on the curriculum revision process. Future patients, employers and, especially, colleagues make demands on the knowledge finally acquired and on the skills of the graduate medical specialist (i.e. product requirements). Apart from the demands associated with *content*, postgraduate students and staff members (i.e. dermatologists) also set requirements with respect to the *form* in which this knowledge and skills are to be learned (i.e. process demands). The discussion with the participants of the stakeholder identification method highlighted that these process demands play a bigger role in the curriculum revision of dermatology than content requirements do.

The identification of decision-makers has resulted in a fairly extensive list. What has become clear, however, is that, apart from a few decision-makers who can base their authority on making decisions according to the law, the majority of the decision-makers can base their decision authority only on specific situational circumstances. In this case the programme director consciously chooses to transfer part of his decision power to these persons.

Also regarding the identification of designers, the decision of the programme director to involve (part of) his staff in the revision is clearly visible. A noteworthy designer that has been identified is the group of representatives of patients.

In the identification of those passively involved, different parties were mentioned that could experience the consequences of the altered process of the postgraduate students. So here also, as with client identification, a process approach has been taken. It is striking that, according to the brainstorming session participants, a large number of these people should be involved regularly in the revision process. It is therefore important at the outset of the process to think about the way in which this kind of stakeholder involvement should be managed.

About the instrument

To apply the stakeholder identification method to the dermatology curriculum revision, two members of the O&D staff group participated in a three-hour brainstorming session. It is likely that a three-hour session would be too long if others, such as the programme director, postgraduate students and staff members, were required to take part.

After all, curriculum revision is not the core task of these medical specialists. Identification of active and passive stakeholders should not, however, take so long. The session described here considered the extent to which this instrument could be used in a curriculum revision of one of the medical specialties within the UMCG. Two possible adjustments were mentioned.

First, as was the situation at the meeting described here, the choice can be made to have only members of the O&D staff group participate in the brainstorming session. If a number of O&D staff members are involved in a curriculum revision, they can identify those involved and their different roles, and assign them to the different phases. Next, they can report these results at meetings with the staff members of the departments concerned. A major disadvantage of this adjustment, however, is that the staff members of the departments involved are not themselves engaged in studying the different roles and their phasing.

A second possible adjustment is to apply the instrument in a reduced form. For each role, show the participants a list of people who could possibly be involved and ask whether those listed fit the role and whether the list is complete. Then, ask participants to identify the phases in which each person on the list can play a role.

Apart from the possible application of the instrument in projects aimed at curriculum revisions, members of the O&D staff group could also use it in other projects, such as the IpGME.

Subproject 3: feasibility of the 'ideal way of learning'[2]

The UMCG surgery department wanted to introduce an innovative educational form in the ETR NE-Netherlands. At UMCG, first- and second-year postgraduate students follow six rotations—emergency room, trauma surgery, abdominal surgery, vascular surgery, oncology surgery and intensive care—in order to acquire specific surgical skills. The UMCG surgeons wanted to deliver a number of mostly off-patient educational modules during each rotation to prepare the students for surgical procedures in practice. In the practical sense this means that each module has to be run three times a year. Eventually, all first- and second-year postgraduate students in the ETR NE-Netherlands will complete the modules.

The educational modules consist of the following steps:

1. Studying literature
2. Watching how things are done in practice
3. Studying anatomy
4. Practising on models (e.g. computer simulations)
5. Practising on animal tissue
6. Practising on human cadaver tissue
7. Treating real patients

---

2 The text given here corresponds to the summary in the master's thesis of Erik Jippes (2004).

The plan is to realise steps 3 to 6 via a two-day training session in the UMCG. The last step, during which the student applies the knowledge and skills acquired to an actual patient, would take place in the hospital where the students have their rotations. In other words, the training session would be delivered centrally within the UMCG and the last step would take place at the teaching hospitals.

This final subproject aims to develop a model (see Fig. 16.3) to help UMCG surgeons determine the organisational attainability of the modular education described above. In addition, this research is directed at starting discussions in the ETR NE-Netherlands about the provision of education in general, and modular education specifically.

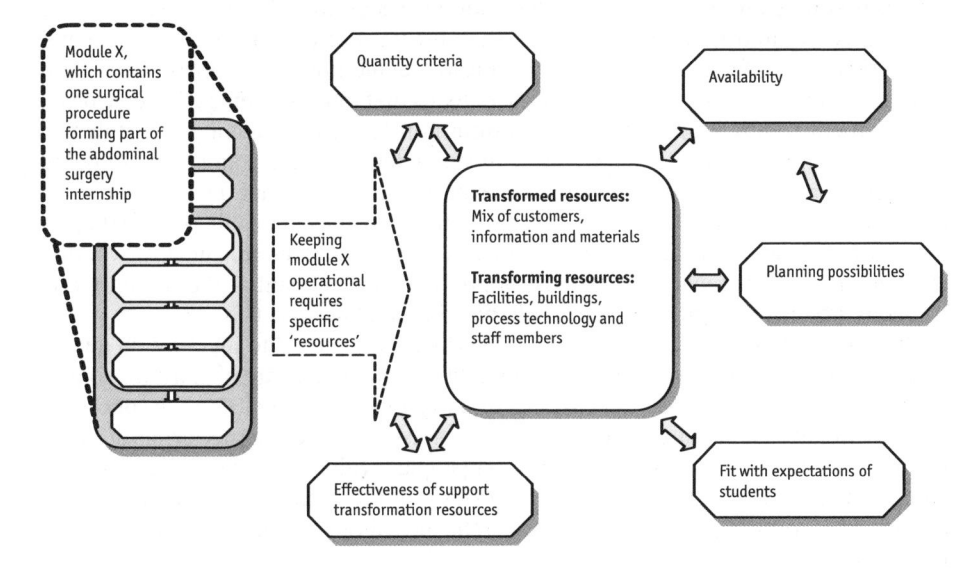

FIGURE 16.3 Model for organisational attainability

Source: Jippes 2004

From an organisational point of view, it is feasible to offer surgical procedures in modules, provided that the necessary resources are available within the ETR NE-Netherlands to meet the necessary training standards (e.g. availability of rooms and educational materials, as well as supervising surgeons and availability of patients).

First, an assessment needs to be made of the suitability of each medical procedure for modular delivery. A procedure is deemed suitable if each training hospital has sufficient patients available (at the final step of the module) for the procedure in question. Next, the resources required must be determined. The resources needed depend on the attainment level required to complete each step of the module, and on how often the students are able to expand their knowledge and practise their skills in order to achieve the required level. The quality of the resources is dependent on their effectiveness, and this is determined by testing the degree to which they meet the expectations of both the surgeons and the students. Finally, it his important to ensure that the required resources can be spared from the primary process of patient care and whether they can be scheduled within the module.

The criteria mentioned above have been applied in a case study on the procedure 'executing an inguinal hernia operation'. The UMCG and three non-academic teaching hospitals have examined whether it is, in organisational terms, feasible to deliver the educational goals for this procedure through a modular approach . To this end, interviews were conducted with a UMCG surgeon, two surgeons of the non-academic teaching hospitals and three postgraduate students. Data were also collected on the numbers of available patients.

The case study indicated that the necessary resources *are* available in the required quality and quantity. However, the question remains whether this is true for other surgical procedures and rotations. This does not always seem to be the case, but more research is required here. Further, given the outcomes of the case study it does not seem possible to offer a larger number of educational modules simultaneously without making structural changes. A larger number means that more students will be involved in off-patient training and that surgeons from non-academic teaching hospitals will have to participate in off-patient training, meaning fewer students and staff attending to the primary process of patient care. It is expected, however, that the modular training better prepares students for surgery on real-life patients; as a result, their first operations will take less time and be more effective. As yet, however, it is unclear whether this benefit will compensate for the loss of production as a result of the students' and surgeons' absence. Further research could possibly shed light on this.

The case study shows that the method described can be used to measure, in a well-ordered manner, the organisational attainability of 'the ideal way of learning' to perform a surgical procedure. By specifically defining and operationalising the concept of 'organisational attainability' we have tried to address all aspects of this term. Although the business theories used are new to (most) people involved in postgraduate medical education at the UMCG, the case study indicates that they can easily be applied to the organisation. With regard to further research, the following recommendations have been made:

- Investigate which procedures in the individual rotations are suitable for the modular approach
- Investigate how much time is saved in (the first) surgical procedures after the postgraduate students have attended the skills laboratory session
- Investigate the financial attainability of the educational form

Implementation

In concrete terms, the NIDO/UMCG project has resulted in three instruments: an innovation scenario, a stakeholder identification instrument and an instrument for testing the organisational attainability of educational innovations. The O&D staff group can use each of these instruments for providing support and advice on curriculum innovations. The usability of each instrument will, however, become apparent only when O&D has worked with it a number of times. The instruments will possibly have to be adjusted to a certain extent before they can be properly applied. However, in each of the projects, a first step has been made to look at curriculum innovations in a more structured and, possibly, more sustainable manner.

Conclusions

In this project, the innovation consisted of revisions in the curricula of postgraduate training programmes for medical specialists. Here, questions play a role on different levels: What are good innovations? What are good innovation processes? How is knowledge shared among different medical departments?

The educational innovation projects at the UMCG differ from 'standard' product innovation projects in the corporate world in a number of ways. The most important differences lie in the composition of the innovation team and the time spent on the project. The programme director of the medical speciality concerned leads the UMCG projects. The programme director and most of the members of the project team are medical specialists. Their medical know-how as regards content is very high and they know what issues in their fields of expertise have to be dealt with during postgraduate training. But in the area of educational models and (didactic) innovation they often possess less experience and it is here that the members of the O&D staff group can play a supportive role.

The programme directors themselves are in an extraordinary position. In conjunction with their directors' responsibilities, they also have so-called production responsibilities (i.e. patient care) as well as responsibilities for the scientific output of their departments. With regard to training, there is a clear tension between patient care ('running production') and training; this tension is even higher when curricula are subject to revision. An innovation process is always under severe time pressures. It is for this reason that a clear but tightly structured innovation project is of great importance. The scenario from the first subproject could be used for this.

The second and third subprojects highlighted how many people are involved in (the consequences of) a curriculum innovation. Although the programme director takes a highly central position, in the actual execution of a revision he or she is dependent on a large number of parties not only within the UMCG but also at regional level. A stakeholder analysis, as described in the second subproject, can provide insight into the roles played by each party. This insight is, however, merely a first step. Stakeholders' involvement in the project then needs to be determined: for example, which activities they can carry out and in which phase of the project these activities take place. Apart from the insights acquired on organisational feasibility, the third subproject highlighted the fact that large projects require the support of a large number of people. A first step in garnering this support could be to involve people proactively in a project.

The subprojects described here have dealt in particular with the improvement of innovation processes and their outcomes. However, sustainable innovation also implies that this knowledge is shared. In the field of educational innovations little knowledge is shared between different departments. The O&D staff group is involved in various educational innovations and will, therefore, be able to build bridges. In this respect it is essential that the knowledge and experience acquired within the staff group becomes common property.

Recommendations, discussion and future research

In this project a number of instruments have been developed that the O&D staff group can use in curriculum innovation projects. The instruments can be applied in a broader field than that of the UMCG. The stakeholder identification instrument is broadly applicable (see Chapters 7, 17 and 23 which describe its various applications). The innovation scenario can be applied in service organisations, especially healthcare organisations. Finally, the feasibility instrument, as developed in subproject 3, can be used in all kinds of projects requiring a broad deployment of different resources.

The NIDO/UMCG project was initiated in order to speed up the starting phase of the IpGME project. The NIDO/UMCG project may certainly have led to a number of usable solutions, but also to several key questions that need to be addressed as the project progresses.

17
Grontmij
CO-OPERATION IN THE LIGHT OF SUSTAINABILITY

Janita F.J. Vos and Nico J. Rommes*

Grontmij is one of the biggest engineering companies in the Netherlands. Operating in the building, infrastructure and environment sectors, it specialises in consultancy, design, engineering, management and turnkey project delivery. By virtue of its primary processes, Grontmij has acquired a great deal of experience in co-operating with other organisations. Despite this empirical expertise and its positive attitude towards collaboration, Grontmij has found the process of co-operation strewn with pitfalls. This study demonstrates the importance of individual staff members, not just for Grontmij itself but also for its co-operative alliances with other organisations.

This chapter describes the results of the NIDO/Grontmij research study conducted within Grontmij, focusing on diversity. An important feature of Grontmij's service provision is its often intense collaboration with other organisations. This, combined with the assumption that third-party involvement makes sustainability more effective and the view that co-operative alliances of this kind can be improved, has been the main driver for the research project discussed here. The research question considered in this chapter is: under what conditions can co-operation be realised in the light of sustainability? In this respect it should be added that choosing a particular form of co-operation could lead to future innovation. This is because innovation can come from the organisation itself or, more importantly, it can develop through collaboration with others.

* In the process of writing this chapter we made use of the masters' theses in business management of Tim Levert and Bart van der Stege. The 'identification of those involved' subproject was executed in co-operation with Marjolein Achterkamp. Further, the authors thank the managing director of Grontmij North, Jeroen Rijnhart, for his comments on an earlier version of this chapter.

The Grontmij research study consists of three subprojects:

1. Sustainability and knowledge sharing in alliances
2. Knowledge sharing within Grontmij
3. Identification of stakeholders

A preliminary research study was conducted as part of the first subproject, and the findings helped to determine subsequent steps in both the first and the second subprojects. The three subprojects deal in different ways with achieving sustainability through co-operation. They will be examined from different perspectives later in this chapter, following a brief description of Grontmij.

Grontmij

Grontmij is a consultancy and engineering firm operating in the international market and employing around 3,300 people in the Netherlands. It offers assistance in developing and realising plans and projects in the fields of construction, infrastructure and environment. In the Netherlands Grontmij is organised in a decentralised way, with an office in each province. The company provides a range of services, from research input and advice through design and engineering to realisation and exploitation. The main lines of the strategy and the resulting market approach have been summarised by Grontmij as follows:[1]

- **Multidisciplinary solutions.** Grontmij is consulted by the government and other companies to solve complex problems in both rural and urban areas. The organisation's ability to offer multidisciplinary solutions is considered its main strength

- **Network organisation close to the customer.** Knowledge of local circumstances is the basis for Grontmij's approach to planning and project management. This is the reason for its decentralised structure. Positioning employees in close proximity to customers enables Grontmij to realise entrepreneurship at the local level

- **Home markets:** Grontmij has chosen to pursue the same organisational formula and market strategy in Belgium and Germany as in the Netherlands. Making use of its knowledge and experience within a network of engineering firms offers extra market opportunities

- **Challenging work.** Grontmij invests in the knowledge and skills of its staff. Offering interesting work and exciting career prospects are key features of its human resources strategy

- **Entire value chain.** Grontmij can be called in at any stage of a project, from advice and engineering to management and exploitation

1 www.grontmij.com.

- **Sustainability.** Finding sustainable solutions is one of Grontmij's core themes, as expounded in its mission statement:

  > We offer our customers solutions in making their residential, working and living environments sustainable. We invest in the quality of our staff and aim at a constant improvement of our achievements. We add value in each stage of a project. We design concepts, give advice, direct, realise and exploit. Our organisational abilities as well as our flexibility characterise us. We are a network organisation and operate in close proximity of the customer. We take initiatives and think along with the customer in finding optimum and sustainable solutions. Co-operation is our point of departure. We are aware of our role in society and the effect our work has on the environment. To deliver a fine job is our challenge.

  Grontmij thus embraces both the 'planet' and 'people' dimensions of the 'triple P' approach. As a quoted company, Grontmij also gives the 'profit' dimension sufficient attention.

- **Alliances.** Co-operation with other organisations is a key issue for Grontmij. This co-operation often consists of complementary activities to provide a complete solution to a customer's problem. To achieve this, Grontmij applies various forms of co-operation. Collaboration is not only aimed at expanding and honing expertise but is also meant to broaden knowledge and stimulate awareness of sustainability. Some co-operative alliances are described in the following sections

Sustainability and sharing knowledge in alliances

The NIDO/Grontmij programme sought answers to a number of questions of interest to Grontmij:

- What are the factors that determine success or failure in co-operative alliances?
- To what extent does knowledge transfer take place in co-operative alliances?
- To what degree is sustainability a common theme for co-operative alliances?

Accordingly, six different alliances were studied in two rounds of research. The alliance concept was defined as co-operation exceeding the usual relations with suppliers or purchasers (Maljers 1995; Nooteboom 1994).

The first round served as a general preliminary investigation to establish a detailed characterisation of the alliance and to further clarify the research question. In selecting alliances for this first round, the following considerations were important:

- There was sufficient documentation available
- The project was neither too complex nor too large
- All parties were prepared to participate in the research study

In the first round, the alliances were mapped out through document analysis and semi-structured interviews so as to verify how they had developed, what form of alliance had been chosen, the nature of the projects executed by the alliance and the various parties' views on co-operation, the sustainability concept and the role of stakeholders. The first research round also looked at how knowledge was created and shared within the alliances and at how competencies were divided between the partners. The next section will describe the results of the first round.

Analysis of the six alliances: results of the first round

One of the first salient results showed that the alliances' form and objectives vary considerably. For example, one alliance is aimed at jointly launching a 'total product' on the market while another focuses on playing a complementary role in the creation of public support for Grontmij projects. The consensus was that the alliance partner can contribute to the sustainability image of Grontmij, while the complementary nature of the co-operation appears to broaden Grontmij's market share.

The alliances were found to have developed on the basis of personal, informal contacts. These personal contacts remained important at the later stages of the projects, with ongoing partner relationships strongly dependent on them. However, as a result, some alliances were formulated with no or few explicit co-operation objectives. Although this might be seen as a disadvantage, it does enable the parties to realise a particular form of co-operation (i.e. mutual trust) during the course of the process in order to meet the expectations of both. This appears to have been the case for a number of alliances, making a shift to the mutual provision of services possible.

Another striking aspect of the alliances is that the original NIDO programme themes, such as knowledge sharing and sustainability, do not explicitly play an important role. Two points are of interest here. First, knowledge sharing is important when there is co-operation on the level of a specific project. This is because co-operation within a project stimulates the knowledge transfer of individual knowledge of people. Coded knowledge can, by definition, be obtained by anyone who has access to it; so co-operation does not add much here. In this respect, it is interesting to observe that not a great deal of the knowledge obtained in this way is written down. Thus, knowledge remains bound to the individual concerned. Second, the focus within co-operation is clearly on areas with complementary competencies. If there is an overlap in competencies, the participating parties are more inclined to put up barriers and keep the knowledge in question to themselves. By dividing the activities and responsibilities in the best way possible, knowledge and expertise transfer is neither necessary nor deemed desirable.

Most of the alliances were not set up with sustainability in mind. It plays a significant role in only two of the alliances studied. In both these cases sustainability is related to the alliance partners' objectives. In the first case, the organisation's objective is preserving and restoring the natural world. In the second case, the focus of the alliance partner is on the development and supply of products resulting from the biosciences. The aim of this partner is to clearly distinguish itself from its competitors as an environmentally and socially responsible organisation.

With regard to the other four alliances, the party that commissioned the project must be willing to pay for a sustainable solution. So the final choice of whether a project should be carried out in a sustainable or non-sustainable way lies with Grontmij's customer. This is surprising for an organisation that has sustainability as a core value. Grontmij explicitly states, for example, that: 'based on the ISO 14001 certificate the customer may expect from us that in our advice, products, product processes, technologies and materials we draw his or her attention to sustainable alternatives'.

Several conclusions can be drawn. The first is that Grontmij is less sustainable than it wants us to believe. However, it is possible that, to Grontmij, sustainability is so self-evident that the company is simply unaware of its distinguishing value on the market. If this is the case, then Grontmij is not making sufficient use of sustainability as a product concept. This concludes the first round of analysis.

For the remainder of this chapter the following points are of importance. First, a further exploration of sustainability within alliances is justified by asking:

- Under what conditions does sustainability have an added value?
- In what way is knowledge on sustainability stored by one or both partners?

Second, it appears that there is only a limited amount of knowledge sharing between alliance partners. This led to the decision to study this research theme within Grontmij itself. Since knowledge sharing around sustainability does not appear to be a theme that plays a significant role in the alliances, the question has been posed whether the organisational conditions regarding this issue could be improved within Grontmij. Initially it was assumed that the selected alliances would also guarantee the sharing of knowledge on sustainability. A more detailed analysis of the alliances shows, however, that there is hardly any knowledge sharing between the partners. Furthermore, the storage of knowledge takes place marginally. This was the reason why, with regard to the issue of knowledge sharing, the alliances were initially not approached. Co-operation with others in order to share knowledge also suggests a climate suitable for knowledge sharing within one's own organisation.

Third, it appeared to be difficult to integrate the role of stakeholders into the alliances' perspective. With regard to this theme it was decided to partly let go of the co-operation perspective. Here the emphasis will be on the way in which the identification of stakeholders relevant to Grontmij can take place. In this respect it is worth mentioning that attention is especially paid to this identification issue in the development of sustainable industrial locations. It should be obvious that collaboration with other organisations is crucial here.

The second round: the added value of sustainability within alliances

As already indicated, Grontmij aims to actively promote sustainability to its customers and clients. However, it appears that Grontmij is not clear about the consequences of this objective. Moreover, the views of the various alliance partners on sustainability diverge somewhat. After the first round of research, it was therefore decided to investigate the terms used by Grontmij and its partners when referring to sustainability. Out of the six alliances from the first round, two were dropped from further analysis because of their marginal status and unclear interpretation of sustainability. Of the remaining four, two consider sustainability important and one does not. Due to a long time horizon, a truly close collaboration does not really exist in the fourth alliance; however, the sustainability component again plays a significant role here.

To gain insight into the perceptions of sustainability within the various alliances, a key representative from each of the alliance partners was interviewed. In the case of two alliances a stakeholder introduced by the alliance partners was interviewed. The limited number of interviews is justified by the personal component of the various co-operation alliances, as previously observed. The initiators of the alliances clearly leave their mark on the nature of the collaboration and, as a result, also on the interpretation of sustainability. In the interviews a conscious decision was made to offer an ambiguous definition of sustainability, because the object of the research was to explore what the concept of sustainability and its added value meant to each of the alliance partners.

In defining the concept of added value, Porter's (1985) notion of tenable competitive advantage led to the following definition: 'a distinguishing value leads to a positive change in the positioning of Grontmij and its alliances, ultimately resulting in a tenable competitive advantage'. Apart from a focus on sustainability, the interviews were also aimed at finding out where the occurring knowledge is being stored and to what extent it is made accessible to others.

The views of the alliance partners on sustainability vary. One of the Grontmij representatives characterised sustainability as continuity and quality, characteristics that are particularly valued by the company's customers. Offering a product that requires less maintenance and that has a longer lifespan is often more expensive. If the customer can be convinced of an ultimate financial advantage, one assumes they will be willing to pay for it. However, at the same time, it is recognised that unless legal rules and regulations apply, the customer will be inclined to opt for a cheaper and possibly less sustainable variant.

The view of another alliance partner on sustainability is similar to that of Grontmij. This partner speaks of a 'pleasant co-operation'. Mutual complementarity in services makes it possible to deliver a good end product. Because their views on sustainability are so similar, the almost self-evident result is, according to these organisations, a sustainable product. In the context of Grontmij's vision, this can be described as 'controlling activities and using resources, materials and energy in such a way that the environment is ultimately preserved and the interests of other parties and future generations are properly taken into account'. This approach has been applied to all relevant parties and laid down in a general policy framework, forming a binding guideline for the entire organisation.

The company that operates in the biosciences field has distinct views on sustainability. It has its own practical interpretation of sustainability which it calls the '4 M Method'. This method is similar to the triple-P approach. The 'Ms' stand for *mens* (man), *maatschappij* (society), *meerwaarde* (added value) and *milieu* (environment). On the basis of these criteria the organisation tests its own products as well as those of its suppliers. In this regard it is similar to Grontmij as both attach value to conducting business in a broadly sustainable manner.

The fourth alliance partner (which focuses on restoring and preserving nature) starts from a so-called commonsense approach to the concept of sustainability. This means that, in this organisation's view, customers will mainly act in their own interest, which is understandable. This is why the decision to embrace sustainability should be based on the customer's interest. If the customer sees no financial or other advantages, sustainability will not be on the agenda. The customer will determine the value ascribed to sustainability and the price it is willing to pay for it.

What applies to all four alliance partners is that the storage of knowledge (even of sustainability) appears to be of little significance. The greater part of the knowledge is person-bound. Mutual exchange of this knowledge is the main method for knowledge transfer and storage. This means that little is laid down, so when a staff member leaves there is a risk that knowledge will be lost. Only one of the alliances studied here is aware of this; it consciously aims to increase the number of people possessing this knowledge in order to minimise the risk.

Conclusions and discussion

In ending this section some preliminary conclusions can be drawn, starting with those regarding sustainability. The alliances studied were not started for reasons of knowledge exchange or for the development of knowledge of sustainability (KoS). In some alliances, however, sustainability actually does play a role: for example, in strengthening Grontmij's image or because there is a large degree of consensus on the concept. A notable fact is that a partner's affinity with sustainability largely determines the way in which it is interpreted within the alliance. In this respect it seems that, as far as customers are concerned, the long-term advantage of a sustainable solution still insufficiently sets off the extra initial costs. A well-focused market strategy and solutions that are more customised could possibly redress the balance. In this context it is important that the organisation's staff members are aware of the added value of their KoS to third parties.

This not only shows that sustainability itself is relevant, but also that knowledge about it can yield considerable profit. However, because of the nature of the alliances, which is often based on trust, the developed knowledge is laid down only marginally. A great deal of knowledge is largely embedded in the minds of individual staff members. In this stage of the analysis it is important to place this conclusion in the light of the risks inherent in alliances, as recognised by Nooteboom (2002) who states that alliances are subject to two types of risks: spillover risks and dependence risks. Here we will limit ourselves to the former. In order to establish complementary competencies, knowledge must be exchanged. This is when spillover risks tend to emerge, as knowledge exchange increases the danger of core competencies spilling over to competitors. However, according to Nooteboom, this danger should not be overestimated. It depends on various factors, such as the degree to which the knowledge is tacit (sensory; see Chapter 6). Individually bound knowledge can of course be sold, and this also holds for those parts of the organisation where the knowledge is stored. Its effectiveness depends on the time the receiving organisation needs to integrate and efficiently exploit the knowledge acquired. The receiving organisation's capacity to absorb knowledge is of crucial importance (see also Cohen and Levinthal 1990; Waalkens 2006). If the tempo of knowledge exchange is fast, the risk of spillover is minimised—by the time the competitor is able to exploit the knowledge acquired, it is often no longer up-to-date. Because knowledge within alliances is largely embedded in the minds of individuals, there is little chance of a spillover problem. However, preservation of knowledge is particularly vulnerable during personnel changes. Increasing the number of people privy to the knowledge and/or registering it structurally will diminish vulnerability and increase usability.

Finally, it can be concluded that trust, as the basis of an alliance, has the significant advantage that, should the objectives of the alliance change after some time, co-operation can be continued quite easily. This is why trust largely stimulates flexibility in the co-operation process.

Sharing knowledge within Grontmij

The first round of analysing the alliances led to the decision to examine sharing knowledge in more detail within Grontmij itself. Where there is a culture of co-operation within an organisation, there is also likely to be a climate for sharing knowledge. However, transferring knowledge takes time. The organisation's culture—that is to say, the prevalent values and norms of staff members—influences the amount of time and resources allocated to knowledge transfer. It is important to make a distinction between focal areas and prevalent values.

With regard to focal areas, there are several possibilities. For example, there can be a strong internal focus on efficient working. Or the focus may be turned outwards to market pressures (see also Chapter 5). At the same time, attention needs to be paid to the business process. This process can be directed at creating new opportunities, but can also be aimed at structure and management. Focal areas are, of course, subject to change depending on internal and external circumstances. For example, sometimes the management of business processes requires a great deal of attention while at other times the development of new products is given priority.

The prevailing values have been dealt with in accordance with the concept of culture as defined by the Focus Group. The Focus Group is an international group of researchers which, during the period 1992–97, conducted research into the culture of organisations in different European countries. The group defines culture as a collection of values, norms, expressions and behaviours which partly determine the way that people within an organisation deal with each other and the degree of effort they put into their work and the organisation (van Muijen 1994; van Muijen, Koopman and De Witte 1996; Cameron and Quinn 1999). This definition shows the coherence between the organisational culture and the value assigned to knowledge creation and knowledge sharing.

The research study

The questionnaire developed by the Focus Group, complemented with questions specifically aimed at knowledge sharing, was used to investigate the perceptions of Grontmij employees about the company. The original Focus Group questionnaire had the following four orientations:

1. Orientation on support
2. Orientation on innovation
3. Orientation on regulations

4. Goal orientation

Within these orientations the focal areas and prevailing values are brought together. The orientation on support is characterised by a strong emphasis on the involvement of staff members. Here, issues such as participation, co-operation, mutual trust, group cohesion and individual growth are referred to. The orientation on innovation is characterised by seeking new information from the surrounding environment, being open to changes, taking risks, creativity, competition, anticipation, room for experimentation and the desire for success. The orientation on regulations constitutes respect for authority, rational procedures and the division of work. Much value is attached to authority and the powers laid down in procedures. Finally, the goal orientation is mainly aimed at rational short-term planning for the realisation of goals. Goals are mostly determined in consultation with the employer.

The knowledge section of the questionnaire, which complements the Focus list, is aimed at five subjects. These are:

- Knowledge sharing and reflection
- Development of new ideas
- Consultation with colleagues
- Solving problems together
- Distributing and gaining knowledge

The questions about knowledge sharing and reflection concern learning 'best practices', sharing knowledge with colleagues and evaluating projects. The emphasis is on the extent to which colleagues mutually learn from the experiences gained. Questions concerning the development of new ideas deal with the amount of time staff members think they need for this and whether it is possible to experiment. The issue of consultation with colleagues is about consulting or being consulted by colleagues. Using a colleague's expertise is likely to contribute to a better product. Another part of sharing and developing knowledge is the way in which problems are solved. Problem-solving within a group helps to develop knowledge collectively and enables a problem to be looked at from different angles. So, the chance of finding a better or completely new solution is increased. The questions on 'solving problems together' focus on this type of group learning. Finally, distributing and gaining knowledge deals with how employees use their knowledge and how they acquire it. Knowledge is gained by individuals: for example, through training or by attending a conference. Knowledge can be distributed by, for example, giving a presentation at a seminar, but also by exchanging knowledge with other organisations in a project.

The questionnaire was completed by 178 employees from different departments within Grontmij. As the questionnaire was filled in via the company's intranet, the sample could be biased towards office workers. The scores of Grontmij's value orientations lie close together in a so-called balanced profile. An organisation with this kind of profile is characterised by the thorough way in which each action and renewal is analysed from various angles. However, as a result of the strong emphasis on analysis there is sometimes a lack of decisiveness. Before taking action, it is important to ensure there is sufficient support, the necessary procedures are established, the objectives are clear and that any innovation is sufficiently renewing (van Muijen et al. 1996). Still, there is somewhat more focus on the mutual relations within the organisation and relatively little on the external market.

As regards the knowledge component, colleagues regularly consult each other. Grontmij employees often contact one another for advice. This indicates a large reservoir of individually based knowledge. Sharing knowledge and reflection on the work performed is less relevant. However, reflection on actions undertaken is an important source of knowledge development, although it does not happen very often. Consciously choosing to solve problems mutually is not common either. This also holds for experimentation as a means of creating new ideas.

Conclusions and discussion

Within Grontmij, the four culture orientations are considered equally relevant, albeit with some slight differences. For example, comparatively more attention is paid to the 'people side' of conducting business (i.e. orientation on support). The goal orientation has the lowest scores. These results indicate that the culture of Grontmij can be characterised as a fairly open one with an employee-oriented style of leadership. Before taking action there will usually be a thorough analysis, looking at a problem from various angles. For this reason the decisiveness has a relatively lower score, corresponding with the relatively lower goal orientation.

The high score on consultation among colleagues illustrates the large reservoir of knowledge existing within Grontmij, although much of this is not stored in a systematic way. However, a comprehensive knowledge storage system may not be appropriate, since knowledge development within Grontmij is very much driven by employee interactions which thrive in the company's open climate with its focus on support, participation and involvement.

The proposition that learning from one's own experiences is, in most cases, the best way of learning also applies to organisations (Argyris and Schön 1978). Sharing knowledge can therefore be stimulated by giving room to mutual reflection on the projects carried out and by asking what lessons have been learned and what could be done differently or better? Given the low score for goal orientation an obvious thing to do is to increase customer involvement in evaluation meetings. This serves to stimulate the development of new knowledge, both within Grontmij and the customer, particularly with larger projects. The multidisciplinary character of such evaluation meetings increases opportunities to develop new insights. Bringing together staff members with various kinds of expertise who have worked on a project will stimulate the development of knowledge. In addition, as long as no commercially sensitive information is at stake, it is important to put the results at the disposal both of the organisation and the customer. Such an open approach has a favourable effect on the knowledge development process within Grontmij. As already argued, given that much knowledge is embedded in the minds of individual employees, the chance of such knowledge being exploited by third parties is slight.

In summary, multidisciplinary sharing of knowledge and reflection are important opportunities for the further development of knowledge. This especially holds for those particular projects in which various knowledge areas have to be integrated into a whole. Also, the involvement of the customer in the evaluation can contribute a great deal. Customer involvement in Grontmij projects and the role of other stakeholders in the light of the resulting identification problems are therefore the topics of the next section.

Identification of stakeholders: the development and application of a method

Owing to the nature of its services, Grontmij often has to deal with a large number of different stakeholders. For Grontmij it is of the utmost importance to have an adequate picture of these stakeholders, so that it can support the execution of projects in the best possible way. Within the overall NIDO programme a method has been developed that supports stakeholder identification. This method is described in more detail in Chapters 7 and 23.

This section will address a number of specific circumstances in the research study conducted within Grontmij which were particularly important for the development of the stakeholder identification method. In this context, attention is paid to the possible use of the method in a specific type of project: namely, the development of sustainable industrial areas. We then describe the application of the method and, finally, draw some conclusions from the analysis.

Execution of the research study in two parallel processes

In this part of the research study a distinction was made between the development of the method (including testing) and its application. Both elements will be dealt with here.

At the start of the programme, a prototype of the method was available, mainly based on the literature (Achterkamp and Vos 2003). This formed the basis for the further development of the method. In the case of Grontmij this took place in two ways. Several researchers worked on the method in two relatively independent research processes. In the first process the emphasis was on the usability of the method in (the development of) sustainable industrial locations. The other process focused on the method's more general usability, in connection with research conducted within other organisations (see Chapters 7, 10, 15 and 16).

In spite of these different perspectives, the processes mutually influenced one another. Indeed, two parallel research processes brought about an extra development impetus. As described in Chapter 7, the method concentrates on two issues: involvement roles and involvement phasing. Both these issues deal with different definitions that have to be formulated during the application of the method. In specifying the definitions, the research conditions within Grontmij were crucial. This applies to both the roles (client, decision-maker, designer and passively involved parties) and the phases ultimately integrated into the method.

Since the prototype was sufficiently embedded in the literature, the further development of the method was mainly aimed at its empirical testing. For this purpose a number of interviews were conducted in two rounds. The first round dealt with gaining insight into the various phases of the projects executed by Grontmij, in particular with respect to the development of industrial locations. This resulted in the revision of the phasing model already referred to. The second round dealt with testing the definitions of the roles of involvement. This round also led to adjustments, in this case to the role definitions (see also Chapters 7 and 23).

Before going into the application of the method, we will first make some remarks on the specific context of sustainable industrial locations. From the corporate world's point of view, interest in sustainability has developed through increasing interest in the management of industrial locations. In the UK and the US there has been intense interest in this where the term 'park management' is used. This term, as well as the working method accompanying it, blew over to the Netherlands a couple of years ago and was adopted by Grontmij. However, the organisation considers park management in a broader sense than merely the sustainable management of industrial locations. As far as Grontmij is concerned, park management is more an overall approach to realising the sustainability of industrial areas.

Grontmij describes park management as maintaining the life-cycle of industrial parks. The concept is aimed at managing the industrial location and realising operational co-operation among the companies settled there. The objective of park management is threefold. First, it is about the development of the real-estate value of the area. Through a more adequate management of the space and the buildings, the value of the real estate is retained. In this way stakeholder investment in the real estate of industrial locations is encouraged. Second, the intention is to offer the most optimal form of business management. Companies can focus on their 'core business' while park management deals with peripheral activities. Third, park management offers the possibility of optimising the settlement and working conditions. An industrial estate should be more than simply a place where businesses are located. It is also where individuals spend large parts of their lives. Attractive surroundings and facilities such as a day nursery or a fitness area promote employee well-being and motivation.

If we consider these three objectives in the light of the identification method, it is possible that each one will lead to different results. This will depend on the type of company that settles in the area, the conditions under which they locate and the co-ordinating facilities available at the park; in each particular case the identification will result in different parties involved.

Application of the method

The empirical test described above was particularly aimed at parts of the method. The integral test took place in applying the method. Within Grontmij, a so-called brainstorming session was organised, in line with the way in which the method works. During this meeting stakeholder groups in three closely linked Grontmij projects were identified, in accordance with the method's operating procedure. In this case it concerned a project consisting of three subprojects, all dealing with restructuring activities at a harbour in a medium-sized municipality. Apart from the two panel chairs and a person taking minutes, three staff members of Grontmij attended this meeting: an accounts manager, the head of the execution department and the project leader.

17. GRONTMIJ: CO-OPERATION IN THE LIGHT OF SUSTAINABILITY

Without going into too much detail about this meeting (see Chapter 7), the following conclusions can be drawn. Given the fact that the meeting concerned three subprojects, there was at times some confusion during the session. However, the subprojects were clearly connected and it was important for Grontmij to achieve added value by overseeing the three together. In addition, the meeting demonstrated that nearly all the stakeholders identified played a role in all three subprojects.

The identification of clients did not pose many problems. Apart from the formal client, the following were also identified as clients—the council, local residents and the users of the area. Almost all clients had the same objectives: namely, accessibility and liveability. These objectives may not mean the same to each client, however. A municipality, for example, could interpret 'liveability' in a completely different way to a person living in the harbour on a houseboat.

The municipality was identified as the most important decision-maker. The identification of decision-makers mainly resulted in a large number of parties who, by making demands or applying a veto, could delay the project. Early consultation with these stakeholders is, therefore, a necessity rather than a luxury.

With regard to the role of designer there were two important parties: the municipality at the start-up phase (i.e. drawing up the programme of prerequisites) and Grontmij in subsequent phases. It became clear that the role of designer was fulfilled well in the field of technical knowledge, but not so well in other areas such as risk analysis, stakeholder management and communication. In particular, the division of the designer role between the municipality and Grontmij was not always clear. This indistinctness is partly due to the various roles played by Grontmij in earlier projects on behalf of this client. For each project it is therefore important to clarify the tasks Grontmij actually has to perform and those that it does not have to perform. The role distinction, in accordance with the method, can be helpful here.

In identifying those passively involved, local residents and other users of the area were proposed. However, looking at our definitions of 'client' and 'passively involved', it became clear that this is actually not correct because a client (as opposed to someone who is passively involved) influences a project. The client's wishes and demands should be known in an early stage, and should serve to guide the project's development. The fact that inhabitants and users of the area are labelled as passively involved leads to the suspicion that too little attention has been paid to their demands and wishes. In the case of the houseboat inhabitants, this was certainly the case as at a certain point they had tried to obstruct the project. Another notable passively involved party was Grontmij itself. The insight that this project, and in fact each project executed by Grontmij, should have consequences (i.e. affected)—for example, for the organisation's image as regards sustainability—could lead to a curtailment of the choice of projects, and as a result to a decrease in potential clients.

In conclusion, three general comments can be made here. First, although it is remarkable that the client partly coincides with the passively involved, the very nature of the projects makes this likely. It seems sensible to make a clear distinction between the groups, by limiting the client group to only include those who are actually paying Grontmij for its services. However, by recognising the broad nature of the client concept, the awareness of the passively involved group will emerge almost automatically. Moreover, it appears that the objectives of the paying clients can be influenced by those passively involved. This is especially relevant when projects are carried out in the public domain. Second, with regard to the phasing of the process of involvement, the project conditions within Grontmij gave rise to the decision to expand the phasing model with an extra phase (i.e. maintenance). Furthermore, a large number of projects have no clear starting point, making it hard to determine who should perform the analysis and when. Third, it became clear that the analysis of Grontmij as described above was, in fact, carried out too late. The analysis revealed a number of stakeholders who had been wrongly excluded from the process. This is a problem that Grontmij is likely to face more often in future, due to the fact that its involvement does not always begin during the first phase of a project, and also because it is not always clear at what point exactly the first phase starts.

Conclusions and discussion

The identification of stakeholders is of crucial importance to Grontmij. The projects executed by Grontmij are often complex and involve a large number of stakeholders. In this respect the development of industrial parks, either with or without a sustainability objective, is exemplary. Furthermore, there is often intense public interest in the environmental planning projects executed by Grontmij, as the projects are aimed at the exploitation of a resource that is highly scarce (especially in the Netherlands): namely, land. Consequently, changes in the zoning plans are often required.

The role(s) adopted by Grontmij will vary, depending on the nature of the project and its positioning in the value chain. Sometimes the organisation plays a mediating role between parties while at other times its role is to execute a project. Although a stakeholder analysis is important in both cases, the outcome will be highly diverse. The brainstorming session showed that this diversity of roles sometimes contributes to confusing relationships between Grontmij and other parties and may distort role demarcation. The method could help clarify mandates and role divisions assumed in projects.

We conclude that, although the applicability of the method for (sustainable) industrial estates has only been partly tested, no adjustments are required. However, we suggest linking the method to the park management concept used by Grontmij.

Conclusions and discussion concerning the three subprojects

Now that the various themes have been discussed, it is useful to return to the main reason for this research project and to the associated research question. As mentioned at the start of this chapter, Grontmij was mainly interested in improving its co-operation alliances with other organisations in the light of innovation. So, what are the conclusions? In most cases a co-operative alliance appears to begin with a personal contact. If this is good, it can provide a reasonable basis for co-operation at the organisational level, particularly in decentralised organisations such as Grontmij. Agreement can then be reached on which services and/or products are to be jointly brought to market. At this stage things can still go wrong: for example, as a result of competitive considerations or too much overlap between the alliance partners. Nevertheless, personal contacts remain important. Should circumstances result in a diminishing overlap, it is again possible to co-operate with this partner properly.

The knowledge component is also of great importance for the success of the alliance. Where both partners possess similar knowledge of a particular issue (or they think they do), then co-operation is impeded and considerations of competitiveness become more important. If, on the other hand, there are large differences in knowledge, this problem is far less severe.

Within Grontmij there is a great deal of knowledge. Staff members know how to get hold of the knowledge they need, but sharing knowledge and developing new knowledge also require mutual reflection. Supporting one another is an important factor in the creation of the proper climate in which knowledge can be shared in an open interaction. The larger multidisciplinary projects could, in particular, provide a wealth of new insights and so serve as a sound basis for innovation.

When discussing the stakeholder identification method, various conclusions have been drawn about its usability for Grontmij. A major focal point of the method—namely, the classification of stakeholders on the basis of roles of involvement—could also help assess any possible co-operation problems within a specific project. If Grontmij and its partner(s) occupy closely connected roles, co-operation problems may occur in the future.

Conclusion: a retrospective of some central terms

In the last section of this chapter we look back on some concepts discussed in Chapters 1–6 of this book, such as sustainability, stakeholders, knowledge creation and knowledge sharing. It is extremely difficult to draw conclusions about the sustainability of Grontmij in order to arrive at an unambiguous characterisation of the organisation. As the preliminary study showed, it seems that Grontmij is sometimes inclined to present itself in a more favourable light than it merits. Thus, only when the partner or client places importance on sustainability is it is clearly expressed in the co-operation alliance concerned. This means that sustainability (in the sense of 'mutually launching sustainable products or services on the market') is relevant only to a limited extent. Yet it has to be said that this conclusion does not do justice to Grontmij. Indeed, it may tell us more about Grontmij's attitude towards both its alliance partners and sustainability. So, although the company assigns great importance to its alliance partners who, to a large extent, determine the nature of the co-operation, it also rates sustainability very highly. It should be noted that Grontmij agreed to continue this research during a difficult reorganisation, which bears testament to this.

Defining sustainability as reducing offload has not been part of the Grontmij investigation, although it has, in fact, considered which parties should be protected from offload. Within Grontmij there are many possibilities for using the method, based on the assumption that it has a positive influence on sustainability. Of particular importance is the identification of (and focus on) the category of the passively involved. However, the client category in its broad sense (as applied in Chapter 7) is just as important, for a number of reasons. First, it may necessitate a critical reflection on (potential) clients, as not all consider sustainability important. Sometimes it may be better to turn down a client in order to maintain integrity with regard to sustainability. In addition, clients are not always well informed about sustainable alternatives, in which case they will need to be provided with the necessary information. Clearly, this will influence the client–contractor relationship. Second, in the section on knowledge sharing within Grontmij, we stated that the client should be involved in reflecting on the projects that are being carried out. We believe that the term 'client' should be interpreted in the broadest way. At the outset of this research study the supposed innovation was 'knowledge creation and knowledge sharing in the context of alliances'. Reflection both *with* the client but also *on* the client can give an additional impetus to this innovation.

We conclude this chapter with a comment on the system levels on which the analyses are based and to which sustainability is also related. The research study was aimed at both the individual employees of Grontmij and at the organisation itself. In order for sustainability to be realised, there needs to be cohesion between these levels. This is one of the significant messages of this chapter.

18
Sociocracy and the sustainability of knowledge
REEKX, ATOL AND ENDENBURG ELEKTROTECHNICS

René J. Jorna and Nico Rommes

In this chapter we will discuss a social structure especially designed for organisations that favour social sustainability, as presented in the literature (Endenburg 1998). This social structure is called **sociocracy**. The basic principle of sociocracy is the consent principle, which means that everyone who is qualified and involved in decision-making within an organisation is not opposed to an intended decision. This, and the other principles of sociocracy as well as its background and its implementation within a large number of firms and organisations, will be discussed later in the chapter. First, however, we will start with a specific question posed by Reekx, one of the sociocratic organisations that participated in the NIDO programme: how can we convince the accountants and our clients of the surplus value of social profit, and how can we operationalise social profit? We will then discuss some aspects of another organisation—Endenburg Elektrotechnics in Rotterdam—which started to structure its organisation according to sociocratic principles in 1970. After that, we will deal with ATOL, another sociocratic organisation that participated in the NIDO programme. Finally, we will discuss the advantages and disadvantages of sociocracy with regard to the overall topic of sustainable innovation. Is sociocracy a sustainable social concept and is it fit to deal with knowledge of sustainability (KoS) as well as sustainability of knowledge (SoK)?

Reekx: can a sociocratic organisation conduct sustainable business?

An organisation that wants to operate in a sustainable way needs to take account of the possible effects on the ecological and social environment of its activities, as well as being aware of its internal environment. For example, if the economy is performing poorly, this may affect the internal environment of the organisation: if orders decrease, a number of employees may become redundant and have to be laid off. This has three consequences. First, part of the organisation's responsibility will be offloaded onto society. Second, there will be an individual cost to those (and their families) who have lost their jobs in terms of a decrease in income and status. There will also be a cost to the organisation as a result of the loss of knowledge and expertise. Third, firing employees will affect the morale of those remaining. Nevertheless, many organisations take this short-term perspective instead of looking for other solutions. Reekx prefers a different approach: looking for alternatives and long-term solutions. This does not mean that people are never made redundant at Reekx in response to external pressures; it is, however, not the company's first option.

Because of its short-term cyclic nature, thinking only in terms of costs and benefits is not a sustainable approach. The problem is that from a traditional economics perspective, an organisation may need to reduce its costs as quickly as possible. From this perspective reducing the wage bill through discharges will reduce costs immediately, thereby restoring profitability in the short term. Although this issue is generally recognised, from the classic economics perspective it is not easy to identify other options. The first problem is that discharges will result in a long-term loss of **human capital** and hence innovative power, learning power and organisational stability (i.e. the sense of security felt by employees). The second problem is that the value of the long-term advantages of holding on to employees can often not easily be quantified in financial terms. In addition, if other kinds of quantifications are used, it is often very difficult to compare them with financial measurements.

Suppose an organisation decides against widespread discharges, how could it justify a short-term loss against financial gains in the long run? One way could be by redefining human capital in terms of investment rather than cost. Reekx tries to do this, but has had problems in justifying this new definition to its employees who are not threatened by dismissal, as well as to its accountants. One way or another, Reekx wants to establish that an organisation can be judged not only in terms of its financial bottom line. Social sustainability is a value standing on its own and has to be integrated into an overall view.

Reekx implemented the **sociocratic circle organisation** method ten years ago. This starts from the principle that the views of *all* members or employees of an organisation are of equal value. Within certain boundaries all employees are allowed to make an input to the organisation's policies. The assumption is that employee involvement results in improved organisational performance. The aim of Reekx is to present a social annual report in which social sustainability is expressed in terms comparable to financial figures. By introducing these annual reports, Reekx hopes to demonstrate its social sustainability to both internal and external audiences.

18. SOCIOCRACY AND THE SUSTAINABILITY OF KNOWLEDGE *Jorna and Rommes*

Reekx was launched in 1985 as a consultancy firm providing a broad range of documentation and information services. The organisation is divided into three divisions (units)—office management, finance and projects—and employs around 70 people. Most employees are information specialists, consultants, librarians, archivists, 'information searchers' and new media experts. Reekx advises on information management, seconds experts to clients, provides training and education, and collects strategic information on behalf of its customers. Most employees work in the projects unit. Employees who are seconded work in the customers' offices. The company is based in the Netherlands with offices in the north at Groningen and in the centre at Almere.

The organisational structure of Reekx is based on the sociocratic circle structure, with separate policy and operational arms. On the operational side, the various units are managed vertically. This implies that Reekx's operational processes have a normal hierarchical structure. The situation is different in the management group, however. In conjunction with the company's other policy-making bodies, the management group uses a circle structure based on sociocratic principles. Circles are semi-autonomous units that manage task performance within their decision domain.

In the management unit the principle of equality is guaranteed by the sociocratic circle structure (see Fig. 18.1). The equality principle concerning activities and tasks does not apply to the operational lines.

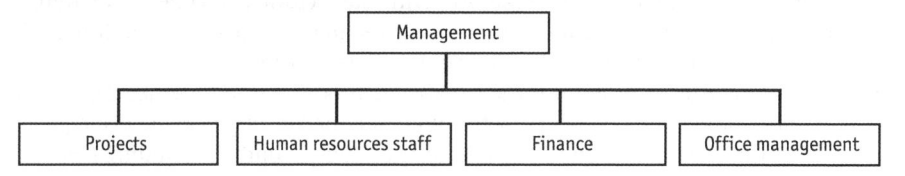

FIGURE 18.1 Organisational description of Reekx since September 2003

Policy-making is realised by employees by means of circles that are coupled. In this context, Reekx uses the **double linking pin** model. The elements at the bottom of the structure are the units' circles (see Fig. 18.2). From each of the circles, two employees are represented in the company circle. This can be compared with the management team or the board of directors. The company circle is coupled to the top circle by at least

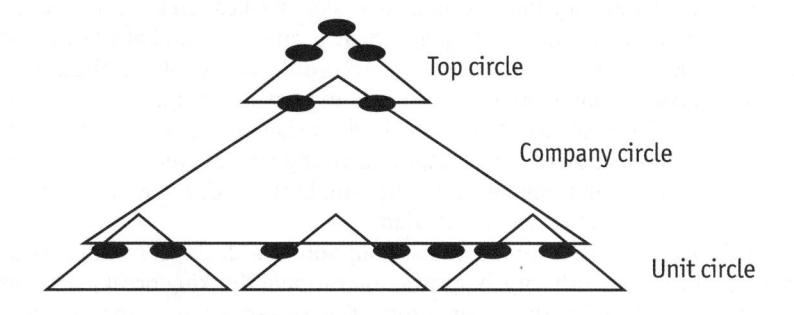

FIGURE 18.2 Policy circle structure with double coupling

two members, comparable with the board of supervisors (a legal structure in the Netherlands to control the board of directors). At this level of aggregation two (or more) persons are always managers and one (or more) are elected representatives from the company circle. Figure 18.2 shows the circles' hierarchy and the black bars depict the various representatives.

Sociocracy: a theoretical introduction

As a movement and a practice sociocracy began in Rotterdam in 1970 (Endenburg 1998). The movement was inspired by the ideas of Kees Boeke, an engineer who founded a school in which equivalence in decision-making was central. The ideas of Kees Boeke originated from Quaker principles regarding the role of authority, co-operation and teaching. The Quakers' main ideas were related to peace and justice for everyone. In 1926 Boeke founded a school in Bilthoven called the Working Place (de Werkplaats), based on the principles he had developed.

Disappointed by the experiment in workers' councils in the 1960s, Endenburg became influenced by the ideas of Boeke. Applying sociocratic principles, Endenburg established his own company, Endenburg Elektrotechnics in 1970, although it took more than five years to partially realise the company as a sociocracy.

Important sources of inspiration for sociocracy can be found in engineering. Both Boeke and Endenburg were engineers by training and one key engineering principle is that of cybernetics. This is the study of communication and control, including positive and negative feedback mechanisms in machines as well as in living systems, including humans. Interest in cybernetics peaked in the 1940s, but subsequently declined because of its almost unlimited scope. It can now be recognised in various disciplines, such as complex adaptive systems, dynamic systems theory, artificial intelligence and control theory. We see sustainability as an aspect of dynamic systems (see Chapters 3 and 22). The essential notion of 'circle' is derived from cybernetics. Endenburg uses the example of a central heating system to explain the control loops in systems, including social systems, such as organisations.

One other essential source of inspiration comes from political theory. Endenburg contrasts tyranny and democracy with sociocracy. Tyranny means that one small group rules whereas democracy implies that the majority rules. So tyranny and democracy involve dictates from a tyrant and a majority respectively. Thus, both cases involve large and small groups that are unable to agree. According to Endenburg, the mistakes made in the 1960s concerning workers' self-regulation within organisations and companies can be traced back to so-called majority discussions in companies. To reach a majority in these situations, numerous meetings and voting rounds were required. These were counterproductive, emotionally damaging and, in the end, always left a small or large group within the organisation dissatisfied.

A third source of inspiration is the assumption that decision-making should not be based on power and authority, but rather on rational thinking or, at least, on thinking as rationally as possible. Apart from production or service provision an organisation's basic activity is decision-making, and this activity is so important that it should never take place on the basis of power. Decisions based on power and authority jeopardise an organisation in the long run.

Based on, among others, the circle principle of cybernetics, the negligence of larger minorities and the attempt to be as rational as possible in decision-making, Endenburg formulated a new social design for both organisations and society. This new social design was based on four basic rules: consent; circles; double links; and elections. The literal meaning of sociocracy is 'the sovereignty of the socius: I myself, the next person, the later ego, the otherness' (Endenburg 1998: 23) We will discuss the four principles consecutively:

- **Consent.** With regard to consent, the most elementary aspect is that it does not hamper or stop decision-making. Not all decisions have to be realised using the consent principle. With respect to operational processes, decision-making can be done as a result of habit or authority but, in cases of doubt, one can fall back on the consent principle. Even elections and discussions about individuals take place with the aid of the principle of consent. Endenburg formulates explicitly that consent does not mean that all people are equal. People are and will remain unequal, but that does not mean that some are leading others on the basis of principles other than that of consent. If one withholds consent, a decision will not be taken (Endenburg 1998: 51):

    > This principle governs the decision-making process (consent = no reasoned or paramount objection). This means that a policy decision can only be made if nobody raises a reasonable and paramount objection against it.

    Consent and consensus are not the same. Consensus means overall agreement, whereas consent means no objection. Neither does consent imply the use of a veto. A veto blocks decision-making. If someone withholds consent, a discussion has to take place about what can be done to change the direction of the decision. If that is not possible, one has to go one level deeper to realise a result. In the case of consent, all parties have to come up with reasonable and alternative solutions. This process may take some time, but much more time may be lost if a decision is reached by means of authority or power resulting in guerrilla tactics or other activities harmful to those who are forced to obey later on

- **Circles.** According to Endenburg (1998: 51):

    > The organisation consists of semi-autonomous groups. Each circle has its own objective, performs the three functions of directing, operating and measuring/feedback, and maintains its own memory system by means of integral education. Making decisions that determine policy takes place within a sociocratic circle.

    Endenburg calls a circle a 'functional group or working unit of those engaged in the realisation of a common goal or purpose' (Endenburg 1998: 53). A circle is a forum that integrates horizontal and vertical lines within organisations. The practice of working with circles varies at different levels within organisations. At the higher level of management policy-making is very important, whereas at the level of the business processes what particularly matters is operational continuation. At the management level, functions and tasks are delegated; that is to say partitioned and, of course, co-ordinated. By means of circles the positive and negative feedback loops are guaranteed, which is especially important for the vertical lines. In Figure 18.2 the black bars depict individuals who participate in normal horizontal functioning but, at the same time, some individuals who participate at that level are also part of higher-level circles. Notably, Endenburg remarks that circles at the higher and lower levels are relative. At each level there are various kinds of limits that occur at the level itself as well as at the higher levels. These levels are also connected to the lower levels

- **Double links.** The double link between lower and higher levels guarantees that hierarchies do not exist forever, that lower levels understand why higher levels make certain decisions, and that higher levels do not lose contact with the shop floor. This does not mean that everybody is talking with everybody else, but that only relevant and productive communication takes place. This double link can also be called the linking pin structure (Endenburg 1998: 51):

    > The connection between two circles consists of a double link. This means that at least two persons from one circle participate in decision-making in the next higher circle: the functional leader and one or more elected representatives.

    Within certain boundaries every organisation has a hierarchy and that hierarchy will remain, but the double link ensures that a hierarchy does not exist for its own sake. The top circle is responsible for contacts with people outside the organisation who can be part of the top circle. The double link structure also guarantees that circles are connected. However, they can also function semi-autonomously

- **Elections.** Elections are open and constructive. Anyone can be chosen, but it is, of course, most productive if those chosen are the most eligible (Endenburg 1998: 51):

    > Persons are elected exclusively by consent, after open discussions. This has the status of an additional procedural rule.

    Various rules can be formulated regarding how long the chosen candidates stay as representatives, how many representatives are suitable and whether re-election is possible. In any case, voting is done on the basis of consent and open discussion so that the pros and cons of the candidates can be balanced but, as Endenburg says, always in the presence of those involved

The four rules are discussed in relation to organisations, but they can also be applied to a society as a whole. Endenburg (1998: 55) considers a sociocratised society as:

> a coherent whole to the degree that all organisations (i.e. the social organisations and social entities) are connected by mutual circle organisations, either directly or indirectly, by double linkage. *Un-socialness* is a social given where persons, groups, social processes (for example, events in a residential

neighbourhood) and institutions (businesses, scientific company, local council, laws, property, patents, etc.) are concerned. It can be gauged by the degree of isolatedness within the social whole.

Because of its circles and double links, in this way a sociocratic society is able to realise a better social service. In a society of this kind, business practices and communal living are interwoven. The top circles include people from external parties, and people in all circles participate in the various communal living situations, such as neighbourhoods, religious communities, sport clubs or leisure groups.

Other basic principles of sociocracy not yet touched on but relevant in organisations as well as in societies are the 'no one is owner' approach and the 'profit-sharing as measurement' perspective. These are in strong contrast with present-day society in which the ultimate goal sometimes seems to be to make everyone an owner while, at the same time, to share as little profit as possible. In sociocracy however, profit-making is seen not as a good but as a means. The reason for both principles is quite simple. If people are owners they are able to break the circle and so isolate themselves from social networks. And if profit optimising takes place, the possibilities and motivation to engage in circles will be minimal. According to Endenburg, profit-sharing should be considered as a reward for active participation in an organisation.

The above is only a very small outline of the many theoretical and practical principles of sociocracy. The sociocratic movement has, for a long time, been considered a utopian and unrealistic activity. However, there is evidence that contradicts this view. For many years now, more than 60 companies in the Netherlands, Canada, the US and other countries have been working according to sociocratic principles. Some companies have been operating successfully for more than 30 years. They survive in what they see as a very hostile environment. Workers' circle participation and no-ownership is in strong contrast with the now-dominant neoliberal economic theory. Sociocratic organisations seem able to adjust their practices to dynamic environments as well as to the ingrained ideas of organisational members in practice. The step towards sociocracy can be realised if a 'powerful someone' in an organisation turns a switch, and if much time and effort is put into education and training. Then a sociocratic structure can work. Finally, sociocratic organisations are not limited to a profit orientation; non-profit and governmental organisations can also be structured in a sociocratic way.

The effect of applying the four simple rules of consent, double links, circles and elections within an organisation is surprising. Improving organisational safety helps to realise optimal creativity in the circle with respect to finding solutions as well as developing new knowledge. Power inequalities impede creative knowledge development. In a sociocratic circle, power inequalities are not possible because everyone has an input into policy-making and an opportunity to jointly formulate and realise organisational goals. The sociocratic method itself is free of content. It is a social structure, not a social content. The method provides the boundary conditions for debates on, and experiments in, organisational behaviour itself. However, one important warning is needed. Although the formal power to enforce decisions is diminished, the issue of psychological differences remains unaddressed. Giving or withholding consent always is influenced by psychological factors. Uncertainty of one's own knowledge, emotional involvement and group pressures will influence consent procedures. Individual experiences will also influence the decision to give consent. In this sense safety is a subjective matter. The positive side of this warning is that this influence can also be detected within other non-sociocratic organisations; however, within a sociocratic organisation the method performs best in counteracting misconduct. It is, after all, always possible to withhold consent. In this sense everyone is responsible for the processes and success of the organisation. It is, therefore, quite understandable that creating a sociocratic organisation takes time and effort, with long training programmes for all employees, from shopfloor workers to senior management.

In a sociocratic organisation it is sometimes difficult to make a distinction between operations and policy. At first sight, this may seem to result in excessive bureaucracy because everyone has the right to put policy and management issues on the circle's agenda. In practice it is not that bad because the feeling of being safe in the organisation prevents these counterproductive activities. The benefit of a sociocratic policy is that, in the decision-making process, it is not just financial economic factors that are relevant, but also the employees' interests. Organisational activities are judged from different angles. The oligarchic structure of the management team is replaced by a balanced representation of the entire workforce. This seems time-consuming, but Reekx and Endenburg have been able to calculate precisely how long it takes to make an important decision—more than 50% of the time is saved. In addition, as the decision-making process is more equitable, any solution is likely to be widely accepted. In non-sociocratic organisations, unpopular or unworkable decisions may be made which are not accepted by the workforce and so prove, in the long term, to be time-consuming and costly.

Sociocracy in practice: Reekx, ATOL and Endenburg Elektrotechnics

Reekx

Reekx has had more than ten years' experience working with the sociocratic circle method. As the method is a co-ordination mechanism, it is normally not directly visible in organisational practice. The company is convinced of the many advantages of the method and it wants to demonstrate these advantages to the outside world.

To stimulate a discussion about how to demonstrate the value of the sociocratic circle method to an external audience, Reekx developed a 'helping circle' in which members of management and researchers participated in research into sociocracy and SoK. A helping circle can be seen as equivalent to a project. The study began by looking at the possibilities of quantifying social profit and comparing them to financial profit. It quickly became obvious that this approach was too limited and that the scope of the research would need to be broadened to encompass an overall assessment of the social performance of Reekx. This assessment explored two issues:

- Employees' 'mental maps' (see cognitive mapping in Chapter 8) of Reekx's social sustainability and sociocracy as they function internally

- The coherence of the company's mission, vision and goals in connection with product–market–technology combinations

Specific results of the first investigation are too detailed to discuss here but can be found in Wevers (2004). The general outcome was that within the organisation there is no coherent view on social sustainability. Given Reekx's tradition of ten years of sociocracy, in which social sustainability has always been a key concept, this was a surprise. We will come back to other general aspects of knowledge and sociocracy later.

ATOL

ATOL is a semi-autonomous business unit of Hanze Higher Vocational Education in Groningen. ATOL applies a specific product–market combination and has its own identity. The organisation is engaged in consultancy activities for managers and offers various types of management training. The unit is financially independent and consists of 25 members, of which 20 are consultants/trainers. The consultants are highly educated and very experienced. They seem to share knowledge, but only to a certain degree. About two years ago ATOL simultaneously introduced the sociocratic circle method and Investors in People (IiP). The sociocratic method is intended to redesign the organisation. The emphasis of the ATOL study was on knowledge sharing and knowledge development. The aim of the study was to find answers to questions, such as: 'what kind of improvements are possible within the various knowledge processes, such as sharing, creation, re-use and development?' and 'will the sociocratic circle method improve these knowledge processes?' (see Riemersma 2004)

ATOL as a business unit is based on the philosophy of the **living organisation** (van Berkel 2002). This philosophy states that every organisation deals with three essential problems: flexibility, control and decisiveness. Every organisation is looking for its own balance, depending on the nature of its work, turbulence in the environment, the organisation's history and its growing phase. Organisations often focus on only one of the three problems and this can result in 'illnesses'. According to ATOL a living organisation is one that constantly and actively searches for a balance when dealing with these problems, and tries to complete the circle by going through phases of development, design, adjustment to changes, trial and error, undertaking action, registration and communicating publicly what works and what does not work.

ATOL can be characterised by an informal atmosphere. Adjusting and decision-making take place informally. Every member of the company acts according to what he or she thinks is suitable for the organisation as a whole. Although this results in maximum flexibility, it sometimes leads to ineffective governance. Several measures have been taken to change this. The organisation is and will remain flat, but the establishment of five teams around core tasks, the appointment of team leaders and the introduction of the sociocratic circle method have created more transparency. ATOL tries to realise a combination of central governance and decentred self-governance. In the centre of the ATOL circle, organisational policies are created. By means of double coupling and the principle of consent maximum input by employees is guaranteed. The teams are each responsible for the realisation of the goals, but are independent in the way they carry them out within their own domains.

Endenburg Elektrotechnics

In 1970, Endenburg Elektrotechnics was the first major organisation to apply the sociocracy principle in the Netherlands. Two years later, it appeared that the introduction of the method had had a very positive effect. In 1990, after 20 years' experience in applying the method, Endenburg proposed the following implementation route. The first step is to start internally with only a few departments. Once this is working successfully, new financial and legal systems can be formulated and realised. The sociocratic organisation had to be embedded into a legal and financial societal structure prepared beforehand. The next step is to involve the labour unions. Although unions are generally in favour of employee participation, the sociocratic method is likely to be new to them and in conflict with their decision-making structures which function on the basis of majority approval rather than consent. With the unions on board, the sociocratic method can be introduced throughout the whole organisation, but only on condition that significant resources are put into education and training. One of the important initiatives taken at Endenburg Elektrotechnics was the introduction of a logbook to record decisions and discussions; this made the employees feel that policy-making and decision-making were transparent and controllable. In 1984 Endenburg decided to relinquish his ownership of Endenburg Elektrotechnics in order to make the transition from the company 'as a property' to the company 'as a means' for the happiness of employees and society. Despite its novel structure, the transition was successful and the company continued to grow. It is now one of the leading technical companies in the Rotterdam area, and it continues to work in a sociocratic manner. Details of the company's development can be found in Endenburg's book, *Sociocracy as Social Design* (1998).

The influence of sociocracy on knowledge sharing and development

Because of the double coupling approach, the sociocratic circle method truly facilitates the exchange of information and knowledge. In the decision-making process all viewpoints are considered equally so no internal interests are ignored. Any decisions made could, therefore, be considered to be internally sustainable. First and foremost the method is a co-ordination mechanism at the group and organisational level. It gives each individual member of an organisation sufficient opportunities to participate in key decision-making.

The culture of organisations such as Reekx, ATOL and Endenburg Elektrotechnics, with their clear focus on support and innovation, stimulates a climate of knowledge sharing in line with the sociocratic method (van Muijen 1994). Sociocracy is hard work, however, requiring a continuous focus on remaining up-to-date and considerable resources devoted to education and training to keep people sharp and creative.

From another theoretical perspective, sociocratic circles resemble communities of practice. The important difference is, however, that in communities of practice cohesion is established on the basis of knowledge within the primary processes whereas in sociocratic circles the orientation is on the secondary processes. Sociocracy favours giving employees freedom to act on their own responsibility and makes it safer to criticise colleagues. However, this does not mean that employees are constantly criticising each other. Where people who have been subject to criticism choose to withhold their consent in important policy meetings, the consent principle forces the exchange of arguments and offers a vehicle for dialogue. In this way, dissenting opinions can be tolerated. And, when decisions are taken, support for them within the organisation is likely to be universal. The sociocratic method involves more people in what is going on in the organisation.

The sociocratic circle method has a positive effect on the sustainability of knowledge processing, at the individual as well as the organisational level. The reasons are that decisions are taken more carefully, that the exchange of opinions is more solid and that there is greater transparency. In organisations that have worked with the sociocratic method for several years, one can see dialogues starting *before* the circle meetings take place. Everyone is actively looking for solutions, and may even approach those who may be expected to withhold consent with a view to persuading them otherwise. As Endenburg (1998) puts it, within a sociocratic organisation no one can be denied.

One issue that is still debatable is the difference between policy and operations. The consent principle holds only for policy decisions. Operational activities are determined by the expertise and knowledge of the employees. A colleague who withholds consent cannot overrule the advice of an expert. In this situation, rational decision-making means that the less skilled employee must give way to the more skilled. So as regards the issue of policy-making the position of the employee within the organisation is in fact of clear importance. This does not rule out the possibility that within this method inequality—that is to say, individual differences—can occur. This is another reason why the sociocratic method requires ongoing training and education.

Apart from its influence on knowledge sharing, the sociocratic circle method also affects an organisation's culture. According to von Krogh, Nonaka and Kazuo (2000), knowledge creation requires specific relational patterns within an organisation. Von Krogh *et al.* (2000) depict a climate of mutual care and attention based on mutual trust, active empathy, a situation in which there is room for posing questions, leniency in judgment and courage. Sharing sensory or tacit knowledge is particularly susceptible to this climate. Socialisation is the proper method to share this knowledge which takes place within so-called **microcommunities**. The sociocratic community would argue that sociocracy is the best method to organise this socialisation. Simply by virtue of the fact that there is a mutual dependency to reach the formulated common goal, the sociocratic circle can function as a suitable platform to develop such a climate. It is up to the participants to nurture this climate responsibly.

Part D
Theory and practice: results from the organisational projects

19
The focus of innovation
WHAT HAVE WE ESTABLISHED?

*René J. Jorna**

In the final four chapters we will discuss what we have classified, analysed and concluded from the nine business projects. This chapter is about the focus of this book—innovation. We have looked at organisations with different structures and cultures at different stages of the innovation process. In Chapter 2 we described the various aspects and characteristics of innovation. In this chapter we will give a detailed list of these characteristics, as described in Chapters 10–18. We will start on a small scale by dealing with the business projects in a concrete manner and from there will make general categorisations for the two higher-level (leap) projects: knowledge of sustainability (KoS) and sustainability of knowledge (SoK).

In Chapters 20 and 21 we proceed thematically: the first theme is sustainability and the second is knowledge and organisation. In Chapter 20 the classification of aspects of sustainability is again based on actual practice. However, because this classification can be interpreted in many different ways (see Chapter 3) there is ambiguity in the different business projects. Chapter 21 deals with knowledge and organisation. With regard to classification characteristics, we make use of the explanations given in Chapters 4 (levels of aggregation), 5 (organisational forms) and 6 (knowledge). In Chapter 21, the material about knowledge and organisation relates to content that is even more elaborate than the material about sustainability in Chapter 20. Thus, it is very difficult to place the knowledge and organisation aspects of the nine business projects in a classification framework. We consider the variety and the particular ways in which the organisations have developed during each of the knowledge projects as an invitation to

---

* With due thanks to Henk Hadders and Jo van Engelen for their comments on earlier versions of this chapter.

continue our exploration. Although in Chapter 21 we also describe and compare the content and the type of knowledge per business project, this chapter is mainly about the typical qualities of the organisations that participated in the different projects. For example, the mental healthcare sector (Chapter 15) is clearly engaged in a knowledge centre and knowledge infrastructure. It is a debatable point whether this is also the case for KunstStoffenHuis (KSH) (Chapter 11), Biosoil (Chapter 10) or the other business projects. In Chapter 21, the method of analysis and drawing conclusions is adopted more from the programme level than the business projects level (i.e. from top to bottom). In the main, this chapter applies the opposite approach (i.e. from the projects level to the programme level).

In Chapter 22 we consider a future theory of sustainability. This theory starts from the perspective that making something sustainable comes down to a **reduction in offload** where offload is an operator consisting of at least four variables. The following formulation will be used: 'A offloads X to B within time horizon T' or 'X_1 transfers Y to X_2 within a Z period of time'. A reduction in offload can affect any of X_1, X_2, Y, Z or a combination of them. We go into this in more detail in Chapter 22. In Chapter 23 we pull all this together to discuss the four ingredients of a questionnaire on the 'people' aspect of sustainability: stakeholders, knowledge, learning and organisations. This questionnaire is not yet a diagnostic instrument by which organisations can measure themselves; rather, it is an assessment aid by which organisations can describe and assess aspects of what we think belongs to social sustainability (the P from 'people'). We will start, however, by focusing on the concept of innovation.

Innovation

As regards the nature of innovations, the business projects all varied in nature and the innovations themselves were at different stages of development and execution. Moreover, very large organisations (such as Philips and Grontmij) as well as very small ones (such as Reekx and KSH) participated in the projects. Furthermore, the innovations themselves were different, as was their orientation on the development of the organisation (i.e. business development). This last point deals with whether the focus was internal (product or service) or external (market or user).

In Table 19.1 we have indicated for each business project how it should be classified on the basis of characteristics such as type of innovation (i.e. product, service, production process or organisation), nature and phase (i.e. from radical to imitative and from invention to evaluation). Finally, in terms of business development, we will indicate whether an innovation results from a focus on the organisation's own environment (i.e. innovation in the product, service or product process) or whether it is instigated by external pressures or demands (the market, users or purchasers).

We will discuss the different organisational projects as follows. First, in accordance with the different innovation characteristics, we will characterise each organisation by means of a number of terms. Next, we will move to a higher level and try to make general statements applying to all organisations, first considering the leap projects KoS and SoK followed by the programme in its entirety.

	Biosoil	Synthetics House	Optichem	Philips	AVEBE	Mental healthcare (GGZ)	AZG (UMCG)	Grontmij	Sociocracy (Reekx)
Type of innovation	Service; production process	Service; organisation	Product; service	Service; production process	Service; organisation	Service; organisation	Service; production process	Organisation	Organisation
Nature of innovation	Really new	Radical	Discontinuous	Discontinuous	Really new	Really new	Discontinuous	Really new	Incremental
Phase of innovation	Implementation	Invention and creation	Invention and creation	Evaluation	Implementation	Invention and creation/implementation	Implementation	Implementation	Evaluation
Internal (product/service) External (purchaser/user/market)	Internal	Internal	Internal	Internal	External	Internal/external	Internal	Internal/external	Internal

TABLE 19.1 Business projects in relation to innovation

Innovation in the organisational projects

Biosoil (Chapter 10)

The *in situ* soil remediation company Biosoil is mainly considered innovative because it offers new services in combination with possible adjustments to the remediation process itself (i.e. the production process). In the discussion about the application of *in situ* remediation it is important to map out the different kinds of parties involved (i.e. stakeholders). Here, the incompatibility of some parts of the existing legislation and the immediate interests of the large number of stakeholders in the remediation debate play a role. Supporting this process is new to Biosoil. Therefore, we are dealing here with a service innovation that is 'really new' in nature, because both the service and the organisation's environment will change, as will the organisation's working methods. The phase of the innovation is that of its implementation. Within Biosoil the ideas already existed before NIDO joined in. From a business development perspective, the innovation has mainly found its origins in the internal environment rather than in the market and the purchasers. Indeed, according to Biosoil, the market or external environment is mostly unco-operative.

KSH (Chapter 11)

KSH has come up with many innovations in the field of synthetics. These activities mainly take place within the Technical University Eindhoven. KSH's problem is that starting an innovation and seeing it through within the small and medium-sized business sector (SME) is a difficult process, both because of the costs involved and the severe competition. For KSH, the innovation is mainly aimed at a service: namely, introducing synthetics innovations and linking these within the SME sector. Thus, we are talking here about product innovation. In the KSH context, organisational innovations are pursued from the chain perspective. To KSH, this service and the organisational innovations are 'radical' or, at the very least, really new. In the development process of KSH, NIDO became involved in a renewal that started only recently, which is why the emphasis is on the invention or creation phase. In this business project, however, part of the implementation had already been started. The impetus to start with these innovations was provided by KSH itself. In terms of business development, we speak of a development stemming from the internal environment.

Optichem (Chapter 12)

The Optichem project involved the introduction by consultancy firm Big River Innovation of decision-support software (DSS) to interconnect the different knowledge domains that lie at the heart of paper production. There is nothing new about DSS systems. What is new, however, is the fact that knowledge from one domain (chemistry) is offered to another (paper/cardboard). Thus, it is partly a product innovation (i.e. DSS) and partly a service innovation (i.e. helping operators in the paper and cardboard sector). To Big River Innovation, it is a service innovation. We consider this innovation to be discontinuous because the renewal has a bearing on the environment of Big River and the chemical industry as well as on the paper and cardboard industry. Although the initiator of this innovation was Big River, in terms of business development the impetus came from the paper and cardboard organisation itself.

Philips (Chapter 13)

Philips aims at further realising the social dimension of sustainability in order to use it in its continuing development of new products and production processes. Better knowledge of the social dimension of sustainability is a service innovation or, possibly at some time in the future, a product or product process innovation. The innovation is discontinuous because there are no innovations in the field of science or technology linked to it, and neither is there a change in the environment. The phase of the innovation is that of the creation or invention of a social sustainability list. The development of a method for assessing this aspect of sustainability is, in Philips' case, still in its infancy and has certainly not yet reached the phase of implementation or evaluation, although Philip's has started to generate social indicator lists. Philips has always had internal motives to stimulate social sustainability. From a business development perspective, there is an external market demand for products that score high on social sustainability, but this demand is ambiguous. In this respect, the European and US markets differ from the Asian market, as discussed in Chapter 13.

AVEBE (Chapter 14)

AVEBE has developed DSSs used by potato growers or cultivation supervisors. These systems have been developed on the basis of theoretical models and are in line with the most up-to-date knowledge in this field. It is therefore disappointing that these systems have not been implemented more successfully. The growers and cultivation supervisors have a view on the cultivation of potatoes which is different to that presented by the theoretical models. The ways of studying and adjusting these systems show that we are dealing with a service innovation aimed at growers and supervisors, although the systems themselves are not innovative. The intention is to realise a product–process innovation by means of this kind of service innovation in a short period of time. The nature of the innovation in relation to the growers and the supervisors is that of a really new innovation, so that a new service as well as a new business activity are being realised in this way. The innovation phase consists of an evaluation followed by an improved implementation of the system. Furthermore, as a result of AVEBE's co-operative form, the impetus in terms of business development to achieve renewals stems from the organisation's own environment rather than from the market or purchasers. This is because the growers are the joint owners of the co-operative.

Mental healthcare (Chapter 15)

The mental healthcare sector in the Netherlands is, among other things, engaged in setting up a new infrastructure on behalf of the Dutch Health Authority. This infrastructure can be used to support the co-ordination, management, control and improvement of knowledge in the mental healthcare sector. On a high level of abstraction a new systematic method is laid down. The nature of this innovation is that of a really new one which, at present, is still in the creation and invention phase rather than the implementation stage. It is difficult in such a complicated healthcare structure to speak in terms of business development, but the ultimate goal is to improve knowledge of the diagnosis and therapy of patients and clients. This means that, in the abstract sense of Dutch society, users and purchasers have been the instigators of the renewals.

A special part of the mental healthcare discussion is related to how knowledge itself is organised. CasusConsult works in a case-based paradigm. In itself, this is not innovative. However, although it is a well-known approach, the 'reasoning with cases' method has never gained full momentum as a technology. CasusConsult means an innovation of a service and, eventually, also of a production process. The nature of the innovation is not radical, for the technology is already there, but it is really new with respect to its application domain and the consequences thereof. The focus is on implementation rather than on creation or invention. In terms of business development CasusConsult has been developed from within the organisation itself; it has not been instigated by the clients or patients.

The innovation to be implemented within the Mental Health Authority Drenthe concerns the introduction of a systematic method for knowledge management. We are dealing here with a really new service innovation in the area of content. The innovation itself is clearly in the transitional phase from creation to implementation. Studies are being conducted in the field of knowledge management that have to provide a basis for the decision-making process throughout the whole organisation. In terms of business development this innovation has clearly been initiated internally by the organisation itself rather than by the users, such as patients and clients.

UMCG (Chapter 16)

In the case of the University Medical Centre Groningen (UMCG), a service innovation is being implemented with the aim of facilitating specialist training courses and realising a better separation between on-the-job training and practical medical work. This will have consequences for the process of curing patients (i.e. the production process). The nature of the innovation is discontinuous and its phase is that of implementation. The concept has been designed and is to be executed in a step-by-step manner. The innovation has been initiated on the basis of internal considerations rather than as a result of pressure from patients or patient groups.

Grontmij (Chapter 17)

Grontmij is looking for possibilities to expand existing alliances or to start new ones in the form of an organisational innovation. Alliances—for example, to combine KoS—can be considered as a really new type of innovation. However, because these are built on either active or dormant combinations, the focus here is not on the creation phase, but on the further implementation of the innovation. The emphasis in this innovation is on creating new complementary knowledge internally. The start of the innovation can therefore be regarded as internally initiated. The situation is, however, complicated, because Grontmij has noticed that within its external market (i.e. the government and the corporate world) there is a growing demand for bundling the knowledge of differ-

294 SUSTAINABLE INNOVATION

ent organisations. This means that purchasers or the market also play a role in the initiation of this innovation. Therefore, it is partly instigated by the external environment as well as internal considerations.

Sociocracy (Chapter 18)

Reekx and ATOL used and started to implement a new organisational form—sociocracy—which involves innovation of the entire organisation. For Reekx this form had already been in existence for ten years, but for ATOL it was completely new. This organisational form had already been invented and realised earlier in other companies. In the case of Reekx there is a clear focus on innovation within the organisation. It wants to gain more insight into the social 'profit' resulting from its organisational structure based on the sociocratical perspective. Although this innovation may once have been really new for Reekx, it can now be said to be 'incremental'. Creation or implementation are not the issues here; instead the focus is mainly on evaluating the organisational innovation. In terms of business development, the renewal has been initiated by the organisation itself. For ATOL, however, it is a really new innovation grounded firmly in the creation phase with a clear focus on implementation. In terms of business development this innovation has mainly been internally initiated by ATOL itself.

The leap projects and the organisations

The nine business projects fall under two leap projects: Biosoil, KSH, Optichem, Philips and AVEBE under KoS; and mental healthcare, UMCG, Grontmij and sociocracy under SoK. Given the nature of the projects and the status of the organisational developments at the time, this division was consciously made beforehand. When we first look at the nature of the innovation, we see no difference between KoS and SoK as regards the degree of innovation (see Table 19.2). From this we conclude that both production companies and service-oriented organisations are innovating drastically.

Innovative nature	Radical	Really new	Discontinuous	Incremental	Imitative
KoS (5 projects)	1	2	2	0	0
SoK (4 projects)	0	2	1	1	0

The numbers in the cells refer to the various business projects and are the summation of the descriptions from Chapters 10–18.

TABLE 19.2 Innovative nature of the leap projects KoS and SoK

The type of innovation has a bearing on the distinction between product, service or something else. Service innovations form a majority (seven projects) for both KoS and SoK (see Table 19.3). The fact that in the case of SoK there are more organisation innovations shows that this leap project is successful from a goal perspective. If SoK is about

Innovation type	Product	Service	Production process	Organisation
KoS (5 projects)	1	5	3	1
SoK (4 projects)	0	2	1	3

Note: The number of projects in each row add up to more than five and four for KoS and SoK respectively because business projects can fall under more than one innovation type.

TABLE 19.3 Innovation types within the leap projects

the preconditions for knowledge creation and for the management, control and re-use of knowledge, support in this area has been intensive. An additional conclusion is that within the framework of sustainability, service innovations are highly important. We have further observed, though this has not been indicated in a table, that in the division of the innovation's creation, implementation and evaluation phases there is no difference between KoS and SoK. Furthermore, the projects have been properly divided over the different phases.

Apart from the aggregation level of the leap projects, we can also look at the separate business projects. Here we see very clearly that most innovations are really new and discontinuous (see the first five columns in Table 19.4). And, although no radical new science or technology is involved, it is a fact that new products and services as well as new external environments and organisations are emerging. It has again become clear to us that a myth is being created around radical innovations. It has already been concluded in Chapter 2 that they occur sporadically (once in every five or ten years), that they have a long incubation period and that they require a radical conversion of both the organisational forms and the knowledge and mental landscapes.

Through the mythologisation of radical and, in particular, technical innovations the importance of other types of innovations remain underexposed. This is in line with a conclusion drawn in the 2003 documentary by Jeremy Rifkin on sustainable energy (see Chapter 2) which promoted the hydrogen cell as a sustainable energy carrier. The new technology of the hydrogen cell is already here, but will certainly require a great deal of technical adjustments. The most important innovations will, however, emerge as a result of different ways of thinking and other organisational forms. For example, at present cars use energy, regardless of the fact that they are equipped with batteries (power *from* the mains). But suppose that the car works on hydrogen cells; in that case it can function as an energy supplier to households (power *to* the mains). This would mean a tremendous impulse in the field of service and other innovations, which will also be much more radical than the development of the hydrogen cell itself (see Chapter 2).

In addition, many initiatives for the development of new products, services or processes are started internally by organisations themselves (see the last two columns in Table 19.4). We consider this as self-evident. If an organisation does not generate new ideas it is likely to lose its position and so go out of business. The best situation, of course, is where the internal and external drivers are connected by some form of feedback loop. However, this does not occur very often. The second best, and most common, situation is where an organisation itself introduces innovations. Although the market is often regarded as the driving force behind innovation, if the organisation

	Radical	Really new	Discontinuous	Incremental	Imitative	Internal	External
Innovation nature	1	4	3	1	0	–	–
Business development	–	–	–	–	–	8	3

Note: In the business development row, two organisations fall under both internal and external.

TABLE 19.4 Innovative nature and business development of the nine organisational projects

itself has no desire or capacity to innovate, little progress will be made. In this respect it is surprising that economists and business analysts do not make use of knowledge gained from other disciplines, such as psychology, education and sociology, where it is commonly accepted that whenever people are not interested in change, or are unwilling to work to achieve it, external pressure does not work.

When looking once more at the organisational projects, we see a picture identical to the one we saw in the leap projects (see the first four columns in Table 19.5). Product innovations are the least common. The majority of innovations are service- and organisation-related. Here the most striking thing is that this applies both to large companies, such as Philips, AVEBE and Grontmij, and the smaller ones, such as Biosoil or KSH. Perhaps we could provocatively state that product innovations are the exception and service innovations the rule. This is in strong contrast with the prevailing view that innovation mainly has to be sought in products rather than in services.

	Product	Service	Production process	Organisation	Creation	Implementation	Evaluation
Innovation type	1	7	3	5	–	–	–
Innovation phase	–	–	–	–	3	5	2

Note: The figures are frequencies. They total more than nine because there can be several innovation types and phases within an organisation.

TABLE 19.5 Innovation type and phase

With respect to which innovation phase the organisations are in, most business projects are in the implementation phase. With regard to the creation phase, the organisations we co-operated with did not start at zero. They had already been engaged in the creation process for some time. Creation cannot be accomplished in a single instance; it takes place over a period of time and, in most cases, our participation started at the end of the creation phase.

Conclusions

We do not pretend to test hypotheses. The amount of business projects studied is too small for this. Moreover, the random sample was highly selective and the possible variables were not measured adequately enough. We can nevertheless observe a number of tendencies. These could, if necessary, be formulated as hypotheses for the benefit of further research. We will return to this in Chapters 22 and 23. Our observations emphasise the explorative character of the NIDO programme. The following general conclusions can be drawn.

- Innovations take a long time, especially those in the field of services and organisations, such as mental healthcare, Philips, Grontmij and KSH. We also observe that radical innovations are rare. Innovations that really affect society usually take more than ten years to be realised
- Innovations do not have a definitive start- or end-point; they evolve in a continuous process. Examples include sociocracy, mental healthcare and UMCG
- There is no clear division between service and product innovations; and in product environments service innovations are common. This applies to AVEBE, Optichem, Philips and Biosoil
- Innovations can take place within a company or organisation, but also between companies and organisations. The latter, in particular, are worthy of praise, because they require changes to more than one organisation. KSH, Grontmij and Optichem are clear examples of this
- Innovations cannot be predicted, controlled or managed in terms of content. It is not possible to control the generation of ideas. What is important is that management is capable of recognising and facilitating conditions for innovative thinking (von Krogh, Nonaka and Kazuo 2000; McElroy 2003). This sometimes requires making an effort—for example, at the start of KSH's and Optichem's innovation process—but sometimes innovation unfolds naturally as, for example, in the case of Biosoil or sociocracy
- Innovations are more favoured by an intrinsic motivation for product and service renewal than by external pressure from users and the market. The best situation is when these factors are combined. In any case, innovations are about people and knowledge; thus, the attention paid to innovation in these terms should have no limit

20
Business (organisational) practices
RECURRING THEMES OF SUSTAINABILITY

René J. Jorna

In Chapter 19 we presented a structured overview of the innovation activities carried out in the various business projects. The overview started from the actual practice of the various projects because our focus is to bring together and stimulate innovations in companies and organisations. In this chapter, about sustainability, and in the next, about knowledge, our approach will be more thematic. The various innovation projects dealt with sustainability and knowledge. However, we have not so far set out all the characteristics of sustainability and knowledge in the various projects. We used a limited structure (as discussed in Chapters 3 and 6) and we also looked at the projects afresh. Thus, we do not consider the classification of sustainability and knowledge developments in the nine business projects as rigid. Rather, we speak of the start of a process of further elaborating and establishing a generic perspective with respect to sustainability. This perspective, in which sustainability is considered as a **reduction in offload**, is developed further in Chapter 22 and in terms of an assessment questionnaire in Chapter 23.

In this chapter, we address aspects of sustainability. First, we deal with the 'triple P' of 'planet', 'people' and 'profit'. According to the sustainability definition of Elkington (1997), these three aspects have to be in balance. For each business project we assess the balance of the different Ps. We labelled the Ps in the projects as ecological sustainability (planet), social sustainability (people) and economic sustainability (profit). We dealt with these aspects thoroughly in Chapter 3. Second, the question of 'sustainability of what' is a relevant issue. In this context, we refer to the artefacts, divided into entities (concrete) and constructs (non-material or mental) that we also discussed in Chapter 3. Third, there is the distinction between absolute and relative. As explained in Chapter 3, one can see sustainability either as the ultimate goal or as a result of an observed deficiency in the 'here and now'. The first perspective of sustainability we have called 'sustainability considered from an absolute point of reference' and the second 'sustainability considered from a relative point of reference'. Finally, we discussed the development of sustainability from a static or a dynamic perspective. Static means that a stable relationship with the environment is assumed. Although the artefact can adjust itself internally, it is not dynamically linked to the environment. A dynamic perspective means that this flexible relation with the environment does, in fact, exist.

The business projects

Biosoil (Chapter 10)

Since its launch in 1993 Biosoil has focused on ecological sustainability. Biosoil's orientation is on improving the technologies applied in the process of *in situ* soil remediation. In the past few years Biosoil has noticed that social sustainability is gaining momentum. Of course, without economic sustainability neither social nor ecological sustainability are achievable as the company would cease to exist. However, Biosoil believes that economic sustainability is a means to achieving social and ecological sustainability rather than an end in itself.

KunstStoffenHuis (Chapter 11)

KunstStoffenHuis (KSH) places ecological and economic sustainability second to social sustainability. KSH benefits from good internal organisation and an effective chain that structures its innovations.

Optichem (Chapter 12)

The development of a decision-support system (DSS) is directed mainly at ecological sustainability by decreasing or improving the use of chemical substances in the paper and cardboard industry. Although economic sustainability is used as an argument to realise this system of improvement, it is not really important. Social sustainability plays a minor role. However, this may change when safety, as well as sharing knowledge between the domains of chemistry and the paper and cardboard industry, becomes more important.

Philips (Chapter 13)

Philips specifically aims at the social dimension of sustainability. The company has already developed a list of indicators of ecological sustainability for its products. According to Philips, the development of a list of indicators of social sustainability is very important with respect to economic sustainability. However, the question remains whether this could be realised without too many problems.

AVEBE (Chapter 14)

AVEBE is in the process of developing a software system for economic sustainability in potato starch production. The development of this system goes hand in hand with ecological sustainability as it will lead to a decrease in the use of pesticides and artificial fertilisers. This will have consequences for the entire northern region of the Netherlands ten years hence, implying that only in the long run will social sustainability play an essential role.

Mental healthcare (Chapter 15)

This innovation is entirely aimed at social sustainability. Ecological sustainability plays no role at all whereas economic sustainability is involved only because a better knowledge infrastructure makes it possible to reduce costs, re-use knowledge and share knowledge more effectively.

UMCG (Chapter 16)

The renewal of training courses and the curriculum of specialists at the University Medical Centre Groningen (UMCG) mainly concerns social sustainability. Ecological sustainability is not an issue and economic sustainability only plays a minor role.

Grontmij (Chapter 17)

Through its innovations Grontmij tries to find a proper balance in its perspective on sustainability. From the company's launch in 1915 ecological sustainability has been very important. In addition, of course, economic sustainability plays a key role. When looking for possible inter-firm alliances, there is now a much greater emphasis on social sustainability, both internally and externally.

Sociocracy (Chapter 18)

The discussion about sustainability within sociocracy focuses on the tension between social and economic sustainability with respect to which of the two should have priority. Sociocratic organisations have the view that better social sustainability stimulates economic sustainability. Ecological sustainability does not play a significant role.

Table 20.1 gives an assessment of the various dimensions of sustainability in terms of their relative importance in the nine different business projects. For each business project the cells in the table contain the figures that for the rows add up to 100%. The figures in the cells are estimates of the relative weight. They have no absolute status.

20. BUSINESS (ORGANISATIONAL) PRACTICES: RECURRING THEMES OF SUSTAINABILITY

	Biosoil	KSH	Optichem	Philips	AVEBE	MHC	AZG (UMCG)	Grontmij	Sociocracy
Planet	50%	20%	60%	20%	50%	0%	0%	40%	0%
Profit	20%	30%	20%	30%	20%	30%	30%	30%	30%
People	30%	50%	20%	50%	30%	70%	70%	30%	70%

TABLE 20.1 Sustainability assessment of the three Ps within the nine organisations

The business projects considered in the light of sustainability aspects

Determining the relative significance of the above-mentioned sustainability dimensions is difficult. Nonetheless, the business projects do generate information about the various dimensions, enabling us to estimate their relative importance (see Table 20.1). First, we consider that the planet component is a priority in organisations engaged in production and the commercial provision of services. This applies to AVEBE, Optichem, Grontmij and Biosoil. The people aspect is well represented in the mental healthcare sector, UMCG, sociocracy, Philips and KSH. Second, we observe that the profit dimension has similar relative importance across all the projects. Third, and as discussed in Chapter 3, we can look at a number of other aspects of sustainability, notably: the sustainability of 'what'; the absolute and relative perspective; and the static versus the dynamic sustainability perspective.

When listing these aspects, Table 20.2 shows that in almost all of our innovation projects the object of sustainability is a construct rather than a physical object. Only Philips' innovations could be described as 'objects': namely, social sustainability indicators for products, appliances and product processes.

With respect to the absolute versus relative and dynamic versus static aspects, we had to interpret the situation within the business projects. It is clear that the business projects that are part of the KoS (knowledge of sustainability) leap project advocate a more absolute view while those in the SoK (sustainability of knowledge) leap project share a more relative view. Biosoil, Philips, Optichem and AVEBE have a more absolute view on sustainability. Their goal is to be as sustainable as possible. This means that waste has to be minimised and the re-use of materials maximised. Starting from this optimum, the ideal situation is 'downgraded' or 'readjusted' so that it fits in with the existing situation. The other projects apply a relative perspective to sustainability, starting from their existing situations. However, it appears that an absolute perspective is more characteristic of the ecological dimension of sustainability than of the social dimension.

	Biosoil	KSH	Optichem	Philips	AVEBE	MHC	AZG (UMCG)	Grontmij	Sociocracy
Sustainability of 'what'	Construct	Construct	Construct	Object	Construct	Construct	Construct	Construct	Construct
Absolute or relative	Absolute	Absolute / relative	Absolute	Absolute	Absolute	Relative	Relative	Absolute / relative	Relative
Static or dynamic	Dynamic	Dynamic	Dynamic	Dynamic	Dynamic	Dynamic	Dynamic	Dynamic	Dynamic

TABLE 20.2 Characteristics of sustainability in the business projects

With respect to the static and dynamic aspects, all the projects respond dynamically to changes in the external environment and with respect to their internal situation (see Chapter 3). However, we acknowledge that this is likely to be an artefact of the sample bias, since participants had either already started to innovate, or were planning to do so, and so were more likely to be selected to take part in the programme.

In light of the aforementioned factors, it is not surprising that knowledge plays an essential role in all the business projects. Chapter 21 further elaborates and clarifies this.

21
Business practice
RECURRING THEMES IN AND AROUND KNOWLEDGE

René J. Jorna and Henk Hadders

Knowledge is central to the knowledge of sustainability (KoS) and sustainability of knowledge (SoK) 'leap' projects as well as to the separate business projects. This means that all the projects can be considered as knowledge management initiatives. There are many reasons for introducing these kinds of initiatives; for example, quality improvement, increasing professionalism, the development of new products and services, and improving the length of time taken to launch a product on the market. In the next section we discuss the types of knowledge (in terms of content) that play a role in the different projects. In doing so we will make a distinction between knowledge within the primary processes and knowledge within the secondary processes. We go on to discuss categorisation of the types of knowledge: sensory, coded and theoretical. In both sections we stay close to what we have observed in the business projects. After this, we consider a number of aspects which, although linked to knowledge, do not belong to the project categorisations. We present our findings on three key areas within the framework of humans, organisations and the dynamics of knowledge creation: namely, policy and practice, characteristics of the knowledge infrastructure and learning.

Knowledge in terms of content within the business projects

Apart from building on existing knowledge, the different projects have also yielded new knowledge. This new knowledge can differ in terms of content or type from the knowledge already in existence in the organisations. Content of the knowledge means knowledge that plays the most important role in the innovation project. We do not claim that this always concerns the organisation's domain knowledge of the primary process. Philips, for example, manufactures all kinds of electric and electronic devices. When the focus is on indicators of social sustainability, however, it is not this technical knowledge that is important, but rather the knowledge of customers, customer groups and areas such as product and consumer safety. By 'types of knowledge' we mean the types of knowledge that are dominant, given the content. First, we briefly discuss knowledge in terms of content within each of the business projects. Then we look at the types of knowledge in more detail: sensory, encoded and theoretical.

Biosoil (Chapter 10)

In the case of Biosoil three knowledge domains are important: knowledge of biological and chemical remediation, knowledge of the social legislation for *in situ* remediation and knowledge of methods for mapping out the interests of the different parties involved. Biosoil possesses considerable knowledge in the first field and, to a lesser extent, in the second, but hardly any in the third.

KunstStoffenHuis (Chapter 11)

In the case of KunstStoffenHuis (KSH) three knowledge domains are important: knowledge of synthetics, knowledge of the interests and expertise of organisations in the small businesses sector, and knowledge of realising forms of co-operation in chains. KSH knows a great deal about the first of these, but little about the other two.

Optichem (Chapter 12)

For Optichem three knowledge domains also play an important role: knowledge of chemistry, knowledge of the paper and carton production, and knowledge of the development of decision-support systems (DSSs). For its part, Big River possesses knowledge of paper and cardboard production and, to a lesser extent, of chemistry. Knowledge of software development is absent.

Philips (Chapter 13)

In the case of Philips, the major knowledge domains in the field of social sustainability are product development and knowledge of customers and customer groups.

AVEBE (Chapter 14)

In the case of AVEBE three knowledge domains are important. These are knowledge of the cultivation of potatoes, knowledge of software development in the field of simulation and optimisation, and knowledge of how users deal with system support. In the areas of potato cultivation and system development there is a great deal of knowledge within AVEBE, but there is much less knowledge about software users.

Mental healthcare (Chapter 15)

Although mental healthcare (GGZ) in the Netherlands in general possesses a considerable amount of knowledge in the content or domain area, this knowledge is not especially relevant to the innovation project. The knowledge content concerns knowledge of developing an infrastructure. This could be called organisational knowledge. Some groups within GGZ—for example, Trimbos—possess a great deal of knowledge. In the special project on case-based reasoning (CasusConsult) three knowledge domains are important: knowledge technology, knowledge of specific healthcare divisions and knowledge of the users of knowledge technology. As regards the latter knowledge domain CasusConsult possesses less knowledge in terms of content. In the case of the specific GGZ Drenthe three different knowledge domains play a role: knowledge of mental healthcare, knowledge of how knowledge is managed both from a people's and an organisational perspective, and knowledge of a method for implementing knowledge management at the organisational level. Knowledge concerning the last domain is notably absent.

UMCG (Chapter 16)

At University Medical Centre Groningen (UMCG) knowledge of managing innovation projects and dispersing this knowledge internally is important. Medical and nursing-oriented knowledge is not especially relevant in this project.

Grontmij (Chapter 17)

In the case of Grontmij three knowledge domains are relevant: knowledge of water, infrastructure, construction and environment, organisational knowledge and knowledge of how to build and expand alliances. Grontmij possesses a large amount of knowledge for the first two domains, but very little for the last.

Sociocracy (Chapter 18)

Two knowledge domains are important for Reekx: knowledge of economic processes, measures and criteria, and knowledge of how to work out the concept of sociocracy. Reekx's primary knowledge domain, information and file management, is not relevant. Reekx knows a lot about the sociocracy concept, but much less about the different ways of applying economic concepts. For ATOL two knowledge domains play a role: knowledge of education and the consultancy component linked to it, and organisational knowledge, especially sociocracy and knowledge management. ATOL is particularly focused on organisational knowledge which, although available to staff members, has not as yet been applied to the organisation itself.

Table 21.1 estimates the proportions for knowledge content in each of the nine business projects. Because, given the scope of our research, we cannot possibly go into all types of knowledge content, we restrict ourselves to distinguishing between the primary and secondary processes.

	Biosoil	KSH	Optichem	Philips	AVEBE	Mental healthcare (GGZ)	UMCG (AZG)	Grontmij	Sociocracy (Reekx)
Knowledge content in primary process	30%	30%	70%	20%	70%	30%	0%	40%	0%
Knowledge content in secondary process	70%	70%	30%	80%	30%	70%	100%	60%	100%

TABLE 21.1 Importance of knowledge content in primary and secondary processes in the business projects

The classification of knowledge types within the various business projects

It is too great a task to give a detailed representation of all the different knowledge types relevant for the various business projects. We have therefore confined ourselves to distinguishing between sensory, coded and theoretical knowledge for the whole knowledge domain (see Table 21.2). In light of the discussion about knowledge types in Chapter 6, readers may wish to make their own categorisation.

	Biosoil	KSH	Optichem	Philips	AVEBE	Mental healthcare (GGZ)	UMCG (AZG)	Grontmij	Sociocracy (Reekx)
Sensory knowledge	20%	40%	40%	30%	30%	30%	40%	30%	30%
(En)coded knowledge	50%	40%	40%	50%	30%	40%	40%	50%	30%
Theoretical knowledge	30%	20%	20%	20%	40%	30%	40%	20%	40%

TABLE 21.2 Categorisation of knowledge types

Conclusions

This section provides a summary of the most important findings and conclusions about the key areas of social sustainability: policy and practice; knowledge infrastructure; and learning. Including themes from Chapter 6, the following processes are also relevant: 'aiming at' and 'carrying out'; and 'structuring'. These lead to the mutual goal of learning and applying knowledge. Individual knowledge is the starting point of the organisational knowledge and value creation spiral. For each key area we reach one or more conclusions and illustrate these with relevant findings from the nine business projects.

Policy and practice

Sustainable knowledge initiatives should be in accordance with the mission, vision, objectives and strategy of the organisation. As an example we consider the mental healthcare sector which was looking for a method to structurally embed knowledge management within its planning and control systems and procedures. Within Biosoil, Philips and KSH there is a similarly clear link between sustainable knowledge initiatives and mission. In the case of sociocracy in Reekx the current mission and vision are being reconsidered.

Knowledge and knowledge activities should be integrated into the daily working practices of knowledge workers. To this end, AVEBE, Optichem and the mental healthcare sector have introduced DSSs. Although the domains differ in terms of content, in essence there is no difference between the approach to 'knowledge in the field' (AVEBE) and 'knowledge at the bedside' (mental healthcare and UMCG). In addition, UMCG is looking for effective learning facilities in the form of a skills laboratory.

Knowledge infrastructure

The knowledge infrastructure forms the backbone of a learning organisation. In this respect sustainable and proper knowledge transfer within a knowledge infrastructure is only possible if organisational, staff, technological and cultural prerequisites are being met simultaneously and coherently.

Organisation

The selected organisational form and structure should facilitate sustainable knowledge creation. In this context the company system level is not suitable for the flow of knowledge. The system level has to be distinguished more clearly from the knowledge level. With regard to sociocracy it is obvious that the organisational form selected (in this case the sociocratic circle method) stimulates the sharing of existing knowledge and developing new knowledge. In addition, transparency and the influence of staff members on the policy-making process are of great importance. The findings support the view that within other organisational types and forms issues such as self-management and direct involvement are of the utmost importance for the realisation of an innovative, knowledge-intensive organisation.

Personnel

Knowledge workers should have sufficient resources, including time, to engage in sustainable knowledge creation. Often, production pressures and organisational culture provide little opportunity for this. This was seen particularly in the healthcare sector projects. Both within mental healthcare and UMCG there was a visible tension between the production and exploitation of knowledge on the one hand and the creation of new knowledge on the other.

Knowledge infrastructures consisting of networks of organisations such as universities, knowledge institutes or public–private partnerships at national, sectoral and local levels are increasingly becoming the success factors for knowledge transfer between science and practice. As a result, knowledge management is moving into knowledge network management. Within KSH, mental healthcare and AVEBE there are chain networks between the organisation and knowledge institutes. The most important mission in this respect is the diffusion and implementation of new insights and knowledge gained in practice.

Within both national knowledge institutes and local organisations an adequate organisational structure and embedding of the knowledge management function are of great importance. In this context, the knowledge worker (as a user and knowledge manager) is central. How should the (supporting) knowledge organisation be structured? Both at the local executive level (for example, within mental healthcare, KSH, Grontmij and AVEBE) and on the national and international levels (within the knowledge centre of mental healthcare [Trimbos] as well as within Philips and AVEBE) this plays a role.

Technology

Knowledge management is often simply seen as the deployment of ICT. Although access to suitable ICT is important for the knowledge worker, knowledge management initiatives will fail if existing structures, patterns, behaviour and systems remain as they are.

Organisations make use of several functionalities/systems simultaneously, focusing on sensory knowledge (personification strategy) or, at other times, on coded and other types of knowledge (codification strategy). The business projects of mental healthcare, UMCG, AVEBE and KSH show various forms of technological support around knowledge management. Communities of practice—groups of people who focus on working with sensory knowledge—are essential for sharing existing and developing new knowledge. Mental healthcare, sociocracy, Biosoil and KSH are, in one way or another, engaged in setting up or facilitating these communities.

Language will affect the sharing of knowledge. Examples are the development of a thesaurus for a particular branch (mental healthcare), the development of an object model for product development (KSH) and a network instrument (Grontmij).

Culture and leadership

Management is often aimed at structuring scarcity. This does not apply to knowledge. What should be central is exploring and supporting a latent abundance rather than managing scarcity. The middle managers of tomorrow will have to become knowledge engineers in an enterprise focused on knowledge creation. In this way the dynamic exchange between individually bound knowledge and the explicit knowledge of the organisation will be facilitated. In line with this approach, middle managers will act as engineers of change, directing the processes of knowledge enrichment and renewal and, as a result, expanding horizontal networks.

Trust in staff members, safety and empowerment are the most important success factors for sharing existing knowledge and developing new. Within the sociocracy project, the important role of trust and safety in relation to knowledge sharing and development is obvious. The same holds for alliances in Grontmij.

A strongly supportive culture offers a great deal of scope for sharing and reflecting on knowledge. The culture research studies conducted in the context of sociocracy show that a structure focused on support is an important success factor.

Learning

Within a number of projects an integral approach to learning was undertaken whereby three types of knowledge were combined and used. These are:

- Knowledge gained by experience (customers, clients, stakeholders)
- Practical knowledge (professionals, knowledge workers)
- Theoretical knowledge (scientific researchers)

Learning is a natural phenomenon. One learns by behaving in a certain way in an environment. Organisations should therefore take particular care to provide the necessary environment for successful learning.

Learning from stakeholders is of decisive significance in the pursuit of sustainable innovation and the development of new products, services, processes and organisational forms. The Biosoil, UMCG, mental healthcare, Grontmij and Philips projects put emphasis on the identification of stakeholders and, subsequently, on initiating a dialogue with the most important ones.

Learning from systematically collecting, filing, combining and distributing the experiences of staff members (i.e. shopfloor wisdom) is of great importance for sharing knowledge within an organisation. Experiences may be collected and filed both at the project level ('after-action review' in the case of Grontmij, cultivation supervisors in the case of AVEBE and redesigners in the case of Philips) and for individual cases (mental healthcare) when the professionals meet to discuss and codify the lessons learned.

The fact that professionals are learning leads to demand for new learning facilities with new forms of education and training in which new methods and educational programmes are implemented, in some cases with the support of ICT (e-learning, virtual reality, electronic libraries and professional journals). Within Grontmij, KSH, UMCG, mental healthcare and AVEBE, knowledge of experts is being laid down and distributed or opportunities are provided to consult experts.

Learning from science as well as from the application of knowledge by knowledge workers (i.e. the implementation of scientific insights in actual practice) appears to be complex and difficult to manage, requiring new theoretical insights or approaches in order to achieve a change in the behaviour of professionals. Within KSH, AVEBE, Biosoil and the mental healthcare sector, the available scientific knowledge is being applied in actual practice. In this context the problem is whether knowledge workers are prepared to accept and use the (scientific) knowledge developed by others.

Final remarks

This chapter has looked at the content of the knowledge that plays a role in the business projects. This knowledge has been subdivided according to its type and association with process (primary or secondary). Some preliminary conclusions have been drawn and these will be included in Chapter 22. The final chapter of this book (Chapter 23) endeavours to make the concept of social sustainability more operational by postulating a theory of sustainability in which the reduction in offload principle is central. To this end, it will attempt to formulate social sustainability in terms of an assessment instrument—a questionnaire. This is not a diagnostic tool, but it is hoped that the answers will lead to reflection and further radical thinking (see Chapter 23).

22
Further steps towards a systematic perspective on sustainability

Niels R. Faber, René J. Jorna and Jo van Engelen

In the previous chapters we looked both theoretically and practically at many aspects of sustainability, innovation and knowledge. This has resulted in theoretical categorisations and classifications in the field of innovation and knowledge and generated a large number of practical innovations in the different business projects. All this work is descriptive, analytical and (partly) diagnostic. Nevertheless, it remains difficult to realise a total perspective on sustainability. Our aim is to develop a systematic perspective on sustainability based on the lessons learned from theory and practice. Apart from providing a means of diagnosis, this should also enable us to take action, to intervene and to carry out treatment. In this chapter we attempt a first step towards such a system. We do not intend to be exhaustive. We will, however, try to establish a further refinement of the definition of sustainability as a **reduction in offload**. Making sustainability operational has already briefly been dealt with in Chapters 3 and 6. In the next and final chapter we present a first attempt at a questionnaire on social sustainability.

Developing a systematic view on sustainability is based on three concepts that are mutually connected:

- Disturbance and retrieval of an equilibrium or balance
- The various aggregation levels that play a role in these situations of balance, such as the individual, group, company and society
- The particular issue that has to be kept in balance (e.g. the pollution or an organisation)

In order to make the reduction in offload terminology concrete we will briefly discuss two examples: the hydrogen fuel cell and the PET (polyethylene terephthalate) bottle. Hydrogen fuel cells have a number of advantages over fossil fuels. They have negligible emissions and they are very resource-efficient. Both advantages mean a reduction in offload onto later generations. The widespread introduction of the fuel cell would bring about a revolution in our ways of thinking and organisation as well as in logistics. With regard to our second example, PET bottles are, at present, recyclable, with a deposit. This is about to change in the Netherlands and probably the rest of Europe. The industry wants to replace the PET bottle by one that can be used only once, with no deposit. Environmental groups are against this and consumers are either indifferent or do not understand the issues. The cost calculations show a clear case of 'subjective colouring' by the different parties. The sustainability concept is used to their own advantage: transport, storage, cleansing, hygiene, raw materials and energy. These issues can be captured in the 'reduction in offload' terminology, but, with regard the various aspects of transport, energy, etc., no one is using this terminology.

We will start by giving a quasi-logical formulation of the reduction in offload concept and by presenting the design methodology as an aid for analysis, diagnosis and intervention. Next, we will focus on offload and the notion of homeostasis, a concept with various consequences for both natural and artificial systems. Finally, we present a research agenda.

A logical and methodological formulation of reduction in offload

Making sustainability operational in terms of a reduction in offloading begins with the term 'offload' itself and with the elements that are related to it. This will be discussed in the next section. First, we will deal with who and what is being subjected to the offload.

Whenever something is being offloaded this means that the unfavourable consequences of a particular activity are transferred from one party to the other. In some cases this happens immediately; in others after a longer period of time. Take, for instance, the example of the hydrogen fuel cell. We know that this is less environmentally damaging than coal, gas and oil. We also know that the supplies of the latter are not infinite and are predicted to be insufficient to serve the world's population in 40–50 years' time. Thus, current generations are transferring a problem to future generations. On the other hand, changing the energy production and distribution infrastructure by moving to a hydrogen-based energy system would cause huge upheaval and be crushingly expensive. Reduction in offload can therefore take various turns. It can refer to present-day situations and to future or hopefully future situations. Comparisons can be made, but they have to be treated very carefully.

The example of the PET bottle can be reformulated in terms of offload. The industry is in the process of subjecting society to the offload of harmful environmental effects under the pretext of the higher costs of recyclable bottles because of distribution. At a certain point these disadvantages will be transferred to society via taxes (bottles are thrown away and require collection by refuse collectors). The individuals will not be able to offload these disadvantages, but they may change their buying behaviour, join an environmental group or change their political preferences. There is a clear pattern in which one aggregation level of offload influences the other. This again leads to a reduction or compensation taking place in different time horizons.

To give another example, in the 1980s the labour market was in turmoil in the Netherlands with the threat of high unemployment. As a result, the government, the trade unions and the employers' organisations decided that a large number of older employees and those in poor health should retire compulsorily via the Wet Arbeids-Ongeschiktheid (WAO) (Disablement Insurance Act). Although ostensibly this was intended to provide protection for employees with a long-term illness, it also offered the option of retiring early at a higher salary level. The outcome was a type of offload. Three important groups in society chose to transfer an 'unpleasant effect' to a facility that was meant for society as a whole. In the short term the actual costs of offload were accounted for by society itself. The WAO is and was funded by the Dutch taxpayers. On the other hand, in the long term this offload has undermined the WAO system itself. We are referring here to future generations. Also in this case the three parties transfer the costs of labour discontent and loss of salary to future generations and society on a long-term basis. In the 2000s the WAO system in the Netherlands was completely reorganised due to its high costs.

These three examples have a bearing on two aspects of sustainability: ecological sustainability in the case of the hydrogen fuel cell and the PET bottle, and social sustainability in the WAO case. From the three examples we can distil a more general description of sustainability as a problem of offload. In general, not being sustainable (in the ecological or social sense) means that an actor X transfers something or what (W) to an actor Y within a certain time horizon (t). Thus, logically, we can state that offload is a functional concept involving at least four arguments (i.e. it is a four-place operator). In order to get to grips with sustainability and the reduction in offload concept, it is essential to determine X, Y, W and t.

Although the term offload has negative connotations, we use it in a neutral sense. A particular entity X or Y is always in interaction with something outside its own system boundaries. The negative aspect of offload emerges when the interaction is no longer there and when only the negative consequences of a W caused by an X on a Y prevail.

A reduction in offload can concern any one of the W, X, Y or t as well as a combination of the four. In the description and analysis of a change trajectory all these elements are required. When, from a business science point of view, we consider the reduction in offload as a design issue, the description and analysis is followed by continuing phases, such as diagnosis, developing a design, change and evaluation. In accordance with the methodology used in business studies, we then speak of DDC (diagnosis, design and change), preceded by description and analysis and followed by evaluation (DDCDAE). After first developing a concept, the earlier mentioned reduction will then consist of change, intervention, taking action and the possible restoration of the balance. In this context, the formulation by means of the quadruple {X,Y,W,t} serves as a descriptive and analytical tool.

Balance, homeostasis and the capability of undertaking sustainable action

In Chapter 4 we already introduced the terms 'homeostasis' and 'systems theory'. The concept of homeostasis seems to lend itself well to the description of processes around sustainability in which sustainable action is taken. In Chapter 3, Figure 3.1 depicts this schematically in the form of three (static) states or modalities of homeostasis. Here, homeostasis should be aimed at the fragile balance and intensive interplay of human activities within and among systems. In the past the 'planet' dimension of sustainability has often been dominant. Our broader approach emphasises the balance between the different dimensions of physical/ecological, mental/social and economic (i.e. the three Ps of planet, people and profit). These activities are connected with one another in a circular fashion. In this respect homeostasis is a mechanism that partly takes place automatically (among other things within biological and physiological systems) and partly consciously. This is because people have an influence on their environment and when adaptive self-stabilisation is lacking they also try to influence their (social) environment.

Is homeostasis a usable concept within this framework? In Chapter 4 we formulated our preliminary working definition of homeostasis as: 'Adjusting processes and structures within the human and organisational environment in such a way that the sustainability of both the human system and the social subsystems are being stimulated'. In short, how could we achieve a good balance among the three Ps, keep the balance maintained or avoid it being disturbed? Although we speak of sustainability, we are actually seeking an adequate description of an artificial system capable of remaining sustainable (i.e. the capability of sustainability).

The starting points of systems theory (von Bertalanffy 1951) are a useful supplement to the homeostasis concept, especially in terms of the organisation and analysis of data at the various system levels. Based on systems theory we have distinguished a number of aggregation levels of human or people-oriented (sub)systems whereby relations and interactions are of particular importance. In this context imbalances occur between different levels at the tangent planes or boundary areas of entities X and Y. In a more dynamic sense one could then speak of a tendency towards ever alternating (un)balanced or more or less stable situations around the boundary area: for example, caused by threats to, or interventions by, other aggregation levels and changes in the behaviour of entities X and Y.

Within our approach, reduction in offload is considered as the action or operational aspect (e.g. action aimed at goals, processes, behaviour, knowledge and learning). In accordance with our line of reasoning the reduction in offload should, of course, be aimed at homeostasis. The homeostasis will be supported, protected and repaired by means of a whole spectrum of measures or interventions that exert their influence on exactly the right level of human existence, individually and socially. Reduction in offload itself can also be seen as a balanced amount of 'care measures' offered in the form of a proper 'balance of 3P care' which equates to a reduction in offload. The objective of reduction in offload in this context is to maintain or increase the capability of sustainability. This means shaping and realising (by oneself) ideas and interactions (by people and the human environment) in such a way that they are aimed at the natural and biological as well as the organisational, mental and knowledge environment, and (being capable of) undertaking action to maintain and continue this harmony and directedness.

Reduction in offload constitutes a range of measures with the aim of increasing the capability of sustainability of an individual or group via homeostasis. So reduction in offload concentrates on homeostasis and is most effective when targeting the cause of the imbalance or the intervening phenomena. This can be explained by phenomena that have their impact on other levels than the biological or physiological. However, we will limit ourselves here to human or social systems. In order to take the right measures, a proper insight into the situation as a whole is crucial. As regards the reduction in offload a distinction is therefore made in phases of analysis and diagnosis as well as execution or intervention.

Analysis and diagnosis of this kind is not a simple matter since various disruptions may occur that either reinforce or cancel each other out. And where does the spiral of reactions begin? There is also the question of whether there can be a sufficient degree of completeness when tracing threat factors. In summary, our system of and for sustainability concerns the 3P care (the reduction in offload) which supports the coherence and co-operation of a large number of 3P balances within human systems on various levels.

However, working on sustainability is fundamentally paradoxical. We will clarify this by referring to the natural sciences. The paradoxical aspect is exemplified by the second law of the thermodynamics, also called the law of entropy. This states that all natural (and social) activities contribute to an increase in entropy. Thus, all human activities will increase entropy. Whether the activity is a technical intervention focused on ecological sustainability or whether it concerns social sustainability, entropy will always increase.

But what is entropy? It describes the aim of each system to reach the most probable state, the so-called state of equilibrium. It sounds appealing, but we are not sufficiently aware of what it means. The most probable state is the one in which a system is the least recognisable. For example, many sequences are possible in a pack of cards. Only a few sequences are likely to be meaningful: for example, when the cards are arranged in accordance with their colour or value. In various card games different sequences have meaning. If we shuffle the pack the chance of a meaningless sequences is much bigger than that of a meaningful one. This is why any system is aimed at the most prevalent state, which is the most meaningless one, and this is indicated as balance. So balance is something that is generally *not* desirable. Or as the physicist Wiener put it once: 'For an organism to be in equilibrium, it is to be dead!' This is not what we have in mind when pursuing sustainability.

It is enough to make the pursuit of sustainability feel like a hopeless cause as each effort takes us farther from our purpose. But one thing we know for sure: if we do not do something, things will get a great deal worse. The sharp observer may also see a silver lining in the discussion about entropy and balance—a ray of hope on which this entire book is based. If the measure of entropy can be indicated in terms of the improbability of the occurrence of a state of the system, entropy is also a measure of the information of that system. Indeed, formal definitions of the term 'entropy' (see, for example, Maxwell 1885; Shannon 1948) state that it is the counterpart of information. This is because, by asking questions, the composition and therefore the meaning of the arrangement of the pack of cards can be determined. This is why the literature also refers to information as **negentropy**. The antidote, as it were, for entropy is therefore information. In this context, we take the step towards knowledge as a refined form of information for the sake of convenience without any further explanation. This is exactly what we do when striving for sustainability: we observe systems, we define goals, we measure where we stand, we redesign and we change. All activities which, by means of the input of knowledge, reshape the systems that are important to us into a more meaningful and therefore improbable configuration.

The systems (biological, human and social) in which we live are highly complex. They are (or seem) too complicated for us to grasp in their entirety. The objectives we set and the changes we make are always limited to parts of those systems. And each subsystem that we can define forms part of a larger, all-embracing system. The only way to study and influence systems is by demarcating them. Moreover, no matter how bounded systems are, there are always more aspects that play a role—more aspects than we could reasonably study and/or influence. The objectives we set for ourselves with respect to systems are **multiform**. This means that we pursue a number of goals at once which are seldom in harmony with each another. In most cases, objectives are subject to internal inconsistencies and require a weighing of interests. In other words, intentions to intervene in a system are multi-issue in nature. The researcher, manager or civilian will have to weigh which interests should be given priority and why. The 3Ps are interests from the perspective of sustainability and are also only seldom in harmony.

An example of this is exporting mopeds to India or Africa. Through the increasing mobility of the population, healthcare will become more accessible and the average life expectancy will increase which is good for the people dimension. Increased mobility will stimulate business which is good for the profit dimension. But the emissions from the mopeds will burden the environment which is bad for the planet aspect. What is more important: the quality of life and life expectancy of the human population in the short term or the environment in the long term? Will the urgent focus on the current health problems possibly lead to environmental problems in a few decades which are much more severe? These are very difficult decisions which cannot be ignored. The aim is to achieve a balance in which the various considerations play a role, in which the perspectives are both local and global, and in which both short-term and long-term effects are assessed. Sustainability is a multi-issue problem whereby the development and deployment of (re-usable) knowledge has to lead to a balance in which the offload within the chain is minimised. Only then can a homeostatic system be approached as closely as possible.

Systems, levels of aggregation and knowledge (= refined information)

The previous section positioned the discussion on sustainability as a discussion on systems and system levels of aggregation. However, the term 'system' is not unambiguous (see Chapter 4). The system concept is used to demarcate what is and what is not

22. FURTHER STEPS TOWARDS A SYSTEMATIC PERSPECTIVE Faber, Jorna and van Engelen

involved in analyses (von Bertalanffy 1951). Furthermore, not all demarcations are alike. Systems can be defined at different levels of aggregation, implying different levels of analysis (Boulding 1956). Hence, the question is: what systems do we consider in relation to sustainability or, to word it another way, to what systems do we ascribe sustainability as an issue of importance?

We argue that sustainability specifically concerns artificial or human-made systems. These systems are generally described in terms of function, objective and adaptation, and are able to imitate natural systems without being natural themselves (Simon 1969). Simon defined an artefact as the boundary between an internal and external environment. His concept of artefact refers to any construct that is human-made, taking many different forms and lying somewhere on the continuum between the concrete and the abstract. In contrast to artificial systems, biological systems are considered inherently sustainable because when the equilibrium between a biological system and its environment is disturbed these systems behave in such a manner that the equilibrium is restored. If there are too many members of a certain species, the environment (in a broad sense) will take measures to restore the balance by shortage of food, increased predation, disease, etc. Unless explicitly programmed, artificial systems lack such equilibrium-restoring capabilities which may cause them to stay in a non-sustainable situation until they collapse.

To explain what is meant by the equilibrium-restoring capabilities of biological systems we use the an concept of ecosystem. An ecosystem consists of living organisms and their environment, including rocks, sand and water. A food web connects all living organisms within an ecosystem, based on their function. Producers transform non-living material into organic material. Primary consumers eat producers and are subsequently eaten by secondary consumers. Reducers transform dead organic material into non-living material and so the cycle of the ecosystem is closed. Relationships between predators and prey within an ecosystem can be described by mathematical equations of Volterra (1959).[1] These equations indicate that over-consumption by one species within an ecosystem affects the whole food chain, and therefore the existence of all the species in the ecosystem.

Artificial systems are also different in complexity, ranging from the very simple to the very complex. Simple artificial systems have a simple structure which makes their behaviour predictable. In contrast, complex artificial systems behave unpredictably. For example, a car as a transportation unit is a reasonably simple artificial system with predictable behaviour. A society in which all individuals over 18 years of age drive a car is of a different complexity. In this case, the simple units combine to make an extremely complex traffic system. When issues such as greenhouse effects, air pollution, diminishing oil supplies or traffic problems come into play, the increase in complexity makes it very difficult to predict how such a system will develop.

Natural systems, of which biological systems are a subset, limit our possibilities to construct artificial systems. Their sources provide us with the raw materials used for building artificial systems and the energy that makes these artificial systems function. Renewable sources provide us with an unlimited supply of raw materials and energy. In contrast, non-renewable sources can provide us with raw materials or energy only

---

[1] Parallel to Volterra, an American biologist called Lotka drew similar models describing relations between predator and prey. These models are therefore referred to as Lotka–Volterra models.

for a limited amount of time. Natural system **sinks** absorb the waste our artificial systems generate. Sustainability concerns the cycle from source, through artificial system, to sinks.

The notion of sustainability is important for artificial systems because the cycle that is part of an artificial system is often left out of consideration. The neglect of aspects of sustainability especially concerns complex artificial or social systems, largely because these systems cannot easily be designed. Social systems often autonomously develop in a direction that is mostly unknown beforehand. However, because knowledge determines individual behaviour and because social systems consist of individuals, knowledge can influence a social system's sustainability.

Summary

As we believe that the discussion on sustainable innovation is far from over, we end our contribution for now and provide a brief summary of the main topics we have addressed. In preceding chapters we explored the concept of sustainable innovation. Chapters 1–6 provide the theoretical framework in which various concepts such as knowledge, organisation and innovation were discussed. We use these concepts throughout the book. Chapters 7–9 introduce different techniques which we applied in several case studies, reported in Chapters 10–18.

Although sustainability remains a complex concept, we believe we have shown that sustainable innovation is more than the sum of its parts. Sustainable innovation is more than innovating to improve the sustainability of something. Sustainable innovation goes, for example, beyond the development of a car with a new engine that runs 100 kilometres per litre, although we would certainly endorse this development and technology.

We have explained sustainable innovation using the concepts of knowledge of sustainability (KoS) and sustainability of knowledge (SoK). In formulating these concepts, we emphasise the idea that humans play the leading role in innovation in general and sustainable innovation in particular. Innovation was explained in terms of the human capabilities of problem-solving and learning whereby innovation is translated into both actively searching for solutions to encountered problems and adopting the chosen solutions in everyday situations.

In relation to innovation, the concept of sustainability constantly focuses on the internal and external environments of innovation efforts. First, regarding the internal environment of innovation, sustainability demarcates innovation content (i.e. KoS). In this first role, sustainability identifies problems relating to current human activities which can be used to identify which knowledge domains we need to focus on in innovation. Second, sustainability shapes the internal and external functionality of innovation (i.e. SoK). Knowledge is developed in innovation. In order for people to apply this knowledge now and in the future, the knowledge has to be preserved. SoK implies the organisation of innovation processes in such a fashion that the knowledge that is developed is also spread and preserved. The two foci that sustainability adds to innovation have been illustrated in the nine case studies in Chapters 10–18.

22. FURTHER STEPS TOWARDS A SYSTEMATIC PERSPECTIVE *Faber, Jorna and van Engelen* 319

Additional to the concepts KoS and SoK, the concept of reducing offload is central to our approach on sustainable innovation. In Chapter 3, sustainability was defined initially as a two-place predicate. There we stated that X is sustainable in relation to Y. With this formulation, we implied that a system X might exist in some sort of balance with its environment Y. Our notion of reduction in offload extended this initial formulation, logically formulating offload as the four-place operator in terms of X, Y, W and t whereby a system X offloads a certain W to a system Y over a period t. In stricter terms, offload is defined as follows:

- X is the set of states of a system X; $X = x_1, x_2, x_3, ..., x_n$, whereby x_a ($a \in 1..n$) is a dimension of X
- Y is the set of states of a system Y; $Y = y_1, y_2, y_3, ..., y_m$, whereby y_b ($b \in 1..m$) is a dimension of Y
- t equals time
- W is the set of states of a system W; $W = w_1, w_2, w_3, ..., w_p$, whereby w_c ($c \in 1..p$) is a dimension of W

Using these definitions, offload becomes a function that transforms the initial state of variables X, Y and W into a new state of these variables over a period t. In other words, offload is defined as: $X \times Y \times W \times t \rightarrow X \times Y \times W$.

Although appealing, the above formula visualises only the principle of offload. Until we are able to connect the different variables to empirical indicators, the formula on its own is a conceptual, quasi-logical refinement. Reduction in offload is a function of the offload formulation above. Reduction complicates the already complex combination of offloading. This twofold complexity has to be investigated further. In both cases, offloading and in reduction in offloading, making the connection to empirical indicators will prove to be the hardest task that lies ahead. At the moment, we do not consider ourselves able to exactly specify the connection between the given formula and empirical indicators. Instead, we pinpoint several problems that arise when attempting to make this connection.

Throughout this book, we have applied a system theoretical approach. This proved helpful in structuring the discussion on sustainability, in conceptualising sustainable innovation, in building a framework for sustainable innovation and in our analyses of the different business projects or case studies. However, although a system theoretical approach is helpful, we also foresee some problems with it. The formal approach towards reducing offload we presented earlier and above incorporates these problems. In our formal approach, reduction in offload is transformed into an abstract notion, independent from any empirical domain. For instance, we have not provided any indication of the kind of systems we have in mind regarding systems X and Y. Neither have we provided a specification of the offload function nor of the activities to reduce.

In order to apply the provided function in practice, several choices regarding the variables X, Y and W have to be made regarding system boundaries. Additionally, the level of aggregation at which the system resides needs to be determined. Both the system boundaries and the level of aggregation determine the exact shape of the offload function and, consequently, its reduction activities. Von Bertalanffy (1951: 146-51) provided five formal properties of systems that are helpful in establishing the system boundaries of X and Y. In order to build the offload function whereby systems X and Y are connected, the underlying variables need to be comparable. Regarding levels of aggregation, Boulding's (1956) system hierarchy might be of use. Both issues require further exploration.

In addition to the problems we identify regarding the formal approach towards reduction in offload, we also identify several concrete topics for further research. The following topics concern both further theoretical as well as empirical exploration:

1. Reduction in offload implies different issues to be considered on a case-by-case base. But how is reduction in offload connected to learning and knowledge from individual cases?

2. Which organisational forms and co-ordination mechanisms do reduction in offload and sustainable innovation require?

3. Which business model is most appropriate for each phase of sustainable innovation?

4. More methods and instruments need to be developed for reusable KoS. Which methods and instruments need to be developed first?

5. Research into reduction in offload requires a multidisciplinary approach and is a multifaceted problem. How do we cope with these characteristics?

6. Is a further operationalisation of the quality of homeostasis and partial balances in social and artificial systems possible? And what defines the existence of a balance?

7. How can the connection between corporate social responsibility and managing stakeholders be enhanced, and what role can internal entrepreneurship, knowledge workers/professionals and new business models play?

8. What other tools for diagnosis and intervention regarding (un)sustainability are available, in addition to those that enhance knowledge creation, instruments for stakeholder analysis, case-based approaches of complex problem and techniques such as MDSA (multi-dimensional scaling analysis)?

The research agenda above is not supposed to be complete. Moreover, it is a first attempt to trigger further development of theory, operationalisation and empirical research in companies and organisations regarding sustainable innovation. The research agenda completes the circle. Together with the theoretical notions discussed in Chapters 1–6, the models and instruments in Chapters 7–9 and the case studies Chapters 10–18, Chapters 19–23 attempt to move theories of sustainability and sustainable innovation to a better level of understanding. We hope that individuals, both researchers and practitioners working in the sustainability domain, can use our findings to formulate new hypotheses that can be scientifically tested and applied in practice.

In the next and final chapter of this book, we present some of our ideas on how sustainable innovation might be operationalised.

23
Assessing and determining social sustainability
AN ONSET AND AN ATTEMPT

Niels R. Faber, Laura Maruster and René J. Jorna

In the previous chapters we explored the relevance of sustainability with reference to the various business projects, with particular emphasis on the people dimension (i.e. social sustainability) of the three Ps (the triple bottom line of planet, people, profit). We have said little about the planet aspect (i.e. ecological sustainability). However, in line with McElroy (2003), we suggest the profit aspect be recategorised to come under the heading of social sustainability. Profit is normally expressed in terms of money and is itself the result of a particular kind of valuation of individual or organisational activities. Where effort, materials and labour are input and products and services are output, a profit is made when the ratio of output to input is >1 and a loss is made when the ratio of output and input is <1. The fundamental perspective we take is that the profit or loss discussion is the result of individual human and organisational activities. Therefore, profit in the triple bottom line is related to social sustainability; in other words, it is a kind of social sustainability.

With regard to both ecological and social sustainability, we take the stance that sustainability is a two-place predicate to which, as an operator or function, two arguments apply. Saying that X is sustainable means that X is sustainable in relation to Y (see Chapters 3 and 22). Furthermore, sustainability is never a static state. One can never say that something is sustainable in the sense that a stable utopia has been reached. Finally, sustainability implies adaptation. A system behaving in an environment is only sustainable if the system itself is capable of changing in relation to a changing environment (Faber, Jorna and van Engelen 2005). In our opinion, these aspects of dyadic relationships, dynamics and adaptation are essential in any discussion about sustainability, regardless of whether it is ecological or social.

Social sustainability is a complex construct. Many aspects of human and organisational activities can be included in it. In Chapters 10–18 several concrete examples of social sustainability were discussed. In Chapters 3 and 22 we tried to make a first systematisation. In this chapter we will continue this systematisation by adding an assessment aid, although a word of caution is needed. We do not believe that we are able to deliver a finished, well-balanced and operational instrument. On the contrary, we can present only different aspects that we believe are relevant to any notion of social sustainability.

We operationalise social sustainability in terms of stakeholder, knowledge, learning and organisational issues, where the last can be seen in terms of co-ordination mechanisms and organisational structures. We are familiar with ethical interpretations of social sustainability, such as justice, fairness, labour conditions, child labour and religious ideologies. The Global Reporting Initiative[1] has developed many questionnaires on these issues. No matter how important these ethical issues may be, we believe that focusing on ethical aspects reverses cause and effect. If one wants to assess and measure social sustainability we believe that descriptions, analyses and measurements come before ethical discussions and normative statements which most often are not primarily based on (empirical) scientific research. Besides, ethical and normative interpretations are abundantly available whereas in issues of sustainable innovation and social sustainability, knowledge, learning and organisational aspects are almost completely neglected. We attempt to explain these issues in the next section, following which we will give answers based on the Optichem case (Chapter 12). We will try not to qualify or disqualify our answers. At this moment, that is a bridge too far.

The aforementioned four aspects dealt with in this chapter are (besides adaptation, dynamics and dyadic relationships) grounded in two underlying principles addressed in previous chapters. The first is the notion of sustainability as a reduction in offload (Chapter 3). The second concerns the observation that sustainability is an attribute of artificial systems (Chapter 22). The reduction in offload implies that a system reduces its offload of activities as externalities towards other systems (Coase 1960) at either similar or different levels of aggregation (see also Chapter 4). Furthermore, sustainability expresses the existence of an equilibrium between the artificial system (Simon 1969) and its environment. Hence, these two views on sustainability are complementary.

We then go on to describe and demonstrate the instrument. In general, an instrument in the form of a questionnaire can have at least three forms. First, it can be a categorisation structure. By means of questions posed under several headings, various aspects can be made public for internal organisational discussion. At the moment we aim at a straightforward assessment structure. Second, it is possible to attach ordinal scales to answers (e.g. where 5 is more than 2 and 2 is more than 1). Third, a questionnaire can have the form of a construct that is measured and of which the outcome is an indication of a certain correct or incorrect state of affairs. In the latter case, one needs a set of norms that makes it possible to determine the measured present situation on the basis of a criterion.

---

1 www.globalreporting.org.

We believe that the questionnaire in this chapter falls under the first of these forms. Questionnaires can be used in a variety of ways: describing; analysing; diagnosing; fault determination; and providing directions of change and evaluation. The aim of the questionnaire in this chapter is to describe and assess. One could argue that radical new thinking about social sustainability has to start somewhere and this is exactly what we do. The questionnaire is not an instrument for disqualification. Disqualification requires a norm or a standard, and we know that standard is not yet available. In the questions belonging to various categories, we do not use norms. With respect to both the individual level of description and the various kinds of organisational levels of description, we try to operationalise units, teams, groups, firms and societies.

Various aspects of social sustainability to be included

Stakeholder issues

As the main thesis of this book is to understand sustainability issues such as reducing offload, the legitimate question arises: what precisely constitutes the offload that should be reduced and who are the parties that should be unburdened? In the following, we aim to determine who these parties or stakeholders are.

Chapter 7 emphasises that stakeholders play a crucial role in reducing negative externalities and explicitly formulates the reasons why stakeholders should have such a role. In the short term, an organisation will have a genuine desire to involve stakeholders in order to improve sustainable innovation because:

- They are the representatives of the organisation's social and ecological environment
- They can help the organisation define the criteria for sustainable innovation
- Stakeholder involvement might lead to more commitment to the sustainability of innovation

In Chapter 7, which discusses the stakeholder identification method, a clear-cut separation is made between 'actively involved' and 'passively involved' parties. From the perspective of sustainability, and especially with respect to reducing offload, there is an important argument for expanding the passively involved group, and their interests, as widely as possible.

The method consists of four phases (see also Fig. 7.1 in Chapter 7):

1. Defining (the goal) of the project
2. Individual brainstorming to identify those involved
3. Group brainstorming to identify those involved on the basis of roles
4. Group brainstorming to identify those involved on the basis of phases

In this chapter, we provide questions that can be used as an aid to identify the stakeholders. We formulate the questions based on the method presented in Chapter 7. Our intention is to provide an aid for anyone interested in questioning sustainability issues in their organisation. We therefore suggest that phases 3 and 4 can be realised not just via group brainstorming but also by means of individual brainstorming.

Note that the requirements of this method are on the project level rather than the organisational level. Within an organisation, a number of projects may run simultaneously. Applying the instrument on the project level allows a refined identification method of stakeholders. Whenever required, the instrument presented here may then be used in one or more projects, or in all projects running within the organisation.

We also adapt the method, which was specifically developed for innovation projects, to be applicable to the broader context of any kind of project running within organisations. So we assume that each project consists of four basic steps: initiation, development, implementation and maintenance. The aid formulated below in A–D should make it possible to investigate several aspects, and the resulting answers may provide insights into aspects that have never been addressed before.

A. Who are the real-world parties or stakeholders involved?

B. Who are the passively involved parties?

Attention should be drawn to the passively involved category. When parties are identified as passively involved, and thus become visible, management can choose to involve them in the project and, by doing so, allow them to strive for their interests. In fact, these parties may then be designated one of three new roles: that of client if their wishes are taken into account; that of decision-maker if they are given some sort of right of veto on the project; or that of designer if their knowledge and expertise actually contributes to the project. Moreover, with respect to each role, the degree of importance can be indicated.

C. How do different stakeholder roles need to be managed?

Connecting the stakeholder role classification with the four-phase model of the project reveals the dynamic circumstances of the project life-cycle. Some of the identified parties will shift to another role or can be given a second role. In this way, the identification method provides a basis for the next step, managing stakeholder involvement or, in terms of this method, managing stakeholder roles. Managing stakeholder roles involves several management questions, such as:

1. What will be the actual activities of the actively involved?
2. Which of the identified passively involved should actually be involved in the project?
3. When should this involvement take place?
4. What should this involvement look like?

D. What is the overall effectiveness of the project?

This instrument can be used as a diagnostic tool for project analysis. The following questions are useful in providing insights into the overall effectiveness of the project:

5. Are all roles fulfilled (e.g. those of client, designer, decision-maker, passively involved/representative)?
6. How clear a division is there in roles between the different parties?
7. Is there a party that fulfils (too) many roles?

Knowledge issues

In Chapters 1, 3 and 6 we distinguished between knowledge of sustainability (KoS) and sustainability of knowledge (SoK), whereby the former was said to relate to knowledge content and the latter to ways of exchanging and preserving knowledge. Both relate to sustainability. KoS is required to ensure that behaviour directly contributes to the improvement of sustainability. SoK is required to ensure that knowledge is distributed among individuals and that knowledge is preserved for those individuals who, in the future, will participate in the improvement of sustainability. In terms of organisational processes, we perceive KoS to be a matter for an organisation's primary processes whereas SoK is a matter for secondary processes. Primary processes are the organisation's main processes while secondary processes are the organisational supporting processes (see Chapter 5). Secondary processes are addressed later in this chapter. Here, we will elaborate on primary processes.

By arguing that knowledge is an important factor in the context of sustainability, questions instantly spring to mind such as: what knowledge are we talking about; what is it used for and by whom? We will provide footholds to gain insights into these questions.

Before we continue, we have to make explicit some basic assumptions that underlie our approach to knowledge. Knowledge can be characterised in a multitude of ways. For instance, it can be typified based on content. Using a content-based typology we can, for example, distinguish between knowledge of medical domains, knowledge of engineering or knowledge of biology. Another way to characterise knowledge is to distinguish between common and specialised knowledge. In this characterisation, common knowledge is knowledge shared by many individuals which allows them to communicate with each other. In contrast, specialised knowledge is not shared, but is possessed by just a few individuals, allowing them to think and act in domains others cannot.

Although interesting, we do not investigate human behaviour in general, but focus on human behaviour in the organisational context. Schreiber *et al.* (1999) specify that individuals in an organisational context perform tasks in business processes. Gaining insight into human behaviour in an organisational context implies gaining insights into the individuals involved, the tasks they perform and the knowledge they use. Therefore, to understand human behaviour in organisational contexts, it is necessary that the individuals involved, the tasks they perform and the knowledge they express, are made explicit in one form or another. In the following, we focus on knowledge, tasks and individuals.

Knowledge and its representation

Knowledge can be represented in multiple ways, through the written or spoken word or by using propositional logic and set theory (see, for example, Russell and Norvig 1995; Luger and Stubblefield 1998). Using language closely connects to how parts of knowledge are stored in individuals' minds. However, words bring about a great deal of ambiguity, since individuals use different terminology to describe their knowledge. In contrast, logic and set theory force individuals to formalise their knowledge, although this might strike them as unnatural and artificial. Besides, the use of formal language requires much knowledge and training in order to understand the symbol systems used.

Taking a stance somewhere in the middle between (ambiguous) words and logic, we use the CommonKADS methodology (Schreiber *et al.* 1999). This method is suitable for representing knowledge and is an approach commonly used for knowledge engineering purposes (see also Chapter 12). We will not provide a complete overview of the methodology; instead, it is our intention to indicate how knowledge can be represented. Despite its strong focus on knowledge engineering, CommonKADS is equally suitable for descriptive and representational purposes; it is a systematic approach to mapping out the knowledge within an organisation.

In order to describe knowledge, the CommonKADS methodology builds on six models, starting from a global description of the organisational context, zooming in on specific tasks of individuals and finally ending up with a model of the knowledge used by these individuals—the domain model (Schreiber *et al.* 1999). In addition to the set-term **knowledge**, the terms **knowledge element** and **knowledge domain** are used. A knowledge element denotes the smallest particle that comprises an individual's knowledge. So, here, a knowledge element is a representation within the individual's mind (Newell and Simon 1972; Newell 1990). Knowledge elements are treated as primitive elements which cannot be decomposed any further. Schreiber *et al.* (1999) use knowledge elements to represent knowledge content in terms of declarative and procedural knowledge. Declarative knowledge concerns knowledge elements that represent facts. Facts are depicted in a general sense by using concepts and in a specific sense by using instances (Schreiber *et al.* 1999). Procedural knowledge can be represented as rules or inferences. An inference is a primitive step in human reasoning which can be formulated as 'if–then' rules. Schreiber *et al.* (1999) specify that a task is built up of inferences. A coherent set of knowledge elements is labelled a knowledge domain. Using the CommonKADS methodology enables us to construct, in a systematic way, detailed models of knowledge domains that individuals use to perform tasks.

We will not elaborate any further on how such domain models are constructed; instead, we refer to Schreiber *et al.* 1999 for details. The main idea is that knowledge that resides in the minds of individuals within an organisation can be represented. This can be done in a detailed manner, using the CommonKADS approach. It can also be done in a rough fashion whereby different knowledge domains that exist within the organisation are mapped out. In relation to the latter, the CommonKADS approach also provides footholds. Using CommonKADS, one should be able to answer the following questions:

8. What knowledge domains exist within my organisation?

9. Are models of these knowledge domains available?

10. What is the level of detail of these models?
11. What is the level of formalisation of these models?

The tasks

The second element required to assess human behaviour within organisations concerns the tasks individuals perform. During task execution human activity is moulded into goal-oriented behaviour. This means that individuals use their knowledge to achieve the task's goal. However, two problems may arise. First, the knowledge of the individual is not always adequate for the task he or she performs. Second, the task may be shaped in such a way that it forces the individual to use certain knowledge, while ignoring the knowledge he or she would normally use.

In order to determine whether the above-described problems occur in the organisation, a clear view of the organisation's tasks is required, and especially of tasks in the primary processes. We perceive a task as an artefact. Postulating a task as an artefact implies that two interactions exist between task and environment. First, a task transforms inputs into outputs that have value for a certain individual. We specified earlier that processes consist of tasks. In other words, tasks are not situated in a vacuum inside an organisation. They are connected. Outputs of one task are inputs of another. Assessing these input and output connections helps to determine dependencies between the different tasks in business processes.

Second, a task interacts with the individual who performs it (i.e. the task performer). Earlier (Chapter 5) we argued that individuals can be seen as information-processing systems. The interaction between task and task performer concerns the exchange of information. The task provides the task performer with certain information and the task demands certain information from the task performer. Schreiber *et al.* (1999) define the former flow of information as **output objects** and the latter as **input objects**.

Information exchange between individual and task generates and triggers the knowledge of the individual (based on Card, Moran and Newell 1983). Hence, this information exchange can also be formulated as exchanging representations coming from different knowledge domains or knowledge possessing entities (i.e. the individuals). Mapping out the tasks of one's organisation should provide an answer to the following questions:

12. Which tasks constitute the organisation's primary processes?
13. What are the objectives of the tasks in the primary processes?
14. What are the inputs and outputs of every task in the primary processes?
15. What dependencies exist among tasks of the primary processes?
16. What knowledge is required to perform the tasks in the primary processes?

Individuals/actors

Individuals as actors in the multi-actor system of an organisation are the third and last aspect we will discuss in the context of knowledge issues. The previous section connected knowledge and tasks from a task perspective. However, as indicated before, we deal with knowledge solely carried by humans. Therefore, to make the connection between knowledge and tasks, a perspective on the individuals involved in the tasks and possessing knowledge is necessary.

In organisations one finds individuals who differ in experience, education and skills. For instance, older employees may have a great deal of experience in their field, but may lack knowledge about new technologies or developments. In contrast, young employees have less experience, but may be more familiar with the newest methods and techniques. Hence, different individuals perform their tasks on the basis of different experiences and insights.

The involvement of an individual in a certain task brings forth issues that are similar to those that concern the task. Again, interconnectedness with other parts of the business process is a key factor. From the perspective of individuals, however, interconnectedness refers to the connections or communication of the individual with other individuals within the organisation. Additionally, through its specification in terms of limitations, a task requires a particular kind of knowledge. From the perspective of the individual, it relates to knowledge that resides in the individual's mind. Thus, an individual may possess knowledge that is different from the knowledge that is required to perform the task. Furthermore, the task environment determines the individual's responsibilities and constrains his or her behaviour, as exemplified in our previous discussion on tasks. The questions that can be formulated are:

17. Which individuals are involved in which tasks?
18. Which individuals possess knowledge from which knowledge domains?
19. Is there a match between the knowledge possessed by an individual and that required by his or her tasks?

Learning issues

The discussion about knowledge automatically brings forth a discussion about learning issues. Learning issues are identified as the next important aspect of social sustainability. Again, we derive the importance of learning issues from the starting point that human behaviour determines sustainability. In contrast to knowledge, learning adds the extra dimension of adaptation to human behaviour. And, although every human being has the capability to learn and hence to adapt his or her behaviour to changing circumstances, individuals differ in their ability to adapt.

The phenomenon of learning takes many shapes. For instance, the field of artificial intelligence (AI) distinguishes between supervised and unsupervised learning (Luger and Stubblefield 1998; Russell and Norvig 1995), a distinction that is based on the type of feedback an individual (i.e. an intelligent actor) receives. Supervised learning refers to situations in which a teacher teaches an intelligent actor. In unsupervised learning, the actor learns from their own interactions with the environment without the benefit of a teacher. AI is a fairly new discipline dealing with learning. Within the older disciplines of biology, psychology and pedagogy, much empirical data are available, combined with a large number of theories. In the field of the educational disciplines, ideologically and empirically founded ideas about how people learn co-exist and parasitise each other; currently, ideology prevails at the multiple levels of the educational system: for example, in the Netherlands (van der Werf 2005).

Bower and Hilgard (1981) report that with respect to theories on learning there are two contrasts: that of the division between empiricists and rationalists and that of the distinction between stimulus–response (i.e. behaviourist) theories and cognitive theories. The distinctions are not orthogonal. Bower and Hilgard (1981) indicate that many, but not all, empiricists, form part of the stimulus–response theorists. In addition, not all cognitive scientists are rationalists. The division between empiricists and rationalists is based on their different opinions about the origins of knowledge. Empiricists believe that knowledge is formed only through experience. At the opposite end, rationalists argue that knowledge is the result of reason, and is based on the idea that humans are born with a basic set of understandings of the world.

Bower and Hilgard (1981) recognise three elements which demarcate the distinction between learning theorists from the stimulus–response and cognitive schools of thought. Stimulus–response adherents take the stance that learning occurs in peripheral systems (i.e. perceptual and motor systems). Those in favour of the cognitive approach ascribe learning to processes central in the mind. Additionally, stimulus–response theorists argue that humans acquire habits whereas the cognitive approach states that mental representations are stored in the human minds through learning. The third difference between the stimulus–response and the cognitive schools concerns the way people learn. The stimulus–response schools favour trial-and-error/success processes; the cognitive schools consider insightful problem-solving as a more appropriate description of learning (Bower and Hilgard 1981).

Apart from the two aforementioned distinctions, Bower and Hilgard (1981) recognise several other issues of dispute. We mention the discussion about continuous learning and learning in phases. This discussion concentrates on the progress of learning through time. On one side of the spectrum, learning is seen as a process whereby individuals learn gradually and continuously, whereas at the opposite end of the spectrum learning is considered as a phased process with individuals learning in a step-by-step fashion.

In Chapter 6, a reference is made to Bower and Hilgard's (1981: 17) definition of learning:

> Learning refers to the change in a subject's behaviour to a given situation brought about by his repeated experiences in that situation, provided that the behaviour change cannot be explained on the basis of native response tendencies, maturation or temporary states of the subject (e.g., fatigue, drugs, etc.)

With this definition they attempt to define learning in such a way that it incorporates the different schools of thought. However, in its current form, their definition emphasises behaviour, leaning strongly on the stimulus–response theories on learning. Following the cognitive school of thought, we argue that a change in a subject's knowledge also forms part of learning. The idea behind the incorporation of a change in an individual's knowledge is that this change potentially alters the individual's behaviour. Hence, rather than directly adopting Bower and Hilgard's (1981) definition of learning, we suggest that an adaptation is required that also incorporates the views presented in cognitive theories on learning.

In this way, learning can be seen as a change in an individual's behaviour or thought processes. In this respect, we perceive three different kinds of change. First, the individual may display an acceleration of behaviour and thinking. If this takes place, learning not only refers to the acquisition of a new skill, but also to the ability to rapidly apply this skill. Second and third, **quantitative expansion** and **qualitative expansion** are also expressions of learning. Quantitative means acquiring more of the same knowledge and qualitative means acquiring complementary knowledge. An example of the former is someone who first learns up to the 10× table and then learns up to the 100× tables. An example of the latter is someone who, in addition to multiplication, also acquires long-division skills.

At the individual level we see learning as a process that underlies innovation. Innovation is a phenomenon of change and adaptation at the organisational level. At the aggregate level, innovation processes involve multiple individuals who realise a change in, for example, the organisation, the production process, a new product line, etc. (following West and Farr 1990). At the level of the individual, innovation implies learning which involves both the innovating individuals and the individuals affected by the innovation. In other words, it is the individuals who are engaged in the innovation processes who learn.

As indicated, individuals differ in their learning capabilities or learning styles. This was shown, for example, in the AVEBE project (Chapter 14). This demonstrated that failure to take account of individual differences when trying to realise knowledge transfer hampers achievement of the objective; in AVEBE's case, changing farmers' behaviour so they can respond to contextual changes, including the application of KoS.

Although the ability to learn is an innate human quality, willingness to learn is, in general, often low. Learning requires cognitive effort, which people often prefer to avoid. The reason is that many people interpret any kind of change as a threat. Hence, in order for individuals to learn and adapt (and thus for innovation to occur), individual differences in the motivation to learn need to be taken into account.

This motivation to learn is part of an individual's learning style. Pintrich and de Groot (1990) divide learning styles into two underlying constructs. The first, learning strategy, refers to an individual's learning skills. The underlying dimensions are cognitive strategies, meta-cognition and resource management. Cognitive strategies concern the means individuals utilise to train their memory, and hence to be able to remember. Meta-cognition denotes the strategies that individuals adopt to change their cognition. Resource management refers to whether the individual is able to focus on and organise his or her time in order to learn. The issues concerning learning strategies result in the following questions:

20. What methods do my employees use to acquire new knowledge and to learn?

21. How do my employees plan and monitor their learning efforts?

22. How do my employees organise their learning time?

The second construct that underlies learning style is motivation itself, consisting of the dimensions expectancy, value and affect. Pintrich and de Groot (1990) indicate that these dimensions determine an individual's motivation to learn. The dimension expectancy refers to individuals' beliefs about their ability to learn. They summarise the expectancy dimension in the question: 'Can I do this assignment?' (Pintrich and de

Groot 1990: 34). Pintrich and de Groot specify an individual's intrinsic and extrinsic values with respect to learning, and the appreciation the individual will receive when he or she is able to learn. The value dimension refers to the question: 'Why am I doing this task?' (Pintrich and de Groot 1990: 34). The affective dimension denotes individuals' emotions regarding learning. They state that the affective dimension equals the question: 'How do I feel about this assignment?' (Pintrich and de Groot 1990: 34). We believe that in relation to motivation the following questions are relevant:

23. I have insight into the ideas my employees have about their ability to learn new things

24. I know my employees' reasons for learning

25. My employees give me their views about changes in the organisation

In addition to Pintrich and de Groot's (1990) perspective on motivation, which concentrates on the individual's motivational factors of learning, we recognise the role of organisational context in individuals' approach to learning. Regarding the organisational context, Newell and Simon (1972) use the term 'constraint'. In this line of reasoning, individuals are constrained by their organisational context. The argument is that organisational constraints force the individual to accomplish a task 'at a specified level of intelligence or adaptivity' (Newell and Simon 1972: 83). While the organisational context is helpful in making an individual focus on accomplishing a task, it also influences their freedom of movement to learn and adapt. A context for learning should, on the one hand, allow the individual to learn and, on the other, motivate and stimulate them to do so. Regarding the context in which learning takes place, we believe the following questions to be relevant:

26. To what extent are employees able to deviate from tasks and to explore and learn?

27. In what way does the organisation stimulate employees to learn?

Organisational issues: structures/forms

In an attempt to assess a reduction in offload (i.e. to promote sustainability), we have discussed how to identify stakeholders. The central point here is the distinction between active and passive parties. In addition, when referring to organisational issues we will use a knowledge management perspective.

As noted in Chapter 5, we distinguish between the primary processes of an organisation (i.e. what an organisation produces, yields or brings forth) and the secondary or organisational processes (i.e. the way these primary processes are structured and interrelated) (see also Porter 1985). Previously in this chapter we focused on knowledge issues concerning the primary processes; in this section we focus on knowledge issues relating to secondary processes.

Organisational processes can be described in terms of their constituent tasks (e.g. control, planning and administration). These tasks are executed by (groups of) individuals using knowledge. Considering the task orientation, we emphasise the perspective of the individual to clarify where the knowledge of the task execution can be found (Vicente 1999).

Organisational processes are steered by co-ordination mechanisms. Because knowledge plays a central role in organisational processes, we claim that both co-ordination mechanisms and the management of knowledge determine the organisational structure (or form). The questions we formulated in helping organisations to assess their organisational forms and co-ordination mechanisms are based on two types of approaches.

The first approach includes **organisational forms** (see Chapter 5) as discussed by Thompson (1967), Mintzberg (1983) and Boisot (1995). Here, we take into account the representation of organisational forms, the design of structures and forms, and the reasons why the co-ordination mechanism is used and why it works. In our assessment, we will work with bipolar characteristics that are formulated as leading principles (Sorge and Warner 2001). Moreover, we will discuss the organisational forms by characterising them in terms of knowledge types (sensory, coded and theoretical) and addressing the prevailing learning modalities of these forms.

The second approach is based on the openness principle, employed in the new knowledge management approach developed by McElroy and Firestone (McElroy 2002; Firestone and McElroy 2003).

Organisational forms

Thompson, Mintzberg and Boisot have proposed such organisational forms as fief, clan, divisional form, machine bureaucracy, professional bureaucracy, adhocracy, market or web. They characterise these forms in terms of authority relation, leading principles and informational aspects. Here, we refer to the six forms we consider as being the most illustrative: clan; feudal system; machine bureaucracy; professional bureaucracy; market; and web (see Chapter 5 for a broader discussion). Other organisational forms can be assessed in a similar way. We characterise these organisational forms by using the ten dimensions referred to in Chapter 5: autonomy–dependence; co-operation–competition; rules–own initiative; shared knowledge–private knowledge; hierarchy–heterarchy;[2] openness–closedness; specialisation–generalisation; centralisation–decentralisation; knowledge types in question 29; and learning in question 30 (see below).

The following questions may help in assessing the characteristics, dominant knowledge types and learning modalities of the organisational forms:

28. In your organisation, the prevailing principle is:
    a Autonomy or dependence?
    b Co-operation or competition?
    c Rules or own initiative?
    d Knowledge is shared or not shared (private)?
    e Hierarchy or heterarchy?
    f Openness or closedness?
    g Specialisation or generalisation?
    h Centralisation or decentralisation?

2 A form of organisation resembling a net.

29. In your organisation, knowledge is:
   a Sensory or weakly coded; namely, knowledge is rather expressed as rules of thumb, customs, experiential practices, feelings, etc.?
   b Generally difficult to put into words (i.e. sensory)?
   c Coded to a large extent (e.g. through regulations, reference books, manuals, jargon and terminology)?
   d Hardly coded?
   e Theoretical (rules, models, theoretical explanations)?
   f Members of the organisation do not precisely know what they are doing and why they are doing it?
   g Is a means of power?

30. In your organisation, the prevailing learning modality is:
   a Learning by doing or imitating?
   b Learning from documents or other materials?
   c Learning by education and training or self-study?

The open enterprise

The concept of the **open enterprise** was inspired by Karl Popper, the 20th-century philosopher of science, who developed his vision of the **open society** (1945) in opposition to dictatorship and other totalitarian forms of government. Karl Popper's ideas are known as **fallibilism** and **falsificationism**, according to which:[3]

> all knowledge is seen as impossible to prove, but error and error correction are necessary to discover and eliminate. Doing so (hopefully) moves us closer to the truth. Thus, the quality of our knowledge steadily improves as we eliminate the errors inside of it

According to Firestone and McElroy (2003: 229):

> The open enterprise is open in the sense of participation and open in the sense that knowledge claims, or as Popper called them, conjectures, are unrestrictedly open to criticism and refutation, no matter what their source.

'Do not block the way of inquiry' is the suggestion by Firestone and McElroy (2003), based on a statement by the logician and semiotician S.C. Peirce (1931–35).

In an open enterprise, the conditions for knowledge processing are set in such a way that relative openness prevails. This means that organisational knowledge can evolve in a transparent way and enables the participation of most members of the organisation. This contradicts the approach taken by many firms, according to which knowledge is kept secret and not diffused, which often results in poor ideas being adopted. Correction is necessary and, as Firestone puts it so eloquently, 'kill your worst ideas before these worst ideas will kill you' (Firestone 2005).

The openness concept not only enables sustainability in terms of its 'ethical' sense of transparency (e.g. 'it is nice/good to inform our employees what is going on in our com-

---

[3] www.macroinnovation.com/nkm.htm.

pany'), but also in a practical way, by promoting the ideas and plans of parties other than the organisation's own management. To formulate it in McElroy's words (2003: 22), the management and the board of directors have to ensure that there is 'sufficient openness in the knowledge claim formulation and knowledge claim evaluation along the knowledge-making process'. The following questions refer to the openness of organisations:

31. Is your organisation open to:
    a New problems recognised by any of the organisations' employees and in what sense?
    b New ideas generated by any of the organisations' employees and in what sense?
    c Continuous criticism of previously generated ideas by any of the organisations' employees?
32. In your organisation, is organisational knowledge (knowledge claims, meta claims, knowledge processes) visible, disclosed and open to criticism (with the exception of private or secret information), although rules of privacy and secrecy are also visible, disclosed and open to criticism?
33. In your organisation, are organisational knowledge processes open to stakeholder participation (with the exception of private or secret processes), although rules of privacy and secrecy are also visible, disclosed and open to criticism?

A questionnaire instrument to determine and discuss social sustainability: the Optichem example

In this section we enumerate the various questions discussed so far, using the Optichem case study as an example (Chapter 12). We do not intend to give complete answers to the questions below which are for illustration only.

Identification of stakeholders

1. In what activities are the parties involved?
    - A certain activity/task
    - A project (Optichem Infonet: enhancing the knowledge of chemicals within the paper production in the paper industry)
2. Who are the parties involved?
    - Organisations:
        • Optichem Foundation
        • Big River Innovation

Party ID	Client[a]	Decision-maker[b]	Designer[c]	Passively involved representative[d]
Optichem Foundation	Not important	Important	Important	Not important
Big River Innovation	Not important	Important	Important	Not important
Chemical producer	Important	Important	Not important	Not important
Transportation organisation	Important	Important	Not important	Not important
Industrial cleaner	Important	Important	Not important	Not important
Machine builder	Not important	Not important	Not important	Important
Five paper mills	Important	Important	Not important	Not important
University	Not important	Important	Important	Not important
Software house	Not important	Not important	Important	Not important
Chemical experts	Not important	Important	Important	Not important
Safety experts	Not important	Important	Important	Not important
Truck drivers	Important	Not important	Not important	Not important
Mechanics	Important	Not important	Not important	Not important
Cleaners	Important	Not important	Not important	Not important
Cleaners' project manager	Not important	Important	Not important	Not important
Local production manager	Not important	Important	Not important	Not important
Responsible expedition employee (paper mill)	Important	Not important	Not important	Not important

a Client is the party whose purposes are being served through the innovation.
b Decision-maker is the party that sets the requirements for the innovation and evaluates whether the innovation meets these requirements.
c Designer is the party that contributes expertise to the innovation process and is responsible for the (interim) deliverables.
d Passively involved is the party that is affected by the outcome of the innovation project without being able to influence these outcomes. A representative is a person who has been selected to act on behalf of others (i.e. the passively involved).

TABLE 23.1 Question 3: roles and importance of stakeholders

- A producer of chemicals
- A transportation organisation
- An industrial cleaner
- A machine builder
- Five paper mills
- University
- Software house
    - Groups of people:
        - Chemical experts
        - Safety experts
        - Truck drivers
        - Mechanics
        - Cleaners
    - People:
        - Cleaners' project manager
        - Local production manager
        - Responsible expedition employee (paper mill)

3. Determine for each party identified in the previous step which role that party can fulfil (or will fulfil or ought to fulfil) and indicate its importance (assigning multiple roles to the same party is possible)

4. Assuming that the activity you have specified at Q1 consists of four phases (initiation, development, implementation and maintenance), indicate for each party specified in Q2 the way in which they should be involved in the four phases (see Table 23.2)

5. In the Optichem Infonet project, all stakeholder roles are fulfilled (see Table 23.1)

6. In principle, each party involved is aware of the role it plays. However, decision-makers tend to behave as designers every now and then

7. No party fulfils too many roles. The Optichem Infonet project originated from the users of the intended decision-support system. Therefore, the parties that are currently involved by default fulfil both the roles of client and decision-maker. In addition, multiple parties are involved in multiple phases of the project

Knowledge issues

Questions concerning the knowledge domains that are relevant in the Optichem case are grouped in Table 23.3. These concern the following questions:

8. What knowledge domains exist within my organisation?
9. Are models of these knowledge domains available?

Party ID/phase	Initiation	Development	Implementation	Maintenance
Optichem foundation	a	a	a	a
Big River Innovation	a	a	a	b
Chemical producer	b	a	b	b
Transportation organisation	b	a	a	b
Industrial cleaner	b	a	a	b
Machine builder	b	b	b	b
Paper mill (5 factories)	b	a	b	b
University	a	a	a	b
Software house	b	b	a	a
Chemical experts	c	a	c	a
Safety experts	c	a	c	a
Truck drivers	c	a	a	a
Mechanics	c	a	a	a
Cleaners	c	a	a	a
Cleaners' project manager	c	a	a	a
Local production manager	c	a	a	a
Responsible expedition employee (paper mill)	c	a	a	a

TABLE 23.2 Question 4: involvement of different stakeholders in project phases

	Question 8: knowledge domains?	Question 9: availability of model?	Question 10: level of detail?	Question 11: level of formalisation?
a.	Chemicals	Yes	Detailed	High
b.	Paper making	Yes	Very detailed	Medium
c.	Engineering	Yes	Detailed	High
d.	Electronics	Yes	Detailed	High
e.	Organisation	Yes	Rough	Low

TABLE 23.3 Questions 8–11: knowledge domains

338 SUSTAINABLE INNOVATION

10. What is the level of detail of these models?

11. What is the level of formalisation of these models?

The letters a–e in Table 23.3 label the different knowledge domains, and we use these in subsequent tables. With regard to Q10, we use the labels 'rough', 'detailed' and 'very detailed' to indicate the level of detail of the models of the different knowledge domains that are available. In Q11, we use the labels 'low', 'medium' and 'high' to express the level of formalisation of these models.

Questions concerning the tasks focused upon in the Optichem case are displayed in Tables 23.4, 23.5 and 23.6. They concern the following questions:

	Question 12: task	Question 13: objective	Question 14: Input	Question 14: Output
1.	Paper making	Make paper	Wood fibres	Paper
2.	Chemical production	Make chemicals	Minerals	Chemicals
3.	Chemical transport	Transport chemicals from A to B	Chemicals	Chemicals
4.	Installation building	Make paper/dosage machines	Steel	Machine
5.	Fitting	Install paper/dosage machines	Machine	Installation
6.	Maintenance	Repair/maintain paper/dosage machine	Broken machine	Functioning machine
7.	Cleaning	Clean paper/dosage machine	Dirty machine	Clean machine

TABLE 23.4 Questions 12–14: tasks and characteristics in Optichem's primary processes

From: \ To: Task	1	2	3	4	5	6	7
1	–	–	–	–	–	–	–
2	X	–	X	X	X	X	X
3	X	–	–	–	–	–	–
4	X	–	X	–	X	X	X
5	X	–	X	–	–	X	X
6	X	–	–	–	–	–	X
7	X	–	–	–	–	–	–

TABLE 23.5 Question 15: task dependencies

	Knowledge domain				
Task	a	b	c	d	e
1	X	X	X	X	X
2	X	X	–	–	–
3	X	–	–	–	X
4	X	X	X	X	–
5	X	–	X	–	X
6	X	–	X	–	X
7	X	–	–	–	X

TABLE 23.6 Question 16: tasks require knowledge from domains

12. Which tasks constitute the organisation's primary processes?
13. What are the objectives of the tasks in the primary processes?
14. What are the inputs and outputs of every task in the primary processes?
15. What dependencies exist among the tasks of the primary processes?
16. What knowledge is required to perform the tasks in the primary processes?

In Table 23.4 the different Optichem tasks are labelled 1–7. These numbers are also used in subsequent tables to refer to these tasks. In Tables 23.5 and 23.6 we use the symbols X and – to indicate whether a task dependency exists or not respectively or whether a task requires knowledge from a certain knowledge domain or not.

Questions concerning individuals involved in the Optichem case are displayed in Tables 23.7, 23.8 and 23.9. These concern the following questions:

17. Which individuals are involved in which tasks?
18. Which individuals possess knowledge from which knowledge domains?
19. Does the knowledge an individual possesses match what is required by his or her tasks?

The individuals mentioned in Tables 23.7 and 23.8 originate from our earlier stakeholder analysis. We consider only the group and individual stakeholders here. Groups are treated as collections of similar individuals. In Tables 23.7 and 23.8, the X indicates that an individual is involved in a task and that the individual possesses knowledge from a certain domain. The – denotes that the individual is not involved in the task or does not possess knowledge of that particular domain.

In Table 23.9, we use the notation { and } to indicate what knowledge domains are actually used in a task and what knowledge domains are required in the design of the task.

	Task						
Individual	1	2	3	4	5	6	7
Chemical expert	–	X	X	–	–	–	–
Safety expert	–	–	–	–	–	–	–
Truck driver	–	–	X	–	–	–	–
Expedition employee	–	–	X	–	–	–	–
Project manager cleaning	–	–	–	–	–	–	X
Production manager	X	–	–	–	X	X	–
Operator	X	–	–	–	–	–	–
Mechanic	–	–	–	–	–	X	–

TABLE 23.7 Question 17: individual task combinations

	Knowledge domain				
Individual	a	b	c	d	e
Chemical expert	X	–	–	–	–
Safety expert	–	–	–	–	–
Truck driver	X	–	–	–	–
Expedition employee	–	X	–	–	–
Project manager cleaning	X	–	–	–	–
Production manager	–	X	–	–	–
Operator	–	X	–	–	–
Mechanic	–	–	X	X	–

TABLE 23.8 Question 18: individual knowledge combinations

Task	Knowledge domains	
	Actual	*Required*
1	{b}	{a, b, c, d, e}
2	{a}	{a, b}
3	{a, b}	{a, e}
4	{-}	{a, b, c, d}
5	{b}	{a, c, e}
6	{b, c, d}	{a, c, e}
7	{a}	{a, e}

TABLE 23.9 Question 19: actual knowledge versus required knowledge per task

Learning issues

	Question	Answer Yes	Answer No
20	I know what methods my employees use to acquire new knowledge and to learn	☐	☑
21	I can explain how my employees plan and monitor their learning efforts	☐	☑
22	I am able to tell how my employees organise their learning time	☐	☑
23	I am acquainted with the ideas of all of my employees about their ability to learn new things	☐	☑
24	I know my employees' reasons for learning	☐	☑
25	My employees give me their views about changes in the organisation	☑	☐
26	To a certain extent, my employees are able to deviate from their tasks and explore and learn	☑	☐
27	Our organisation stimulates its employees to learn	☑	☐

TABLE 23.10 Questions 20–27: learning strategies, motivation and context

Organisational forms and open enterprise

In this section we continue with the Optichem example to illustrate how the organisational forms are assessed. The following eight questions, representing Q28 about organisational forms, refer to the dimensions: autonomy–dependence; co-operation–competition; rules–own initiative; shared knowledge–private knowledge; hierarchy–heterarchy; openness–closedness; specialisation–generalisation; and centralisation–decentralisation.

In your organisation:

1. Autonomy–dependence
   - ◉ Autonomy prevails
   - ○ Dependence prevails
   - ○ Neither prevails

2. Co-operation–competition
   - ◉ Co-operation prevails
   - ○ Competition prevails
   - ○ Neither prevails

3. Rules–own initiative
   - ○ Rules prevail
   - ○ Own initiative prevails
   - ◉ Neither prevails

342 SUSTAINABLE INNOVATION

4. Shared knowledge–no shared knowledge
   - ◉ Knowledge is shared
   - ○ Knowledge is not shared
   - ○ Neither

5. Hierarchy–heterarchy
   - ○ Is based on hierarchy
   - ◉ Is based on heterarchy
   - ○ Is based on neither

6. Openness–closedness
   - ◉ Is based on openness
   - ○ Is based on closedness
   - ○ Is based on neither

7. Specialisation–generalisation
   - ◉ Is based on specialisation
   - ○ Is based on generalisation
   - ○ Is based on neither

8. Centralisation–decentralisation
   - ○ Is centralised
   - ◉ Is decentralised
   - ○ Neither

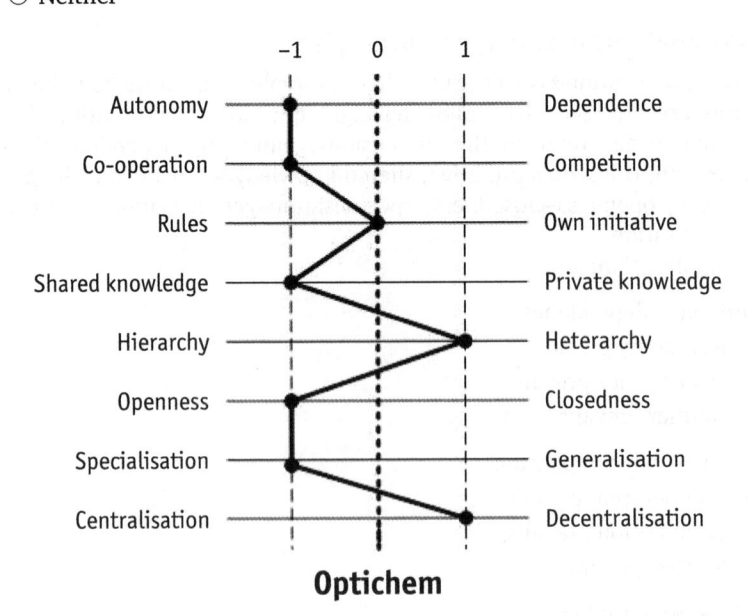

Optichem

FIGURE 23.1 Characterisation of the Optichem project with respect to the eight dimensions

23. ASSESSING AND DETERMINING SOCIAL SUSTAINABILITY *Faber, Maruster and Jorna*

In Figure 23.1 we present the chart that helps us to profile Optichem. This can be compared with the charts in Table 5.1 (Chapter 5). We observe that the Optichem organisational form is close to a professional bureaucracy. This result is not surprising as the goal of Optichem's project was to enhance the knowledge of chemicals within paper production through knowledge exchange between highly educated and specialised people. In the figure, –1 indicates that the concept on the left of the figure predominates whereas 1 indicates that the concept on the right predominates; a value of 0 reflects that neither concept is dominant or that the dimension is not relevant.

The following questions refer to knowledge types and learning modalities in the context of Optichem.

29. Knowledge types

    In your organisation:

    a Knowledge is weakly coded (sensory). Namely, knowledge is rather expressed as rules of thumb, customs, experiential practices, feelings

    ☐ yes   ☑ no

    b Knowledge is generally difficult to put into words (sensory)

    ☐ yes   ☑ no

    c Knowledge is coded to a large extent (e.g. through regulations, reference books, manuals, jargon and terminology)

    ☑ yes   ☐ no

    d Knowledge is hardly coded

    ☐ yes   ☑ no

    e Knowledge is theoretical (rules, models, theoretical explanations)

    ☐ yes   ☑ no

    f Most members of the organisation do not know precisely what they are doing and why they are doing it

    ☑ yes   ☐ no

    g Knowledge means power

    ☑ yes   ☐ no

30. Learning modalities

    In your organisation, learning modalities are:

    a Learning by doing, imitating

    ☑ yes   ☐ no

    b Learning from documents, other materials

    ☑ yes   ☐ no

    c Learning by education/training, or by self-studying manuals

    ☑ yes   ☐ no

In Table 23.11 we show how six organisational forms (clan, feudal system, machine bureaucracy, professional bureaucracy, market, web) can be represented in terms of knowledge types (sensory, coded, theoretical) and learning modalities. We translated the characterisation provided in Table 5.2 (Chapter 5) in order to answer Q29 and Q30. Given these responses, it is possible to identify the organisational form that best matches the Optichem project.

344 SUSTAINABLE INNOVATION

Organisational form	Question 29: knowledge types							Question 30: learning		
	29a	29b	29c	29d	29e	29f	29g	30a	30b	30c
Clan	Y	Y	N	N	N	N	N	Y	N	N
Feudal system	N	Y	N	Y	N	Y	N	Y	N	N
Machine bureaucracy	N	N	Y	N	N	Y	Y	N	Y	N
Professional bureaucracy	N	N	Y	N	Y	N	N	N	Y	Y
Market	Y	Y	Y	Y	Y	N	N	Y	Y	N
Web	Y	N	Y	N	N	N	N	Y	Y	N
Optichem	N	N	Y	N	N	Y	Y	Y	Y	Y

TABLE 23.11 Questions 29 and 30: The six organisational forms in terms of knowledge types and learning modalities

As we can see in Table 23.11, this time the best-fit organisational form with respect to knowledge types is machine bureaucracy. With respect to learning modalities there is not such a clear match between a specific organisational form and our Optichem example. However, the ones that are closest are market and web.

The last three questions 31–33 relate to the open enterprise and aim to assess the extent to which an organisation is open, transparent and inclusive. The answers should give an indication of how well employees participate in the process of knowledge creation. In the case of Optichem, the principles of openness and epistemic inclusiveness are fairly dominant. With regard to the transparency principle, however, the situation is quite the opposite.

31. Openness

    Is your organisation open to:

    a New problems recognised by any of the organisations' employees?

    ☑ yes   ☐ no

    b New ideas generated by any of the organisations' employees?

    ☑ yes   ☐ no

    c Continuous criticism of previously generated ideas by any of the organisations' employees?

    ☐ yes   ☑ no

32. Internal transparency

    In your organisation, is organisational knowledge (knowledge claims, meta-claims, knowledge processes) visible, disclosed and open to criticism (with the exception of private or secret information), although rules of privacy and secrecy are also visible, disclosed and open to criticism?

    ☐ yes   ☑ no

33. Epistemic inclusiveness (external)

In your organisation, are organisational knowledge processes open to stakeholder participation (with the exception of private or secret processes), although rules of privacy and secrecy are also visible, disclosed and open to criticism?

☑ yes   ☐ no

Abbreviations

3P	people, planet and profit
AI	artificial intelligence
APZ	algemeen psychiatrisch ziekenhuis (general psychiatric hospital, Netherlands)
AVB/AVEBE	Aardappelmeel Verkoop Bureau (Potato Starch Sales Agency) (Netherlands)
AZG	Academisch Ziekenhuis Groningen (Netherlands)
BEST	Business Excellence through Speed and Teamwork (Philips)
CAP	Common Agricultural Policy (EU)
CBMS	Central Board for Medical Specialties (Netherlands)
CBR	case-based reasoning
CBS	Central Bureau for Statistics (Netherlands)
CFT	cognitive flexibility theory
CG	corporate governance
CoMPASS	Concept Mapped Project-based Activity Scaffolding System
CSO	Corporate Sustainability Office (Philips)
CSR	corporate social responsibility
CST	critical systems thinking
DDC	diagnosis, design and change
DDCDAE	diagnosis, design and change; description and analysis; evaluation
DIY	do-it-yourself
DJSI	Dow Jones Sustainability Index
DSS	decision-support system; decision-support software
EDR	Ems Dollar Region (Netherlands/Germany)
EFQM	European Foundation for Quality Management
EU	European Union
FFPI	Five-Factor Personality Inventory
GGZ	Geestelijke Gezondheids Zorg (Mental Health Care) (The Netherlands)
GMO	genetically modified organism
GRI	Global Reporting Initiative
HPA	Hoofdproductschap Akkerbouw (Agricultural Agency, Netherlands)
ICT	information and communications technology

ABBREVIATIONS

IiP	Investors in People
IpGME	Innovation of (post)Graduate Medical Education (University of Groningen, Netherlands)
ISO	International Organisation for Standardisation
KADS	Knowledge Acquisition and Documentation System
KB-DSS	knowledge-based decision-support system
KCSI	Knowledge Creation for Sustainable Innovation
KMS	knowledge management system
KoS	knowledge of sustainability
KPI	key performance indicator
KS	knowledge system
KSH	KunstStoffenHuis (Netherlands)
KT	knowledge technology
LCD	liquid-crystal display
MDSA	multi-dimensional scaling analysis
MHP	model human processor
MSLQ	Motivated Strategies of Learning Questionnaire
NGO	non-governmental organisation
NIDO	Nationaal Initiatief Duurzame Ontwikkeling (National Initiative for Sustainable Development, Netherlands)
O&D	Organisation and development staff group (UMCG)
OECD	Organisation for Economic Co-operation and Development
OLM	online monitoring
PES	Philips Environmental Services Knowledge Centre
PET	polyethylene terephthalate
R&D	research and development
RBR	rule-based reasoning
REC	risk, environment and costs
SAE	socially accountable entrepreneurship
SD	standard deviation
SME	small or medium-sized enterprise
SoK	sustainability of knowledge
SPSS	Statistical Package for the Social Sciences
SUMI	Software Usability Measurement Inventory
UMCG	University Medical Centre Groningen (Netherlands)
WAO	Wet ArbeidsOngeschiktheid (Disablement Insurance Act, Netherlands)
WBCSD	World Business Council for Sustainable Development
WTO	World Trade Organisation

References

Achterkamp, M.C., and J.F.J. Vos (2006) 'A Framework for Making Sense of Sustainable Innovation through Stakeholder Involvement', *International Journal of Environmental Technology and Management* (in press).
Adriaanse, D.J., and P.Ch.A. Malotaux (1975) *Model voor het Beschrijven van Verandering voor Organisaties in het Kader van Organisatie-ontwikkeling* (Delft, Netherlands: Delft University Press).
Alexander, P.A. (1992) 'Domain Knowledge: Evolving Themes and Emerging Concerns', *Educational Psychologist* 27.1: 33-51.
Anderson, J.R. (1983) *The Architecture of Cognition* (Cambridge, MA: Harvard University Press).
Andriof, J., and S. Waddock (2002) 'Unfolding Stakeholder Engagement', in J. Andriof, S. Waddock, B. Husted and S. Sutherland Rahman (eds.), *Unfolding Stakeholder Thinking: Theory, Responsibility and Engagement* (Sheffield, UK: Greenleaf Publishing): 9-16.
Andriole, S., and L. Adelman (1995) *Cognitive Systems Engineering for User–Computer Interface Design, Prototyping and Evaluation* (Mahwah, NJ: Lawrence Erlbaum Associates, 1st edn).
Argyris, C., and D.A. Schön (1978) *Organisational Learning: A Theory of Action Perspective* (Reading, MA: Addison-Wesley).
Armengol, E., and E. Plaza (2003) 'Relational Case-Based Reasoning for Carcinogenic Activity Prediction', *Artificial Intelligence Review* 20.1-2: 121.
Asakawa, K. (1995) 'Managing Knowledge Conversion Processes across Borders: Toward a Framework of International Knowledge Management', *INSEAD Working Paper Series* 95/91/OB.
Ashby, W.R. (1956) *Introduction to Cybernetics* (London: Methuen).
Asper, C., A. Donker, L. Greer, E. Olano and S. Twigge (2003) *Philips Team II: Final Report* (Rotterdam, Netherlands: Erasmus University).
Baker, W. (1990) 'Market Networks and Corporate Behaviour', *American Journal of Sociology* 96: 589-625.
Bakkenist Management Consultants (1997) *Rapportage CasusConsult GGZ* (The Hague: Transparant).
Barletta, R. (1991) 'An Introduction to Case-Based Reasoning', *AI Expert*, August 1991: 42-49.
Beier, E.B., and P.L. Ackerman (2005) 'Age, Ability and the Role of Prior Knowledge on the Acquisition of New Domain Knowledge: Promising Results in a Real-world Learning Environment', *Psychology and Aging* 20: 341-55.
Berg, M. (2000) *Kaf en Koren van Kennismanagement: Over Informatietechnologie, de Kwaliteit van Zorg en het Werk van Professionals* (Rotterdam, Netherlands: Institute BMG Erasmus University).
Beth, E.W. (1959) 'Aristotle's Principle of the Absolute', in E.W. Beth (ed.), *The Foundations of Mathematics* (Amsterdam: North-Holland Publishing Company).
Bhatt, G.D. (2000) 'Organising Knowledge in the Knowledge Development Cycle', *Journal of Knowledge Management* 4: 15-26.

Billet, S. (2001) *Learning in the Workplace: Strategies for Effective Practice* (Crows Nest, NSW, Australia: Allen & Unwin).
Block, P. (1998) *Empowerment in Organisaties: Werken met Positieve Tactische Vaardigheden* (Schoonhoven, Netherlands: Academic Service).
Boden, M.A. (1994) *Dimensions of Creativity* (Cambridge, MA: MIT Press).
Boisot, M.H. (1995) *Information Space: A Framework for Learning in Organisations, Institutions and Culture* (London: Routledge).
Bolwijn, P.T., and T. Kumpe (1990) 'Manufacturing in the 1990s: Productivity, Flexibility and Innovation', *Long Range Planning* 23.4: 44-57.
Bos, J.H., P. Veenstra, H. Verhoeven and P.D. de Vos (1995) *Het Papierboek* (Houten, Netherlands: Educatieve Partners Nederland b.v.).
Bossel, H. (1999) *Indicators for Sustainable Development: Theory, Method, Applications* (Winnipeg, Canada: International Institute for Sustainable Development).
Boulding, K.E. (1956) 'General Systems Theory: The Skeleton of Science', *Management Science* 2.3: 197-208.
Bourdieu, P. (1986) 'The Forms of Capital', in J.G. Richardson (ed.), *Handbook of Theory and Research for the Sociology of Education* (New York: Greenwood).
Boutkan, E.J.M., H. Canter Cremers, A. Van Diem and J.E. Wieringa (2004) 'BioSoil Initieert Duurzaam Saneren', *Bodem: Tijdschrift over Duurzaam Bodembeheer*.
Bower, G.H., and E.R. Hilgard (1981) *Theories of Learning* (Englewood Cliffs, NJ: Prentice Hall, 5th edn).
Breuker, J., and W. van de Velde (1994) *CommonKADS Library for Expertise Modelling: Reusable Problemsolving Components* (Amsterdam: IOS Press).
Bunge, M. (1998) *Philosophy of Science: From Explanation to Justification* (Sumerset, NJ: Transaction Publishers).
Burns, T.R., and G.M. Stalker (1961) *The Management of Innovation* (Oxford, UK: Oxford University Press).
Cameron, K.S., and R.E. Quinn (1999) *Diagnosing and Changing Organisational Culture: Based on the Competing Values Framework* (Reading, MA: Addison-Wesley).
Card, S.K., T.P. Moran and A. Newell (1983) *The Psychology of Human–Computer Interaction* (Mahwah, NJ: Lawrence Erlbaum Associates, 1st edn).
Carson, R.L. (1962) *Silent Spring* (Cambridge, MA: Houghton Mifflin/Riverside Press)
Castells, M. (1996a) *The Information Age* (Oxford, UK: Blackwell Publishers).
—— (1996b) *The Rise of the Network Society* (Cambridge, UK: Blackwell Publishers).
Cavaleri, S.A., and D.S. Fearon (2005) *Inside Knowledge: Rediscovering the Source of Performance Improvement* (Milwaukee, WI: ASQ Quality Press).
—— and S. Seivert (2005) *Knowledge Leadership: The Art and Science of the Knowledge-Based Organisation* (Burlington, VT: Elsevier Butterworth-Heinemann).
CBS (Centraal Bureau voor de Statistiek) (2004) *Kennis en Economie 2003: Onderzoek en Innovatie in Nederland* (Report No. 0515904010; Voorburg, Netherlands: CBS).
Checkland, P.B. (1981) *Systems Thinking, Systems Practice* (Chichester, UK: John Wiley).
Choo, C.W. (1998) *The Knowing Organisation* (Oxford, UK: Oxford University Press).
Churchland, P.M. (1984) *Matter and Consciousness* (Cambridge, MA: MIT Press).
Churchman, C.W. (1971) *The Design of Inquiring Systems: Basic Concepts of Systems and Organisations* (New York: Basic Books).
Cijsouw, R.S., and R.J. Jorna (2003) 'Measuring and Mapping Knowledge Types', in H.W.M. Gazendam, R.S. Cijsouw and R.J. Jorna (eds.), *Dynamics and Change in Organisations: Studies in Organisational Semiotics* (Dordrecht, Netherlands: Kluwer): 215-43.
——, R.J. Jorna, B. Verkerke and G. Rakhorst (2004) 'Knowledge Matters in Medical Device Development: The History of the Artificial Kidney Development Process from a Knowledge Management Perspective', paper presented at the BMSA (Biomedical Study Activity) Conference, Schiermonnikoog, Netherlands, 2003.
Clarkson, M.B.E. (1995) 'Stakeholder Framework for Analysing and Evaluating Corporate Social Performance', *Academy of Management Review* 20.1: 92-117.
Coad, P., and E. Yourdon (1991) *Object Oriented Design* (Englewood Cliffs, NJ: Yourdon).

Coase, R.H. (1960) 'The Problem of Social Cost', *Journal of Law and Economics* 3: 1-44.
Cognitive Systems (1993) *The Application of Case-Based Reasoning in the Healthcare Industry* (Boston, MA: Cognitive Systems Inc.).
Cohen, W.M., and D.A. Levinthal (1990) 'Absorptive Capacity: A New Perspective on Learning and Innovation', *Administrative Science Quarterly* 35.1: 128-52.
Cooper, R.G. (1998) *Product Leadership: Creating and Launching Superior New Products* (Reading, MA: Perseus Books).
—— (2001) *Winning at New Products: Accelerating the Process from Idea to Launch* (Reading, MA: Addison-Wesley).
—— and E.J. Kleinschmidt (1990) *New Products: The Key Factors in Success* (Chicago: American Marketing Association).
Csikszentmihalyi, M. (1996) *Creativity: Flow and the Psychology of Invention* (New York: HarperCollins).
Daft, R.L. (2001) *Organisation Theory and Design* (Cincinatti, OH: South-Western College Publishing).
—— and K.E. Weick (1984) 'Toward a Model of Organisations as Interpretation Systems', *Academy of Management Review* 9: 284-95.
Damanpour, F. (1987) 'The Adoption of Technological, Administrative and Ancillary Innovations: Impact of Organisational Factors', *Journal of Management* 13: 675-88.
Damhuis, G., G. Davits, P. Elshout, K. Lombarts, K. Verschure and G.G. de Vries (2002) *Leven en Werken in Netwerken* (Den Bosch, Netherlands: DamhuisElshoutVerschure; www.homozappens.nl).
Davenport, T.H., and J. Glaser (2002) 'Just-in-time Delivery Comes to Knowledge Management', *Harvard Business Review* 80.7: 107-11.
Davis, G.B., and M.H. Olson (1985) *Management Information Systems: Conceptual Foundations, Structure and Development* (New York: McGraw-Hill).
De Groot, A.D. (1961) *Methodologie: Grondslagen van onderzoek en denken in de gedragswetenschappen* (The Hague: Mouton).
De Hoog, R., and B. Wielinga (2003) *Expertsystemen: Past, Present* (Amsterdam: University of Amsterdam).
De Leeuw, A.C.J. (1986) *Organisaties, Management, Analyse, Ontwerp en Verandering: Een Systeem Visie* (Assen, Netherlands: Van Gorcum).
Dendermonde, M., and H.N. Sierman (1979) *Hoe Wij Rooiden: De Veenkoloniale Aardappelboer en Zijn Industrie* (Veendam, Netherlands: AVEBE).
Dennett, D.C. (1978) *Brainstorms* (Brighton, UK: The Harvester Press).
—— (1987) *The Intentional Stance* (Cambridge, MA: MIT Press).
—— (1991) *Consciousness Explained* (London: Allan Lane/Penguin).
—— (1998) *Brainchildren: Essays on Designing Minds* (Cambridge, MA: MIT Press).
Donald, M. (1991) *Origins of the Modern Mind: Three Stages in the Evolution of Culture and Cognition* (Cambridge, MA: Harvard University Press).
Donaldson, T., and L.E. Preston (1995) 'The Stakeholder Theory of the Corporation: Concepts, Evidence and Implications', *Academy of Management Review* 20.1: 65-91.
Doppelt, B. (2003) 'Overcoming the Seven Sustainability Blunders', *The Systems Thinker* 14.5: 2-7.
Dosi, G. (1988) 'The Nature of the Innovative Process', in G. Dosi, C. Freeman, R. Nelson, G. Silverberg and L. Soete (eds.), *Technical Change and Economic Theory* (London: Frances Pinter).
Duivenboden, H., M. Lips and P. Frissen (1999) *Kennismanagement in de Publieke Sector* (The Hague: Elsevier Bedrijfsinformatie b.v.).
Edelman, L.F., M. Bresnen, S. Newell, H. Scarbrough and J. Swan (2004) 'The Benefits and Pitfalls of Social Capital: Empirical Evidence from Two Organisations in the United Kingdom', *British Journal of Management* 15: 59-70.
Edwards, P. (1967) *The Encyclopaedia of Philosophy* (New York: Macmillan).
Elkington, J. (1997) *Cannibals with Forks: The Triple Bottom Line of 21st Century Business* (Gabriola Island, BC: New Society Publishers).
Endenburg, G. (1998) *Sociocracy as Social Design* (Delft, Netherlands: Eburon).
European Commission (2004) *Newspaper NRC Handelsblad* (Rotterdam), 14 April 2004: 19
Faber, N.R., R.J. Jorna and J.M.L. van Engelen (2005) 'The Sustainability of "Sustainability": A Study into the Conceptual Foundations of the Notion of "Sustainability"', *Journal of Environmental Assessment Policy and Management* 7.1: 1-33.

Fastrez, P. (2001) 'Characteristic(s) of Hypermedia and How They Relate to Knowledge', paper presented at the *International Council for Education Media Conference*, Geneva, Switzerland, 2000.

—— (2002) 'Navigation Entailments as Design Principles for Structuring Hypertext', *Education, Communication and Information* 2: 7-22.

Firestone, J.M. (2003) *Enterprise Information Portals and Knowledge Management* (Boston, MA: Butterworth-Heinemann).

—— (2005) *Reducing Risk by Killing Your Worst Ideas* (KMCI; Boston, MA: Butterworth-Heinemann).

—— and M.W. McElroy (2003) *Key Issues in the New Knowledge Management* (Boston, MA: Butterworth-Heinemann).

—— and —— (2004) *A Governance-Based Approach to Knowledge Management: A KMCI Position Statement* (Hartland Four Corners, VT: Knowledge Management Consortium International).

Fodor, J.A. (1975) *The Language of Thought* (New York: Thomas Y. Crowell).

Fortune (2003) 'Ten Great Companies to Work for in Europe', www.fortune.com/fortune/bestcompanies/articles.

Freeman, R.E. , and D.L. Reed (1983) *Stockholders and Stakeholders: A New Perspective on Corporate Governance* (Los Angeles, CA: UCLA Extension).

—— (1984) *Strategic Management: A Stakeholder Approach* (Boston, MA: Pitman).

Frooman, J. (1999) 'Stakeholder Influence Strategies', *Academy of Management Review* 24.2: 191-205.

Garcia, R., and R. Calantone (2002) 'A Critical Look at Technological Innovation Typology and Innovativeness Terminology: A Literature Review', *Journal of Product Innovation Management* 19.2: 110-32.

Gardner, H. (1984) *Frames of the Mind: The Theory of Multiple Intelligences* (London: Heinemann).

Gazendam, H.W.M. (1993) *Variety Controls Variety: On the Use of Organisational Theories in Information Management* (Groningen, Netherlands: Wolters-Noordhoff).

——, R.J. Jorna and R.S. Cijsouw (2003) *Dynamics and Change in Organisations* (Dordrecht, Netherlands: Kluwer).

Gezondheidsraad (2000) *Van Implementeren Naar Leren: Het Belang van Tweerichtingsverkeer Tussen Praktijk en Wetenschap* (The Hague: Gezondheidsraad).

Giel, R., and F. Sturmans (eds.) (1996) *Psychiatrische Casus-Registers in Nederland: Regionale Informatie in de GGZ* (Groningen, Netherlands: University of Groningen).

Gierl, L., M. Bull and R. Schmidt (1998) 'CBR in Medicine', in M. Lenz, S.B. Bartsch and S. Wess (eds.), *Case-Based Reasoning Technology: From Foundations to Applications* (Berlin: Springer): 273-97.

Gold, A.H., A. Malhotra and A.H. Segars (2001) 'Knowledge Management: An Organizational Capabilities Perspective', *Journal of Management Information Systems* 18.1: 185-214.

Goodman, N. (1968) *Languages of Art* (Brighton, UK: The Harvester Press).

Goodpaster, K.E. (1991) 'Business Ethics and Stakeholder Analysis', *Business Ethics Quarterly* 1.1: 53-73.

Goodwin, P., and G. Wright (2003) *Decision Analysis for Management Judgement* (Chichester, UK: John Wiley).

Grant, R.M. (1996a) 'Prospering in Dynamically-Competitive Environments: Organisational Capability as Knowledge Integration', *Organisation Science* 7: 375-87.

—— (1996b) 'Toward a Knowledge-Based Theory of the Firm', *Strategic Management Journal* 17: 109-22.

Greene, B.A. (1995) 'Comprehension of Expository Text from an Unfamiliar Domain: Effects of Instruction that Provides Either Domain-Specific or Strategy Knowledge', *Contemporary Educational Psychology* 20: 313-19.

Gupta, A.K., and V. Govindarajan (2000) 'Knowledge Flows within Multinational Corporations', *Strategic Management Journal* 21: 473-96.

Hansen, M.T., N. Nohria and T. Tierney (1999) 'What is Your Strategy for Managing Knowledge?', *Harvard Business Review* 77.2: 106-16.

Healy, T., and S. Côté (2001) *The Well-being of Nations: The Role of Human and Social Capital* (Paris: OECD, Centre for Educational Research and Innovation).

Hedlund, G. (1994) 'A Model of Knowledge Management and the N-form Corporation', *Strategic Management Journal* 15: 73-90.

Helmhout, M., H.W.M. Gazendam and R.J. Jorna (2004) 'Social Constructs and Boundedly Rational Actors: A Simulation Framework', in L. Kecheng (ed.), *Virtual, Distributed and Flexible Organisations: Studies in Organisational Semiotics* (Dordrecht, Netherlands: Kluwer): 153-79.

Hendriks, A.A.J. (1997) *The Construction of the Five-factor Personality Inventory (FFPI)*, PhD thesis, University of Groningen, Netherlands.
Hermans, J., J. Iamsakul, A. Susanto and R. Wish (2003) *Philips Stakeholder Dialogue: From Eco-efficiency to Sustainable Entrepreneurship* (Rotterdam, Netherlands: Erasmus University Rotterdam).
Hinds, P.J., M. Patterson and J. Pfeffer (2001) 'Bothered by Abstraction: The Effect of Expertise on Knowledge Transfer and Subsequent Novice Performance', *Journal of Applied Psychology* 86: 1,232-43.
Holsapple, C.W., and A.B. Whinston (1996) *Decision Support Systems: A Knowledge-Based Approach* (Minneapolis, MN: West Publishing Company).
Hoogendoorn, Y. (1996) *Case-Based Reasoning: Een Vergelijking Tussen Theorie en Praktijk* (Groningen, Netherlands: Rijks University).
Hutschemaekers, G. (2001) *Onder Professionals* (Nijmegen, Netherlands: University of Nijmegen/SUN).
IOM (Institute of Medicine) (2001) *Crossing the Quality Chasm: A New Health System for the 21st Century* (Washington, DC: National Academy Press).
Isenberg, D.J. (1986) 'The Structure and Process of Understanding: Implications for Managerial Action', in H.P. Sims and D.A. Gioia (eds.), *The Thinking Organisation* (San Francisco: Jossey Bass).
Jameton, A., and J. Pierce (2001) 'Environment and Health: Eight Sustainable Healthcare and Emerging Ethical Responsibilities', *Canada Medical Association Journal* 164.3: 365-69.
Janszen, F.H.A. (2000) *The Age of Innovation: Making Business Creativity a Competence, Not a Coincidence* (London: Prentice Hall).
Jentjens, V.L.M. (2001) *Mensen Leren, Organisaties Niet* (Amsterdam: Ricent Consultancy and Research).
Jippes, E. (2004) *Intensivering Vaardigheidsonderwijs Opleiding Chirurgie: Een Studie Naar de Organisatorische Haalbaarheid in de Onderwijs en Opleidingsregio Noord en Oost-Nederland*, master's thesis, Faculty of Management and Organisation, University of Groningen, Netherlands.
Joenje, R. (2004) 'Van CasusConsult Naar een GGZ Kennisnet', in R.J. Jorna, J. van Engelen and H. Hadders (eds.), *Duurzame Innovatie: Organisaties en de Dynamiek van Kenniscreatie* (Assen, Netherlands: Van Gorcum).
Johnson, S.C., and C. Jones (1957) 'How to Organise for New Products', *Harvard Business Review* 35.3: 49-62.
Jorna, R.J. (1990) *Knowledge Representation and Symbols in the Mind* (Tübingen, Germany: Stauffenburg Verlag).
—— (2001a) 'De Cognitieve Kant van Kennismanagement: Over Representaties, Kennistypen, Organisatievormen en Innovatie', in A. Witteveen and P. van Baalen (eds.), *Kennis en Management* (Schiedam, Netherlands: Scriptum).
—— (2001b) 'Decision-making, Semiosis and the Knowledge Space: The Case for Studas', *Semiotica* 133: 97-119.
——, W.H.M. Gazendam, H.C. Heesen and W. van Wezel (1996) *Plannen en Roosteren: Taakgericht Analyseren, Ontwerpen en Ondersteunen* (Leidschendam, Netherlands: Lansa).
—— and J.L. Simons (1992) *Kennis in Organisaties: Theorie en Toepassingen van Kennissystemen* (Muiderberg, Netherlands: Coutinho).
——, J.M.L. Van Engelen and H. Hadders (eds.) (2004) *Duurzame Innovatie: Organisaties en de Dynamiek van Kenniscreatie* (Assen, Netherlands: Van Gorcum).
Kanter, R.M. (1983) *The Change Masters* (New York: Simon & Schuster).
Kaptein, M., and J. Wempe (1999) *Sustainability Management: Balancing and Integrating Economic, Social and Environmental Responsibilities* (Report No. 51; Rotterdam, Netherlands: School of Management).
Keen, P.G.W., and M.S. Scott-Morton (1978) *Decision Support Systems: An Organisational Perspective* (Reading, MA: Addison-Wesley).
Kingma, J., and J. Rienstra (2002) *Kennismanagement in het Beroepsonderwijs* (Amsterdam: Max Groote Kenniscentrum voor Beroepsonderwijs en Volwasseneneducatie).
Kirakowski, J. (1994) *The Use of Questionnaire Methods for Usability Assessment*, www.ucc.ie/hfrg/questionnaires/sumi/sumipapp.html.

REFERENCES 353

Klein, M.R., and L.B. Methlie (1995) *Knowledge-Based Decision Support Systems* (New York: John Wiley, 2nd edn).

Kleinknecht, A., J.O.N. Reijnen and W. Smits (1992) 'Innovatie-indicatoren: Vernieuwing in het Nederlandse Bedrijfsleven', in J.W.A. van Dijk and L. Soete (eds.), *Innovatiebeleid in een Economie Met Open Grenzen* (Alphen aan de Rijn, Netherlands: Samson): 95-117.

Klos, T.B. (2000) *Agent-Based Computational Transaction Cost Economics*, SOM PhD thesis, University of Groningen, Netherlands.

KNMG (Koninklijke Nederlandse Maatschappij ter bevordering van de Geneeskunde) (2002) *De arts van straks: Een nieuw opleidingscontinuum* (Utrecht, Netherlands: KNMG, DMW-VSNU, VAZ, NVZ and LCVV).

Kolb, A.D. (1984) *Experimental Learning: Experience as the Source of Learning and Development* (Englewood Cliffs, NJ: Prentice Hall).

Kolodner, J.L. (1991) 'Improving Human Decision-making through Case-Based Decision-aiding', *AI Magazine* 12.2: 52-68.

—— (1993) *Case-Based Reasoning* (San Francisco: Morgan Kaufmann Publishers).

Kratzer, J. (2001) *Communication and Performance: An Empirical Study in Innovation Teams*, SOM PhD thesis, University of Groningen, Netherlands.

Lekanne Deprez, F.R.E. (2003) *Van Elementair Belang: Kennismanagement als Waardeversneller* (Heerlen, Netherlands: Hogeschool Zuyd).

Linschoten, J. (1964) *De Idolen van de Psycholoog* (Utrecht, Netherlands: Bijleveld).

Lit, A.C. (1992) *Integrale Psychiatrie: Een Systeemtheoretische Basis voor Multidisciplinair Werken* (Amsterdam: Swets & Zeitlinger).

Lubbers, M.D. (2004) *Kennismanagement binnen GGZ Drenthe*, master's thesis, University of Groningen, Netherlands.

Luger, G.F., and W.A. Stubblefield (1998) *Artificial Intelligence: Structures and Strategies for Complex Problem-solving* (Harlow, UK: Addison-Wesley Longman, 3rd edn).

Maljers, F.A. (1995) *Strategisch alliantie: Over Lat-relaties in het Bedrijfsleven* (Rotterdam, Netherlands: Erasmus University).

Malthus, R. (1798) *An Essay on the Principle of Population* (Oxford, UK: Oxford University Press).

March, J.G. (1991) 'Exploration and Exploitation in Organisational Learning', *Organisation Science* 2.1: 71-98.

—— and H.A. Simon (1958) *Organizations* (New York: John Wiley).

Martens, P. (2005) *Duurzaamheid: Wetenschap of Fictie?* (Inaugural Lecture; Maastricht, Netherlands: University of Maastricht).

Maxwell, J.C. (1885) 'On Faraday's Lines of Force', in W.D. Niven (ed.), *The Scientific Papers of James Clerk Maxwell* (Cambridge, UK: Cambridge University Press, 1890; New York: Dover, 1952): 155-59.

McElroy, M.W. (2002) ' "Deep" Knowledge Management and Sustainability', www.macroinnovation.com/images/DeepKMbyM.W.McElroy.pdf.

—— (2003) *The New Knowledge Management: Complexity, Learning and Sustainable Innovation* (Boston, MA: Butterworth-Heinemann).

Meadows, D.H., D.L. Meadows, J. Randers and W.W. Behrens (1972) *The Limits to Growth: Report for the Club of Rome's Project on Predicament of Mankind* (London: Earth Island Ltd).

Mennin, S.P., and S. Kalishman (1998) 'Issues and Strategies for Reform in Medical Education: Lessons from Eight Medical Schools', *Academic Medicine* 73.9: Supplement S72.

Meyer, D.E., and D.E. Kieras (1997a) 'A Computational Theory of Executive Cognitive Processes and Multiple-Task Performance. Part I. Basic Mechanisms', *Psychological Review* 104: 3-65.

—— and —— (1997b) 'A Computational Theory of Executive Cognitive Processes and Multiple-Task Performance. Part II. Accounts of Psychological Refractory-Period Phenomena', *Psychological Review* 104: 749-91.

Michon, J.A., J.L. Jackson and R.J. Jorna (2003) 'Semiotic Aspects of Psychology', in R. Posner, K. Robbering and T.A. Sebeok (eds.), *Semiotics: A Handbook on the Sign-theoretic Foundations of Nature and Culture* (Berlin: de Gruyter).

Midgley, G. (1996) 'What is This Thing Called CST?', in R.L. Flood and N.R.A. Romm (eds.), *Critical Systems Thinking: Current Research and Practice* (New York: Plenum Press): 11-23.

—— (2000) *Systemic Intervention: Philosophy, Methodology and Practice* (New York/Boston/Dordrecht: Kluwer/Plenum).

Miles, R.E., and C.C. Snow (1978) *Organisational Strategy, Structure and Process* (New York: McGraw-Hill).

Mintzberg, H. (1983) *Structures in Fives: Designing Effective Organisations* (Englewood Cliffs, NJ: Prentice Hall).

Mitchell, R.K., B.R. Agle and D.J. Wood (1997) 'Toward a Theory of Stakeholder Identification and Salience: Defining the Principle of Who and What Really Counts', *Academy of Management Review* 22.4: 853-86.

Mowat, H., and D. Mowat (2001) 'The Value of Marginality in a Medical School: General Practice and Curriculum Change', *Medical Education* 35: 175-77.

Muller, P.C. (1999) *Team-Based Conceptualisation of New Products: Creating Shared Realities Using Information Technological Support*, PhD thesis, University of Groningen, Netherlands.

Naess, A. (1973) 'The Shallow and the Deep. Long-Range Ecology Movements: A Summary', *Inquiry* 16: 95-100.

Nagel, E. (1961) *The Structure of Science* (London: Routledge & Kegan Paul).

Nahapiet, J., and S. Ghoshal (1998) 'Social Capital, Intellectual Capital and the Organisational Advantage', *Academy of Management Review* 23.2: 242-66.

Newell, A. (1982) 'The Knowledge Level', *Artificial Intelligence* 18: 87-127.

—— (1990) *Unified Theories of Cognition* (Cambridge, MA: Harvard University Press).

—— and H.A. Simon (1976) 'Computer Science as Empirical Inquiry: Symbols and Search', *Communications of the Association for Computing Machinery* 19: 113-26.

—— and —— (1972) *Human Problem-solving* (Englewood Cliffs, NJ: Prentice Hall).

Nijkamp, P., A.L. Bovenberg and L. Soete (2000) *Kennis is Kracht: Het Belang van Goede Kennisinfrastructuur in Nederland* (The Hague: Notitie Ministerie van Onderwijs, Cultuur en Wetenschap).

Nilsson, M., and M. Sollenborn (2004) 'Advancements and Trends in Medical Case-Based Reasoning: An Overview of Systems and System Development', in V. Barr and Z. Markov (eds.), *Proceedings of the 17th International Florida Artificial Intelligence Research Society Conference* (Miami Beach, FL: AAAI Press).

Nonaka, I. (1994) 'A Dynamic Theory of Organisational Knowledge Creation', *Organisation Science* 6.1: 14-37.

—— and H. Takeuchi (1995) *The Knowledge Creating Company: How Japanese Companies Create the Dynamics of Innovation* (New York: Oxford University Press).

Nooteboom, B. (1994) *Management van Partnerships: In Toeleveren en Uitbesteden* (Schoonhoven, Netherlands: Academic Service).

—— (2000) *Learning and Innovation in Organisations and Economies* (Oxford, UK: Oxford University Press).

—— (2002) *Vertrouwen* (Schoonhoven, Netherlands: Academic Service).

Norman, D.A. (1989) *The Psychology of Everyday Things* (New York: Basic Books, 3rd edn).

O'Connor, G.C. (1998) 'Market Learning and Radical Innovation: A Cross Case Comparison of Eight Radical Innovation Projects', *Journal of Product Innovation Management* 15.2: 151-66.

OECD (Organisation for Economic Co-operation and Development) (1991) *The Nature of Innovation and the Evolution of the Productive System, Technology and Productivity: The Challenge for Economic Policy* (Paris: OECD): 303-14.

—— (2003) *Health at a Glance: OECD Indicators 2003* (Paris: OECD).

Open Clinical (2000) *The Medical Knowledge Crisis and its Solution through Knowledge Management* (London: Open Clinical).

Pahl, G., and W. Beitz (1995) *Engineering Design: A Systematic Approach* (Berlin: Springer, 2nd edn).

Pantazi, S.V., J.V. Arocha and J.R. Moehr (2004) 'Case-Based Medical Informatics', *BMC Medical Informatics and Decision-making* 4: 19.

Parsaye, K., M. Chignell, S. Khoshafian and H. Wong (1989) *Intelligent Databases: Object-Oriented, Deductive Hypermedia Technologies* (New York: John Wiley).

Peirce, S.C. (1931–1935) *The Collected Papers of Charles Sanders Peirce Vol. I–IV* (Cambridge, MA: Harvard University Press).

Phillips, R. (2003) 'Stakeholder Legitimacy', *Business Ethics Quarterly* 13.1: 25-41.
Pieters, D. (2005) *Stijlvol Leren en Kennis Overdragen: Aen Onderzoek Naar Leer—En Persoonlijkheidsstijlen bij Zetmeelaardappeltelers van AVEBE,* master's thesis, University of Groningen, Netherlands.
Pintrich, P.R., and E.V. de Groot (1990) 'Motivational and Self-regulated Learning Components of Classroom Academic Performance', *Journal of Educational Psychology* 82: 33-40.
Plesk, P. (2003) *Complexity and the Adoption of Innovation in Healthcare* (Rowell, GA: Paul E. Plesk & Associates).
——, C. Lindenberg and B. Zimmerman (1997) *Some Emerging Principles for Managing in Complex Adaptive Systems* (Working Paper; Allentown, NJ: Edgeware Filing Cabinet).
Polanyi, M. (1967) *The Tacit Dimension* (London: Routledge).
Poole, P.P., D.A. Gioia and B. Gray (1989) 'Influence Modes, Schema Change and Organisational Transformation', *Journal of Applied Behavioural Science* 25.3: 271-89.
Porter, M.E. (1985) *Competitive Advantage* (New York: The Free Press).
Postrel, S. (2002) 'Islands of Shared Knowledge: Specialisation and Mutual Understanding in Problem-solving Teams', *Organisation Science* 13.3: 303.
Puntambekar, S., A. Stylianou and R. Hübscher (2003) 'Improving Navigation and Learning in Hypertext Environments with Navigable Concept Maps', *Human–Computer Interaction* 18: 395-428.
Pylyshyn, Z.W. (1984) *Computation and Cognition* (Cambridge, MA: MIT Press).
Quinn, D., and T.M. Jones (1995) 'An Agent Morality View of Business Policy', *Academy of Management Review* 20.1: 22-42.
Rajlich, V. (2003) 'Case Studies of Constructivist Comprehension in Software Engineering', *Brain and Mind* 4: 229-38.
Ravensbergen, J., and W.M.C. Mik (2003) *In Zicht: Nieuwe Wegen voor Implementatie* (Assen, Netherlands: Van Gorcum).
Reber, A.S. (1993) *Implicit Learning and Tacit Knowledge: An Essay on the Cognitive Unconsciousness* (Oxford, UK: Oxford University Press).
Rice, M.P., G.C. O'Connor and L.S. Peters (1998) 'Managing Discontinuous Innovation', *Research Technology Management* 41.3: 52-58.
Riemersma, S. (2004) *Kennis en Consent? Het verduurzamen van kennis in een Sociocratische organisatie,* master's thesis, University of Groningen, Netherlands
Riesbeck, C.K., and R.C. Schank (1989) *Inside Case-Based Reasoning* (Hillsdale, NJ: Lawrence Erlbaum Associates).
Robson, C. (2002) *Real-World Research* (Oxford, UK: Blackwell Publishing, 2nd edn).
Rogers, E.M. (1962) *Diffusion of Innovation* (New York: The Free Press).
Rotmans, J. (2003) *Transitiemanagement: Sleutel voor een Duurzame Samenleving* (Assen, Netherlands: Van Gorcum).
—— (2005) *Maatschappelijke Innovatie: Tussen Droom en Werkelijkheid Staat Complexiteit* (Inaugural Lecture; Rotterdam, Netherlands: Drift).
Rowley, T.J. (1997) 'Moving beyond Dyadic Ties: A Network Theory of Stakeholder Influences', *Academy of Management Review* 22.4: 887-910.
Russell, S.J., and P. Norvig (1995) *Artificial Intelligence: A Modern Approach* (Upper Saddle River, NJ: Prentice Hall) .
Sauvante, M. (2001) 'The "Triple Bottom Line": A Boardroom Guide', *NACD Director's Monthly* 25.11: 2-6.
Savery, J.R., and T.M. Duffy (2001) *Problem-Based Learning: An Instructional Model and its Constructivist Framework* (University of Indiana, CRLT Technical Report No. 16-01).
Schank, R.C. (1982) *Dynamic Memory: A Theory of Reminding and Learning in Computers and People* (Cambridge, UK: Cambridge University Press).
Schecter, D. (1991) 'Critical Systems Thinking in the 1980s: A Connective Summary', in R.L. Flood and M.C. Jackson (eds.), *Critical Systems Thinking: Directed Readings* (Chichester, UK: John Wiley): 213-26.
Schellekens, W. (2003) *Leiderschap, Keuze: Slachtofferrol of Voortrekker?* (Presentatie Congres Kennisbeter delen II; Utrecht, Netherlands: Kwaliteitsinstituut voor de Gezondheidszorg CBO).

Scheper, W. (2004) *Innoveren van Medische Vervolgopleidingen: De Ontwikkeling van een Innovatiedraaiboek*, master's thesis, University of Groningen, Netherlands.
Schlegelmilch, B.B., and T.C. Chini (2003) 'Knowledge Transfer between Marketing Functions in Multinational Companies: A Conceptual Model', *International Business Review* 12.2: 215-32.
Schreiber, G., H. Akkermans, A. Anjewierden, R. de Hoog, N. Shadbolt, W. Van de Velde and B. Wielinga (2000) *Knowledge Engineering and Management: The CommonKADS Methodology* (Cambridge, MA: MIT Press).
Schumpeter, J.A. (1934) *The Theory of Economic Development* (Cambridge, MA: Harvard University Press).
Senge, P.M. (1990) *The Fifth Discipline: The Art and Practice of the Learning Organization* (New York: Currency Doubleday).
Senker, J. (1995) 'Tacit Knowledge and Models of Innovation', *Industrial and Corporate Change* 4.2: 425-47.
Sennett, R. (1998) *The Corrosion of Character: The Personal Consequences of Work in the New Capitalism* (New York: Norton).
Sessions, G. (1995) *Deep Ecology for the 21st Century* (Boston, MA: Shambala).
Shannon, C.E. (1948) 'The Mathematical Theory of Communication', *Bell Systems Technical Journal* 27: 379-423.
Simon, H.A. (1945) *Administrative Behaviour* (New York: The Free Press).
—— (1960) *The New Science of Management Decision* (Englewood Cliffs, NJ: Prentice Hall).
—— (1969) *The Sciences of the Artificial* (Cambridge, MA: MIT Press).
—— (1973) 'The Structure of Ill-structured Problems', *Artificial Intelligence* 4: 181-201.
—— (1977) *The New Science of Management Decision* (Englewood Cliffs, NJ: Prentice Hall, rev. edn).
Smolensky, P. (1988) 'On the Proper Treatment of Connectionism', *Behavioural and Brain Sciences* 11: 1-74.
Song, M.X., and M.M. Montoya-Weiss (1998) 'Critical Development Activities for Really New versus Incremental Products', *Journal of Product Innovation Management* 15.2: 124-35.
Sorge, A. (2001) 'Organisation Behaviour', in A. Sorge and M. Warner (eds.), *The IEBM Handbook of Organisational Behaviour* (London: International Thomson Press).
—— and M. Warner (eds.) (2001) *The IEBM Handbook of Organisational Behaviour* (London: International Thomson Press).
Stacey, R.D. (1996) *Strategic Management and Organisational Dynamics: The Challenge* (London: Pitman).
Stanford Medical Informatics (2004) 'The Protégé Ontology Editor and Knowledge Acquisition System', retrieved 2 September 2004, from protege.stanford.edu.
Starbuck, W.H. (1992) 'Learning by Knowledge Intensive Firms', *Journal of Management Studies* 29: 713-40.
Tansley, D.S.W., and C.C. Hayball (1993) *Knowledge-Based Systems Analysis and Design* (New York: Prentice Hall).
Theunissen, N.C.M., R.F. Friele and J.F.E.M. Keijsers (2003) 'Implementeren door kennismanagement: Theorie en praktijk', in J. Ravensbergen (ed.), *In Zicht: Nieuwe wegen voor implementatie* (Assen, Netherlands: Koninklijke Van Gorcum).
Thompson, J.D. (1967) *Organizations in Action* (New York: McGraw-Hill).
Tricot, A., and C. Bastien (1996) 'La Conception d'Hypermédias pour l'Apprentissage: Structurer des Conaissances Rationellement ou Fonctionellement?', in E. Bruillard, J.-M. Baldner and G.L. Baron (eds.), *Hypermédias et Apprentissages* (Paris: Presses de l'INRP/EPI): 57-72.
Turban, E., J.E. Aronson and N. Bolloju (2001) *Decision Support Systems and Intelligent Systems* (Upper Saddle River, NJ: Prentice Hall).
Tweede Kamer (Parliament) (2000) *Noten Tweede Kamer 29* (Report No. TK 29-2530; The Hague, Netherlands).
Ulrich, W. (1983) *Critical Heuristics of Social Planning: A New Approach to Practical Philosophy* (Chichester, UK: John Wiley).
—— (1987) 'Critical Heuristics of Social Systems Design', *European Journal of Operational Research* 31.3: 276-83.

—— (1993) 'Some Difficulties of Ecological Thinking, Considered from a Critical Systems Perspective: A Plea for Critical Holism', *Systems Practice* 6.6: 583-611.

—— (2003) 'Beyond Methodology Choice: Critical Systems Thinking as Critically Systemic Discourse', *Journal of the Operational Research Society* 54.4: 325-42.

Valiant, L.G. (1984) 'A Theory of the Learnable', *Communication of the ACM* 27: 1,134-42.

Van Berkel, K. (2002) *Levende Organisaties* (Antwerp, Belgium: Business Contact).

Van Dale (1996) *Handwoordenboek van Hededaags Nederlands* (Zutphen, Netherlands: Koninklijke Wohrmann).

Van de Ven, A.H.V., D.E. Polley, R. Garud and S. Venkataraman (1999) *The Innovation Journey* (New York: Oxford University Press).

Van den Broek, H. (2001) *On Agent Co-operation: The Relevance of Cognitive Plausibility for Multiagent Simulation Models of Organisations*, SOM PhD Thesis, University of Groningen, Netherlands.

Van der Laan, G. (2001) *Leren van Gevallen* (Utrecht, Netherlands: SWP).

—— (2002a) *CasusConsult: Op Weg Naar een Methodiek* (SPH maandblad; Amsterdam: Uitgeverij SWP).

—— (2002b) *Moderne Technologie als Metafoor* (Eindhoven, Netherlands: Fontys Hogeschool).

Van der Plaats, A. (1994) *Geriatrie: Een Spel van Evenwicht* (Assen, Netherlands: Van Gorcum; Dekker & Van de Vegt).

Van der Putten, T. (2005) *Van CasusConsult Naar een Kennismanagementsysteem voor de GGZ*, master's thesis, University of Groningen, Netherlands.

Van der Spek, R. (2004) 'Een kennisgerichte strategie', in C. Stam (ed.), *Productiviteit van de kenniswerker: Wegwijzer in kennismanagement* (Noordwijk, Netherlands: de Baak-Management Centrum VNO-NCW).

——, J. Hofer-Alfeis and J. Kingma (2002) 'The Knowledge Strategy Process', in C.W. Holsapple (ed.), *Handbook on Knowledge Management* (Heidelberg, Germany: Springer Verlag).

—— and J. Kingma (1999) 'Achieving Successful Knowledge Management Initiatives', in *Liberating Knowledge: Business Guide of Confederation of British Industry* (London: Caspian Publishing): 20-30.

—— and A. Spijkervet (1995) *Knowledge Management: Dealing Intelligently with Knowledge* (Utrecht, Netherlands: Kenniscentrum CIBIT).

Van der Werf, M.P.C. (2005) *Leren in het Studiehuis: Consumeren, construeren, engageren?* (Inaugural Lecture, University of Groningen, Netherlands).

Van Ees, H., and Th. Postma (2002) 'An Enquiry into the Nature of the Relationship between Corporate Governance and Corporate Innovation', paper presented at the conference *Corporate Governance and Firm Organisation*, Oslo, November 2002.

Van Haren, R. (2005) *Innovatie Adoptie Door Telers: Lerend Veranderen of Veranderend Leren* (Groningen, Netherlands: Academie voor Management, University of Groningen).

Van Houten, E.J. (1994) *Anderhalve eeuw Aardappelzetmeelindustrie* (Veendam, Netherlands: AVEBE).

Van Muijen, J.J. (1994) *Organisatiecultuur en Oorganisatieklimaat*, PhD thesis, VU, Amsterdam, Netherlands.

——, P.L. Koopman and K.B.J. De Witte (1996) *Focus op Organisatiecultuur* (Schoonhoven, Netherlands: Academic Service).

Van Raaij, E.M. (2001) *The Implementation of a Market Orientation* (Enschede, Netherlands: Twente University Press).

Van Wezel, W., and R.J. Jorna (2002) 'Planning, Anticipatory Systems and Kinds of Actors', in D.M. Dubois (ed.), *Computing Anticipatory Systems: Casys 2001* (Melville, NY: American Institute of Physics Conference Proceedings): 411-23.

——, R.J. Jorna and A. Meystel (eds.) (2006) *Planning in Intelligent Systems: Aspects, Motivations and Methods* (New York: Wiley Interscience).

Van Yperen, T.A. (2003) *Gaandeweg: Werken aan de Effectiviteit van de Jeugdzorg* (Utrecht, Netherlands: University of Utrecht/NIZW).

Van Zon, H., and K. Kuipers (2002) *Geschiedenis en duurzame ontwikkeling: Duurzame ontwikkeling in historisch perspectief* (Nijmegen, Netherlands: Netwerk Duurzaam Hoger Onderwijs).

Verburg, H. (2001) *Kennis en Kenniscentra in de GGZ* (Utrecht, Netherlands: Trimbos Institute).

—— (2003) 'Nieuwe Kennisinfrastructuur Krijgt in de GGZ Geleidelijk Vorm', *Health Management Forum* 12: 18-20.

Vicente, K.J. (1999) *Cognitive Work Analysis* (Mahwah, NJ: Lawrence Erlbaum Associates).

Visser, A., and A. Gaarthuis (2003) 'Cascade: Een Voorbeeld van Case-Based Learning' in *Maatwerk, Vakblad voor Maatschappelijk Werk* 2003 (1) (February 2003): 7-10.

Volberda, H.W., and F.A.J. van den Bosch (2004) *Rethinking the Dutch Innovation Agenda: Management and Organisation Matter Most* (Rotterdam, Netherlands: Erasmus Strategic Renewal Centre).

Volterra, V. (1959) *Theory of Functionals and of Integral and Integro-differential Equations* (New York, NJ: Dover)

Von Bertalanffy, L. (1951) 'An Outline of General System Theory', *British Journal for the Philosophy of Science* 1.2: 134-65.

—— (1968) *General Systems Theory: Foundations, Development, Applications* (New York: George Braziller Inc.).

Von Glaserfeld, E. (1989) 'Cognition, Construction of Knowledge and Teaching', *Synthese* 80: 121-40.

Von Hippel, E. (1988) *The Sources of Innovation* (Oxford, UK: Oxford University Press).

Von Krogh, G., I. Nonaka and I. Kazuo (2000) *Enabling Knowledge Creation* (Oxford, UK: Oxford University Press).

Vos, J.F.J. (2003) 'Corporate Social Responsibility and the Identification of Stakeholders', *Corporate Social Responsibility and Environmental Management* 10: 141-52.

Waalkens, J. (2006) *Building Dynamic Capabilities in the Construction Sector*, SOM PhD thesis, University of Groningen, Netherlands.

Waddell, S. (2002) 'Societal Learning: Creating Big-systems Change', *The Systems Thinker* 12.10.

Waern, Y. (1989) *Cognitive Aspects of Computer Supported Task* (Chichester, UK: John Wiley).

WBCSD (World Business Council for Sustainable Development) (2005) *Scoping and Construction Phase During 2004 for the Council Initiative Sustainable Health Systems* (Geneva: WBCSD).

WCED (World Commission on Environment and Development) (1987) *Our Common Future* (Oxford, UK: Oxford University Press).

Weggeman, M.C.D. (2000) *Kennismanagement: De Praktijk* (Schiedam, Netherlands: Scriptum).

—— (2003) 'Doorpolderen leidt tot stilstand', *NRC Handelsblad* (Rotterdam), 11 January 2003: 4.

Wenger, E.C. (1998) *Communities of Practice: Learning, Meaning and Identity* (Cambridge, UK: Cambridge University Press).

West, M.A., and J.L. Farr (1990) *Innovation and Creativity at Work: Psychological and Organisational Strategies* (Chichester, UK: John Wiley).

Wevers, J. (2004) *De Duurzaamheid van een Organisatie: Ontwikkeling van Leren en Leren van Ontwikkeling*, master's thesis, University of Groningen, Netherlands.

Wheelwright, S.C., and K.B. Clark (1992) *Revolutionising Product Development: Quantum Leaps in Speed, Efficiency and Quality* (New York: The Free Press).

Wierenga, J.E. (2004) *BioSoil Project Duurzaam Saneren*, master's thesis, Rijks University, Groningen, Netherlands.

Williamson, O.E. (1975) *Markets and Hierarchies: Analysis and Anti-trust Implications* (New York: The Free Press).

Willmot, H. (1989) 'OR as a Problem Situation: From Soft Systems Methodology to Critical Science', in M.C. Jackson, P. Keys and S.A. Cropper (eds.), *Operational Research and the Social Sciences* (New York: Plenum): 65-78.

Wilson, R.A., and F.C. Keil (1999) *The MIT Encyclopaedia of the Cognitive Sciences* (Cambridge, MA: MIT Press, 2nd edn).

Wolfe, R.A., and D.S. Putler (2002) 'How Tight are the Ties that Bind Stakeholder Groups?', *Organisation Science* 13.1: 64-80.

Wood, D.J. (1991) 'Corporate Social Performance Revisited', *Academy of Management Review* 16.4: 691-719.

Wright, P.C., R.E. Fields and M.D. Harrison (2000) 'Analysing Human–Computer Interaction as Distributed Cognition: The Resources Model', *Human–Computer Interaction* 15: 1-41.

Zuurbier, W. (2004) *Kennisinnovatie: Een Marketing en Innovatieperspectief op Kennismanagement* (Noordwijkerhout, Netherlands: Congresbundel Document 2004, 4 November 2004).

About the contributors

Marjolein Achterkamp (Dr. ir. M.C. Achterkamp). Marjolein Achterkamp is Assistant Professor at the Faculty of Management and Organisation, University of Groningen, the Netherlands. In 1994 she obtained her MSc degree in Applied Mathematics, and in 1999 she received her PhD in Sociology on the subject of influence strategies in collective decision-making. Currently her research focuses on sustainable innovation (in particular, stakeholder involvement), innovation in medical education, and research methodology. She teaches various courses on research methodology.

Else Boutkan (Ir. E. Boutkan). Else Boutkan works as an independent consultant on a number of issues related to sustainability. Her focus areas are strategic networks between business and not-for-profit organisations as NGOs and government and the related stakeholder interactions. Else Boutkan received a MSc degree in Chemical Engineering at the Delft University of Technology in 1993 and an MBA degree in General Management at the Rotterdam School of Management in 2000. From 1993 to 1999 she worked at Heineken Research and Development, on projects on environmental affairs, among others.

Cees van Dijk (Drs. C.N. van Dijk). Cees van Dijk was the project leader of the Synthetics House (KunstStoffenHuis) project. Having obtained his master's degree in business administration at the University of Groningen in 1992, he worked as a consultant and project manager for organisations in the profit, as well as not-for-profit, sector. He has carried out projects in the area of quality management, process redesign, business development and organisational change and development. He has worked for consultancy firms such as ACM and Horvath & Partners and has participated in research at the Faculty of Management and Organisation in the field of sustainable innovation. Currently he is responsible for International Implementation at ADP Claims Services/Audatex, creating sustainable claims communities.

Jo van Engelen (Prof. dr. ir. J.M.L van Engelen). Jo van Engelen studied Physics and Mathematics at Eindhoven University of Technology and also Management and Organisation Studies at Twente University. He received his PhD from Twente University on Information Technology in Marketing Management. He has three years' experience as a management consultant and six years' experience at Océ–Van der Grinten (Copying and Printing) in a number of management functions. Since 1991 he has been chaired professor of Business Development and Business Research Methods at the University of Groningen and consultant and board member for several leading companies in the Netherlands. Since 2003 he has been an executive board member of the Royal Dutch ANWB.

Niels Faber (Ir. drs. N.R. Faber). In 1999, Niels Faber received his Master of Science in computer science at the University of Twente. Immediately thereafter, he studied industrial engineering at the Faculty of Management and Organisation of the University of Groningen, which he completed in 2002. He remained at the Faculty of Management and Organisation for PhD research on sustainable innovation and decision support which will be completed in 2006.

Henk Hadders (Mr. H. Hadders). Henk Hadders is a Bachelor of Economics and studied Dutch Law at the University of Utrecht. In 2004 he resigned as Member of the Board of Directors of the Mental Health Institute GGZ Drenthe. For over 25 years he contributed to the building and renewal of mental healthcare in the Province of Drenthe in Holland. He was present at the inception of many national innovative breakthrough projects, such as the Substitution Project. Based on the research of the Knowledge Management Consortium International (KMCI) and the National Initiative for Sustainable Development (NIDO), he is currently conducting a PhD project regarding Societal Knowledge Management. This research combines knowledge management at this level with learning environments (sustainable innovation) and governance structures (sustainable inquiry), in order to realise more sustainable outcomes in future mental healthcare.

Rob van Haren (Dr. ir. J.F. van Haren). Rob van Haren works for the Dutch starch potato processing industry, AVEBE. He is a research manager responsible for production chain innovation programmes. Sustainability is the major motivation for innovations for AVEBE. He previously worked as senior scientist agro-ecology at Plant Research International in Wageningen, Netherlands, where his main duty was to develop crop growth simulation models and decision-support systems for different crops and agro-ecozones. He did his PhD in theoretical biology at the Vrije Universiteit in Amsterdam and his MSc in biology in Wageningen.

René Jorna (Prof. dr. R.J. Jorna). René Jorna is full professor in Knowledge Management and Cognition at the Faculty of Management and Organisation of the University of Groningen. He studied Analytic Philosophy and Logic (Master in 1981) and Experimental Psychology (Master in 1982) and did his PhD in 1989 in Cognitive Science on knowledge representation. His research and publications address cognition, semiotics, knowledge management, sustainable innovation, knowledge technology and decision-support systems especially related to planning and scheduling. In 1990 he published *Knowledge Representation and Symbols in the Mind* (Tübingen: Stauffenburg) and in 1994 *Semiotic Aspects of Artificial Intelligence* (Berlin: Walter de Gruyter). From 1990 to 1995 he was manager of a large research project on planning and scheduling (DISKUS), which resulted in commercial software and five dissertations. From 2001 until 2004 he was programme manager of the NIDO project on Sustainable Innovation. In 2006 the book *Planning in Intelligent Systems* was published (with van Wezel and Meystel; John Wiley). He supervises seven PhD projects on sustainable innovation, planning, scheduling and cognition and social simulation.

Han van Kasteren (Dr. ir. J.M.N. van Kasteren). Han van Kasteren studied chemical engineering and in 1990 received his PhD degree at the Technical University Eindhoven. In 1990 he worked at the Inter-University Environmental Institute Brabant (IMB). From 1991 he has been working as assistant professor at the TU Eindhoven, in the field of environmental technology, specialising in solid waste technology. From 1996 to 1999 he was director of the Polymer Recycling Institute (PRI). At PRI economic and technical feasibility studies of the recycling of wastes are carried out. Since 1998 he has also been founder and chairman of Knowledge Platform Recycling (KPR), a co-operation between industry and research institutes. From 1999 to 2004 he was director of the KunstStoffenHuis at TU Eindhoven, an intermediate between the polymer industry and knowledge institutes. Since 2004 he has been part-time senior advisor of Telos, the Brabant Centre for Sustainable Development, in the field of sustainable energy and innovation. Since 2005 he has also been working part-time as a senior advisor for small and medium-sized enterprises in the field of expertise transfer for Innovation Lab (United Brains), an intermediate between SMEs and expertise institutes in Eindhoven.

Derk Jan Kiewiet (Dr. D.J. Kiewiet). Derk Jan Kiewiet studied mathematics (BSc) and cognitive psychology (BSc and MSc), and has a PhD in management and organisation studies (his PhD is on a mathematical foundation for a decision-support system for information planning). At present he is working at the Faculty of Management and Organisation, University of Groningen, the Netherlands, where he gives courses in business methodology and business development. His current research interests are measurement issues of complex concepts such as sustainability and success, planning, organisational learning, teamwork in product development and methodology.

Laura Maruster (Dr. ir. L. Maruster). Laura Maruster studied Computer Science at the University of Timisoara, Western Romania. She received her PhD degree from Eindhoven University of Technology, the Netherlands, with research on a machine learning approach to understand business processes. Currently, she is a researcher at the Faculty of Management and Organisation, University of Groningen, the Netherlands, working in the field of sustainable innovation. She is also collaborating with the Dutch gas company Gasunie on a Casimir project. Her research interests include sustainable innovation, knowledge management, induction of machine learning and statistical models, process modelling and process mining.

Kristian Peters (Drs. K. Peters MSc). Kristian Peters is a PhD student studying sustainable innovation and decision-support systems. He did his master's in Technology Management at the University of Groningen.

Jan Pols (Dr. J. Pols). Jan Pols (MD, PhD) studied medicine at Groningen University. After several years of internships he continued his career in medical education. Among other things he has developed and introduced a clinical skills programme for the problem-based learning curriculum for undergraduate medical education at Groningen University. He wrote his PhD thesis on research into professional training of medical students. In the last few years he has been working as a senior staff member of the Wenckebach Institute of the University Medical Centre Groningen and is involved in innovations in postgraduate medical training.

Nico Rommes (Drs. N.J. Rommes). Nico Rommes graduated in psychology (1973, University of Groningen). He spent four years on research into human relations in work and organisation. He spent 20 years in human resource management for Dutch telecom and a number of hospitals. In the past ten years he has been a consultant in management and occupational health. He has been involved in all kinds of staff development activities and is increasingly interested in knowledge creation and transfer of knowledge in organisations.

Floortje Smit (Drs. F. Smit MA). Floortje Smit (1979) is a freelance editor. She has a degree in journalism and history from the University of Groningen. Prior work includes articles on sustainability for the Faculty of Management and Organisation at Groningen. She has also written for (national) newspapers and websites and worked as a reporter for the radio.

Janita Vos (Dr. J.F.J. Vos). Janita Vos is an assistant professor at the Faculty of Management and Organisation, University of Groningen, the Netherlands. She received her PhD (1993) in Management and Organisation Science on the subject of the organisational problem of privatisation. Currently, her research focuses on stakeholder management (in particular, stakeholder identification) and cognitive mapping as a means for conceptualising sustainability. She teaches various courses on the subject of Organisational Change and Business Development.

Jan Waalkens (Dr. J. Waalkens). Jan Waalkens is currently director of the Planning Expertise and Innovation Centre (PEIC). From 2001 to 2006 he was lecturer and PhD candidate at the Faculty of Management and Organisation at the University of Groningen. His PhD research was on absorptive capacity and innovation of architectural and engineering medium-sized enterprises. Before he worked for the Faculty of Management and Organisation, he was senior project manager and organised postgraduate courses. He started his academic career in the field of Economic Geography, which he studied at the University of Groningen.

Koos Zagema (Ir. K. Zagema). Koos Zagema (1965) graduated in 1991 as an engineer in management studies from the University of Twente. In the 1990s he worked for the national Dutch Forestry Commission, the Dutch Tax and Customs Administration and Panfox (information architects) as an architect of business processes. Together with two partners in 2001 he founded Pernosco, a consultancy firm involved in the management of sustainable innovations. The key to successful sustainable innovation is the collaboration between businesses, governmental organizations, NGOs and knowledge institutes. Pernosco (Latin, 'I examine, learn thoroughly') has developed models and working methods for project management, knowledge management, competence management and quality management to improve this collaboration.

Index of subjects

4 M Method   264

Absolute approach to sustainability   36
Absorptive capacity of organisations   24
Abstract artefacts   35
Abstract knowledge   79, 82
Accelerating knowledge by learning   93
Accessibility of knowledge   94
'Accommodation'   173
Actions   75
Actively involved, in innovation project   99, 107
Actors   23, 42
   multi-actor system   327
Adaptive organisation   49
Added value, alliances   263
Administration   62
   administrative innovations   20
Aggregation levels   10, 42, 51, 316
   measuring innovations   23-24
Agriculture   204-26
Agrobiokon research programme   207-209, 213
Alliances
   knowledge sharing in   261, 266
Analytic tasks   63
Aristotle's principle of the absolute   36
Artefacts   35
   artefact level of design   180
   concrete   35
   non-material   58-59, 72
   organisation   57
   physical   58
   types of   58
Artificial systems   317
ATOL   283
Authority   66
Automated (compiled) knowledge   81

AVEBE   204-26
   knowledge domains   305
   starch potato production   204-26
   sustainability   300

Balance, sustainability   314-16
Big River Innovation   167, 291-92, 304, 334
Biosoil   136-47
   knowledge domains   304
   sustainable remediation   136-47
   sustainability   299
Bird's-eye view   62, 76
Boekelo Decor   158
Bureaucracy   65, 68
Business architectures, development of   48
Business development   70
Business practices   298-302

Case-based reasoning (CBR)   125-33
   and RBR   129
   case descriptions   123-26
   experts   125
   indexing   126, 128
   keywords   126
   maintenance   62
   mental healthcare   240
   missing data   131
   selection mechanism   126
   solutions   131
Case storytelling   241
CasusConsult   124, 240-46, 293, 305
Change
   aspect of innovation   17, 21
   in organisations   8, 72
Chemicals   20, 164-85
   knowledge domain, DSS   169

364 SUSTAINABLE INNOVATION

Choice phase 216
Circles, sociocracy 279-80
Clan, organisational form 64-67, 70, 332, 343
Classification principles 9
Clients, curriculum revision 252-54
Codes 83-84
Coded knowledge 73, 79, 83-84, 90
Codification strategy 241
Cognition 45-46, 59
  cognition levels 52
  cognitive architecture 59
  cognitive map of sustainability 111, 121
  cognitive mapping 111
  cognitive schemata 173
  cognitive science 45
  cognitive system 78
  cognitive task analysis 63
  cognitively impenetrable knowledge 81
Cohesive group 47
Collective learning 48
Collective memory 49
CommonKADS method 124, 176-80, 326
Communication 62
  communication model, concept level of design 179
Community 47
  community/organisational learning 48
  interaction, in communities 47
Complex adaptive systems 54
Complex systems 54-55
Complexity, deliberate 174
Component loadings 115
Concept level of design 179
Concrete artefacts 35
Concrete knowledge 79, 82
Consent, sociocracy 279
Constructs 35
Contamination, soil 136-47
Context level of design 179
Context of knowledge 231
Contracts, drawing up 62
Co-operation
  improvement 272
  sustainability 259-74
Co-ordination 57, 60, 64, 75
  co-ordination mechanisms 64
Corporate governance 29-30
Corporate repository 49
Corporate social responsibility (CSR) 29
Creativity, definition 18
Critical systems thinking (CST) 106-107
  roles of involvement 106
Culture, organisational 66

Data 77-78
  analysis 114-15
  collection 112-13
    object order 112
  preparation 113
Decision-making
  definition 169
  information sources (for potato growth) 217
  process 170
  sociocracy 278

Decision-support systems (DSSs) 219-20
  paper production innovation 169-86
  starch potato production innovation 208-26
  testing protocol 180
Declarative knowledge 79
Deep ecology 33-34
Deliberate complexity 174
Description levels 42-56
Design
  context level 179
  design phase 216
  designing a prototype 91
  simplicity 174
Discontinuous innovations 21
Discourse management 164
Dispersed knowledge 79, 82
Distrust 66
Durability, concept 31
Dynamic balance 37
Dynamic systems theory 53
Dynamic view of sustainability 37

Ecodesign 189
Ecology 33-34
  deep 33-34
  shallow 33-34
Ecosystem, equilibrium 317
Education innovation, UMCG 254
Efficiency, organisational 72, 232
Emergentism 45
Employees 8, 9, 16-17, 307, 309, 328
  appointing 17
  at Biosoil 138, 142
  at Endenburg Elektrotechnics 284
  at Grontmij 57-58, 60, 71, 121, 137, 259-61, 265-68, 273-74
  laying off 21, 38, 276, 313
  learning 162, 166, 173-74, 309, 330-31, 334, 344
  and Optichem 166
  at Philips 188, 190, 191, 192, 193, 194 201
  safety 176, 180
  and sociocracy 285, 303-304
  at Reekx 276-77, 282
  training 155, 161, 166, 169, 282-83
  see also Personnel
Empowerment, definition 47
Endenburg Elektrotechnics 278, 284
Endurability, concept 31
Entities 35, 42, 51
Entropy 315
Environment and sustainability 30
Equilibrium 315
Evidence-based knowledge 233
Explicit knowledge 79, 80
Exploitation, problem-solving 25
Exploration, problem-solving 25

Falsificationism 333
Farmers
  potato 204-26
  yields 209
Feudal system, organisational form 65-67, 70, 332, 343

INDEX OF SUBJECTS 365

First-order learning 7
Flexibility, organisational 72, 232
Flowlight 158-59
Functional classification, tasks 64
Functional structures 174

Game changers 21
Goals 75
Grontmij 57, 259-74
    case 113
    co-operation 259-74
    knowledge domains 305
    identification of stakeholders 271
    sustainability 300
Group, aggregation level 47

Helicopter view 62, 76
Homeostasis
    concept 53
    sustainability 314
Humans
    behaviour, tasks 327
    brain, information-processing system 59
    human component, in organisation 59
    human decision-making 215-18
    human–computer interface, DSS 174-76, 219-20
Hypertext organisation 48

Identification of stakeholders
    at Grontmij 271
    identification method 99
Imitative innovations 22
Impenetrable knowledge 81
Incremental innovations 22
Indexing, CBR 126
    organising 128
Individuals
    aggregation level 47
    individual learning 47
    multi-actor system 327
Inductive process 127
Industrial parks, life-cycle 270
Information 77
    sources, potato growth 217
    units 78
Innovation
    administrative 20
    AVEBE projects 225
    clusters, KunstStoffenHuis 160
    concept 4
    definitions 17
    dimensions of newness 21
    discontinuous 21
    imitative 22
    importance of 16
    incremental 22
    marketing 20
    measuring 23-24
    newness 17, 21
    Optichem Infonet project 184
    in organisations 71
    performance improvement 17, 21
    phases within 18

Philips 201
positive and negative sides 2
of production processes 19
project
    involved parties 99
    phases 101
    phases of involvement 108
radical 21
really new 21
service 20
technological 20
trajectory 251
    paper production 169
    synthetics 153
transaction 21
types 19
Inside knowledge 233
Institutional factors 65
Integrated organisational processes 61
Intellectual capital, knowledge accumulation 231
Inter-organisational learning 50
Invention, concept 19

Justified true belief 78

KCSI (Knowledge Creation for Sustainable Innovation)
    programme 2-14
    objectives 12
Knowledge 9, 59, 77
    acquisition 123
        CBR and RBR 129
    areas 237
        assessment of 239
        identification of 237
    automated (compiled) 81
    availability of 94
    business projects 304
    coded 73, 79, 83-84, 90
    classical definition 78
    concrete 79, 82
    content 78
        concept 10
    context of 231
    conversion 93
        processes 48
    creation 5, 26, 90
    cycle 230
    declarative 79
    development
        case 250-56
        sociocracy 284
    dispersion 79, 82, 91
        not dispersed 82
        paper production 168
    distinction 10
    domain 316
    element 326
    elicitation, DSS 173
    evidence-based 233
    expansion
        quantitative and qualitative 330
        by learning 93
    explicit 79, 80

impenetrable 81
implicit 79, 80
    sharing of 90
importance of 26
infrastructure 94, 230, 307
inside 233
institute, synthetics innovation 150
main functions model 52
management 88, 308
    action plan 236, 239
    mental healthcare 233, 258
    technology 308
model, concept level of design 179
one-dimensional 82
outcome 231
personal 79, 82
phases, in innovations 26
policy, mental healthcare 230
procedural 79
qualitative, changing 93
representation 326
sensory 73, 82, 90
    sharing of 90
sharing 250
    alliances 261
    sociocracy 284
snapshot 88
space 86
sustainability, mental healthcare 227-46
of sustainability (KoS) 5, 8, 11, 325, 20, 46, 72, 95, 96, 123, 135, 136, 144, 185, 202, 204, 265, 288, 294-95, 301, 303, 318-20, 325, 330
    alliances 265
    definition 5
    and farmers 225-26
    leap projects 11, 13
    remediation 146-47
    and sociocracy 275
systems 123
    development 130
    sustainable starch potato production 204-26
tacit 79, 80
    sharing of 90
theoretical 73, 84, 90
three-dimensional 84
time-to-knowledge 234
transfer 231
two-dimensional 83
types 52, 78, 306
    classification 85
    concept 10
    conversion 93-94
    definitions 73
    organisational forms 65
uncoded 79
workers 51, 308
Knowledge Centre, Philips Environmental Services (PES) 190
Knowledge-guided process 127
KoS
    see Knowledge → of sustainability
KunstStoffenHuis (KSH) 148-64
    knowledge domains 304

knowledge institute 160-61
sustainability 299
synthetics innovation 148-64

Labour/trade unions 194, 206, 284, 313
Leap projects 294
    sustainability 11, 13
    synthetics innovation 150
Learning 47, 309, 328
    CBR 132
    constructivism 173
    definition 92
    first-order 7
    individual 47
    innovation, UMCG 254
    learning community, definition 48
    learning organisation 8, 47
    inter-organisational 50
    second-order 7
    second-loop 48
    single-loop 48
    theory of the learnable 173
    types 49
Levels of aggregation 10, 42, 51, 316
    measuring innovations 23-24
Levels of description 42-56
Living organisation 283
LWB Eindhoven Ltd 157-58, 163

Machine bureaucracy, organisational form 65-66, 70, 332, 343-44
Main function model 52
    policy-making dimension 52
    production dimension 52
Management 66
    of knowledge 88, 308
Mapping 157
Market, organisational form 65-68, 70-71, 332, 343
Marketing 20
Measuring
    innovations 23-24
    methods, social sustainability 199
Medical Association, postgraduate medical training 249
Mental healthcare
    knowledge domains 305
    knowledge sustainability 227-46
    sustainability 300
Mental images, assessing 111-22
Mental representations 59
Model human processor (MHP) 171-72
Modifying tasks 63
Monitoring 62
Multi-actor perspective 77
Multi-actor system 23, 42, 60, 71, 76
    actors 327-28
Multi-compartment stochiometric dynamic crop growth model 208
Multi-dimensional scaling analysis (MDSA) 121, 320
Multiple category co-ordinates 115-20

Natural systems 317-18
Nearest neighbour process 126, 127, 129

INDEX OF SUBJECTS 367

Negentropy 316
Netherlands Initiative for Sustainable Development
  see NIDO
Networks 42, 68, 70
  aggregation level 49
  management 49
NIDO (Netherlands Initiative for Sustainable
  Development) programme 4, 5
  AVEBE 213
  BioSoil 140
  Grontmij 261
  offload model 39
  Philips 190
Non-material artefacts 58-59, 72

Object model for product development 155
Offloading 10-11, 12, 14, 29, 37-41, 43, 55, 56, 72, 98,
  108, 110, 120, 136-37, 142-44, 185, 201, 289, 298, 310,
  311-23
  definition 37
  Grontmij 273
  homeostasis 314
  Reekx 276
  and soil remediation 144-47
  stakeholders 331
One-dimensional knowledge 82
Open enterprise 333
Open system 53
Optichem 165-85
  Infonet Project 123, 165-86
    DSS prototype 176
    paper production 167
  knowledge domains 304
  questionnaire 334
  sustainability 299
OPTIras™ 208-209, 213-14, 217, 221-24, 226
OPTIrob™ 217,18 222, 226
Organisations 57, 307
  adaptive 49
  aggregation level 48
  as artefact 58-73
  classification 8
  concept 8, 51
  culture 66
  definition 75
  flexibility 72, 232
  forms 70, 332
    six types
      clan 64-67, 70, 332, 343
      feudal system 65-67, 70, 332, 343
      machine bureaucracy 65-66, 70, 332,
        343-44
      professional bureaucracy 65-66, 68,
        70, 332, 343
      market 65-68, 70-71, 332, 343
      web 68, 70, 332, 343-44
  hypertext organisation 48
  ideal types 71
  interdependencies 64
  innovation 17
  knowledge types 65
  living organisation 283

main function model 52
  policy-making dimension 52
  production dimension 52
organisational learning 47
  as principle 58-73
  processes 61
    separated 61
  projects 294
  reasons to exist 9
  scope 232

Paper industry 165-86
Park management 270
Passively involved parties 324
  in innovation project 99, 107
Performance indicators, identification 237
Personalisation strategy 241
Personnel 17, 21, 49, 62, 169, 179, 244, 308
  changes 265
  see also Employees
Perturbation 173
Philips 187-203
  Knowledge Centre (PES) 190
  knowledge domains 304
  social sustainability 187-203
  sustainability 299
Planning 62
  definition 170
Polux 157
Polymer production 149
Pooled/common interdependency 65
Postgraduate medical training 248
Potato production 204-26
Power 66
Primary process 60
  knowledge in 10
Problems
  concept 25
  decomposition 171
  definition 170
  problem space 25, 171, 216
Problem-solving 24
  CBR 125
  definition 169
  exploitation 25
  exploration 25
  structured 216
Procedural knowledge 79
Process perspective
  on organisation 62
  sustainability 6-7
Processes 76
  description 76
Products
  development, object model 156
  dimension, main function model 52
  innovation 19
Production processes, innovation of 19
Professional bureaucracy, organisational form 65-66,
  68, 70, 332, 343
Prototypes
  Optichem Infonet project 176, 183

368 SUSTAINABLE INNOVATION

Qualitative expansion   330
Quantitative expansion   330

R&D department   16
Radical innovations   21
Really new innovation   21
Reciprocal interdependency   65
Recognise–act principle   172
Reduction in offload
   see Offloading
Reductionism   45
Redundancy
   see Employees → laying off
Reekx   274, 276-78
   and sociocracy   282-83, 294, 305, 307
Relative approach, sustainability   36
Relevant adoption-unity   18, 21
Remediation, soil   136-47
   legislation and government   139
   sustainable   136-47
Renewable energy   31
Representation, concept   78
Rule-based reasoning (RBR)   124, 129-32
   and CBR   129-30
   missing data   131
   solutions   131

Second-loop learning   48
Second-order learning   7
Second-order primary processes   61
Secondary process   60
   knowledge in   10
Sense making   95
Sensory knowledge   73, 82, 90
Sequential interdependency   65
Service innovations   20
Shallow ecology   33-34
Shareholders, interests   191
   see also Stakeholders
Single-category co-ordinates   115-19
Single fit   116
Single-loop learning   48
Singularly linked cluster   79
SMEs
   need for innovation   148, 159
Socially accountable entrepreneurship (SAE)   29
Social action model   51
Social capital, knowledge accumulation   231
Social developments   50
Social profit   275
Social sustainability   51, 321-45
   case   187-203
   indicators   193
      classification   198
Social-organisational developments   29-30
Society, aggregation level   50
Sociocracy   275-85
   circles   276, 279-80
   consent,   279
   double links   280
   elections   280
   Endenburg Elektrotechnics   284
   knowledge domains   305

knowledge sharing   284
Reekx   282-83, 294, 305, 307
SoK   275-85
   sustainability   300
Soil remediation   136-47
SoK
   see Sustainability → of knowledge
Spillover risks   265
SPSS analysis   114
Staff
   see Employees; Personnel
Stage-gate process   108
Stakeholders   98-110
   BioSoil   141
   curriculum revision   252
   definition   103, 105
   definitive   104
   groups
      classification   104
   identification
      Grontmij   271
      method   99
      problem   103
   interests, in organisation   191
   involvement roles   100, 106
   Philips   191
   reduction in offload   331
   social sustainability   323
   sustainability in alliances   269
Starch potato production   204-26
Structural identity   84
Sustainability
   absolute approach   36
   alliances   263
   AVEBE   207
   balance   314-16
   business projects   301
   components   33
   concept   5
   definition
      authors   10
      and concept   30
      WCED   10, 33
   dimensions   35
   dynamic view   37
   giving concrete form to   112
   ecological   30
   images, retrieving   112
   of knowledge (SoK)   7-8, 11-13, 26, 46, 72, 75, 93,
      95-96, 123, 133, 148, 202, 226, 246, 248, 275,
      282, 288, 289, 301, 303, 318-19, 325
      case   227-46
      compared with KoS   294-95
      definition   5
      leap projects   13
   leap projects   11
   learning   228
   measuring   120
   Optichem Infonet project   184
   paper production   168
      case   165-86
   parameters   141
   Philips   189, 201

process perspective   7
reduction in offload   312
relative approach   36
remediation   141
    case   136-47
social
    see Social sustainability
social-organisational developments   29
sociocracy   275-85
starch potato production   204-26
static view   37
Sustainable development   28
    static interpretation   7
Sustainable society
    see Social sustainability
Synthetic tasks   63
Synthetics Innovation Small Businesses   151, 161
Synthetics innovation, case   148-64
Systems   23, 42
    artificial   317
    complex   54-55
    complex adaptive   54
    concept   51
    homeostasis   314
    levels of aggregation   316
    systems perspective   51
    systems theory   53, 58, 106
    types   53

Tabaksblat Committee   29
Table of quantifications   116
Tacit knowledge   79, 80
    sharing of   90
Target groups   210

Tasks
    classification   62
    environment   218
Technology   308
    technological innovations   20
Terminology, development   91
Theoretical knowledge   73, 84, 90
Theory of the learnable   173
Thesaurus, knowledge-guided process   127
Three-dimensional knowledge   84
Time-to-knowledge   234
TIPSTAR™   208, 214, 226
Trade unions
    see Labour/trade unions
Transaction innovation   21
Triple bottom line   28, 33
Triple P (planet, profit, people)   5, 33, 298
Trust   66
Truth   78
'Tuning'   70
Two-dimensional knowledge   83

Ultimate good   36
UMCG (University Medical Centre Groningen)   247-58
    knowledge domains   305
    sustainability   300
    sustainable innovation   247-58
Uncertainty reduction, innovation trajectory   155
Uncoded knowledge   79

Value chain of paper production   166
Vertical reductionism   45

Web, organisational form   68, 70, 332, 343-44
'Why' chain   84

Index of names

Achterkamp, M.C. 98, 110, 247, 269
Ackerman, P.L. 173
Adelman, L. 169
Adriaanse, D.J. 52
Agle, B.R. 103
Alexander, P.A. 125
Anderson, R.J. 79
Andriole, S. 169
Argyris, C. 7, 268
Aristotle 36
Armengol, E. 124
Arocha, J.V. 124
Ashby, W.R. 42
Asper, C. 187

Baker, W. 231
Barletta, R. 124, 126
Bastien, C. 174
Beier, E.B. 173
Beitz, W. 109
Berg, M. 243
Berkel, K. van 283
Beth, E.W. 36
Bhatt, G.D. 231
Billet, S. 74
Block, P. 47
Boden, M.A. 18
Boeke, K. 278
Boisot, M.H. 64, 65, 67, 79, 82, 83, 332
Bolwijn, P.T. 71, 72
Bos, J.H. 166
Boulding, K.E. 51, 317, 320
Bourdieu, P. 231
Boutkan, E.J.M. 141
Bovenberg, A.L. 231
Bower, G.H. 91, 329
Breuker, J. 63, 124
Brundtland 38
Bull, M. 124
Bunge, M. 43
Burns, T.R. 23

Card, S.K. 169, 171, 172, 215, 327
Carson, R.L. 33
Castells, M. 50
Catalone, R. 22
Cavaleri, S.A. 233, 234
Checkland, P.B. 106
Choo, C.W. 95
Churchland, P.M. 45
Churchman, C.W. 106
Cijsouw, R.S. 3, 59, 79
Clark, K.B. 157
Clarkson, M.B.E. 103, 104
Coad, P. 156
Coase, R. H. 322
Cohen, W.M. 24, 265
Cooper, R.G. 19, 109, 149, 251
Csikszentmihalyi, M. 18

Daft, R.L. 61, 77
Damanpour, F. 19, 21
Davenport, T.H. 243
Davis, G.B. 64
De Groot, A.D. 12
De Groot, E.V. 221, 330
De Hoog, R. 241
De Leeuw, T. 53
Dendermonde, M. 206
Dennett, D.C. 44, 45
De Witte, K.B.J. 266
Donald, M. 84
Doppelt, B. 228
Dosi, G. 19
Duffy, T.M. 173
Duivenboden, H. 231

Edelman, L.F. 231
Edwards, P. 78
Elkington, J. 10, 32, 298
Endenburg, G. 275, 278, 279, 280

Faber, N.R. 31, 35, 37, 72, 321

INDEX OF NAMES

Farr, J.L.   18, 21, 330
Fastrez, P.   174
Fields, R.E.   175
Firestone, J.M.   233, 235, 241, 332, 333
Fodor, J.A.   45
Freeman, R.E.   103, 104, 191
Frissen, P.   231
Frooman, J.   103

Gaarthuis, A.   243
Garcia, R.   22
Gardner, H.   18
Gazendam, H.W.M.   59, 60, 64, 75, 89
Ghoshal, S.   231
Giel, R.   241
Gierl, L.   124
Gioia, D.A.   77
Glaser, J.   243
Gold, A.H.   231
Goodman, N.   78, 80, 83
Goodpaster, K.E.   104
Goodwin, P.   155
Govindarajan, V.   231
Grant, R.M.   72, 231, 232
Gray, B.   77
Greene, B.A.   173
Gupta, A.K.   231

Hadders, H.   176, 228
Hansen, M.T.   241
Harrison, M.D.   175
Hayball, C.C.   179
Healy, T.   28
Hedlund, G.   232
Helmhout, M.   60
Hendriks, A.A.J.   221
Hilgard, E.R.   91, 329
Hinds, P.J.   173
Hofer-Alfeis, J.   235
Holsapple, C.W.   169, 219
Hoogendoorn, Y.   124
Hübscher, H.   175

Isenberg, D.J.   77

Jackson, J.L.   82
Jentjens, V.L.M.   47
Jippes, E.   247, 254
Joenje, R.   234, 240, 241
Johnson, C.S.   109
Jones, C.   109
Jorna, R.J.   59, 62, 69, 77-80, 82 123, 169, 171, 176, 228, 238

Kanter, R.M.   24
Kaptein, M.   32
Keen, P.G.W.   169, 219
Keil, F.C.   169, 170
Kieras, D.E.   172
Kingma, J.   235, 236
Kirakowski, J.   180, 221
Klein, M.R.   169, 215, 219, 220
Kleinknecht, A.   22

Kleinschmidt, E.J.   19, 109
Klos, T.B.   76
Kolb, A.D.   47
Kolodner, J.L.   124, 125, 126
Koopman, P.L.   266
Kratzer, J.   23
Kumpe, T.   72

Lekanne Deprez, F.R.E.   243
Levert, T.   259
Levinthal, D.A.   24, 265
Lindenberg, C.   54
Linschoten, J.   80, 81
Lips, M.   231
Lit, A.C.   42, 53, 55
Lubbers, .   234
Luger, G.F.   220, 326, 328

Maljers, F.A.   261
Malotaux, P.Ch.A   52
March, J.G.   25, 74
Martens, P.   227
Maxwell, J.C.   315
McElroy, M.W.   6, 9, 34, 228, 233, 235, 321-333
Meadows, D.H.   35
Mennin, S.P.   109
Methlie, L.B.   169, 215, 219, 220
Meyer, D.E.   172
Meystel, A.   62
Michon, J.A.   82
Midgley, G.   106, 107
Mik, W.M.C.   55, 229
Miles, R.E.   24
Mintzberg, H.   64, 65, 67, 68, 332
Mitchell, R.K.   103, 104, 105
Moehr, J.R.   124
Moran, T.P.   169, 215, 327
Mowat, D.   109
Muller, P.C.   149, 153

Naess, A.   33
Nagel, E.   45
Nahapiet, J.   231
Newell, A.   18, 25, 43-45, 59, 74, 169-171, 214-16, 326-31
Nijkamp, P.   231
Nilsson, M.   124
Nohria, N.   241
Nonaka, I.   18, 23, 48, 89, 90
Nooteboom, B.   46, 77, 261, 265
Norman, D.A.   175
Norvig, P.   326, 328

O' Connor, G.C.   21
Olson, M.H.   64

Pahl, G.   109
Pantazi, S.V.   124
Patterson, M.   173
Peters, L.S.   21
Pfeffer, J.   173
Phillips, R.   104
Piaget, J.   92
Pieters, D.   221

Pintrich, P.R. 221, 330
Plato 36, 78
Plaza, E. 124
Plesk, P. 54, 228
Polanyi, M. 79-81
Poole, P.P. 77
Popper, K. 333
Porter, M. 23, 264, 331
Postma, T. 2
Postrel, S. 79
Puntambekar, S. 175, 189
Putler, D.S. 104
Pylyshyn, Z.W. 44, 45, 79, 81

Rajlich, V. 173
Ravensbergen, J. 55, 229
Reber, A.S. 81, 82
Reed, D.L. 191
Rice, M.P. 21
Riemersma, S. 283
Rienstra, J. 236
Riesbeck, C.K. 124
Rifkin, J. 295
Robson, C. 180
Rogers, E.M. 23
Rotmans, J. 24, 51, 227
Russell, S.J. 326, 328

Sauvante, M. 28
Savery, J.R. 173
Schank, R.C. 124, 125
Schecter, D. 106
Schellekens, W. 229
Scheper, W. 247, 251
Schlegelmilch, B.B. 232
Schmidt, R. 124
Schön, D.A. 7, 268
Schreiber, G. 63, 173, 176, 179, 181, 183, 219, 325-27
Schumpeter, J.A. 2, 17
Scott-Morton, M.S. 169, 219
Senge, P.M. 48
Senker, J. 19
Sennett, R. 47, 96
Sessions, G. 33
Shannon, C.E. 315
Sierman, H.N. 206
Simon, H.A. 18, 25, 35, 42, 45, 58, 74-77, 155, 169-71, 214-17, 322, 326, 331
Simons, J.L. 123
Smolensky, P. 45
Snow, C.C. 24
Soete, L. 231
Sollenborn, M. 124
Song, M.X. 21
Sorge, A. 64, 66, 67, 89, 332
Spijkervet, A. 235
Stacey, R.D. 54
Stalker, G.M. 23
Stubblefield, W.A. 220, 326, 328
Stylianou, A. 175

Takeuchi, H. 18, 23, 48, 89
Tansley, D.S.W. 179

Theunissen, N.C.M. 232
Thompson, J.D. 64, 65, 75, 332
Tierney, T. 241
Tricot, A. 174
Turban, E. 169, 170

Ulrich, W. 99, 106-108

Valiant, L.G. 173
Van den Bosch, F.A.J. 51
Van den Broek, H. 76
Van der Laan, G. 241
Van der Plaats, A. 53
Van der Putten, T. 240, 243
Van der Spek, R. 235, 239
Van der Stege, B. 259
Van de Velde, W. 63, 124
Van de Ven, A.H.V. 24, 109, 252
Van der Werf, M.P.C. 329
Van Diem, A. 136
Van Ees, H. 2
Van Engelen, J.M.L. 176, 228
Van Houten, E.J. 206
Van Muijen, J.J. 266, 268, 284
Van Raaij, E.M. 8
Van Wezel, W. 62
Van Zon, H. 30
Verburg, H. 230, 343
Vicente, K.J. 63, 331
Visser, A. 133, 243
Volberda, H.W. 51
Volterra, V. 317
Von Bertalanffy, L. 42, 53, 314, 317, 319
Von Glaserveld, E. 173
Von Hippel, E. 17, 24
Von Krogh, G. 90, 91, 285
Vos, J.E.J. 98, 106, 110, 247, 269

Waalkens, J. 265
Waddell, S. 228
Waern, Y. 63, 213, 220
Warner, M. 66, 89, 332
Weggeman, M. 2
Weick, K.E. 77
Wenger, E.C. 47
West, M.A. 18, 21, 330
Wevers, J. 283
Wheelwright, S.C. 157
Whinston, A.B. 169, 219
Wielinga, B. 241
Wierenga, J. 136
Wijffels, H. 10, 37
Williamson, O.E. 65
Willmott, H. 106
Wilson, R.A. 169, 170
Wolfe, R.A. 104
Wood, D.J. 103
Wright, G. 155, 175

Yourdon, E. 156

Zimmerman, B. 54